Margaret
Wise Brown

MARGARET WISE BROWN

Awakened by the Moon

Leonard S. Marcus

BEACON PRESS

BOSTON

Beacon Press
25 Beacon Street
Boston, Massachusetts 02108

Beacon Press books ·
are published under the auspices of
the Unitarian Universalist Association
of Congregations.

99 98 97 96 95 94 93 92 8 7 6 5 4 3 2 1

Text design by Copenhaver Cumpston

Library of Congress Cataloging-in-Publication Data

Marcus, Leonard S., 1950–
Margaret Wise Brown: awakened by the moon /
Leonard S. Marcus.
  p. cm.
Includes bibliographical references and index.
ISBN 0-8070-7048-3
1. Brown, Margaret Wise, 1910–1952. 2. Authors,
American—20th century—Biography. 3. Children's
literature, American—History and criticism. I. Title.
PS3503.R82184Z78 1992
813'.s2—dc20   91-17305
                                    CIP

67 10216

For Amy

Contents

Illustrations

Acknowledgments

This book could not have been written without the generous assistance and cooperation of many people who allowed themselves to be interviewed, responded to questions by letter, lent research materials in their possession, or (in several instances) did all of these things. In particular, I wish to acknowledge the help of: William Albin, Augusta Baker Alexander, Dorothy A. Bennett, Barbara Biber, James Black, Johanna Boetz, Penelope Bordon Boone, Marion Ristine Bowes, Polly Schoyer Brooks, B. Gratz Brown, Jr., Billy Brown, Mary Steichen Calderone, Charles Carpenter, Joan Clarke, Margaret Cousins, Ray Dennis, Katherine A. Dilworth, Lucienne Bloch Dimitroff, Frank and Betta Dobo, Jessica Gamble Dunham, Gerold Frank, the late Josette Frank, Anne Fuller, James P. Gaston, Morrell Gipson, Mrs. J. Wooderson Glenn, the late Luther Ward Greene, Mary Guiheen, Montgomery Hare, the late Marguerite C. Hearsey, the late Peter Heggie, Betty Husting, Sarah Kerlin, Frank E. Kilroe, Ruth Krauss, David C. Lamb, Elizabeth and Condie Lamb, Adrian Lambert, Claudia Lewis, Dorothy R. Luke, Inez Camprubi Mabon, James MacCormick, Richard Mack, Virginia Mathews, Ilse Mattick, John G. McCullough, J. P. Miller, Eileen Moriority, the late Martha Huguley Naftel, Priscilla Newhall, Mrs. Hoffman Nickerson, John H. Niemeyer, the late Ursula Nordstrom, the late Lucille Ogle, John Oelsner, Leonora Alexander

Orr, Julia Lamar Parish, Adelaide Dana Parker, Ted Scott Peckham, Ellen Pettit, the late Mary Phelps, the late Harriet F. Pilpel, Nancy Pittman, Jeffrey Potter, the late Wallace B. Putnam, Richard and Josephine Reeve, Colette Richardson, Elizabeth M. Riley, Dorothy Wagstaff Ripley, Joseph D. Ryle, Margaret P. Scott, William R. Scott, Art Seiden, Judith Shahn, Jane Thurston Shepard, Esphyr Slobodkina, Ellen Tarry, Yvonne Thomas, Charlotte Tiplady, Alvin and Blossom Tresselt, Susanna P. Turner, Gloria de Veyrac, Jeanette Connolly Waddell, Sophie Shoumatoff Ward, Dorothy Warren, Elizabeth Watson, Garth Williams, and Charlotte Zolotow.

I wish to offer special thanks to Roberta Brown Rauch and Bruce Bliven, Jr., coexecutors of Margaret Wise Brown's estate, for permissions granted and for memories, insights, and information shared.

I thank James Stillman Rockefeller, Jr., for making available original source materials, for relating his memories of Margaret Wise Brown, and for allowing me to visit the Only House.

Special thanks also to Leonard Weisgard and the late Phyllis Weisgard, who submitted good-naturedly to what proved to be the longest interview conducted for this book, a series of intensive conversations spanning eleven consecutive days.

I gratefully acknowledge the many helps and kindnesses extended to me by Edith Thacher Hurd and the late Clement Hurd; they gave freely of their time and knowledge, and, by accompanying me on my visit to the Only House, helped make a productive experience an unforgettable one as well.

Institutional archives consulted as part of my research are acknowledged in the Notes. I wish, however, to express here my appreciation to David J. Panciera, Executive Director, Memorial and Library Association of Westerly, Rhode Island, for his friendly and gracious assistance over nine years of periodic visits to the Margaret Wise Brown Collection of books and papers.

Friends and professional colleagues who took an early interest in this project or offered encouragement at critical moments along the way include: Everett F. Bleiler, R. Cat, Tin Shue Chin, the late Elizabeth Cleaver, Gary C. Karshmer, Fran Manushkin, and Susanne Suba. I especially wish to thank Deanne Urmy for her stead-fast support, sound judgment, and good fellowship.

An Ingram Merrill Foundation grant-in-writing was helpful in supporting my preliminary research and writing, and is acknowledged with gratitude.

I thank my friends at the Writers Room, Inc., New York, where I found the quiet to write portions of this book.

I wish to thank my editor, Wendy J. Strothman, and the staff of Beacon Press for their interest in my work and for their high professional standards. I would also like to express my appreciation to my excellent copy editor, Chris Kochansky.

I thank my parents and family for their encouragement over many years.

Introduction

I see the moon,
And the moon sees me.

*The Oxford Dictionary
of Nursery Rhymes*

One never forgot the things *she*
noticed, for she charged them with
her own intense feeling. This power
of enhancing and ennobling life
was felt by all who knew her.

EDMUND WILSON ON

EDNA ST. VINCENT MILLAY,
The Shores of Light

We speak naturally," observed Margaret
Wise Brown, author of *Goodnight Moon* and other classics of the
American nursery, "but spend all our lives trying to write
naturally." [1]

A contemporary of Ludwig Bemelmans, Robert McCloskey,
Virginia Lee Burton, and Dr. Seuss, Margaret Wise Brown was
one of the central figures of a period now considered the golden
age of the American picture book, the years spanning the post-
Depression thirties and the postwar baby boom forties and fifties.
Bemelmans and the others began as visual artists who became au-
thors, as it were, in order to have material to illustrate. In contrast,
Margaret Wise Brown was a picture-book *writer* from the start, the
first such writer, as Barbara Bader has remarked in her splendid
American Picturebooks, "to be recognized in her own right. The first,

too, to make the writing of picturebooks an art."[2] Within the children's book world of that immensely fruitful era, Margaret also occupied a unique place as an inspired author for the very youngest, a group of children for whom few had even thought to write before; and no author before or since has managed so well to shape books that complete what Margaret herself once called the "natural impulse to amuse and to delight and comfort" small children.[3]

Steeped in the moderns and trained at Lucy Sprague Mitchell's progressive Bank Street school, she incorporated insights from these and other vital contemporary sources into a tireless personal campaign to make the picture book new. For a time she was a highly innovative juveniles editor, and throughout her career she played impresario to the entire field, taking pleasure in discovering or furthering the careers of illustrators and writers such as Clement and Edith Thacher Hurd, Garth Williams, Leonard Weisgard, Esphyr Slobodkina, Jean Charlot, and Ruth Krauss. It was at Margaret's urging that Gertrude Stein wrote *The World Is Round*.

As she became increasingly successful, she used her growing influence to fight for juvenile authors' and illustrators' rights in their dealings with publishers. Widely respected by her colleagues, she lived to see her books become extremely popular. Yet Margaret's success was not without its ambiguities. She remained acutely aware of having made her name in a sector of the literary world that most outside it did not take seriously. Extraordinarily accomplished writer that she was, she never freed herself altogether from the suspicion that to have written for adults would have been a greater achievement.

It's possible I knew some of Margaret Wise Brown's books as a child growing up in the early fifties, but if I did I don't remember. This would not have surprised her at all. Of her own childhood memories of books, Margaret once remarked that it had not then occurred to her that books were written by people; what mattered was whether or not they rang true.

In any case, my work on the present book did not begin as a nostalgic quest for a favorite childhood author. As an undergraduate history major at Yale, I had become curious to know what kinds of books were published for young people during the early nineteenth century, when the American republic was itself still in its formative years. As I was also reading and writing a good deal of poetry, my interest in children's literature naturally expanded to include the modern picture book, which at its best has much in common with lyric poetry: an ultimate clarity and compactness of expression, a seamless merging of matter and means.

I first became aware of Margaret Wise Brown's work a few years after graduation, while browsing in a New York bookshop where copies of *Goodnight Moon* were stacked high on a table. As I read the book for the first time, unaware of the author's legendary status within her field (or indeed of anything about her) I was forcibly struck by the realization that the quietly compelling words I was saying over in my head were poetry and, what was more, poetry of a kind I prized: accessible but not predictable, emotional but purged of sentiment, vivid but so spare that every word felt necessary. Her words seemed to be rooted in the concrete but touched by an appreciation of the elusive, the paradoxical, the mysterious. There was astonishing tenderness and authority in the voice, and something mythic in it as well. It was as though the author had just now seen the world for the first time, and had chosen to honor it by taking its true measure in words.

I began looking for other books by her and discovered that there were *lots* of them—over one hundred in all, more than forty of which remained in print over thirty years after publication. Although they varied in overall quality, several seemed memorable to me, many were very good, nearly all were in some sense innovative, and none was without a fresh perception or a jaunty phrase that stuck in the mind. (A train did not go "chug chug" but "picketa-picketa," while another train went "pocketa-pocketa"; a dog could "belong to himself.")[4]

My curiosity was channeled into research—first for a critical essay and a magazine piece, then for this book—and as I proceeded to read the few articles that had been written about her and had my first conversations with people who had known her, I began hearing distinct echoes of the qualities I admired in Margaret's writings. "She was an original," more than one of her friends said. She was "mercurial," "quixotic," "an experimenter," "a perfectionist." Nearly everyone spoke of her in heartfelt superlatives, as an "irreplaceable" friend, as the "most creative" person they had ever known.[5] In more than nine years of research and writing, I have been sustained by a core impression of Margaret Wise Brown as the least complacent of people, as a highly individual personality who time and again bravely tested her limits as a writer and human being.

Some of her experiments in literature and life, I learned, worked better than others. She was a poet of places, a master at shaping (decorating is not the word) her home surroundings into havens that mirrored the emotional warmth and whimsy, and the fascination with the primitive, of her imaginative writings.

However, she seems to have found it exceedingly difficult to meet her peers on equal terms, especially in love. As a lonely but delightfully resourceful child, she had at times to play parent to herself, and she learned the role well, though not without emotional cost, then and later. As an adult, she approached others obliquely, from above and below, with a beguiling mixture of childlike need and proprietary concern for the other person's welfare. She was forever enlisting collaborators, urging artists and writers to enter her new and largely unexplored field. A publishing colleague wondered, years after her death, if the picture book of all literary forms had not suited her so well precisely because it required the involvement of collaborators.

Over the years of the writing of this book, the first reaction of many people has been, "How did she die? She died *so* young!" I suppose this is natural given the fact that mention of her death in 1952, "when she was still a young person" (Margaret was forty-two), is just about the only biographical information supplied on the flap of *Goodnight Moon,* in the note that accompanies the photo of the attractive, open-faced author with a romantic glow.

Nonetheless, for a long time I was puzzled by the sheer intensity of people's curiosity about this one question, and I have come to believe that it has at least two sources. The first of these is the Romantic myth of the creative artist whose genius flares brilliantly but briefly and is then snuffed out in tragic circumstances. The second is the common premise that children's literature is a sentimental repository of innocent thoughts and happy endings, and little more than that—how ironic, then, when a children's author's own story ends so *un*happily.

In some respects, Margaret consciously cast herself in the Romantic poet's role. She lived flamboyantly, liked to say she dreamt her books (sometimes, apparently, she did). But there was no dark secret to her death; she died of a blood clot following a routine operation. Margaret, always something of a fatalist, had often remarked that becoming a children's author had been an accident of sorts. Her early death, sad as it was, simply happened.

This point bears emphasis because Margaret's own approach to children's literature—and to living—was so bravely unsentimental. Her books have an underlying emotional tautness and honesty about them that is both salutary and rare. They express a clear-eyed respect for the young that both children and adults immediately recognize. Margaret herself could be exasperating. She could also be a generous and charming and affirming friend. But most of all, she never pretended to more knowledge or self-knowledge than was properly hers. She never gave up on growing up. Not least of all for that reason, she was among the most memorable of people.

CHAPTER ONE

"A WILD AND PRIVATE PLACE"

Every family constructs a mythology of its talents and qualities.

LIONEL TRILLING

In an autobiographical sketch prepared for her publishers, Margaret Wise Brown once described her earliest childhood memories. Among them were images of a "city street with high iron gates, a red brick church at the end of the street and the sound of boats on the river"; a recollection of the "painful shy animal dignity with which a child stretches to conform to a strange adult social politeness"; thoughts about death, dreaming, "mysterious clock time," and aging; and a "problem of aesthetics I had—why wasn't an airdale's [*sic*] face beautiful, if it was beautiful to me?" [1]

As a child, a favorite pastime of hers was to make up little tunes, to set poems she composed to old melodies, and to croon traditional songs like "Dixie"—an anthem which beguiled her in part through a misunderstanding: "I thought Dixie Land and

Sandy Bottom were two little girls. I envied them and cherished them, as a child does imaginary playmates, and I never understood why Dixie Land kept looking away, but that was just the way she was."[2]

As the author of more than fifty books, Margaret later observed that memory, the ultimate source of her creative work, is a "wild and private place," a place to which "we return truly only by accident"—the writer's inspiration—"as in a dream or a song," or by "beaten paths"—the writer's craft. Whatever the method or the path, she was convinced that "as you write, memory will come out in its true form."[3]

The iron gates were those along Milton Street, in the then fashionable section of Greenpoint, Brooklyn, where Robert and Maude Brown had settled as a newly married couple from Kirkwood, Missouri, and where five years later, on May 23, 1910, their second child, Margaret, was born.

Once a bucolic East River village within easy reach of Manhattan, Greenpoint by the turn of the century had been transformed into an "American Birmingham," a worthy rival to England's industrial leviathan in the variety and quantity of its manufactures and in the declining quality of its air.[4] Robert and Maude Brown, like many of their neighbors, had come to live there largely out of convenience. In 1905, with the promise of a secure future ahead of him in a business that was partly family owned, Robert had moved east to work for the American Manufacturing Company, makers of rope, cordage, and bagging. A short, impatient man, Margaret's father possessed a shrewdly matter-of-fact view of life and a brilliant mind for mechanical problems. In due course he rose to become his company's treasurer and vice president.

By 1912, Robert and Maude were the parents of three healthy children, all of them born on Milton Street. Benjamin Gratz, Jr., named for Robert's father, was nearly two years old when Margaret was born; Roberta, the youngest, arrived when Margaret was not quite two.

It would hardly be noteworthy that an ambitious young company man like Robert Brown was a conservative Republican but for the fact that his own father, the Honorable B. Gratz Brown of Missouri, had been one of the nation's most progressive political leaders during the Civil War and Reconstruction eras.[5] An ardent opponent of slavery, B. Gratz Brown served Missouri as a United States senator and as governor, and in 1872 he ran unsuccessfully for the vice presidency on the Liberal Republican and Democratic tickets, both headed by Horace Greeley.

According to a family anecdote that bears on their relationship, father and son (the boy was not more than nine) were riding one day in an open carriage. Young Robert, having noticed a black person in the street, made some casual remark about "that nigger," whereupon the elder Brown slapped him hard across the face in a show of his utter contempt for bigotry.[6] In later life, Margaret's father turned petulant at the merest approving reference to any progressive political cause. While Maude Brown deferred completely to Robert in matters of politics, each of their three children reacted differently: mechanically inclined Gratz by wholeheartedly embracing his father's views and professional interests, intellectually acute Roberta by veering in the opposite direction to become a vigorous Roosevelt Democrat, and Margaret, the family daydreamer, by becoming more or less apolitical—indifferent to it all.

One senses a tinge of bitterness in Robert Brown's rebellion. The older of B. Gratz Brown's nine children—Lily, Mary, Violet, Margaretta—all had memories of life in the heady, privileged circumstances of a governor's family—a family that could trace its distinguished line of clerics and high government officials back to the days of William of Orange.[7] But Robert missed out on the glory days. The governor's law practice and personal finances had fallen into disarray during his years of crusading public service and remained so at the time of his death in 1885, when Robert was nine. Robert's mother fell ill, was invalided, and died soon afterward. When Robert was ready for college, there weren't enough funds in the family's modest inheritance to send him to Princeton or Yale, where past generations of Brown men had studied. His situation was saved only when members of the Gratz branch of the family intervened on his behalf, arranging a first job for him with the American Manufacturing Company in New York. Clinging doggedly to the bit of security thus put in his way, Robert Brown remained with the firm until his retirement.

Three of the Brown aunts must have cut beguiling figures in young Margaret's imagination, even if she saw them only occasionally. There was an adventurousness, a spirit of fun and extravagance about Lily and Margaretta, both of whom painted and taught art in St. Louis, and about Violet (though she presented a rather more mixed case), which anticipates later descriptions of Margaret herself.

Years later, in a letter to her sister Roberta, Margaret recalled the spectacle of aunts Margaretta and Violet blithely lifting their corsets to show the two girls the scars left from their appendectomies. Another time, Lily and Margaretta ran out of money while touring in Europe and had to cable their prosperous brother in New York for additional funds. (This incident was not soon forgotten in Robert Brown's household. When Margaret and Roberta wanted to make a similar trip abroad in their mid-twenties, their father was hesitant, fearing that family history might repeat itself.)

Violet Brown moved to Manhattan about the same time that Robert and Maude came East. She had always been fond of her younger brother and may simply have wanted to maintain their close ties. In any case, Violet and Maude never got along. As the self-styled protector of the family name, Violet found fault with both Gratz's and Roberta's marriage partners, declaring them "foreigners," by which she meant that they lacked distinguished backgrounds on a par with that of the Browns. Violet sowed further discord by cultivating a lopsided relationship with her nephew, to the near total exclusion of Margaret and Roberta. (As the sole male heir, Gratz was destined to perpetuate the family name.) Not surprisingly, the girls felt a certain resentment toward her for her assorted inattentions; when, as small children, they decided one day to make some money by selling flowers from the family garden, it was the violets they picked.

Margaret's mother, Maude Johnson Brown, was better educated than her husband, having earned an "Eclectic" degree from Virginia's Hollins Institute (afterwards known as Hollins College) in 1899.[8] A striking, well-spoken woman (she had received high marks in elocution at Hollins), Maude had, according to family legend, dreamed of going to New York to become an actress. She seems to have stuck to her goal through college, where she completed advanced classes in dramatic arts, but in opting for the security of marriage, Maude made a decision in keeping with both convention and common sense. With the leisure that married life afforded her she pursued her aesthetic interests along the avenues then open to women of comfortable means: decorating china plates, gardening, reading poetry, collecting early American glass, dressing her children. During her married years, only concern for her children's welfare seems to have emboldened her, as when she insisted, over Robert Brown's strenuous objections, that Margaret and Roberta, as well as Gratz, be given the chance to attend college as she herself had done.

Margaret grew up knowing considerably less about her mother's family than about the illustrious Browns. Maude's father, Berkeley Estes Johnson, had been a Virginian and a fervent supporter of the Confederacy. As a young man he had gone west to Kansas and Missouri, working for the railroads as a civil engineer. Maude's mother, Margaret Naylor Wise Johnson, was the only grandparent whom Margaret, her namesake, ever met. A pious woman whose conversation was laced with quotations from Scripture, Grandma Naylor, as the children called her, was also an opera lover. When she came east to visit, the family gathered for long sessions around the living room victrola and the children were briskly dispatched to Sunday school, which neither Maude (an Episcopalian) nor Robert (Presbyterian) otherwise encouraged them to attend. Grandma Naylor was staying with them in the summer of 1915 as the Browns prepared to leave Brooklyn for the fresh air and unspoiled natural surroundings of nearby suburban Beechurst, Long Island. Margaret, then five, later fondly recalled Grandma Naylor, "that singing Welsh lady," as a great presence sitting beside her on moving day in the open family car.[9]

Popular magazines of the period, like the *Saturday Evening Post, Ladies' Home Journal,* and the *Atlantic Monthly,* were filled with "back to nature" articles extolling the virtues of fresh air and the country—especially for families with children.[10] Margaret's parents—Maude especially—seem to have needed little persuading. Once the decision was made to move, Margaret's father commissioned an architect friend to design the Brown family's new home. That summer of 1915, while awaiting the completion of construction work, the family took up temporary lodgings in a nearby rented house not far from the beach where the children would now be able to play.

Beechurst was a prosperous village inhabited by businessmen, professionals, and show people. A short commute from the city by automobile or rail, it bordered Long Island Sound and had its own yacht club, which the Brown family joined. Houses were spaced far apart, apple and cherry trees dotted the landscape, and the children soon discovered a narrow dirt lane that ran past the elaborate gardens of wealthier neighbors on its way to an expanse of woods abundant with jack-in-the-pulpits, black-eyed susans, and other wildflowers.[11]

The Browns' new three-story brick and stucco home, though far from the largest in the neighborhood, was spacious and comfortable. Off to the left as one entered was the dining room; to the right was the living room with its victrola and upright piano, a chime clock which sounded throughout the house, and the hearth. One Christmas Eve, Margaret, in the ritualistic way of small children, convinced herself that by scrubbing the hearth she could insure St. Nicholas's safe and satisfactory arrival. However, no sooner had she finished her work than bluff, querulous Robert Brown decided that the house was too cold and the time had come to build a fire; Margaret shuffled off to bed that night feeling sullen and furious. It was with utter surprise and gratitude next morning that she found that Christmas presents and a beautifully decorated tree had nonetheless appeared during the night.[12]

Both parents were cautious about money, though Maude Brown was determined to spare no expense over the children and her husband seems generally to have gone along with her, if not always graciously. Margaret and Roberta each took piano lessons for a time but without much success. All three children were enrolled at a local dancing academy.

Occasionally, their father took the initiative in providing for them; each year before Christmas he drove them down to the local hardware store, where toys were also sold, and observed the three-some as they inspected the shelves. By this rather remote but effective means, he determined what their presents should be.

Neither girl ever wanted a doll; they preferred action toys like Gratz's train set and the toy steamer they discovered one year hidden in the closet in its holiday wrappings and secretly launched in the tub before repacking it in hopes their parents would suspect nothing. [13]

The Browns' house did not have a formal library, but they owned the usual sorts of books, including a set of Sir Walter Scott's Waverley novels, a conventional fixture of turn-of-the-century middle-class American homes, especially those of Southern heritage. There was also a set of Mark Twain's works, which, more for its Missouri associations than its literary ones, stirred Robert Brown's enthusiasm to a pitch otherwise foreign to him in aesthetic matters. The only other books he is known to have enjoyed were Joel Chandler Harris's Uncle Remus collections, which, like the Twain novels, he read aloud to the children, sometimes becoming so engrossed in a story that he read ahead in silence, momentarily forgetting his young audience.

The children had a standard set of *The Book of Knowledge,* and along with the *National Geographic,* the family took the popular children's monthly *St. Nicholas.* Books of fantasy were known to the children early on. Margaret recalled having read *The Tale of Peter Rabbit, Black Beauty, The Song of Roland,* and Andrew Lang's Rainbow fairy tale collections. Margaret said later that her favorite story had been "Aladdin and his Wonderful Lamp," while insisting that on the whole she had not read much as a child: "I was too busy." [14] When the girls were old enough for series novels, they preferred adventure fiction published for boys. Among their favorites were the dog stories of Albert Payson Terhune; the Browns named their collie for the hero of Terhune's popular novel *Bruce.*

Margaret and Roberta's large second-floor bedroom was heated by means of a gas grate framed with decorative ceramic tiles depicting nursery rhyme characters—the Three Little Bears and the Cow That Jumped Over the Moon that Margaret would recall in *Goodnight Moon.* Because their parents put the children to bed early, the two sisters had hours each evening in which to devise new games and stories for their own amusement. Some of these revolved around Margaret's black cat, Ole King Cole, and the fireflies they brought indoors in summertime in Mason jars. One night, after all the Browns had gone to bed, a moment's diversion came their way from an unexpected quarter when the sisters heard a suspicious noise in the yard. Margaret leaned out their bedroom window and, borrowing an expression from the family's Irish cook, shouted, "Burglar, you burglar, get going while your shoes are still good!" [15]

Before Roberta was old enough to read, Margaret gallantly read aloud from their Andrew Lang Rainbow series. However welcome at the time, these story hours later caused Roberta some embarrassment when she realized that the tales she had learned were by no means the same as the "Red Riding Hood," "Cinderella," and "Hansel and Gretel" that other children knew. While gazing intently down at the page before her, Margaret had felt free to stray from the printed word, adding horrific details to the plot just to frighten her rapt listener, and taking care that in the stories about three siblings it was not the youngest of the three who triumphed, as is the convention in such tales, but the middle child.

Two more bedrooms completed the second floor, and the sleeping porch occupied its own level a few steps down. Margaret must have loved the phrase "sleeping porch," with its suggestion of a languorous interior life of the woodwork. She stargazed from the porch and by the age of six she held court there regularly, telling outlandish stories of her own devising to other neighborhood children. If, after sitting through one of these tales, someone in the audience demanded to know whether the story was true, Margaret merely referred the questioner to *The Book of Knowledge*, her sole source and authority, she said. She recalled years later with sly satisfaction that "the twenty-four red volumes were too voluminous to betray me." [16]

Under the eaves of the third floor were the cook's room and a playroom with Gratz's coveted electric train as its centerpiece. Once when the rest of the family was out for the day, young Gratz, in search of adventure, climbed out the playroom window onto the roof and, losing his balance, slid down to the rain gutter. There he remained until rescued by the postman. The physical punishment administered by Robert Brown following such escapades could be harsh. Nonetheless, Gratz preserved his reputation with the local girls as an efficient prankster who would deny everything when confronted by his accusers: "Did I do *that?*" [17]

For most of childhood, Margaret and Roberta were a study in contrasts and all but inseparable. Margaret was hale and hardy, Roberta fragile, more prone to illness. Roberta was a model of diligence, persistence, and responsible behavior; Margaret was a trickster who more often than not escaped blame for her misdeeds. Boys found Margaret attractive early on, were drawn to her, as her brother recalled, "like [bees to] honey"; Roberta was plainer. [18] Their mother dressed them in identical outfits which a seamstress who visited the house for a few days each month made under her supervision.

Much of the year the Brown children lived outdoors. In the yard to one side of the house, they had a joggling board—a flexible, narrow, thirty-foot plank that their father had shipped specially by train from California. It came with low, movable metal supports that could be placed under the center of the board or at either end, depending on whether there were two children who wanted to seesaw, or one or more who wanted to stand at the middle and jump up and down. A joggling board was a leveler: two players jumping together on the quavering platform could compete to see who would last longer. Margaret, a sensuous, physical child, was a fine athlete with exceptionally quick reflexes. More often than not it was she who was left standing.

School was a more decisive leveler. While Gratz performed well and Margaret earned a reputation as a keen-spirited daydreamer with reserves of untapped potential, Roberta positively shined. Roberta's intellectual prowess and her efforts to be a dutiful child did not necessarily inspire friendly treatment within the sometimes ruthless subculture of childhood. Margaret and Gratz could put aside their differences long enough to leap on her from behind the woodpile with cries of "Witch, witch!" [19] By the second grade, Roberta had advanced a full year beyond her classmates, to close half the gap in academic standing between Margaret and herself. She repeated the feat a few years later; when the two sisters entered boarding school at Dana Hall, they were members of the same class.

For both girls, schooling would always be associated with disruptive change. After starting in public school (Robert Brown had thought the rough and tumble atmosphere would be good for a boy), Gratz was sent to a Long Island boarding school, where he remained until college. In contrast, by the end of Margaret's seventh year of studies, she and Roberta had changed schools four times.

The vagaries of small town private schooling accounted for some of this fitful shuffling about. The school most convenient to the Brown home did not offer a complete grammar school course; Margaret and Roberta simply moved on after exhausting its limited program. But another factor contributing to the girls' choppy school life was the disruption caused by Robert Brown's business travels; he was periodically dispatched for lengthy intervals to his company's plants in Scotland and India. Before leaving on one such year-long journey in 1919, he closed the Beechurst house and moved the family into temporary quarters in the Garden City Hotel, an arrangement intended to make housekeeping easier for his wife during his long absence. Gratz's boarding school was in Garden City, and the girls were placed in nearby St. Mary's.

Margaret and Roberta could hardly have been expected, under the circumstances, to form lasting friendships with schoolmates, and because few children lived in their neighborhood, they had relatively little companionship, apart from each other, during the Beechurst years. Years later, Margaret recalled having spent much of her childhood playing alone, in the "countries of the worlds I made up."[20]

Summers, children home from boarding school added somewhat to the pool of playmates. Foremost among these was Jane Thurston, an outgoing, athletic child and the daughter of one of the world's best-known stage performers, (Harry) "Thurston the Magician." Jane's lavish home and the ample grounds surrounding it became a focal point for all the neighborhood children. Margaret later recalled with delight the impromptu magic shows Jane's famous father gave for them and the visits he permitted them with the monkeys, snakes, and other exotic animals of his private menagerie. In the Thurstons' attic, which was large enough for Jane's mother to have considered converting it into a ballroom, trunkloads of old theater costumes were stored; it was in these incomparable circumstances that the girls played their dress-up games.

Even summers, however, were not times of uninterrupted companionship. Because Robert Brown suffered from severe hayfever, the family went north to Penobscot Bay, Maine, for a month or more each year. Once in Maine, Margaret's father disappeared on deep-sea fishing expeditions, sometimes taking Gratz along but leaving Maude and their daughters to entertain themselves at their hotel.

Gratz, who had a larger allowance than his sisters, financed the Brown children's animals. During the warmer months, they kept as many as twenty rabbits at a time in mesh cages stacked beside the backyard woodpile. It was the children's responsibility to feed the rabbits and clean their cages (though Margaret was frequently absent when it came time for these disagreeable chores). They learned to hold the soft, wary creatures in their own small hands, and it was from watching the rabbits that the children first learned about sex. Once, when one of the rabbits died, Margaret, in her startlingly fearless and unsentimental way, skinned the carcass for its fur, perhaps recalling as she did so her father's boyhood tales of bear-hunting. She attempted to shock the other children further by insisting that when she grew up she was going to be a "lady butcher."[21] The comforting softness and sensuality of fur, and the quickness and vulnerability of rabbits, captivated her, and later became poignant emblems in her published writings and her personal mythology.

A few blocks from home was a woodlot known as Robin's Woods, where Gratz, while playing one day, discovered an underground chamber, large enough for a grown man to crawl through, which the children afterwards used as a hideaway, as doubtless the bootleggers who dug it must also have done.

For Margaret, as for the others, there were the usual turns of childish mischief that might have had serious consequences, but didn't. Once she was bitten by a squirrel she had foolishly taken in hand. Another time, the two sisters set fire to the woodlot. When the fireman asked if they knew how the minor blaze had started, Margaret and Roberta replied as one, "Oh, no! No!" shaking their heads innocently. [22]

Together, in the privacy of the woods, the children smoked their first cigarettes. (Only Margaret enjoyed the experience and later became a heavy smoker.) There she and Roberta also gave plays for their friends, including a sort of precocious sexual farce concerning a cowherd (Margaret), a milkmaid (Roberta), and a cow (played by the family collie, Bruce), in which the climactic speech, delivered by the dashing swain, went: "It's not her I want [motioning to the cow], but *her!*"[23]

It was also in Robin's Woods that the Brown children buried a small dead animal they had found in the road. Margaret later recalled the incident in "The Dead Bird," one of her first published stories for children. Taking the measure of young children's real (but also quite limited) capacity to grieve, she wrote, "And every day, until they forgot, [the children] went and sang to their little dead bird and put fresh flowers on his grave."[24]

In "Discovery," one of Margaret's many unpublished autobiographical pieces, a six-year-old girl, playing in a woodlot with her older brother and younger sister, announces one day that the woods all around them belong to her. The girl does not explain how this could be so, she simply offers to let the others buy a bit of her property and proceeds to sell her sister a tree stump for a dime and an oak tree to her brother for a nickel. Returning home, the girl enjoys a good laugh in private. "How could they believe it?" she asks herself in amazement, laughing some more. [25]

But this discovery—the gullibility of children less quick-witted (if in other respects more accomplished) than herself—is just the beginning of the knowledge she acquires that day. Late in the afternoon, the girl wanders into the dining room, "cool and empty with the great magic places she knew under the table." Her attention focuses on the sideboard, and a thought "begun over the roast beef on Sunday" is rekindled. She wants to see her father's carving knife, the big long knife he "flourished over the sharpener before he carved, back and forth, back and forth. What a fine thing to do, and that was father. Sharpening the knife and carving the roast."

Opening the drawer in which the knife is kept, she touches the blade very lightly and withdraws her hand. "It was so sharp you could hardly touch it. . . . She picked it up and slowly and solomnly [*sic*] she brought the point of the knife towards the heart in her little flat chest. She held the rough bone handle very tight and very steady. She looked at her arm . . . as it bent and the thought that finished under the tight golden hairs of her head was as big as life itself. It was as big as death. It was bigger. In that small arm that bent as she told it to or stopped bending as she made it do was the power to live or to die. Amazement brought the knife close to her chest. . . . She put the carving knife back in the drawer. . . . She closed the drawer." The little girl's second discovery of the day also concerns power, but power of a different order. Margaret's six-year-old realizes that with selfhood—growing up—comes a certain power to shape one's own destiny.

In *Little Fur Family,* one of her best-known books for children, Margaret recounted in strikingly similar terms the adventures of an imaginary "fur child" just coming into his own in the "wild wild wood" where he lives. Out for a walk, the little hero pulls a fish from the river, takes a good look at it, then throws it back into the river unharmed. Next he catches a bug in mid-flight, examines and releases it. Finally, the fur child spies a tiny fur creature in the grass, a miniature version of himself; the fur child picks him up, as a parent might a child, kisses him on the nose, and lets him run off again. [26]

Both "Discovery" and *Little Fur Family* are stories of life and death—of life over death. As an author, Margaret often returned to the compelling (and at the time largely unexplored) theme of the power struggles implicit in growing up: young children's determination to make the world conform to their will and to acquire a sense of self-mastery. By sparing the lives of the fish, the bug, and his miniature counterpart, the fur child shows that he knows how to use his new-found power benignly and well. In the poignant logic of the tale, acquiring that knowledge is recognizing the power of love.

Robert Brown seems to have been most at home in life when at his office. As a father and husband he was the classic proud provider, a man confident in his views, who expected, in return for the fairly bountiful portion of material security he bestowed on his family, that life at home should largely go his way.

Impatient and quick to anger, he sometimes resorted to physical punishment when it came to disciplining young Gratz. More often, however, he dealt with misbehavior by simply threatening to withhold the offender's allowance. Around the age of six, Margaret developed a rather precocious habit that may have contained her comment on her father's machinations in this domain; whenever she became cross with someone, she would threaten not to leave that person such and such in her will.[27] Where she had heard talk of wills and legacies is not known, but it was altogether like her—and in keeping with the mythologizing imagination later revealed in her books—to recast a prosaic dollars-and-cents ultimatum in more fundamental life-and-death terms. If death was a part of experience, she would reckon with it. She would love the rabbit while it lived and skin the dead rabbit for its fur, extracting from death life's pleasurable essences. She would tell stories to Death, as it were, from *The Book of Knowledge*.

On the one occasion when Margaret tried to run away from home, she laid her plans carefully, publicizing her escape route in advance with their friendly neighbor, Mr. Storms, to assure the drama its full effect. It's not clear how old she was at the time, but she seems not to have made it out of the neighborhood; the ever-resourceful Margaret must have been quite young. Perhaps, like the hero of *The Runaway Bunny*—like virtually all child runaways—Margaret did not so much wish to leave home as to know that someone there would notice her absence and care enough to find her.

Just why Margaret might have wanted to call attention to herself in that particular way is a matter for speculation. She was the middle child, and middle children often feel at a disadvantage in the struggle for their parents' affections. There were Robert Brown's frequent absences, his more than occasionally absent manner when home, and the added strain his comings and goings placed on Margaret's mother, who suffered from chronic high blood pressure severe enough at times to become disabling. Later, as she approached adulthood herself, Margaret seems to have felt an increasingly urgent need to find someone—mentor or friend—to fill the void left unattended by her parents.

An emotionally resilient, sanguine young child, Margaret discovered a refuge of sorts in nature. Deep-seated affections were transferred onto the landscape, to the small animals she observed and kept as pets, to wildflowers, trees, sky, and water. As a writer she would describe the natural world with an intensity that, in Proust's words, "makes us not merely regard a thing as a spectacle, but believe in it as a unique essence."

In *The Little Fir Tree,* a Christmas story, Margaret gave comforting substance to the fearfully intangible feelings of loneliness that all small children know: "Always the little fir tree looked over at the big fir trees in the great dark forest. He wished he were part of the forest or part of something, instead of growing all alone out there, a little fir tree in a big empty world."[28]

And in a passage in *The Golden Sleepy Book,* she transformed a simple stock taking of the natural order into a vision of loneliness banished: "All over the world the animals are going to sleep—the birds and the bees, the horse, the butterfly and the cat.

"In their high nests . . . the fish hawks are going to sleep. . . .

"And the fish in the sea sleep . . . like fish . . . in some quiet current of the sea."[29]

Early in 1923, when Robert Brown learned that he was to make another extended trip in India, Maude decided she should accompany him. An elaborate scheme was devised to allow their daughters to travel with them a part of the way. That summer, Margaret (just turned thirteen), Roberta (eleven), and their parents sailed for Europe in first-class accommodations aboard the Dutch liner *Veendam.*

The Browns toured Holland, then went on to Paris for more sightseeing. From there the girls were taken to Lausanne, where they spent the next two years at an exclusive girls' school, the Château Brillantmont. Robert and Maude boarded a ship for the long journey to India.

The following summer, Maude returned to Europe to travel with the children, including Gratz, who came over on his vacation from boarding school. Though keeping, as always, to a modest budget, she was determined to make the most of their adventure. One evening in Monte Carlo (where minors were barred from the gaming rooms) Maude concealed Gratz under her evening coat rather than have him miss the opulent spectacle of the casinos. In Venice, they all posed for pictures in St. Mark's Square and inspected churches and art museums, as they had done in Florence and Amsterdam. Then Gratz sailed for New York and Maude left the girls in their Lausanne school before returning to Paris for some time by herself.

Because most of the Château Brillantmont's students were English and its classes were conducted entirely in French, two years of study there were bound to be a broadening experience for the suburban New York sisters. The school's rigid disciplinary regime could nonetheless be rather trying, and Margaret in particular found it so. Students were required to keep separate pairs of shoes for indoor and outdoor wear, and once a day they were dispatched out along Lake Geneva, marching in double file with a matron bringing up the rear to keep them in good order. Margaret's knowledge of the French language (and of Swiss ski resorts, which she and her fellow students visited on holidays) would later serve her well. She would not, however, remember her years at the school with much affection, but rather (after the numerous dislocations of the past) as one more personal upheaval she had endured.

By the spring of 1925, when Margaret and Roberta came home to the United States, the house in Beechurst had been sold and her parents were living in temporary quarters on Long Island before leaving for Maine for the summer. The plan was to return in the fall and take an apartment in Forest Hills, in the general vicinity of where they wished to settle, and begin house hunting. (The new house was to be closer than the last to Manhasset, where Robert Brown's motorboat was moored). Anticipating the coming changes, Maude Brown enrolled in an interior decoration class. The girls spent the year at the nearby Kew Forest School.

The family celebrated the Christmas of 1925 at Buck Hill Falls, a Pennsylvania winter resort where an unpretentious holiday atmosphere prevailed. One Sunday, in an incident redolent of their earlier collaborative mischief making, Margaret and Roberta wandered into a Quaker prayer meeting. Feigning ignorance, one of the girls broke the silence by saying to the other in a loud whisper, "Why is everyone so quiet around here?" Then both girls bolted out the door.[30]

Maude Brown had a more serious religious encounter during that vacation. Another hotel guest, a Mrs. Sable of Rockport, Massachusetts, engaged her in a conversation about Theosophy.[31] Back in New York, Maude began attending meetings of the Theosophical Society and visited the Sables in Rockport for a part of each of the following two summers, taking Margaret and Roberta along with her. Robert Brown did not accompany them, preferring to fish off the coast of Maine. As would become increasingly apparent, Maude Brown's newfound interest in a spiritualist philosophy which posited the oneness of humankind with the universal All took root at a time when her relationship with her husband was beginning to unravel.

The two-story stucco house at 8 Ridge Drive which Robert Brown purchased in well-to-do Great Neck, New York, was ready for the family by the fall of 1926, just as Roberta and Margaret were leaving for yet another school.

Dana Hall, the private girls' preparatory school in Wellesley, Massachusetts that the two sisters entered as members of the class of 1928, was known for the rigorous academic training it offered girls bound for the Seven Sisters colleges. Latin and classical literature were emphasized, along with English literature, French, and mathematics. Music and art classes were considered of minor significance, as at most other schools of the time. Most striking about the Dana Hall regime was the importance the school placed on the development of intellectual self-confidence and independence. As Dana Hall's owner and principal Helen Temple Cooke declared, "the task of the School is to help each girl to think."[32]

Dana Hall students were instantly recognizable in their navy blue middy blouses and pleated skirts. On trips to town, which were always chaperoned, they were required to wear gloves and hats as well. High heels were at all times expressly forbidden. But for all the school's nettlesome rules and regulations, Dana Hall's faculty (which included a future president of progressive Sarah Lawrence College) took a generally farsighted view of the social questions of the day—not least of all of the role that educated women might play in the modern world. Anticipating the arrival of a group of visitors from all-black Howard University, Helen Cooke's assistant addressed the Dana Hall girls (all of them white) to ask if any would refuse to eat dinner with a black person.[33] When a few students said they would, she pressed them for their reasons; in this way, the faculty and staff challenged the girls to rethink their received prejudices. Margaret later recalled Dana Hall with gratitude as the first school she had attended that made learning seem worth the effort.

Margaret excelled at sports while remaining in her sister's shadow academically. (She nonetheless managed to place in the first quarter of their class of one hundred and twelve.) She impressed Helen Cooke as a well-groomed, able person of above average intelligence who needed to be prodded a bit to do her best. Classmates nicknamed Margaret "Tim" for her straw-blond hair, reminiscent of timothy. Her fellow seniors voted her "Most Serious"—Roberta was voted "Brightest."[33] But as commencement day approached in the spring of 1928, it appeared that Margaret might not graduate.

She had induced the class valedictorian and its treasurer to join her one evening on a moonlight walk along a remote path off limits to students after dark. A teacher caught the group and duly advised them to report their offense, for which others had suffered expulsion, to the principal. Days passed as the matter was taken under advisement.

Margaret, one suspects, had taken along her friend the valedictorian as insurance. It was finally decided that the three should graduate. At commencement Helen Cooke quoted Browning— "Grow old with me;/The best is yet to be"—and with that, bid Margaret, Roberta, and their classmates farewell.

At Dana Hall Margaret had elected not to take the mathematics and Latin courses required for admission to the more selective northeastern schools. She considered junior college, then (most likely it was her mother's idea) decided instead to apply to Maude Brown's alma mater, Hollins College.[34]

By then Gratz was an engineering major at M.I.T. and, much to Robert Brown's satisfaction, was preparing for a business career. But it was only over their father's objections and after Maude Brown's intervention on their behalf that Margaret and Roberta applied to college at all. Taking a conventional view of the matter, he thought a college education would be wasted on them, that the proper thing for his daughters to do was to marry well, have children, and stay at home. In the aftermath of that disagreement, family members went their separate ways that summer; Robert Brown to Maine for a fishing trip, Margaret south to visit school friends, Roberta and Maude to a quiet New Hampshire retreat. And that fall of 1928, the two sisters did go off to college, Roberta to prestigious Vassar, Margaret to the less demanding Hollins College, near Roanoke, Virginia.

Referred to with pride as "the Mount Holyoke of the South" by its partisans, Hollins College had the more dubious reputation in the North of a Southern finishing school for well-to-do girls, a place of quaint May Day rituals, untaxing academic pursuits, and chaperoned decorum. When Margaret arrived on campus, she found herself a welcome initiate of a warm family-run institution where it was equally possible to slip by with a minimum of strain or to acquire all the basic elements of a well-rounded liberal arts education.

Margaret had applied for admission in the usual way, filling out her application with the affecting candor of one more intent on taking the measure of her own worth than impressing others.

Could she sing? "No." *Play a musical instrument?* "No." *Draw or paint?* "No." *Act?* "I don't know." She enjoyed writing and had already written both stories and poems. *Had she won any academic scholarships or prizes?* "No." *Did she expect to graduate from college?* "I don't know." *Did she feel ready to enter heartily into the life of the school?* "Yes, I do."[35]

The focal point of the Hollins campus was the quadrangle

formed of ambling three-story red brick neo-classical buildings softened by touches of white Victorian gingerbread. Broad wooden porches, balconies, and colonnades edged the central lawn, which was crisscrossed by stone footpaths. East and West buildings, the student dormitories, faced each other like grounded riverboats across a yard shaded by splendid tall white ash trees. "Is it too vain a fancy," wrote Margaret's favorite literature professor, Marguerite Hearsey, in the graduation yearbook, "to find in [the quadrangle's] colonnades and columns, in the very brick and mortar of our physical Hollins, a symbol of our kinship with the Greeks?"[36]

Stately Main building, on the quadrangle's northern rim, was the school's formal center and hearth. In its Old Green Drawing Room students received their guests and took tea with visiting campus dignitaries. Miss Mattie Cocke, Hollins' elderly but formidable president, successor to her equally formidable father, had her office in Main as did her son, the dean; for nearly all of its eighty year history, Hollins had been owned and administered by the Cocke family.

At Hollins, with its small, secluded campus and a student population of fewer than three hundred women, everyone soon got to know everyone. Students took their meals and attended evening chapel together. Throughout the year there were numerous occasions when the entire Hollins community gathered for guest lectures, theater performances, and a full calendar of school rituals: the annual fall trek up nearby Tinker Mountain, the Christmas pantomime, and the gala May Day revel staged in the Forest of Arden. From the first, Margaret gave herself over to these school traditions, to the romance of them. It mattered deeply to her that Hollins had been Maude's school. Just being there allowed her to imagine a special closeness with her mother, a longed-for feeling of attachment that, ironically, remained a good deal more elusive when she was actually at home.

Margaret, who continued to be known by her Dana Hall nickname, "Tim," nonetheless soon acquired a reputation around campus as an individualist. The best of company, she quoted from *Winnie the Pooh* and gave parties to celebrate unbirthdays and the arrival of asparagus at the local market, but Margaret was also something of a loner. Above all fellow students learned to expect the unexpected from her; boarding a train on her way to a date at the University of Virginia, she was observed carrying a rabbit.

A certain mystique attached itself to the beautiful, fair-haired adventuress from the North whose preferred New York meeting place was said to be the last pew of St. Patrick's Cathedral and who once, on realizing she could not keep an appointment there, had sent her friend a telegram addressed to "Last pew, St. Patrick's Cathedral."[37] "A law unto herself," observed history professor Margaret P. Scott, "and definitely *not* a poseur."[38] (Scott had known Margaret almost from her first day on campus; some thirty years earlier, their mothers had been friends at Hollins.)

Entering with advanced standing in French, Margaret took a standard assortment of freshmen courses, but did not apply herself very seriously to her studies. She preferred to take long walks in the forest or up the narrow footpath to the Cocke family cemetery, with its stand of cedars and its commanding view of the Shenandoah Valley's deeply folded terrain. Throwing off her shoes, she might wade into Garvin's Creek, which ran just west of the quadrangle (perhaps coaxing a less adventurous companion in with her) or linger in the apple orchard or by the great weeping willows that lined the main campus road and which, like the fluted white columns of the quadrangle's colonnades, were said to embody the spirit of Hollins.

That spring, a visiting former Hollins professor, Dr. John M. McBride, prefaced a formal lecture on Southern folklore with a nostalgic slide talk on Hollins life as he had known it a quarter of a century earlier. As the professor's slides flashed onto the screen, the audience was amused by each passing glimpse of the vanished youths of this or that senior faculty member; but, as the campus paper reported, the evening's loudest "shrieks of delighted recognition" were reserved for a picture that startled all present with a moment of déjà vu. But for her costume, the image of the strikingly beautiful twenty-year-old Maude Johnson might have been a portrait of Margaret.[39]

As though to further bind the evening in memory for her, Dr. McBride proceeded to give a lecture on the Uncle Remus stories. He remarked in particular on the choice of the rabbit as the story cycle's central character. Although commonly viewed in the West as a lowly creature, the rabbit, McBride said, is revered in many traditional cultures around the world; the stories about Brer Rabbit, a typical trickster hero, came to the New World from Africa. Older still than the Uncle Remus tales are those of the ancient Eastern traditions, according to which the rabbit god, in recognition of his virtue and self-sacrifice, was rewarded by having his image permanently stamped on the face of the moon.

Overall, Margaret's freshman year went well. She earned average grades, was victorious on the hockey field, made friends of teachers and students, and enjoyed the new measure of personal freedom that college life afforded her. She spent most of a restless summer with her family in Great Neck and Maine, eager to be back on campus. Before returning to Hollins in the fall, she made a pilgrimage to historic Liberty Hall, the Brown family home in Frankfort, Kentucky, where, in her finest spidery cursive hand, she copied out pages of notes tracing her ancestry back to the reign of Elizabeth I by way of colonial Virginia.[40]

Radio first came to the Hollins campus that October, and on the evening of October 21, 1929, the entire Hollins community gathered in the student recreation room to "listen in" as President Hoover, Henry Ford, and Thomas Alva Edison spoke in the first radio program ever beamed worldwide, a tribute to Edison on the fiftieth anniversary of his invention of the incandescent light.[41] As part of the ceremony, listeners were asked to flash off and on their own electric lights in homage to the inventor. The "Jubilee of Light" was far and away the most elaborate media event (and public relations coup for the manufacturers of light bulbs) the world had yet seen. In less than a week, however, memories of the evening were eclipsed by news from New York. The following Thursday, the New York stock market dissolved in panic; the Great Depression had begun.

Visiting Hollins that fall, Reinhold Neibuhr lectured on Christian love, exhorting students to remember that although they lived in an "age of disillusionment," a time of faith tarnished by the bitter experience of the World War, it remained each person's responsibility to look inward, make an "intelligent self-analysis," and confront the world's problems without abandoning the idealism that was the special boon of youth. [42]

In the months to come, the Depression's main effect on Hollins life was a quickening of the attrition rate already a standard feature at all-women's colleges, where students often gave up their studies for marriage. In economically good times, about one in three Hollins freshmen might have been expected to drop out. But in 1932, Margaret's graduation year, three quarters of the sophomore class were already gone.

A visiting alumna, addressing students on "The Modern Girl," predicted (inaccurately, as statistics for the period would eventually indicate) that Hollins women would not be content merely to marry and have children, but would also insist on pursuing lifelong professional careers. "The college girl of to-day [*sic*] doesn't want leisure," declared Eudora Ramsay Richardson, class of 1910, "she wants to enjoy life to the fullest, and in these days of modern conveniences and early school age for children, a woman has to work outside her home if she is to be occupied fully." Richardson also observed that a woman might need to work to supplement the household income and should be prepared to support herself and her children in the event of divorce or her husband's death. With a nod to popular concern over the dreaded "mother fixation," she suggested that children might actually be better served by mothers with other interests to occupy them. [43]

Other alumnae, including Dorothy Dix, reportedly the highest paid woman journalist in the United States, spoke at Hollins about career opportunities in advertising, social work, psychology, and newspaper journalism, but of the members of Margaret's class who entered the work force upon graduation—and a majority did so—nearly all gave up their careers on marrying, on average within four years. (Classmates later reported to the *Alumnae Quarterly* their wedding dates, pregnancies, anniversaries, and the like; in marked contrast to the norm, Margaret kept Hollins regularly informed about her publications.) [44]

English composition, as taught by the unsmilingly rigorous Dr. F. Lamar Janney, proved a harrowing experience for one with Margaret's impatience with the proprieties of punctuation and spelling. She had little use for the comma, it seems, and perhaps owing partly to her French studies, her fanciful spellings of many English words more closely resembled Chaucer's than Webster's. On returning an "experimental" theme of hers, composed without the use of a single verb, Dr. Janney, an even-tempered romantic who had written his doctoral dissertation on "The Child in Wordsworth," threw up his hands (and with them a few stub ends of colored chalk) in exasperation. Frustrated, but also somehow impressed by his baffling, headstrong student, Professor Janney was overheard to declare Margaret a "genius without a talent."[45]

She did, as always, excel at sports, and having helped persuade the Hollins administration, at a time of dwindling enrollment, to build a riding ring and stable, Margaret found new scope for her prowess. She enjoyed the physicality and showmanship of riding competitions. Once when it seemed that spectators were not paying sufficient attention as she put her horse through its paces, she salvaged the situation by simply removing her cap. As Margaret's full mane of straw-blond hair flared dramatically behind her, all eyes automatically turned to her.

Stage acting, at which her mother had distinguished herself at Hollins, was more difficult for Margaret, as it required her to project her low, tremulous voice, so unlike Maude Brown's, in public. Margaret was embarrassed by the very sound of her own voice. Nonetheless, she seems to have faced her reluctance as another fence to be cleared. In her freshman year, the campus paper declared her death scene as the fatherly Lorenzo, King of Fiori, in Edna St. Vincent Millay's romantic tragedy "The Lamp and the Bell" to be one of the evening's highlights.[46] As a junior she attained the pinnacle of Hollins dramatics, playing the part of the Madonna in the annual Christmas pantomime, an elective honor conferred by fellow students in recognition of the winner's beauty and composure, not her piety.[47] The role suited Margaret perfectly, placing her at center stage without having to speak a word.

Junior and senior years she roomed with a student from West Point, Georgia, named Martha Huguley, who had become fast friends with her during a walk to the cemetery, when they first discovered that they enjoyed trading tall tales.[48] Martha soon had Margaret helping her improvise stories about her imaginary family, the Gets (This Get, That Get, Other Get, and their various relations). The two friends also read to each other from Proust, Virginia Woolf, and Gertrude Stein, writers for whom the typical Hollins student cared little, and they shared a theory that they and a fortunate few others had remained children in spirit and would always keep within themselves (as Lewis Carroll said of his Alice) the "simple and loving heart of . . . childhood" through all their "riper years."

Much of the time Margaret took a protective attitude toward Martha, cautioning her, as a parent or older sister might, against smoking and drinking, all the while continuing to do both herself. At other times, Tom Sawyer–like, she led the way in mischief, as when she decided that they should have a dog, despite a school rule prohibiting pets. Margaret purchased a pup in town and hastily arranged to board it with one of the staff; technically, the dog was not living in the dormitory. It was this ability of Margaret's to "rise above" without ever quite breaking the rules that Martha most admired. If there was a lesson to be learned from it all, Martha thought it must be that to have one's way in life was not necessarily a matter of asserting one's will, but rather of using one's imagination properly.

During her junior year, Martha recorded her appointments in a small, quaintly illustrated French calendar to which Margaret felt free to add her own notations. The pages for the week in June just after the end of the spring term read like a comedy routine, with Martha, who planned to stay on for a few leisurely days after her roommate left for the North, naturally reduced to the straight-man's role.

> MONDAY. [Martha:] *See Mary all day—the walk, the ride, the dance.*
> [Margaret:] Send Tim a present. TUESDAY. *Hollins at 11:30.* Read
> [Virginia Woolf's] *Orlando.* WEDNESDAY. *The Holy Grail. The
> Horse-back ride. Swim.* Write to Tim. THURSDAY. *See Roanoke.
> Flowers. Swim.* Send Tim a picture. FRIDAY. *Poetry. Good-bye.* Un-
> derline a book you like and send it to Tim.[49]

The unassailable good cheer of Margaret's unsolicited messages—little offerings from "Tim" for her indulgent, doting friend—masked Margaret's secret doubts about her future at the school. She had not told Martha that she had just failed chemistry, a course she needed to graduate; she was all but certain that she would not be returning to Hollins for her senior year.

From her parents' home she wrote the registrar indicating her intention to withdraw and contemplated her own unworthiness, the lack of discipline and inner resolve that was (had Dr. Janney not implied as much?) the dark side of her sparkling impetuosity.[50] The correspondence with school officials took a positive turn, however, when the dean offered Margaret a chance to regain her lost academic ground. With heartfelt gratitude, she accepted the offer as the reprieve it was. Thanking Dean Cocke for his consideration of her "lack of one hour," as she called it, Margaret promptly mailed in her registration fee. Her high spirits restored, she added: "Please remind me to Mrs. Cocke and to 'Cracker Crumb'—that is Albert [one of the dean's grown sons]. Very sincerely yours, Tim."[51]

That fall she signed up for a heavy course load, applied herself more diligently to her studies than in the past, and in Marguerite Hearsey's Chaucer class produced an essay thought good enough for the campus literary magazine, *Cargoes*—her first publication. In Chaucer ("my old teacher," she later called him) Margaret had discovered a benign yet knowing foil for her own self-critical inclinations. "We . . . breathe a sigh of relief," she wrote of Chaucer's robust depictions of human folly, "to find ourselves exposed in a light that makes us appear much less sinister than did the shadow of our own imagination. Our burden of bad conscience becomes merely a humorous deformity that we share with our fellow-men."[52]

The experience, both heady and formal, of seeing her work in print for the first time did not decide Margaret, there and then, on a literary career, but Marguerite Hearsey believed that Margaret might one day be a writer and told her so. The teacher's words came as a much-needed piece of encouragement. In 1937, five years after her graduation, when Harper and Brothers published her first book, *When the Wind Blew,* Margaret inscribed a copy to Hearsey: "Remembering the stumbling of words that led up to whatever clarity is here. And always thanking you for the first encouragement."[53]

Hearsey, in turn, recalled having learned an important lesson or two from her memorable student. Margaret as a rule did not say much during class discussions, but once in the Chaucer seminar Hearsey was reading vigorously aloud from the Middle English when she suddenly came to one of the bawdier passages and hesitated in embarrassment; just then a quavering voice—Margaret's—piped up from across the room, "Is it going to have a red light and a green light?"[54]

Over spring recess, Margaret travelled to Little Rock, Arkansas, to be married—or so she had told Martha—to a young Southern lawyer she had met on the rounds of parties at neighboring men's colleges. The story sounded a bit incredible to Martha. But when Margaret arrived in Little Rock, actually for the purpose of meeting young George Armistead's family (formal engagement plans were indeed in the works), she went so far as to telegram holiday greetings to her roommate in the name of the happy couple-to-be:

NATURE SMILES AND ALL IS GLAD WHY SHOULD MORTAL MAN BE SAD RAISE YOUR EYES AND LOOK ABOVE EASTER JOYS BRING NAUGHT BUT LOVE —*Mr. & Mrs. George Armistead.*[55]

Just what happened next is not clear, except that the engagement was broken off and that it was Margaret who ended it. Martha was taken aback again when her roommate returned to campus alone and unmarried. Astonishingly, close though they were in some ways (especially where Martha's personal affairs were concerned), they never talked about this dramatic incident, even briefly. Margaret's only explanation took the form of a terse note scrawled on a slip of legal paper and left under Martha's bedroom door. "Life," the message read, "is damn queer."[56]

In May, when the campus newspaper canvassed seniors about their future plans, Margaret, with no imminent marriage prospects or other news to report and with her twenty-second birthday fast upon her, answered, "Lord knows."[57] It was as wryly philosophical a good face as she could put on a dubious situation. The following month, Margaret was once again living in her parents' home.

CHAPTER TWO

NEW
YORK
HERE
AND
NOW

There are so many New Yorks
that you can always find the
special one that fits your
special pattern.

LUCY SPRAGUE MITCHELL,
Two Lives

The coming of the Great Depression had no appreciable effect on the Brown household in Great Neck. Robert Brown remained secure in his job and in his Republican politics. He kept his prized motorboat at the Port Washington Yacht Club and took it for long solitary spins on Long Island Sound. Maude Brown continued to drive her own automobile and to employ a cook. While at college, Roberta and Margaret had not been asked to make do with smaller allowances, forego activities not included in their tuitions, or sacrifice in any other way. When Margaret returned home from Hollins in June of 1932, it was not with pressing financial worries on her mind. Relations between her parents were chilly, but this had been the case for some considerable time.

Her overriding concern, simply put, was to decide what next

to do with herself. Roberta, as purposeful and academically successful as always, was bound for graduate studies in physics at Yale.
With no comparable prospects of her own, Margaret over the next
several months did her best to settle in at home and attended the
weddings of friends while contemplating, albeit in the abstract, a
married future of her own.

In the late spring of 1933, Margaret returned to Hollins for
her first class reunion and continued on to West Point, Georgia, to
attend Martha Huguley's wedding as one of eight bridesmaids.
The celebration, with all the elaborate preliminary teas and parties, lasted a week, allowing time for Margaret to get acquainted
with the bride's entire family, which for the purposes of the wedding included not only a full complement of cousins, uncles, and
aunts, but also the local police and fire departments and everyone's
household servants.

Margaret seemed to enjoy herself, dispensing mirth in her cus-
tomary fashion—one evening leading a group in a game she called
Stomach, in which players in a circle took turns resting their heads
on the next person's belly while telling some ridiculous story to
make everyone laugh. She caused Martha's father a little fright
when she announced her intention to wander out alone after dark
along the banks of the treacherous Chattahoochee River, but at
the ceremony Margaret merged effortlessly into the formal wedding
tableau, appearing, as recorded in "Miss Martha's Wedding Book,"
in "violet crêpe with a yoke of beige gorgette finished with fur at
the neck," and a corsage of roses. Margaret presented the newlyweds with an antique French silver and crystal liqueur set. More
tellingly, when the couple returned from their honeymoon, they
were surprised to find a second gift of sorts: "Tim" herself—part
doting, worried mother, part abandoned child—waiting on their
doorstep to greet them. [1]

A year later Margaret received a letter from her married friend
and reported to her Hollins mentor, Marguerite Hearsey, that
Martha did indeed seem very happy, "And I am glad for her." And
yet, she added, considering the shock of separation that comes
with the end of one's college years, a separation measured not just
in the loss of daily contact with old friends but in the sheer diver-
gence of the new lives chosen, "it is strange that we will never again

meet on a common ground of interest. . . . We were once so very close," she wrote Miss Hearsey, "and now we hardly speak the same language."[2]

For Margaret, 1933 and much of the following year passed in this way, her calendar perforated with the weddings of classmates. In late 1933, to occupy herself, she took a sales job at Altman's in Manhattan.

Commuting to New York, she spent weekdays behind Altman's silver counter, an experience she outwardly tolerated, but recoiled from mentally. In "The Meeting," a short story based on her sales job experiences and apparently written at this time, she evoked something of the inner turmoil of her predicament: "The [sales]girl . . . was staring far away. . . . It was a curious expression to find on a salesgirl's face. . . . There was no . . . 'May I help you Madame,' about this girl." Approaching a certain customer, the girl "was not interested so much in a sale as in an uninvolved desire to be of assistance to a person who interested her."[3]

Nonetheless, Margaret was able to amuse herself on occasion. A historian by training, her brother-in-law-to-be, Basil Rauch, had found temporary employment as an Altman's floorwalker. A novice at stealth, he did his best to blend discreetly into the throngs of shoppers, only to have Margaret call out loudly across the selling floor, "Hello, Basil!"[4]

Her own romantic life was at a standstill, and perhaps as much for the sake of a new circle of friends as for other reasons, she became a charter member (in the spring of 1934) of the Buckram Beagles, a group (primarily) of Long Island socialites with an interest in pursuing the sporting life in the form of long strenuous runs through the woods to hounds, with a rabbit as their quarry.

Running to hounds was an ancient pastime when King Edward III of England took it up in the mid-fourteenth century. In the British-inspired American version of the sport, hours of rugged physical exercise were capped by a convivial late-afternoon high tea. While out in the woods, the men and women of the club participated as equals and were judged only on their stamina. As both a formidable runner and a charming companion, Margaret became a much admired member of the group.

Margaret herself provided the most telling clue as to what

hunting meant to her. In an undated poem titled "Running/Running to Hounds," the hunter's quest is a contest in which the victory is won not over a fleeing animal but over time itself: "An old body/Rises up in the new/And leans forward into the wind/Made by its own running/Long strong leaps/As though the fields had springs/And my body hangs from the shoulders/As the shoulders help it along/And my fists climb the air/And the lean/muscles of/an old stomach/Come in my new stomach/And my legs run/on through my/weariness/Keep running."[5]

During the summer of 1934 time weighed heavily on her. Her new club was in suspension till the fall and her job still bored her. With no compelling reason for staying, Margaret quit work and headed north to meet Roberta and Basil at Don Dickerman's Camp, an offbeat resort on Kezar Lake in southwestern Maine frequented by writers and theater people. There she socialized with the other guests, took part in a play reading, and wandered off for solitary afternoons of boating and hiking. "I am leading the lusty life of the woods," she wrote Marguerite Hearsey. "There are roaring fires at night. I plunge naked into the lake in the morning and we . . . laugh deep down in our stomaches like Vikings."[6]

One afternoon, after paddling out alone to the middle of Kezar Lake in a kayak, Margaret became absorbed in a book and, looking up only "at intervals," was surprised to find on finishing it that she had come more than two miles to the Lake's unfamiliar far end. "I moored the boat . . . and wandered up a road to an old country store, to leave the book so that it wouldn't get wet going home against a wind that had come up suddenly. . . . Then I had a wonderful battle against black waves and wind to get home." The battle "brought out all the bad parts of my nature." Taking pride in her honesty as she faulted herself for a serious breech of her personal code, she admitted that she had wanted "to signal three speed boats that passed for a tow. But I didn't. (Only one and they didn't see me, but that halfhearted attempt marred the core of my victory.)"

Evidently, Margaret had also gone to Maine with hopes of proving herself as a writer, perhaps by turning out a polished short story or two; she suffered a disappointment on finding herself too restless and impatient to do so. So out of sorts was she that she felt "as though I were cheating and quibbling with time whenever I read a book" instead of trying to write one. Nevertheless, she wrote her old teacher, she realized that

> there seem to be times of reception and times of creation and it is perhaps difficult not to confuse the two. . . . Now I am living such a rich life of all the senses with pine smoke and clear air and distant mountains and wind and sails, that some good cannot fail to come out of it in the spirit. . . . All of me is responding entirely. That, to respond entirely, is my idea of complete health.

It was largely through Margaret's correspondence with Marguerite Hearsey, the Hollins professor who had encouraged her to think about becoming a writer, that Margaret kept this possibility alive for herself. She wrote Miss Hearsey often, and the dedicated, kindly older woman was happy enough to serve as a mentor and sounding board.

Back in New York in September of 1934, Margaret found in city routine a more problematic kind of intensity, a "strange mixture," she wrote, "of Subway rush and hurried moments of awareness."[7] Roberta had returned home to a Great Neck teaching job, a professional advance which, modest though it was, underlined for Margaret her own lack of direction. Thinking that the enforced discipline of a course might help her get on with writing, she enrolled for the fall semester in a fiction workshop at Columbia University.

Margaret anticipated the course, for which her father had agreed to foot the bill, in fear and trembling. If she was to have a career as impractical, from Robert Brown's point of view, as that of a writer, she would have to prove herself soon. What was more, she had long since internalized the pressure to do so. On the evening before her first class, she scratched out a letter to Miss Hearsey "so horridly full of information" that she felt the need to apologize for it. "Information," she considered, "is like a plot. A plot is like the sound of the word. 'Plot.' . . . I will never be a writer."[8]

The Columbia workshop proved a disheartening misadventure. Years later, in an interview in *Life* magazine, she shrugged off the experience with the wry throwaway remark that she had simply not been able to "think up any plots."[9] But it may not have been just for want of invention that Margaret found the class so trying that she dropped out before the end of the term. In the absence of story ideas, she seems to have fallen back for material on some of her own painful recent experiences with romance and at home. Perhaps writing about these troubles forced her to focus on them all the more intently.

One such story, "In Ten Years,"[10] begins with a scathing account of life with her parents: "Mr. Rabber got in his car. He noticed as he crossed his lawn . . . that it was a good day.—A most irrelevant observation, however, for Mr. Rabber had no time for a good day. As he told his daughter, dollars didn't grow on trees, and he had to get into town and work."[11]

Elizabeth, the grown daughter from whose point of view Margaret told the story, watches her father from a distance. "She didn't make a sound for fear he would speak to her. He would only upset her if he spoke. He might shout at her; and the morning was so beautiful. . . . She shuddered and turned to her book."

It was doubtless tempting to treat as fictions—as characters to be parodied and paraded at will—those people with whom Margaret was not getting along. Paradoxically—and the paradox spoke to her very core—Margaret was never a more conscientious truth teller than as the author of these outwardly fictional character studies. However inconsequential as literature, the pieces seem to have served her as occasions for taking stock of herself, her limitations and prospects, and her capacity for self-knowledge.

Elizabeth longs for the day she will live on her own, and she is evidently on no better terms with her mother than with her father.

> Elizabeth's mother was . . . too quick for her. She called down from her bedroom for her daughter to perform the first of what the latter expected would be an interminable list of small and for the most part unnecessary errands. . . .
>
> "What shall I get?" [Elizabeth asked.]
>
> "Oranges, and see if we need any butter and eggs . . . ."
>
> "I can telephone for all that, Mother; there is no need to make a trip down town."
>
> "No you can't. You must pick things out."

"But there is nothing you have mentioned, Mother, that has to be picked out." . . .

"You grow more like your Father every day. . . . You should go to a doctor. You used to be a sweet tempered child."

The action continues with a scene that in all likelihood was Margaret's fictionalized effort to clarify her emotional confusion at the time of her engagement, two years earlier, to George Armistead. Elizabeth's boyfriend is expected for dinner; the couple has agreed to ask Mr. Rabber's permission to marry.

At five o'clock, Elizabeth bathed and dressed, went out into the garden. She broke some branches from an apple tree, little red flower buds among the pale green of the leaves[,] returned to the house and arranged them. . . . [Then] she drove to the station to meet Jim, who had a good job in New York. The train came in and she heard the rush of it all through her.

The couple's emotionally flat conversations suggest a distant, troubled relationship. Tellingly, this and other short stories that Margaret finished all end vaguely, inconclusively, as though their outcome lay in her own future, a future she could not predict and felt was largely beyond her control. Moreover, in the story "In Ten Years" Elizabeth's point of view remains blurred; it is unclear whether she realizes the irony of her imminent marriage to a young business success well on his way to becoming a difficult man just like her father.

Margaret succeeded in making painfully vivid the troubled atmosphere of an outwardly placid and prosperous home. Among her instructor's criticisms was the comment "Couldn't you manage to convey a little more intensely that they [Elizabeth and Jim] love each other?"[11] In all honesty, Margaret could not.

That fall (of 1934), Margaret had taken an apartment in Manhattan, which her father had agreed to finance. With the help of a new city friend, Inez Camprubi, she found a small place on MacDougal Street, in the proverbial heart of Greenwich Village.

Inez, a painter, lived in the apartment across the hall. She and Margaret began to spend a good deal of time together, talking about art, Gertrude Stein, and their personal crises and passions of the moment. Theirs was an easy-going, companionable friendship. Inez impressed Margaret as a person of great inner resolve. She had had the independence to decide not to go to college, choosing instead to live for a time in Spain, in the household of her uncle, the illustrious poet Juan Ramón Jiménez. In addition to pursuing her art, she was enrolled as a student in the Cooperative School for Student Teachers, an intensive program of the highly innovative Bureau of Educational Experiments. The bureau, which had come to be known by its west Greenwich Village address as Bank Street, was an internationally respected center of childhood development research as well as a functioning nursery school and a training ground for teachers.

In letters to Marguerite Hearsey Margaret praised Inez for her forthright manner and, as she somewhat cryptically put it, for the "more or less social work" of her Bank Street activities. Margaret's talented friend also proved a sympathetic listener when it came time to review her prospects for a literary career. Margaret did not feel very optimistic on that score. At least, she told Inez, she had managed to devise a method for staving off depression. On awakening in the morning, Margaret lay in bed for a time, surveying the room around her to the last detail. One by one she noted every particular of the room and the scene out her window that gave her pleasure. Then—grasping for straws or counting her blessings— she wrote them all down in a list. [12]

The strenuous exercise of running to hounds provided another release. One Sunday Margaret took Inez along with her to Long Island. The two friends had a glorious time. Inez won Margaret's admiration all over again by easily keeping pace with her. Inez, for her part, was richly amused when she noticed that Margaret, instead of staying as close as possible behind the hounds, as beaglers were supposed to do, simply ran off now and then in her own direction.

Margaret spent an evening that fall with Frances Stoakley, Hollins class of 1929 and its leading literary light, who had come to New York to make her reputation as a poet. Together they read aloud poems they both admired, like Thomas Wyatt's "My lute be still, for I have done." ("How complete that is and honest in its mood," Margaret wrote Miss Hearsey.)[13] Through Frances she discovered the poetry of Emily Dickinson, reflecting in another letter,

"I can't understand how I never read her. I must have confused her with Sara Teasdale and some of the 'Ah the pain of it all, girls.' " Margaret also reread the books that had meant the most to her in college, Virginia Woolf's *The Waves* and *Orlando,* some Romantic poetry, and (to "cure to sleep a bad attack of futility") the second part of Chaucer's "The Knight's Tale," which ends with the accidental death of one worthy knight, the triumph in love of his equally worthy rival, and the admonition to bear oneself through life with equanimity, for *"alday meeteth men at unset stevene"* (one is constantly keeping appointments one never made). [14]

That fall, Margaret also thought about studying painting, but after one uninspiring session at the Art Students League she decided "to get a pile of green vegetables and paint by myself at home instead of paying to paint a pile of naked figures." [15]

"In my own life," she wrote her former teacher, "I feel like a green vegetable—peas—that arn't [*sic*] cooked yet but are doing a lot of whirling about in the kettle."

As Margaret whirled, she also trudged through Gertrude Stein's long and arduous *The Making of Americans:*

> In this book I am given new solutions, brand new ideas. . . . There is a rhythm of American day to day existence and relationship that is as certain as the rhthm [*sic*] of the ocean and as binding as the relationship of the ocean to the little waves that crash on our shore. . . . I think she is the first to write of many people without cutting them off from the grandparents who were once little children whose parents produced them and from the flow of life that goes on about them and that went before them and that will go on after them. [16]

One evening in early November, she and Frances Stoakley met to listen to Stein—her "beautiful voice"—on the radio.

> One of my insignificant joys in her clarity was her remark, when her punctuation was challenged, that "If a reader doesn't know that a question is a question when he reads it, then a question mark can't tell him." I prayed to one of God's clerks who handles his lesser business that Dr. Janney was listening. [17]

Later that month Margaret attended one of three lectures given by Gertrude Stein at the Brooklyn Academy of Music. Buddha-like and formidable in appearance, Stein was disarmingly down-to-earth as she spoke and laughed and occasionally teased the audience by asking (a certain reputation for obfuscation having preceded her) whether they were having trouble following her meaning.

Margaret came away exalted. And the memory of that evening stayed with her even as she packed her bags in defeat and moved back in with her parents in time for Thanksgiving. On New Year's Eve, as she closed out 1934 in a letter to Marguerite Hearsey and as the "very solemn" mood that always descended upon her at this time of year asserted itself, she ruefully considered the "weakness of every undisciplined area of my mind, which, as you know, is most of it."[18] On a recent visit to New York, Miss Hearsey had spent an afternoon with her. "After I left you," Margaret recalled, "I found a large bunch of narcissus in the Subway for 15¢, and for 15¢ it was Spring. . . . I pause here being frightened that this sounds like Gertrude Stine [*sic*]. But no. If I think that, I can't write to you so the words had best come out as they will." She was uncertain even of her authenticity as a letter writer.

Over the next several weeks, however, her situation began to change. That winter she found temporary employment as a child's companion, a part-time job that hardly felt like work at all. Her duties consisted of gently prodding twelve-year-old Dorothy Wagstaff to do her lessons and accompanying that very wealthy young girl to dog shows, movies, teas, and on horseback rides, all between the hours of two and five-thirty on weekday afternoons.[19] For her services she received the tidy sum of fifty dollars a month. From Margaret's standpoint, this was clearly an interim measure. She had still to find her own equivalent of the fulfilling lifework, the "something . . . outside of herself" that her friend Inez had committed herself to at Bank Street. Margaret was painting again at the Art Students League, but she saw these exertions too as a stopgap, an "indirect approach to writing" or a limbering-up exercise.

In the spring of 1935, having continued to receive good reports about Bank Street from Inez, Margaret took a first step toward entering the Bank Street program herself. Ordinarily a new student began in the fall, taking a complete battery of courses while at the same time acquiring on-the-job training as a teaching assistant at one of several New York–area progressive schools with which Bank Street was affiliated. Margaret, however, arranged to start as a student teacher that very spring, before even applying for admission to the Cooperative School for Student Teachers. It was rather like her to do her best to bend the rules in a situation about which she felt ambivalent. She wanted to waste no time in finding out whether teaching might satisfy her professionally. Following directly in Inez's path, she reported for work at the Little Red School House, where she was assigned to the second grade class, "the Eights."

Of her regular encounters with the Little Red School House's eight-year-olds, she wrote to Miss Hearsey: "They tell me stories and I write them down. Amazing. And also the pictures they paint. It must be true [as the school's regular teachers and staff believed] that children are born creative. I love best the little colored children. And they give long spontaneous plays." Margaret, however, had already come to an important conclusion: "I don't want to teach." The previous several weeks she had been too tired, or "too over charged," to pursue her writing. "A few poems. But really nothing. . . . And I hear Time whirring by. I am very sorry."[20]

Perhaps, then, it was only for want of an alternative that Margaret proceeded to apply for admission to Bank Street's Cooperative School for Student Teachers. For philosophical reasons (and perhaps for financial reasons as well) Bank Street rarely turned down a serious applicant, but acceptance into the program was not guaranteed. In evaluating candidates, Elizabeth Lamb (the perceptive, down-to-earth staff member who interviewed Margaret) looked for signs of an inquiring, flexible mind and an overall impression of emotional wellbeing.[21] She found Margaret clearly suitable—a good-natured, bright, and exceptionally poised young woman. At twenty-five, Margaret was a year or two older than the average applicant—well and good, as personal maturity was an asset in work with children. It also counted in her favor that she had lived in Europe and in the American South; in theory at least,

Bank Street strove for a broad cultural diversity in its students and staff. She was accepted for the fall of 1935.

Whatever Margaret's private reservations may have been as the semester got under way that October, she soon decided that Bank Street was a truly exciting place to be. For one thing, she had never before been so busy. Mondays through Wednesdays she continued as a teacher's assistant in the Little Red School House. There were thirty-five eight-year-olds, she told Marguerite Hearsey, "and they are all alive."[22] On Thursdays and Fridays academic and arts classes met at 69 Bank Street from nine in the morning till seven in the evening, with little time set aside for lunch, recreation, or rest. With a sense of having pledged herself to what she ebulliently called the "service of discoverie" (quoting Samuel Johnson), she plunged headlong into Bank Street's varied activities.

During the 1930s Bank Street was the scene of a robust social experiment which after nearly two decades of intensive spade work and much progress was ripe for a fresh harvest of accomplishments. One aspect of the school's considerable appeal for Margaret and many others was that it operated as a laboratory where learning proceeded as much by observation and experiment as by formal classroom study. Margaret and her fellow trainees were but one of three main groups working side by side. A dedicated core faculty of psychologists, educational reformers, anthropologists, and artists taught the trainees. Both groups had regular contact with the children and staff of the Bank Street nursery school. The trainees helped the faculty carry out their research studies, in which the children were the subjects; they also helped in the day-to-day supervision of the nursery school and "cooperating" day schools for older children like the Little Red School House and the Rosemary Junior School of Greenwich, Connecticut.

The central idea that unified Bank Street's varied endeavors was the assumption, basic to the American progressive schools movement as a whole, that to teach children effectively one had first to understand how the young experienced reality at every stage of their natural development. At traditional schools, including virtually all American public schools at the time of the founding of the Bureau of Educational Experiments in 1916, children were treated as incomplete adults who chiefly required lessons in disci-

pline and in certain skills—the three Rs, civics, and other subjects—as preparation for their future lives in the marketplace or at
home. Progressive educators maintained that the young had legiti-
mate interests and needs quite apart from these.

Almost from the start, a major goal of the bureau's faculty and
staff had been to contribute to the establishment of an accurate,
flexible definition of children's developmental stages, a tower-
ing intellectual challenge grounded in the work of many others—
theorists as diverse as John Dewey, Edward L. Thorndike, and
Sigmund Freud. The ultimate aim of Bank Street teaching, in
turn, was to provide children with learning situations in which
to develop as fully as possible in accordance with their individual
potentials. Margaret and her thirty-odd classmates were encouraged to discover their own practical means to that end through a
continual open-minded give-and-take between the theories
which they studied in class and their own daily encounters with
children.

Bank Street was unique in the United States as a place where
the three distinct functions of developmental research, teacher
training, and nursery-level education—each of which was a focus
of numerous experimental efforts around the country—had been
thoroughly integrated. The school's organizational scheme was itself an expression of one of the most fundamental principles of
Bank Street's educational philosophy, that of "relationship thinking," the notion that understanding is enhanced whenever the individual elements of a question are seen in relation to each other
and to the larger whole. Even the boxy four-story structure (once a
Fleischmann's Yeast factory) which housed the school offered up to
visitors a striking illustration of the concept of relationship thinking. Indoors at 69 Bank Street, exposed utility pipes had been
color-coded in red and blue, so that the building's interior func-
tioned as a working diagram of itself, a sort of outsize educational toy highlighting the web of technology on which daily life
depends.

Margaret's new environment was an informal, noisy, bustling
place where no one person seemed to be in charge unless, as a staff
member wryly suggested, it was the janitor. It was a "rabbit warren," as one of the school's numerous visiting observers recalled, a

labyrinth of cramped and cluttered offices, chockablock corridors, and spacious nursery playrooms.

The staff of a dozen or so—the "sane maniacs" another visitor called them—were selected with a view toward representing the widest possible range of theoretical outlooks. While a materialist psychologist tracked changes in the children's cranial measurements in a study of the relationship of skull size to intellectual capacity, others watched the nursery children for fresh bits of behavioral data or lectured the staff and students on Freud. When a German emigré who had studied with Maria Montessori appeared one day, eager to enroll in the teacher training program but unable to pay tuition, she was promptly hired as the school's librarian. When an educational toymaker whose ideas interested the staff needed a workshop, space was cleared for his use near the freight elevator. During Margaret's time at the school, an aspiring young publisher of experimental children's books, William R. Scott, was also given space, an "office" in the school's projection closet. As in the Vanderhoef household of Kaufman and Hart's comedy, *You Can't Take It with You,* many who came to visit 69 Bank Street ended by staying.

The one hundred or so children enrolled in the nursery school at any one time came from all parts of the city and from diverse ethnic and religious backgrounds. There were children of celebrities—the son of actress Ruth Gordon and producer-director Jed Harris, the daughter of artist Ben Shahn, and others. While many of the children were from families of privilege, the school also offered a substantial number of scholarships in a deliberate experiment in democracy carried out on the scale of the classroom.

The impression that no single individual had primary authority in the running of the school was, however, largely an illusion cultivated by Lucy Sprague Mitchell, the central figure responsible for the founding of the Bureau of Educational Experiments and a woman of idealism, practicality, and selfless ambition. A level-headed visionary in the progressive mold of Jane Addams and John Dewey, she considered herself above all a social reformer. Her interest in education was rooted in her commitment to democratic values and the belief that a democratic society could flourish only if all its members were given the chance to develop to their fullest potential and taught to work together cooperatively. Lucy Mitchell was genuinely determined that Bank Street should, through all its activities, serve the world as a model democracy based on ultimate respect for children's developmental needs and priorities. However, if it became necessary from time to time to play the benevolent despot in order to further that goal, she was prepared to do so.

In 1935, when Margaret first met her, Lucy Mitchell was fifty-seven years old and at the height of her powers. Everything about her seemed larger-than-life. A taller than average woman, Mitchell had a sparkling but somewhat formal manner that many people found intimidating. "Don't talk while I interrupt," she good-naturedly chided everyone at the school at one time or another.[23]

Her loose-fitting, deep-pocketed dresses and long beaded necklaces presented a curiously unstudied contrast to her patrician bearing. An incorrigible chain-smoker, Mitchell sometimes absently lit a second cigarette while a first still dangled from her hand. She often seemed to be in an extraordinary hurry and she spoke in a rapid but deliberate deep voice which broke off in mid-sentence to begin a different thought without the least regard for those unable to keep pace with her racing intellect.

As a seminar leader, researcher, student advisor, benefactor, and writer, Mitchell continually energized and inspired those around her. With a knowledge of literature, geography, comparative religion, philosophy, history, and current affairs which was at once encyclopedic and lightly held, she displayed a great knack for conveying the clear essence of any subject that engaged her curiosity. Equally important, she made others—Margaret not least among them—eager to learn.

Born in Chicago in 1878 into an enormously wealthy family of transplanted New Englanders (her father, Otho Sprague, was a founding partner of Sprague Warner and Company, the wholesale foodstuffs concern later known as General Foods), she was denied nothing in childhood for "financial reasons," as she later recalled.

> But I was denied, as a child, all the art expressions that I think are
> very deep in me. I was never allowed to choose the color of a dress
> because I was told I wasn't old enough. My father was really upset
> if he found that I had written anything. When I was 7 or 8 I wrote
> poems by the yard, but my terror in life was that he would find
> them. I would actually have been disciplined. [24]

Her mother had been both a "delightful and tragic" person.
"Mother," she recalled, "was an artist by temperament, and . . .
might well have been a professional musician; she had a quality
that I can only describe gently as gypsy-like. She was naturally a
very impulsive and very affectionate person, but shy about expressing her affection." Otho Sprague, ten years older than his wife,
had "very little sympathy with that type of spontaneity." He was,
in his daughter's later estimate, "a very controlled man and a businessman," who treated her mother (to whom she thought him
genuinely devoted) "like an older daughter." [25]

Through her father's philanthropic activities in Chicago,
young Lucy Sprague became aware of the social and educational
experiments of Jane Addams and John Dewey; by the time she was
in her teens, their ideas and activities interested her greatly. At
Radcliffe College, where she majored in philosophy and was
elected president of the Class of 1900, she took full advantage of
the freedom that living away from home afforded her and pursued
her intellectual interests with all her considerable might and main.

Not least of the revelatory insights gleaned in four years of
intensive study was the realization that learning itself might be an
impetuous form of play.

> When I first heard of [William] James' theory that behavior pro-
> duces emotion, as well as that emotion produces behavior, I re-
> solved to test it. These men in the philosophy department were
> highly individualized in their behavior as well as in their thinking.
> If I *behaved* like one of them, would I not *feel* like him? . . . For a
> week, I walked breezily, swinging my arms like William James.
> I let my mind and my speech fly off in a tangent if it felt like do-
> ing so. [26]

This delightful experiment suggests the young woman's deepening accord with James' underlying faith in firsthand experience.

In a series of public lectures (published in 1898 as *Talks to Teachers*) James argued that the mental growth of children was certain to be advanced by regular exposure to non-cerebral, firsthand experiences such as manual work with different tools and materials, play with a variety of toys, and exploratory trips outside the classroom. "A child brought up alone at home"—James might almost have been describing Lucy Sprague's own first years when, as a sickly, house-bound child, she haunted her father's library—"with no acquaintance with anything but the printed page, is always afflicted with a certain remoteness from the material facts of life,"[27] a remoteness that detracted from one's subsequent ability to realize one's potential as a mature individual and citizen.

A few years after graduation, Lucy Sprague won appointment as the first dean of women at the University of California at Berkeley and the school's first female English instructor. In the spirit of James and Dewey, she not only counseled and lectured her students but also marched them down to orphanages, settlement houses, poor houses, and the San Francisco docks in an effort to acquaint them at firsthand with the world that lay beyond the privileged ranges of their academic studies.

Despite her innovative "curriculum of experience" and the challenging responsibilities that went with her dual appointment, she grew restless at Berkeley.[28] In the fall of 1911, she made a three-month visit to New York for the purpose of undertaking a series of exploratory "apprenticeships" with leading figures in the city's progressive reform movement.[29]

In January of 1912 she accepted the long-standing marriage proposal of a respected young Berkeley economist, Wesley Clair Mitchell (known affectionately as Robin), who agreed to move east with her permanently. During the couple's first years in New York's intellectually vibrant Greenwich Village, Lucy Mitchell continued to investigate the city's wide range of ongoing social reformist experiments. As she did so, she collected more mentors.

From John Dewey, whose lectures at Teachers College she began attending regularly, she acquired a powerful conceptual framework within which to focus her own still fragmentary ambitions and ideas. In the series of lectures that formed the basis of his monumental *Democracy and Education,* she heard Dewey argue that education was essentially an organic process whose true end was the nurturing of human growth. It followed from this that democracy, as the social system that allowed for the freest possible exchange of information and ideas, provided the optimal conditions for education to flourish and that, conversely, every classroom ought to be viewed as a democracy in microcosm, as a place where individuality was valued and where children learned to act as responsible members of an interdependent community.

In Edward Thorndike's researches, Lucy saw the promise of a reliable system for measuring individual differences in children's mentalities and thus of acquiring a scientific basis upon which to design educational programs to suit individual needs. Thorndike's use of statistical analysis, moreover, showed her that techniques with which she was already somewhat familiar through her husband's economics research might also be applied to the field of educational reform.

Harriet M. Johnson, whom Mitchell once described as having "a genius for friendship and a genius for work," was among the most original thinkers within the city's educational reform avant-garde.[30] In 1916, when a substantial sum of Sprague family money became available to her, Lucy asked her husband, Harriet Johnson, Evelyn Dewey (the coauthor with her father of *Schools of Tomorrow*), Caroline Pratt (whose radically experimental Play School, in Greenwich Village, had replaced traditional pedagogy with block-building, expressive dance, and a host of other group-oriented opportunities for "self-education"), and a few other trusted advisors to help her plan a central clearinghouse for information about all the varied educational experiments going on nationwide. This Working Council soon greatly enlarged their plan to include the direct sponsorship of a wide range of worthy experiments, all to be coordinated by a newly formed Bureau of Educational Experiments.

Among the bureau's first ventures were projects relating to psychological testing, sex education in the public schools, and nutritional research. Through the bureau, Lucy soon became deeply involved in Caroline Pratt's Play School as a benefactor and teacher. By 1918, she was also the mother of four children, two of them adopted. Determined to resolve the dualism of motherhood and career, she became increasingly interested in the nursery school movement, then a new American phenomenon. In 1919, the bureau adopted Harriet Johnson's plan for a "scientific" nursery school; it opened that year in a building owned by the Mitchells.

It was at this time that Lucy Sprague Mitchell, as a teacher, mother, and frequenter of the bureau's own experimental preschool, embarked on what was to become one of the central focuses of her own (and eventually of the bureau's) research: the study of language development and its relationship to other aspects of the child's emerging self. As Lucy worked with and observed young children, she was struck by the playfulness and inventiveness of their everyday speech. Recalling her own childhood impulse to write poetry, which her father had suppressed, she resolved to understand language development and to discover how parents and teachers might best foster the process.

Her first major goal was to arrive at a general theory of the stages of language development during the child's early years. To do this, she committed herself to recording word for word a significant sample of both the casual remarks and more organized group discussions of the nursery and Play School children—a four-year-old's comment, for example, that "sometimes there is a sunny [i.e., full] moon, sometimes half a moon"; a conversation among five-year-olds about American history:

G: Saturday is George Washington's birthday.
E: But George Washington is dead.
J: Yes, he lived thousands and thousands of years ago.
M: He was the first boss of this country.
J: No, he was the president of New York.[31]

Thousands upon thousands of such linguistic fragments were collected by her and others associated with the bureau. Lucy herself was always ready for impromptu notetaking. In the big pockets of her gypsy-style dresses she kept a supply of small stenographic record books, scores of which she filled with children's words. As the mounds of data accumulated, she patiently sifted for patterns.

Lucy Mitchell's investigations in this field were of pathfinding importance. Among the more striking insights to emerge early on was the observation that "communication is not the earliest impulse that leads to the use of language"—a discovery that ran directly counter to the most basic assumptions of traditional pedagogy, with its emphasis on vocabulary building and early mastery of the mechanics of grammar, syntax, and spelling. "Children," she was convinced, "begin to play with sounds long before words have any meaning to them." It was the "rhythm, sound quality and patterns of sound" they first responded to and which constituted the

> chief elements of language as an *art medium.* . . . Even [Jean] Piaget . . . suggests that children will soon outgrow the childish pleasures in rhythm and sound qualities and speak sensibly like grownups. And so they do! To Piaget, this dropping of art elements from language is progress, the overcoming of an immaturity. To me it is a tragedy, for to me a child's pleasure in rhythm, sound quality and pattern is the seed from which literature grows.[32]

Children's first semantically meaningful utterances, Mitchell believed, continued to reflect that total immersion in what she called the "Here and Now" world of the sensory realm. A four-year-old did not speak (or think) of "climbing a hill"—remote adult conceptualization—but of going up "the place where the legs ache," as one child had put the matter to her in conversation.[33] Everyday language, moreover, was littered with empirically inexact metaphors—"night is falling," for example—which observant young children were constantly improving upon, as when a Bank Street toddler remarked at the onset of evening, "The big shadow is all around."[34] For Mitchell, the lesson to be drawn from the evidence was that young children made such highly vivid "direct observations" as a matter of course, provided only that they were encouraged to express themselves freely.

Less than a half dozen years after the bureau's founding, Mitchell felt confident enough in her findings to take a second step as a researcher and reformer: the creation of a prototype book for an entirely new kind of literature for young children, a developmentally sound here-and-now literature directly based on her own observations of children aged two to seven.

Her introduction to the *Here and Now Story Book,* which Dutton published in 1921, combined a vigorous summary of her theories with practical advice addressed to the teachers and parents who would be reading the book to their children. As she well realized, the *Here and Now Story Book* was certain to be regarded as a strange and controversial work, challenging as it did conventional assumptions about the form and content of stories and poems appropriate for small children. For one thing, she had made extensive use of children's own invented phrases and sound-alike words—"toot, toot!" and the like—less with a view to creating memorable literary works than to providing stories that children would recognize as their own. Mitchell's formal emphasis on rhythmic repetition was another attempt to take a direct lead from children's own speech patterns.

More striking, however, than these features of Mitchell's stories (traditional folktales and rhymes also employed repeating devices and contained some play words) was the emphatically modern urban setting of the *Here and Now Story Book*'s pieces. Much of the children's literature of the period remained rooted in nineteenth-century Romanticism, with its idealized imagery of the happy child at home in harmonious natural surroundings. In stark contrast, Mitchell's stories about skyscrapers and airplanes, tugboats and trolleys acknowledged the demographic and social reality that in 1921 the majority of American children lived in cities.

Mitchell's writing could be witty but was more often overwrought and a bit dull. She made no exaggerated claims for herself in the literary sphere. Her primary objective was to provide other, more gifted writers with a model on which to base fresh experiments in the virtually neglected field of imaginative writing for the nursery ages.

The *Here and Now Story Book* also represented a direct challenge to the widely held view of librarians and publishers that fairy tales, myths, legends, and traditional nursery nonsense—the literature of "once upon a time"—comprised the best introduction to literature for the young. Bank Street research had proven otherwise, said Mitchell. She conceded that the rhythmic language of a "simple folk tale might indeed delight children from the earliest ages. "Moreover, after a child is somewhat oriented to the physical and social world, say at six or seven, . . . he can stand a good deal of straight fairy lore." At the same time, Mitchell declared, "[for] brutal tales like Red Riding-Hood or for sentimental ones like Cinderella I find no place in any child's world." And while she did not wish to reject all fairy tales out of hand, Mitchell argued that "a child's imagination will surely flourish if he is given freedom for expression, without calling upon the stimulus of adult fancies. It is only the jaded adult mind, afraid *to trust to the child's own fresh springs of imagination,* that feels for children the need of the stimulus of magic."[35]

Mitchell's caustic reference to jaded minds seemed calculated to be taken as a declaration of war on the children's book establishment of her day. Chief among the objects of her scorn was the formidable Anne Carroll Moore, the New York Public Library's Superintendent of Work with Children and the olympian authority figure in the field. The struggle of ideas (and to some considerable extent of personalities) that was thus joined in the early 1920s between Mitchell and her colleagues on the one side and Moore and her partisans on the other eventually drew Margaret Wise Brown into its very core.

When Anne Carroll Moore was appointed the New York Public Library's first Superintendent of Work with Children in 1906, library service for the young was still in its infancy. Moore was not the nation's first children's librarian, but during a career that spanned a half century she probably did more than any other individual to establish the importance of providing children with ready access to books through library service. In the process, Moore herself emerged as the nation's final arbiter of the standards by which books for the young should be judged.

A brilliant strategist, Moore went about the business of library reform with Napoleonic boldness and zeal. Under her watchful eye a handsomely appointed Central Children's Room—with carved mahogany bookcases, glassed-in exhibition cabinets, Italian marble countertops, and Welsh quarry-tile floors—opened in May 1911 in the resplendent new New York Public Library building on Fifth Avenue. From this headquarters Moore oversaw the formation of one of the world's finest collections of children's books. To attract the city's children she initiated a full calendar of events which soon became established traditions: candle-lit story hours, Halloween and May Day celebrations, among others. To ensure the continuance of her efforts, Moore personally trained a small corps of librarian-disciples drawn purposefully, in a city of immigrant children, from a wide range of ethnic and cultural backgrounds. These devoted acolytes often went on to assume positions of responsibility in the New York system's local branch libraries, or found library jobs elsewhere throughout the country and beyond; others became juveniles editors at publishing houses.

Under Moore's leadership the selection of books for the Central Children's Room was never a casual affair. A New York Public Library purchase order soon came to be regarded as a major critical endorsement. In 1911 Moore formalized the matter, and greatly enhanced her power, by issuing the first of the library's annual fall lists of new books recommended for holiday gift giving. Such was her reputation nationally that inclusion on the list all but assured a book a respectable sale; omission might just as easily mean oblivion. Editors, authors, and illustrators routinely stopped by to visit with Miss Moore and seek her counsel on their works in progress.

Moore made an indelible impression on others by appearing on many occasions with an eight-inch wooden Dutch doll—Nicholas—in hand. Nicholas, she explained, represented the "spirit of the children's libraries."[36] The vigilant guardian of that spirit had commissioned monogrammed luggage for the little wooden man, as well as a bed and numerous other accessories of appropriate size. Guests who dined with her in her lower–Fifth Avenue apartment were expected to acknowledge the presence of their fellow dinner companion, Nicholas, for whom a place setting was always provided; with finicky caprice, Moore treated such occasions as tests of their capacity for "child-like" fantasy (though one wonders how many of them felt merely put upon).

The growing currency of Freudian psychology, with its powerful rebuff to the Romantic cult of childhood innocence, troubled Moore as a deeply disturbing development. Throughout her long, extraordinary career, she herself remained a Romantic in the mold of Walter de la Mare, whose birthday (along with Shakespeare's and Hans Christian Andersen's) was celebrated at the Central Children's Room. De la Mare, as Randall Jarrell was to observe, still believed in the "romantic's world," but could cling to that belief only as to a "sweet ghost" abroad in the "industrial and scientific world that [had] destroyed it." To such a poet, Jarrell said, the "ordinary rational or practical life resembles the mechanical and rationalized routine, the hysterical anesthesia, of the hypnotized subject: what is real lies above (God, Beauty) or beneath (dreams, animals, children) or around (ghosts, all the beings of myth or Märchen)"[37]—to which Moore herself had of course added little Nicholas. For her, as for the authors of such extraordinarily popular fantasies as *Peter Pan* and *The Velveteen Rabbit,* the mere capacity to believe had become a sort of desperate, last-ditch ultimate good.

"You must write a book about Nicholas, Miss Moore. You make him real," a little girl is said to have urged the librarian one afternoon following a Christmas story hour at which *The Velveteen Rabbit* had been read aloud.[38]

Whether or not the librarian intended *Nicholas: A Manhattan Christmas Story* as a direct rebuttal to Lucy Sprague Mitchell's *Here and Now Story Book,* which had appeared just three years earlier, Moore's book certainly amounted to one. She had set the opening scene of her fantasy in the here-and-now surroundings of the Central Children's Room, but from the first, Moore made her impatience with Bank Street realism felt. A "Brownie," she told her readers, was hiding in the room, "waiting for something wonderful to happen."[39] In her fantasy world, nothing could ever be only what it seemed. A brownie or gnome or Nicholas had always to appear to confer a touch of magic on an otherwise all too prosaic world.

Moore advanced her campaign for high critical standards and increased her great influence in the children's book world through the steady outpouring of articles and reviews she published for more than forty years. In 1918 she inaugurated a quarterly column of opinion and review in the *Bookman.* From 1924 onward she contributed a weekly piece to the *New York Herald Tribune*'s Sunday supplement, *Books.* No critic in America had previously given children's literature such sustained critical attention in print. Moore called her column "The Three Owls" in recognition of the shared responsibility of authors, artists, and vigilant reviewers like herself in the education of the nation's youth. In 1924 Boston's Bookshop for Boys and Girls began a newsletter on various aspects of the juveniles field which grew to become the widely respected *Horn Book* magazine. By the mid-thirties, Moore's own "Three Owls" column had migrated to the *Horn Book*'s pages.

Like Lucy Sprague Mitchell, Anne Carroll Moore was a stoutly self-assured visionary. She never wavered in her criticism of the impact of progressive education on the children's literature of the day. She argued vigorously that literature could not be cut from the cloth of any scientific theory, that aesthetic creation simply did not work that way. She was right, of course, but she failed to conceive the possibility that insights like those gleaned from Bank Street research might serve as a point of departure for writers of real ability.

More basically, philosophical differences had led Moore and Mitchell to very different ideas about childhood. The librarian was a moral idealist who regarded childhood as a fixed state of innocence to be shielded from, rather than shaped by, historical change and environmental factors. Moore remained deeply suspicious of Mitchell's empirically grounded—and thus relativistic—"modern" approach to literature and education. Mitchell, for her part, was convinced that people like Moore lived in a sentimental dreamworld.

As to the Fairy Tale War itself—their acrimonious debate over the value of folk and fantasy literature for younger children—both sides presented a rather mixed case of blindness and insight. Moore's responsiveness to the tales was salutary, but there was something stilted about her unquestioning reverence for the "timeless" classics, as though they were to be venerated as sacred relics, as bulwarks against modernity; Mitchell's tendering of an essentially original view of literature for small children was a worthy contribution to the debate, but her reluctance to recognize that children might appreciate fantastic tales on a symbolic level seems a case of theory winning out over direct observation.[40]

The decade of the twenties was a period of national prosperity and widespread questioning of traditional social codes and institutions. Experimental schools of all sorts proliferated throughout the country. The protestations of Anne Carroll Moore and her colleagues notwithstanding, the *Here and Now Story Book* struck a responsive chord in many critics and educators, who hailed it as an important innovation. The *Journal of Educational Psychology* declared Mitchell's work "quite revolutionary." The *New York Evening Post* said the author's stories were "among the most genuine things that have ever been written" for young children. Arnold and Beatrice Gesell called the book a "new impetus to creative work and artistic expression with little children. . . . If the ability to handle words, to make them into patterns, to regard them as tools of expression can be awakened at an early age, the whole technique of language instruction in the schools will be altered."[41]

The Cooperative School for Student Teachers, the program which Margaret entered in the fall of 1935, had not been envisioned in the early plans for the Bureau of Educational Experiments. Its establishment in 1930 marked an important shift in emphasis away from quantitative studies of child development; the new focus was on preparing the next generation of teachers for work in child-centered experimental schools. Significantly, courses in pedagogy were excluded from the curriculum. When student teachers were not engaged in actual on-the-job training they came to the bureau's new headquarters at 69 Bank Street for classes intended not so much to teach them how to teach as to help them become more experientially grounded, self-aware human beings.

Lucy Mitchell and her colleagues felt that traditional schooling, with its emphasis on rote learning, had a deadening effect that rendered most adults ill equipped to respond with sensitivity to children's own needs. If, as William James had said, young children were little empiricists whose "native interests" lay "altogether in the sphere of sensation," student teachers would have to undergo a wholesale reeducation of the senses, a kind of second childhood, before they would be ready to do their jobs well. For as James had also said, "The child will always attend more to what a teacher does than to what the teacher says."[42]

To heighten their sensory awareness trainees were given classes in painting, dance, pantomime, music—all activities also offered to Bank Street's nursery school youngsters. Both groups were encouraged to enjoy these experiences without concern for the quality of the end result. It was hoped that the trainees would also come to understand the role that art might play in the "fully rounded development of children."

At Bank Street, then, several key elements of the teachers' and the children's educations proceeded along parallel lines. Margaret's dance instructor found her to be "very timorous physically" during their first weeks of work together in the fall of 1935. "Her movements," the teacher observed in an evaluation filed the following spring, had at first been "ineffectual and sentimental," but Margaret had worked hard and toward the end of the course had done "surprising improvisations. . . . I think [the report concluded] the work had a rather profound salutary effect in freeing her."[43]

In her painting class, Margaret seems to have allowed herself a heady taste of artistic license, laying down "sheer color" on canvas, as she wrote Marguerite Hearsey, "without form or cerebral intent." To her own surprise, the results were "most amazing [and] strangely enough, not without meaning, though they are decidedly without coherant [*sic*] meaning."[44] As with her dance class, her instructor noted that after a "very crude start" and "slight growth for several days" Margaret had made "a jump" into "adventurous and extremely sensitive color harmony."[45]

Pantomime was another regularly scheduled activity for both the nursery school children and the teacher trainees. Lucy Mitchell regarded these acting-out exercises as a technique for literally feeling in one's bones (and muscles) the rhythmical aspects and sheer physicality of all manner of experience. (Once, following a field trip to a dairy farm with the trainees, she asked the group to reenact the visit in pantomime. When the group came to recalling the milking parlor's activities, she volunteered to play the part of the cow.)

Bank Street's staff conceived of the child's reality in terms of a sequence of outwardly radiating circles starting at the center with his or her rudimentary sensory awareness and leading by stages to an ever-expanding interest in home, community, region, and world, the past and future, and purely fantastic realms. They thought that the educational needs of two- to five-year-olds, who were focused on here-and-now immediacies, might be fully served by a well-equipped and supervised nursery school environment. Slightly older children were considered ready to relate classroom activities to firsthand experiences outside the school, a trip to the New York waterfront, for example, to taste the salt water, see for themselves that Manhattan is an island, and learn why some objects float when tossed into the river while others sink.

The teacher trainees were also taken on exploratory journeys, including one annual "long trip" far from New York which Mitchell led herself and conducted as an informal total immersion course in relationship thinking. The material of the course encompassed everything from the geological features of the terrain through which they passed in their chartered bus to the political concerns of the communities they visited. Field trips that interested Margaret were apt to be those that engaged her aesthetically. She was in her element when Lucy Mitchell, back in New York, asked her class to find a field, close their eyes and record the rush of sensations that ensued. It was autumn as Margaret conscientiously scribbled down her findings: "Sharp/Cold, in the nose/Feeling younger/Long forgotten/Burning leaves."[46]

At Bank Street, child observation was considered an especially fruitful exercise for the teacher trainees; while honing their knowledge of children's gestures, facial expressions, and speech patterns, they might become keener, less blindered observers.

It was one thing to strive for an intellectually complex understanding of children's behavior and development; it was quite another to reconstitute within oneself even a semblance of the actual perceptual framework of childhood—to see the world, as it were, through a three-year-old's eyes. It amounted to a sobering realization for more than a few of the trainees and staff that children were the only real professionals at childhood, that they themselves were largely destined to remain awkward amateurs. Clever children were quick to point this out to their overseers. Out one day on the rooftop playground, an artistically gifted five-year-old demanded to know what the hapless trainee was writing in her notebook:

"What are you writing now?" (The trainee continued to take

notes throughout the exchange.) "Are you writing about my Dutch costume?"

"Yes," the trainee replied, a little sheepishly. "I'm writing about all the children's costumes."

Whereupon the child issued a stern warning: "I'll follow you till you tell me what you're writing. Or I'll smack you good and hard—'cause I mean what I say!"[47]

Child observation was sometimes conducted less openly. Concealed behind the cheerfully appointed walls of the school's four spacious nursery rooms were observation booths fitted with two-way mirrors. By the mid-thirties, the entire range of investigative techniques in use at Bank Street and the research results that flowed from them had become a matter of such general interest among psychologists and educators that a steady parade of visitors from as far away as the Soviet Union and Australia came to observe the observers observe the children, and to be observed by them in turn.

To her Bank Street colleagues, Margaret, although generally seen as a good-spirited and engaging companion, remained elusive, an indefinable presence who "operated in a highly individual mode," as the staff psychologist, Barbara Biber, put it.[48] Other new arrivals at the school usually "merged" (as Biber said) with Bank Street culture, with certain inbred nuances of the school community's style of thought and talk and behavior. But Margaret somehow managed to remain an ironic observer among observers. She was a wonderchild. What others at the school pored over psychology texts, studied the children, and strained their memories and imaginations to achieve—an unselfconscious identification with the young child's experience—was Margaret's as if by second nature. The very completeness of her identification with the children put her curiously at odds with her peers.

It was a Bank Street custom—an element of the merging process—to adopt a pet name; quaint diminutives like "Clover" and "Boots" were generally chosen. Effecting a characteristic evasion, Margaret allowed herself to be known as "Brownie," a different nickname from the one she was still called elsewhere, "Tim," one she might therefore leave behind at the end of the day, as stacks of paperwork are left at the office.

As for her efforts as a teacher's assistant at the Little Red School House, Margaret's mid-year report (filed in January 1936) indicated that she had tried her best to put in a creditable performance and that she had largely succeeded.[49] The supervising teacher, Dorothy Stall, found her "open and frank" and intensely curious about everything that happened in the classroom. She believed that "Brownie" had won the children's "love and respect"; Her principal shortcoming was in managing groups of youngsters, but even this weakness was related to her overall sensitivity: "Large group problems worried her because in solving them it seemed necessary to forget the individual child or ignore his personality and sometimes perhaps his rights." Margaret, Stall wrote, exhibited a "strong sense of justice . . . as if she remembered her own childhood and wanted to make good to 'the spirit of childhood' for the grown-ups who did not understand her." She also reported that Margaret had decided [again] that she did not want to teach professionally. "[Her] interest in children is no more real than [her] interest in all types of personality." With some candor, she added, "[Margaret is] decidedly not the 'school-teacher' type, and in spite of all the progressive education I'm afraid most of us fall into a 'type.' "

But Margaret was an original, a classroom presence both her supervisor and the children were unlikely to forget. The report concluded, "While many of the details of the work, especially connected with academic work were neglected, . . . the spiritual contribution Miss Brown made . . . far outweighed the defects. . . . The whole tone and attitude of the children toward each other and toward adults owes much to having had her with us."

Lucy Mitchell's abiding faith in learning by firsthand experience had inspired her to attempt her *Here and Now Story Book*. How better to determine children's literary priorities and needs than to write a variety of stories, try them out on groups of young listeners, revise as the children's responses dictated, and thereby gradually refine the manuscript—and one's understanding. Pursuing the logic of the experiment a step further, Mitchell resolved that each of the trainees in the Cooperative School for Student Teachers should try her hand at writing as well. The students' efforts might not be very accomplished, but the primary goal was simply to make them more aware of the range of children's experience as readers and listeners.

Mitchell taught the children's literature workshop herself, and it was as a member of that class, in the fall of 1935, that Margaret first considered the possibility of becoming a children's author. She seems to have recognized Lucy Mitchell from the start as a teacher as worthy of her wholehearted respect as Marguerite Hearsey had always been. Mitchell's immense range of learning, her fiercely independent and playful manner, and her selfless dedication to her work all impressed Margaret. The questions she posed about childhood development in the literary sphere, as in others, stirred Margaret's curiosity deeply. And she was grateful for her new mentor's eagerness to encourage her writing.

The first piece Margaret produced in Mitchell's class was, she afterwards said, a "silly story" that "tried too hard to sound like a children's story." It had been "all decked out like a Christmas tree with echoes of all the fairy stories I had ever read."[50] Nevertheless, Mitchell soon spotted something special in "Brownie": "crazy, penetrating, blind instincts and feeling for language," as she later told the critic Louise Seaman Bechtel.[51]

In Margaret's first term evaluation, filed in December 1935, Mitchell noted, "I'm inclined to suspect she may go precious if not more related to external things. . . . [I] believe her a person of unusual capacities who needs her interests widened. Let her remain an artist but have more to say!"[52] Four months later, Mitchell's next report was equally balanced and appreciative:

> Probably she has the most consistent and genuine interest in language of the group, perhaps of all our students. Her product, though slight, always shows sensitivity to form, sound and rhythm. Her paper on the language of the 8's showed real insight and was quite her own. She might go far—might even make a real writer for children.[53]

As her own recollection of her gaudily embellished first story bears out, Margaret had evidently mounted some initial resistance to the here-and-now view of appropriate subject matter. Mitchell's report continued, "Still inclined to think of our content for children as . . . of 'spinach' variety. I should like a chance to work with her over a period of years. She is waking. . . . Be very careful about next year. Don't let her degenerate to a think specialist." Under Lucy Mitchell's extraordinarily capable guidance, Margaret's Bank Street years continued to be a fertile time of acquiring understanding and of being understood.

A notebook Margaret kept at this time provides a glimpse of the ideas that had begun to focus her attention. She was evidently intrigued by Lucy Mitchell's developmental theory of humor. She noted that for two-year-olds, humor arises out of "physical incongruities; reversals of observed relations"; a year or so later, children are ready to see the fun in "plays on words; obvious untruths; . . . [in a] routine or sequence . . . reversed. 'Suppose we washed our hands after dinner instead of before.' "[54]

Margaret also formulated (or copied into her notebook), assorted aphorisms, exhortations, and study exercises related to writing for children: "In the development of an expressive act, the emotion operates like a magnet drawing to itself appropriate material"; "To make words give a vicarious experience"; "Whenever a child says something that expresses a pattern, tells his interest, analyse, or tell why a child likes one thing, not another. To what extent are they quoting. What springs from them?" To what extent she quoted Lucy Mitchell in these passages or was recording her own observations is not always clear. "The ruthlessness of theory vs. the sympathy of experience—limitations in both"—*that*, more than likely, was Margaret, who was always quick to view any matter as a contest of wits and who in the end was rather more willing than her teacher to set theory aside as the moment dictated.

One reason she may have enjoyed the prolonged hours of child observation that she and her fellow students were required to perform was that Margaret viewed the experience as another battle of wits, a type of sport. A note to herself concerning one of her research projects renders the assignment in the language of the hunt, almost as though she were contemplating an afternoon outing with the Buckram Beagles: "A behavior record of the child I will chase . . . Take [George] because he's an imaginative child still in the half-tones of reality." Some years later, recalling the feverish note-taking she was obliged to carry out as part of her field research, Margaret again chose a hunting metaphor: "One had to be absolutely still and write very fast to catch" the stories and poems the children improvised.[55]

In all likelihood, Bank Street's exacting regimen was more than matched by the internal demands Margaret placed on herself. She was doubtless as aware as her instructors whenever her work fell short. She admonished herself in her notebook not to forget that "subconscious maturation precedes creative production in every line of human endeavor." If she had not yet become the writer she wished to be, she had at least begun attending to the prerequisites. That there were also moments when waiting for the egg to hatch seemed almost too much for her to bear is also plain. "I'm about to boil over," Margaret sighed one day into her notebook, "with nervous energy and apprehension."[56]

For much of her long, relentlessly productive writing career, Lucy Sprague Mitchell spoke almost apologetically of her "art expressions" and "art indulgences" rather than of her literary art.[57] She considered her substantial output as an author—essays, magazine articles, lectures, and radio talks for adults; stories, poems, and nonfiction for children—as primarily a form of social service, only marginally as creative work done for her own satisfaction.

It was reason, the mind exercised in conscious witness of itself, that Mitchell had learned from early childhood to trust as her own best parent or guardian. Her poetry necessarily suffered as a consequence and would always be self-consciously methodical, emotionally tepid. Yet her powers of introspection were such that she had also devised ingenious stratagems for tricking herself—and later her students—into a less deliberately controlled, more "childlike" state of mind. Some of these ruses became the assignments—the "five-finger exercises"—she gave the Bank Street student teachers. Time and again she exhorted them to trust, not disparage, their imaginative instincts, for, as she assured a group of teacher trainees one day, "All that glitters is not guilt!"[58]

Mitchell was always to remain skeptical of any force or fact or system that could not be clearly charted or consciously known. Hers was a brilliant daylight intelligence. Content, in the spirit of intellectual inquiry and democratic fair play, to have Freudian theory taught at Bank Street, she was made uncomfortable by the notion of applying Freudian analysis as a practical means of resolving one's personal difficulties; the idea doubtless offended her Sprague sense of rugged individualism and Puritan self-abnegation, a cast of mind she had perhaps not fully succeeded in shedding after all.

"Sally," she began one day, in a mischievous stage whisper addressed to a student sitting beside her in class, "You don't think *everyone* needs to be psychoanalyzed, do you?"

"Why no, Mrs. Mitchell," came the correct response.

"Sally," she continued, her voice rising so that others might also hear. "Don't you think there is too much psssssychoanalysis around here?"[59]

In contrast, mapmaking and the study of geography were among Lucy Mitchell's most absorbing interests. She taught a class in geography for the teacher trainees in which maps were presented as tools by means of which older children might learn to generalize from their earlier here-and-now experiences. To prove her point, Mitchell proposed to the trainees the puzzle of a European map on which major rivers, mountain ranges, and mineral deposits were indicated but not political boundaries. She asked the class to speculate, based on the distribution of natural resources, where conflicts leading to war were likeliest to be centered. This exercise typified Mitchell's engrossing, game-like teaching methods. It illustrated as well her deep-seated and characteristically American preference for environmental explanations of human behavior, whether on the scale of the individual, the classroom, or society.

Margaret had heard and been properly amused by her teacher's quip about psychoanalysis, but she had also long taken a more than passing interest in her dreams and suspected that the unconscious interior life, in all its mysterious operations, was a resource that writers ought not to shun. One day in geography class she turned to the teacher she respected and adored, and in her own loud stage whisper inquired pointedly, "Mrs. Mitchell, what are sssssocial studies?"[60]

CHAPTER THREE

BANK
STREET
AND
BEYOND

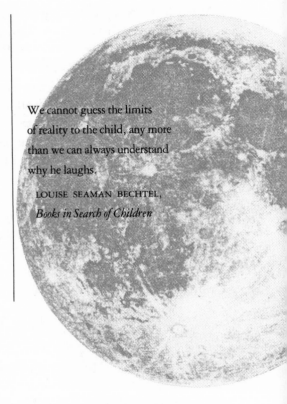

We cannot guess the limits
of reality to the child, any more
than we can always understand
why he laughs.

LOUISE SEAMAN BECHTEL,
Books in Search of Children

Margaret's arrival at Bank Street could hardly have been better timed. By temperament and training, Lucy Sprague Mitchell was a teacher supremely suited to guiding Margaret toward the vocation she so urgently required. In turn, Margaret's emergence as a writer presented the Bank Street founder with an extraordinary opportunity to advance her own life-work a step further. Lucy Mitchell realized that "Brownie" and a handful of others at the school represented the potential core of a whole new generation of here-and-now authors. She proposed a new collection, a sequel to the landmark *Here and Now Story Book,* as a collaboration in which Margaret and the others might all become involved.

Always a steady seller, the original *Here and Now Story Book* was in its eighteenth printing in 1936. Not surprisingly, the publisher, E. P. Dutton, was quite receptive. In typical fashion, Lucy Mitchell threw herself completely into all phases of the project, with Margaret as her assistant. "I am in the process of looking over recent publications for children," Mitchell wrote Dutton's president, John Macrae, who was editing the anthology personally.[1] She was determined to hold the retail price of the book to two dollars (about average for the time) so as to make it widely affordable, and studied similar books to determine how much color art might be feasible at the price. (She was convinced that the earlier book's quaintly stylized black-and-white drawings by Hendrik van Loon were "of no significance for small children"; a new illustrator would be needed.)

Taken together, Mitchell's introductions to each section of the new volume were a book in themselves, a substantial monograph composed of subtly observed, year-by-year developmental profiles of children from two to six. Describing a typical two-year-old, Mitchell wrote:

> Mollie . . . has got her legs, though she often loses them. For she still has a baby's legs—short and weak. . . . She has not far to fall, and her frequent sudden sitting-downs seem to amuse rather than to discourage her. . . . "Da, Mollie, da," she says solemnly each time. To whom? To herself, of course. For at two Mollie's conversation is not cramped by lack of an audience. It burbles on, accompanying almost every activity. To practice new words? To reinforce the emotional quality of the activity? Who but two-year-olds know? And they never tell us! . . . Sometimes Mollie's remarks are repeated over and over until they trail off into a rhythmic chant. . . . Mollie is still changing. . . . But while she is two, the stories that Mollie seems to enjoy (presumably because she understands them) are about Mollie and Mollie's emotional waverings between dependence and independence, her adventures with her own bed, her own dinner, her own blocks, her own places to sit, her own kitty. . . . She enjoys very brief stories about her intimately personal world.[2]

The import of these observations was not lost on the future author of *Goodnight Moon,* but little by Margaret and her fellow contributors to the anthology proved memorable. There were, to be sure, occasional flashes of wit and signs of promise—in Margaret's "Fifteen Bathtubs," for example (a story for four-year-olds about a young contrarian who for all the numerous tubs in his parents' house managed to remain the "dirtiest little boy in the world"), and in Lucy Mitchell's own buoyantly titled "How Jimmy Jim Jam Got His Name," a story for "Fives."

Although Mitchell remained adamant about the validity of the here-and-now approach, she was willing to strike a moderate tone in a prefatory note addressed directly to those critics who "felt that [her] philosophy might be jeopardizing something precious to children—the sheer beauty of classical literature."[3] After restating unequivocally that children under the age of seven were not yet ready to appreciate classical mythology and folklore, she wrote: "If the stories in this book are less lovely than Cinderella or Little Red Riding Hood or Pandora's Box, it is because we lack the requisite artistry, not because we do not value loveliness. The great writer for the young children of the 'here and now' period is still to come."

In mid-October of 1936, just weeks before the manuscript was due at the publisher, Margaret moved out of her parents' house for good, taking a ground-floor apartment in a well-kept brick row house at 21 West Tenth Street in Greenwich Village, within a few minutes' walk of Bank Street.

Among the first things Margaret did on settling in was to scratch out a letter to Marguerite Hearsey. Miss Hearsey had recently left Hollins College to become principal of Abbot Academy, Andover, Massachusetts. Reporting her own change of address, Margaret vowed as before a higher authority that the opportunity represented by having thus secured a room of her own would not be lost on her. "I'm going to write every morning from nine till eleven," she said, "or hate myself forever."[4] That evening, she told Miss Hearsey, her sister and Basil were giving her a party. She expected to meet more of their interesting friends, an Englishman and a "titled lady who [sang] cowboy songs" and ran the Drama Bookshop in mid-town, among others. Over the coming weeks, she said (sounding rather like a delinquent student promising to make good on an overdue assignment) she hoped to frequent the city's art galleries and to reflect on the "artist's medium of perception."

All this was written on assorted scraps of paper, the ragtag informality of which now struck her as fresh evidence of the mental disarray against which she intended to take her stand in these new quarters. "I will write you again, a clear logical letter all on the same piece of paper in good handwriting," she assured her former teacher.

Margaret's Greenwich Village address was at least as fashionable as it was bohemian. Within a few blocks of her door stood all the Village landmarks one read about in the *Saturday Evening Post:* Washington Square Arch, the Provincetown Playhouse (where new works by Eugene O'Neill and Edna St. Vincent Millay had premiered in the 1920s), the art galleries and black-and-orange tea rooms of Eighth Street (the latter more often now the way stations of tourists than of poets, libertines, and revolutionaries), and the row houses, brick or brownstone, tumbledown or stately, that had at one time or another been home to Henry James, Mark Twain, Theodore Dreiser, Willa Cather, Gellet Burgess, and John Dos Passos.

Artists and writers like John Sloan, e. e. cummings, and William Glackens still lived in the neighborhood, but Greenwich Village during the 1930s was largely a genteel gloss of bohemias past. (Real estate values actually rose for most of the decade.) Intellectuals continued to make their homes in Margaret's new neighborhood, but they were less often the wild-eyed garret types for which the Village had been known than the respectable salaried varieties—college professors, magazine editors, publishers. Among Margaret's neighbors were the Mitchells; the *New Republic*'s gallantly indignant managing editor, Bruce Bliven, Sr., and his wife Rosie, a Bank Street staff volunteer; Margaret's own sister Roberta and Basil, who taught history at a Manhattan private school; and *Time* magazine editor Robert Cantwell, whose apartment, always well stocked with reviewer's copies of the latest books, doubled as an unofficial lending library.[5]

An informal, collegial atmosphere prevailed among Village residents, a great many of whom shared Ivy League affiliations as well as social and professional ties. Neighbors knew each other, attended the same poetry readings, gave small dinner parties, socialized at gathering places like the White Horse Tavern and Jai Alai restaurant, and left their doors unlocked at night.

Two blocks north of Margaret's apartment was a crossroads of another sort, the New School for Social Research, with its streamlined modern quarters designed by Joseph Urban, heroic murals by Thomas Hart Benton and frescoes by Orozco, and an extraordinary faculty comprised in part of the cream of European scholars in exile.

The New School had been conceived as a progressive experiment in continuing education, a kind of secular people's temple of learning, open to all and dedicated to exploring new approaches to the humanities, social sciences, and the arts. But as Edmund Wilson caustically observed, at a dollar-fifty a ticket, few among the ranks of the working classes and the unemployed could afford to take advantage of the school's numerous public programs; to become better informed about "The Advantages and Disadvantages of Capitalism," "Movies and Talkies," or "The Abnormal Mind," one had to have a certain amount of capital of one's own.[6] Thanks to the allowance her father gave her, Margaret had the necessary funds and attended many New School programs.

Within a block of Margaret's door, in the shadow of the massive, soon-to-be-demolished Sixth Avenue El, bell-ringing volunteers daily collected donations in support of the anti-Franco fighters in Spain. For many at Bank Street, though not for Margaret, the Spanish Civil War was the most closely followed, passionately discussed event of the years immediately preceding the Second World War. To some at the school concern over the plight of Spain and participation in other activities of the Left were bright badges of political and social involvement wholly compatible with the progressive education movement's idealistic determination to reshape society on more humane grounds. Bank Street as an institution had no official ideology or political slant (though it was widely enough perceived as being left-leaning for some upper middle class parents to think twice before sending their daughters there to study). The depth of political commitment of the students and staff certainly varied considerably. Margaret's friend Jessica

Gamble, a popular staff member, was a dabbler in radical reform, who enjoyed the romance of whispered phone messages about clandestine political rendezvous—"Comrade! The place: Coney Island. Bring your tennis sneakers!"—as she did any sport.[7] For sport, Margaret preferred running to hounds with the Buckram Beagles.

To help pay the rent and to lend added respectability (in her father's eyes) to her new living arrangements, Margaret persuaded a beagling friend, Sophie Shoumatoff, to room with her. Among the amenities of their floor-through were a marble fireplace in the living room and a modern convenience, Venetian blinds. The rear windows faced a small enclosed garden. The street-side windows provided material for lighthearted speculation about the comings and goings of well-dressed gentlemen at the townhouse next door; the discreet brass and mahogany sign reading Marshall Chess Club was a thin cover indeed—or so Margaret assured gullible Sophie—for the thriving high-toned brothel that she insisted flourished within.

The apartment's unremarkable furnishings gave the desired impression of well-bred conventional taste, but the effect was offset rather strongly by the shifting menagerie that Margaret maintained at home. Visitors became flustered when the goat entrusted to her temporary care (awaiting transport to the family farm of Dorothy Wagstaff, the girl Margaret had tutored after college) leapt from table to chair. Margaret's flying squirrel, solitary and nocturnal, kept to the upper reaches of the window curtains until one evening, during a dinner party, it found its way into the bathroom, became disoriented, dived impulsively, and plunged into the toilet, where—a hapless minor player in Margaret's screwball comedy—it drowned. A foppish, overarticulate young man who lived upstairs knocked at Margaret and Sophie's door one evening to say he believed his Persian cat might "benefit psychologically" from a few hours spent in the company of her cat, Sneakers.[8] In this way, life at 21 West Tenth Street proceeded.

Sophie stayed on for about two months, keeping her share in the apartment a while longer as she planned her wedding to the Buckram Beagles' hunting master, Edward Ward. Thereafter, she and Margaret would see each other mainly on Sunday afternoons of exhilaration and exhaustion, in pursuit of hares and hounds in the Long Island woods.

Friends who visited Margaret in New York remarked on the wide circle of her casual acquaintances, including not only her neighbors but the policemen on the beat and the local shop-keepers—the French grocer, for example, who happened to be a former hunting master. Margaret was taking lessons from him, she told Dorothy Wagstaff, on the hunting horn. She had a kind word for everyone they passed in the street.

New, lasting professional friendships were also forming. Bruce and Rosie Bliven's apartment was a gathering place for everyone affiliated with Bank Street. There Margaret met their son Bruce, Jr. A journalist just out of Harvard, he shared a Village apartment with E. J. Kahn, Jr., a *New Yorker* staff writer still in his early twenties. By day, young Bruce wrote editorials for the liberal *New York Evening Post;* after work, he scoured pawnshops for second-hand musical instruments—saxophones, snare drums, trom-bones, and the like—and toted them home (as he explained) more because he liked to look at them than because he liked to play them. This was quite enough to win Margaret's admiration. (A similarly playful idea about cross-mixing the aural and visual realms later gave rise, in the spring of 1939, to Margaret's and Leonard Weisgard's *Noisy Book.*) Bliven and Kahn invited her over for all-night sessions of youthful noise making which was jazz to the noise-makers if not to their neighbors. They met regularly on Thursday evenings to paint. Irwin Shaw was among the literary friends who sometimes joined them during these evenings of irre-medially bad painting and smart conversation.

It was gratifying to Margaret to be included in this group of accomplished young writers. That fall of 1936, however, there were also discouraging reminders of her own contrasting lack of accomplishment and independence. Although Margaret now lived in Manhattan, her legal residence was still her parents' home. Early that fall, Robert Brown accompanied his daughters to the local Great Neck polling place to get them registered to vote in the upcoming presidential election (Roosevelt versus Landon). Ro-berta had been too young to vote in the previous election; Marga-ret, though of age, had not registered. Their father was well enough acquainted with his younger daughter's views (he must have thought Roberta's Democratic politics plain stubbornness) to realize that his one chance for paternal influence lay with the day-dreamer, Margaret. In the car, he played his favorite card, threatening to cut off her allowance unless she registered as a Republican. Roberta countered that Margaret ought to register with the party of her choice (if she had a choice), that registration, like voting, was a private matter. (Whether Robert Brown had his way on this occasion is not known; Margaret never told Roberta.)[9]

Roberta and Basil Rauch were married on Saturday, October 31, 1936, in the parsonage of New York's Saint Patrick's Cathedral. Although no longer a practicing Catholic, Basil had agreed to a religious ceremony to please his parents. Free-thinking Roberta, aware that her mother and father would be irritated by the arrangements, had little choice but to go along.[10] Robert and Maude Brown did attend the ceremony, as did Robert's older sister, Violet, who, vigilant as ever in matters concerning the Brown family name, had already made known her doubts as to the groom's worthiness. Margaret, Gratz, and a friend of Basil's completed the wedding party, the younger members of which adjourned after the ceremony for a celebratory Russian dinner in the Village.

The newlyweds, both of whom now had teaching jobs, planned in the modern way to postpone their honeymoon until the following summer. As Robert Brown believed that married people ought to take financial responsibility for themselves, he promptly terminated his younger daughter's annual allowance.

Roberta's marriage was the latest reminder to Margaret of the unsettled state of her own situation. With deepening resolve, she worked at her writing. Evenings, she labored over short stories while also turning out more of the children's manuscripts that came so easily to her, often at the rate of a story or more a night.

Gathering up her courage, Margaret began submitting stories to the *New Yorker*. Nothing came of these efforts, however, and she seems not to have mentioned her submissions to her various friends associated with the magazine; what Margaret plainly wanted was a clear and solid literary triumph, honestly come by, or none at all. She also sent off some of her children's stories to Harper and Brothers. Her decision to try Harper (rather than, say, Dutton, the Here and Now books' publisher) had been made quite casually after Jessica Gamble, whose judgment Margaret trusted, remarked one day that she thought highly of the firm. Some time around the first of the new year of 1937, Margaret fatalistically deposited her packet of manuscripts in the mail and did her best to forget about them.

In February no word had yet come from Harper when Margaret left for Virginia for a week of hunting and socializing. In Richmond she unexpectedly crossed paths with a Hollins schoolmate, Adelaide Dana and her husband. Delighted to see each other, the three made a sidetrip together to Hollins. Even though Marguerite Hearsey was no longer at Hollins, Margaret enjoyed the visit. She and Adelaide went hiking in Happy Valley, waded in Garvin's Creek, and sighted the year's first robin. Crossing the quadrangle, they met Dr. Janney, who without skipping a step declared, "For Heaven's sake! Here comes Bad—and Worse!" (Relating the incident in a letter to Miss Hearsey, Margaret took pride that she had been merely the "Bad" of the pair.) Most of all, being at Hollins reminded her that "New York City and the world today is not everything."[11]

Gratifying news awaited Margaret on her return to Manhattan. Harper and Brothers had accepted one of her stories. The editor, Louise Raymond, reported that she did not wish to change a word (though before the manuscript found its way into print, Margaret's original title, "The Blue Gray Kitten," somehow became *When the Wind Blew*).[12] Raymond said she greatly admired the qualities of "color" and "extraordinary light" in Margaret's story about an "old, old lady" who "lived by the side of the ocean . . . in a little shack made of wooden planks all whitened and silvered by the ocean winds."[13] Harper intended to make it a "swagger book," with special printing and hand-blocked illustrations by Rosalie Slocum, the illustrator of *Another Here and Now Story Book* and a well-known figure in the Greenwich Village art scene.

"I am excited," Margaret wrote Marguerite Hearsey.

> For all the long groping and aspiring letters I used to write you in my struggles for coherance [*sic*], I never really dreamed that I would write, last of all be published and have other publishers asking for manuscripts. . . . I only pray that this beginning goes

a long way before it ends and that someday I will be able to write grown up writing as well. Or write something for children that is literature. [14]

When the check for her royalty advance came in the mail soon afterward, Margaret cashed it immediately. Horse-drawn flower carts were still a familiar sight in the Village; fresh from the bank, Margaret hailed a cart, told the vendor that she wanted to buy everything he had, and directed him to her front door, where the entire cartload was deposited. She decorated her apartment, then called her friends over for a party.

Margaret's contribution to *Another Here and Now Story Book* led to other opportunities. Dutton's president, John Macrae, proposed to her that she write a children's collection of her own. When the "man in a salmon-pink necktie" (as she later happily described the dapper if grandfatherly publisher) asked if she would accept the assignment, Margaret responded with caution. [15] She would first have to know "how thick" a book he had in mind. A Dutton title of appropriate girth was brought in for her inspection. Having taken the measure of matters, she nodded her ascent. Terms remained to be worked out. Macrae generously offered a base royalty rate of $12\frac{1}{2}$ percent (10 percent was standard), to which Margaret, her sporting instinct aroused, countered, "Fifteen!" Taken aback and eager to secure her services for Dutton, Macrae agreed. Margaret also arranged for her sister Roberta, who she assured Macrae drew in a "child-like way," to illustrate the book (afterwards known as *The Fish with the Deep Sea Smile*). "In those days, fifty dollars was fifty dollars," Roberta recalled years later with a little laugh. [16] She had had no previous training or experience as an illustrator, and although she did an adequate job on the book, she never tried her hand at children's book art again. For Margaret the project was the first of many in which she took part not only as author but as an impresario enlisting new talent for the field.

In the spring of 1937, flush with this quick succession of accomplishments and with a drawerful of newly printed stationery at her disposal, Margaret wrote Marguerite Hearsey a letter brimming with pride. [17] Harper had offered her a second contract for an adaptation from the French of Y. Lacôte's *The Children's Year,* a calendar for young readers, and had accepted two more of her own manuscripts. There was the Dutton story collection and the possibility of an offer from Viking. One editor was even urging her, prolific author that she had become, to consider publishing under two or more different names. In all, it was an impressive showing.

Romance, or something like romance, had also entered her life in the shadowy form of a "good quiet man from Virginia" (unnamed and not mentioned again in future letters to Marguerite Hearsey) whom Margaret thought she might marry the following spring, unless in the meantime "some ruthless bounder" should come along "that I could love and then if such a strange felicity should happen I would give anything for two children before I'm thirty."

The bright, independent-minded "modern girl," Margaret and her fellow Hollins students had been told by a visiting lecturer, did well to choose a career first and afterwards find a husband. Having put the first decision behind her—"it is all so sudden and amazing that I can laugh loud over it"—she hoped now to complete the business. Meanwhile, she wrote, "one submits to the unexpectedness of existence."

A passage from Virginia Woolf's new book, *The Years,* had lately stuck in her memory. " 'But you must come and see it for yourselves,' North was saying. They had asked him to describe Africa. . . . He stopped; it was difficult to describe a place to people who had not seen it."[18] She wondered why this bit of narrative so preoccupied her, why it hovered like a talisman in her mind. Apparently, North's quiet satisfaction over his recent adventure mirrored her own delight in the life she now led; like him, she found it hard to put the experience into words. *But you must come and see it for yourselves.* She invited Miss Hearsey to visit her in New York: "Have tea with me before June 1st"—evidently, in Margaret's Africa certain of the proprieties were still to be observed—"or will your children [the students of Abbot Academy] be having commencement then?"

By almost any standard, *Another Here and Now Story Book* had been a success. Sales of the book were excellent, with a third printing required within a month of its publication in March of 1937, and reviews were generally favorable. The United Press news service called the new anthology "an important contribution to progressive child education."[19] The *New York Times,* in its thoughtful and balanced appraisal, found the book better than the earlier Here and Now volume, which the reviewer noted had pioneered a significant new kind of literature for young children.

> Sixteen years ago, . . . [Mitchell's] idea was so new as to be startling, even a little shocking, but with the passage of time this type of story has come to be better understood. What the story of everyday things does for the little child is recognized; also the fact that its advocates are not bent on driving out the tale of imagination and fancy.[20]

The progressive education movement itself seemed a good deal less startling to large segments of the American public than it had just fifteen or twenty years earlier. In the early 1920s, when Mitchell's first *Here and Now Story Book* was published, there were perhaps two dozen nursery schools in the United States; by 1936 such schools numbered well into the hundreds. A *Time* magazine cover story would soon declare that progressive education had entered the American mainstream.[21]

A striking indication of this shift in attitudes can be found in the *Horn Book* magazine's May/June 1937 number. The journal's editor, Bertha E. Mahony, hailed the new Bank Street book with respectful appreciation and a changed mind. Recalling that when Mitchell's first story collection appeared she had been among the doubters, Mahony explained, "We feared that, if the boundaries in the content of stories for little children were fixed too tightly to familiar and *seen* things, the element of wonder would be lost."[22]

Another Here and Now Story Book included pieces about rural life as well as those about urban experiences. (Evidently Mahony, like many of her colleagues in the children's book field, continued to associate "innocent" childhood primarily with rural nature and to mistrust the urban as artificial and spiritually debased.) The new anthology was more varied in other ways as well, with stories "centering in emotional situations and [with] frankly humorous ones." As the critic gracefully conceded, the sheer gaiety of the book "lowered our defences and made us the freer to examine Mrs. Mitchell's point of view."

The May/June issue of the *Horn Book* also reprinted a poem by Mitchell from the book and a profile of her coauthored by Margaret and a fellow contributor to the volume, Mary Phelps. Seizing the moment, they proclaimed that

> when Mrs. Mitchell began to publish, in 1921, there appeared a new kind of author for children. Combining a scientist's command of modern child study with the insight of an unusually gifted teacher, she knew children well enough to understand what is their reality, what their confusion, at different levels of growth. Believing the art experience in all its beauty and delight is their proper heritage, she realized that it can be given them in full measure only by writers in whom the creative genius unites with real understanding of how children grow. [23]

However, resistance within the library world had by no means come to an end and would linger on to cloud, to some extent, the reception of some of Margaret's most original books.

It had been largely a matter of chance that enough more or less talented writers were available to Lucy Mitchell to produce *Another Here and Now Story Book.* She now moved to replace chance with something like scientific predictability. Mitchell conceived of creating an elite group within the school whose primary objective would be to develop their craft as writers. Margaret and her colleagues became the charter members of the Bank Street Writers Laboratory. The group met for the first time in October of 1937.

In principle, the Bank Street community had always aspired to ethnic and racial diversity. But in practice, as most of the school's active recruitment of teacher trainees was done at Radcliffe and the other Seven Sisters colleges, nearly all of the twenty to thirty annual entrants to the program were white, middle-class women.

Mitchell saw the Writers Laboratory as an opportunity to take a concrete step toward rectifying this situation. Early in the summer of 1937, she established a special scholarship to support a young black writer interested in joining the new workshop. In her usual practical-minded, well-intentioned, and proprietary way, she dispatched Margaret as an envoy to Harlem to recruit a suitable candidate.

Margaret headed uptown to West 136th Street, to the Countee Cullen Branch of the New York Public Library, where she found the children's librarian, Augusta Baker, waiting for her. Baker, who was well known to the city's children as a storyteller, escorted Margaret past the ranges of shelves, answering her many questions.

On the whole, Baker explained, Harlem children read what other city youngsters read: *Peter Rabbit, Peter Pan, The Wind in Willows,* Andrew Lang's Rainbow fairy tale collections—the "classics," most of them imported from England. There were pitifully few books that reflected black children's own experiences and cultural heritage. Only a handful of black writers had attempted such books. James Weldon Johnson, the patriarch of the Harlem literary renaissance, was not among them, although he took a keen personal interest in the young people of the Harlem community and Johnson's bravura creation poem, "God's Trombones," was read by older children who came to the library.

The classic work of African-American folklore, the Brer Rabbit stories, sat unread on the shelves. The children, Baker reported, found it hard to make out the dialect of the centuries-old tales, which had been written down and published during the 1880s by a white Southern journalist, Joel Chandler Harris. In most important respects Harris had been faithful to the traditional black storytellers' narrative art and to the Gulla dialect. But there had also been patently racist blackface Brer Rabbit parodies, like *Uncle Pappy Sings,* a copy of which Baker showed Margaret and which the latter described in her report to Mitchell as a "white (trash) imitation" of the original. "It had good rythm [*sic*]," Margaret noted, straining for objectivity, but, as the librarian had told her, children "both resented and didn't understand the dielect [*sic*]."[24] The children Baker read to did enjoy the stirring poetry of Paul Laurence Dunbar, even though Dunbar himself sometimes resorted to dialect and did not write specifically with children in mind. A few African adventure stories were also available. Baker expressed her delight in Lucy Mitchell's eagerness to encourage the writing of books about black children's own lives. The librarian, whose husband was a local WPA administrator, promised to pass the word about the Writers Laboratory scholarship.

Baker's comments on the Brer Rabbit tales were of particular interest to Margaret, who was just then working on her own edition of the stories—attempting a simplification of the dialect that she hoped would retain the flavor and energy of the original. Baker invited her to return to Harlem to test her manuscript, Bank Street–style, at the library's story hour.

This Margaret did from time to time over the summer of 1937, which she spent partly in New York and partly on a rented potato farm, Ploughed Fields, at the far end of Long Island. She wrote Lucy Mitchell from the farm, "The more I work on [Brer Rabbit] the more inevitable it seems and the more lost I am in admiration of the form and vitality of some of those stories."[25] Struggling with the knotty problem that Augusta Baker had alluded to, Margaret wondered how much of the dialect as set down by Harris to leave intact. "It is the rythm [*sic*] and timing and the underlying cadence that gives strength and charm, not the dielect [*sic*]." But she wavered on this point, fearful of draining the tales of their character. Baker's comments had reminded her of the delicate balance between authenticity and simplicity that she would need to strike.

There seemed a good chance that Harper would publish the book (they eventually did, in the fall of 1941), "but whether they decide to take it or not I'm going to do it. It seems one tangable [*sic*] thing that can be done"—one contribution, that is, to the cause of racial equality. "If any one can do it better, I hope they do, sooner or later, only I think I can do it."

Margaret's versions of the stories gradually emerged. In "The Wonderful Tar-Baby Story," the best known of all Brer Rabbit tales, Harris' line "Brer Rabbit come prancin' 'long twel he spy de Tar-Baby" became "Brer Rabbit he came prancing along until he spied the Tar-Baby."[26] Harris' "Youer stuck up, dat's w'at you is . . ." became "You're stuck up, dat's what you is . . . and I'm gwineter cure you."[27]

In addition to modifications of the dialect, Margaret made another, more significant change, eliminating the narrative frame that Harris had devised in order to render the tales more palatable to his overwhelmingly white audience. Harris had interposed a seven-year-old "little white boy" who was heard to converse with the old slave storyteller in the passages introducing each tale. One by one, Remus told his beguiling tales for the boy's amusement. By discarding Harris' device and presenting the stories on their own, Margaret brought them a full step closer to their authentic origins in the culture of African-Americans and their African ancestors. She proudly told Augusta Baker when the manuscript began to assume its final form, "Now we are taking them [the stories] out of slavery."[28]

Margaret was in high spirits that summer of 1937 as she reported to Lucy Mitchell on her first Harlem trip. She was fairly bursting with other news as well. One day not long before, while observing a kitten playing by the hearth at Ploughed Fields, she had improvised a story about the cat—writing, as it were, from life, as Gertrude Stein was said to do when making her word portraits of her artist friends. She had also taken up the habit of composing impromptu verses about the paintings she saw on visits to New York museums, scribbling these on the backs of postcard reproductions. Another day, fishing off Long Island, she hauled in a "fish that our boatman . . . said had a 'deep sea smile.' " The winsome phrase, whether recalled or invented by her, had inspired a ballad of sorts, "The Fish With the Deep Sea Smile," which became the title piece of her collection for Dutton:

> They fished and they fished
> Way down in the sea
> Down in the sea a mile
> They fished among all the fish in the sea
> For the fish with the deep sea smile . . .[29]

Remembering with gratitude her teacher's patient encouragement over the past two years, Margaret offered to dedicate *The Fish with the Deep Sea Smile,* still in progress, to Lucy Mitchell ("if," she added with the gallantry of the Canterbury Knight, "you will accept it").

A new facility as a writer, one that nearly two years of Bank Street note taking and training had done much to cultivate, had become hers. When a royalty advance arrived from Harper in the form of a check made out to "Margaret Wise Brows," she smiled with quiet satisfaction at the accidental caricature and confessed to Louise Raymond to feeling very flattered—though she trusted the error would not be repeated in print.[30]

Later that summer, Margaret sailed for England, where she bought a bicycle and together with "some very chivalrous American boys I met on the boat" spent a week touring Cornwall. "This being of dubious convention," she wrote Marguerite Hearsey, "is between us."[31] Her Chaucer was evidently standing her in good stead; for all this portion of her journey she felt like a "part of a pilgrimage, half prioresse half wife of Bath." Pubs had been investigated. "It would have been only half of literature not to have gone in them." The travelers had lodged at youth hostels, farms, and fisherman's houses. In all, it had been "just beautiful."

Splitting off from the others, Margaret headed northeast through the Devonshire moors, through a fine rain with "nothing but rabbits, sheep, heather and the great waves of mist that blow up" all around her. "England is so like England should be that I have yet to feel real in it," she told her old teacher. She was writing stories for the Dutton collection and painting landscapes as she travelled—to Oxford, then to London for a brief rest at stately Brown's Hotel, then on to Canterbury, where the British leg of her self-styled pilgrimage came to an appropriate close. She met Roberta and Basil, who had come over to Europe on their belated honeymoon, in Paris. They all had planned to stay in the same modest Left Bank hotel, but Margaret had failed to write ahead to reserve her room. After much discussion, the concierge agreed to rent her one of the common bathrooms.

The Paris Exposition was on, and Roberta and Basil had the most moving experience of their visit on viewing Picasso's heroic new work of political protest, *Guernica,* large as a billboard, which compressed with the bluntness of a telegram horrific images of the slaughter and desolation of the Spanish Civil War. What Margaret may have thought of the painting is not known. The world situation was in any case not in her thoughts as she wrote her Harper editor, Louise Raymond, from Paris. She was spending time alone each day in one of the city's open air markets, observing a certain

white goose—"Josephine" Margaret called her—that came and
went with equanimity and determination amid the looming human traffic.[32] Cheering news arrived for her in Raymond's next
letter; Harper had received the first bound copies of *When the Wind
Blew,* and they looked "perfectly stunning."[33]

In September, Margaret continued on to Ireland by herself,
again touring by bicycle. In high spirits, she confided to Marguerite Hearsey, "I don't know where I'm going . . . , but Time, the
Lord and good taste will provide, I hope."[34] A few weeks later, a
large clump of peat, unwrapped except for a heavy cord to which an
address tag had been secured, arrived at 69 Bank Street—a bit of
the old sod for her friends, with postage due, from "Brownie."

Feeling rested and renewed, Margaret returned to New York
in October to begin the three-quarter-time job that she had persuaded Mitchell to offer her.[35] She planned to devote every fourth
week to writing plays; perhaps writing for the theater was the adult
work she was really cut out for. (She was considering enrolling in a
play-writing workshop at Columbia.) Or perhaps, as she told Miss
Hearsey, she would simply dedicate the off-weeks to "playing and
mankind—or both." Her Bank Street salary of $110 a month
would be supplemented by royalties and her allowance from home.
In the previous year she had written a great deal of poetry. "But I
am still too uncertain of what it is, to do more than put it away in a
folder." By one means or another, she said, she was determined to
put children's writing behind her, to "graduate," as her friend
Bruce Bliven, Jr., later described her ambition, to writing literature for adults.[36]

Apparently it was not fear of her new-found success that
prompted this acute longing for a different kind of literary career.
On the contrary, Margaret was proud of all she had achieved. Reviews of *When the Wind Blew,* which began appearing in September, were uniformly favorable. The *New York Times* was typical in
noting that "the musical flow and repetition of the text make it an
admirable story for reading aloud." The *Horn Book* also praised the
musicality of Margaret's prose.[37] But to flourish within Bank
Street's rarefied precincts and gain acceptance within the still distinctly marginal domain of the book world known as juvenile publishing represented only a qualified success. Pioneering figure that

Margaret was as a serious writer and as a poet of picture books for the nursery ages, she remained subject to periodic misgivings when family or friends poked fun at her for being the author of "baby books"—books of only fifty or a hundred small words intended for persons not yet old enough to read. And as Margaret's Hollins friends continued to marry—in the *Alumnae Quarterly*'s class notes, her litanies of forthcoming books presented a striking contrast to the nuptial tidings—she could not help but wonder in her darker moments whether the gift that allowed her to write so knowingly for the very young did not harbor within it the curse of perpetual immaturity.

Starting in October 1937, the dozen or so women of the Bank Street Writers Laboratory met on Wednesdays throughout the school year for late-afternoon sessions that generally stretched on into the evening. In a top-floor room with a battered green plush sofa as its centerpiece, Lucy Mitchell, a stack of papers in hand, took her place each week in the sofa's shapeless depths as the others gathered round. Mitchell rarely seemed in a hurry on these occasions, and for everyone in the group the meetings were eagerly anticipated.

A heady, informal workshop atmosphere prevailed, with less rivalry among the participants than one might have expected from ambitious young writers routinely putting their work on the line for their fellows' scrutiny. Lucy Mitchell's fair-mindedness and contagious enthusiasm did much to set the cooperative spirit of the group. Sherry, tea, and delicious pastries also helped. When Margaret acquired a Kerry Blue terrier, she began bringing the dog to meetings. Curling up at her feet, Smoke often dozed through the literary discussions, but if a manuscript being read aloud happened to bore Margaret, a little kick to the dog's ribs produced a mournful howl that spoke volumes for them both and gave the group as a whole a few tension-shattering moments of laughter.

Because the members all had regular contact with young children, there were always fresh nuggets of "language data" to report. ("I come from Alabama," a three-year-old had warbled into one researcher's ear, "with a Band-aid on my knee.")[38] "The Emotional

Effect of Stories on Children" and other prearranged discussion topics also provided a focus for a portion of some meetings.

Distinguished guests periodically sat in—Pearl Buck, psychologist Alice Keliher, Max Lerner, poet and folklorist Sterling Brown, and many others. They commented on the members' work and spoke about their own contributions to the fields of literature, child development, intelligence testing, and current affairs. Such encounters were considered an integral part of the here-and-now writer's education. Talks by Margaret's Harper editor, Louise Raymond, and by respected illustrators like Kurt Wiese kept the group grounded in the practical realities of writing for publication. The main business of each meeting, however, was the critiquing of work. The effectiveness of a particular image, the appropriateness of this or that word, and similar matters of craft were ardently debated as the group explored the central issue of how purely literary considerations and those brought to light by developmental research might be reconciled in the new kind of children's literature.

The new writing of Gertrude Stein, Virginia Woolf, and other modernists excited them greatly and was understood to have a particular relevance to writing for young children. The modernist aesthetic of recreating in art the immediacy of sensory impressions seemed to coincide with young children's natural reliance on their senses as the primary means of both experiencing and expressing themselves about the world.

Stein's work was considered especially pertinent. The inherent playfulness of her verse and prose, her exuberant manner of cadenced repetition (and of subtle variation within repetition), and her peculiar genius for making words seem to speak directly from the page were all elements of attitude and style that Margaret and the others were eager to incorporate in their own work.

Lucy Mitchell generally listened more than she spoke and resisted the temptation to take charge, except to propose occasional group assignments of one kind or another. She once asked everyone to rewrite a finished piece of theirs for a different age-level of readers. Such experiments forced Margaret and the others to test their assumptions. It was Mitchell's gift as a teacher to make doing so seem like a form of play.

Ellen Tarry, the young Harlem journalist with the Federal Writers' Project who had responded to Lucy Mitchell's scholarship offer, unsettled the group with the first story she read to them. "Janie Belle" told about a black baby who had been abandoned in a garbage pail on the Harlem streets. A white nurse found the infant, fed and cared for her and—this was the story's happy ending—adopted the child.

As Tarry finished reading the piece in her thick Virginia drawl, the others in the room sat stone silent. At last Lucy Mitchell spoke up to wonder aloud whether all children, even those born into well-off "happy" homes, might not at times experience the fear, if not the actual fact, of abandonment by their parents; after an earnest discussion the group agreed that children did know such fears. Over the next several months it was Margaret who most openly befriended Ellen Tarry, though the initial awkwardness felt by both women is plain from a running private joke they shared. When the fair-skinned Harlem woman told Margaret that her ancestors were thought to have been slaves of a wealthy Virginia family named Brown, Margaret replied that in that case the two of them were probably related. [39]

Gradually the real writers in the group found each other. Margaret and Edith Thacher, who already knew each other from Bank Street, now became close friends, continuing their discussions over dinner at the Grand Ticino Restaurant on nearby Thompson Street or at Monte's on MacDougal—both quaint, candle-lit, Italian family establishments a few steps down from the street, where for a dollar one got a big bowl of spaghetti, a bottle of chianti and hours of undisturbed conversation.

Margaret and her friend, known to everyone as Posey, complemented each other. Posey was a sensitive, hard-working intellectual with a quiet orderly resolve that seemed unshakable. Margaret was quixotic, unpredictable, a sensualist and a poet. Both were astute observers, but in characteristically different ways. What Posey might have seen as a fire engine hurrying past to perform a vital civic function, Margaret registered as a "big, powerful, noisy red color."[40] The two friends poked gentle fun at each other and at Bank Street constantly. Among their "theories" was one concerning inferiority complexes. Dogs, they posited, were as susceptible as humans to this fearful disorder which Alfred Adler had first explicated for the world during the 1920s. Margaret and Posey discussed at length a tongue-in-cheek experiment for testing their idea. They would name a puppy "Nothing" (Posey eventually did so), then observe the effect ("Here, Nothing!" "Nothing, lie down!") on the poor creature's self-esteem.[41]

For all the good-natured fun that she and Margaret had at Bank Street's expense, Posey Thacher probably resembled Lucy Mitchell more closely in talent and temperament than anyone in the Writers Laboratory group. Missouri-born and educated at Radcliffe, she was a tall, attractive woman of keen intellect, with a lyrical prairie cadence in her voice, an easy but firm way with children, an unshowy elegance in her writing, and a reserved but determined manner that made her a much admired figure among her colleagues. Thirty years earlier Posey's mother and young Lucy Sprague had been students together at Radcliffe. The elder Thacher remembered Lucy as one of the chief campus troublemakers; Gertrude Stein had been another. In the fall of 1933, Posey's parents had resisted the idea of their daughter enrolling in Lucy Sprague Mitchell's "communist" school.[42] Posey, who had found Radcliffe a genteel, intellectually arid place, had remained adamant. From their first meeting she had been deeply impressed by Mitchell's spirited commitment to discovering the underlying patterns of childhood experience and using these discoveries as tools for effecting concrete change in the world.

After completing her Bank Street studies one year later, in the spring of 1934, Posey had continued to be a presence at the school, first as a part-time instructor and then as a member of the Writers Laboratory. A short story by her, a droll satirical piece in the Just So vein called "The Elephant's Delicate Taste," had appeared in *Another Here and Now Story Book*. For Posey, as for Margaret, Bank Street would prove to be a way station on the road not to a teaching career but to the literary life; Lucy Mitchell's ambitions for the Writers Laboratory were starting to be realized.

Among the parents of the toddlers enrolled at Bank Street in the fall of 1937 was William R. Scott, an engaging man in his late twenties, with a serious interest in books. An English major at Yale, Scott was a skilled letterpress printer and book designer. He had a great reserve of family money at his disposal, and was eager to become a publisher. But a publisher of what? Scott had brought out a miscellany of limited edition art books and poetry broadsides, and he had discussed possible future directions with his wife, Ethel, and his brother-in-law, John McCullough, but without coming to any decisions. Then he met Lucy Sprague Mitchell.

Mitchell and Jessie Stanton, who directed the Bank Street nursery, told Scott that in juvenile publishing a chance lay open to him to make a significant contribution to the book world, the education field, and society as a whole. They urged him to become the first publisher to devote his list to experimentally tested, here-and-now-style children's books.

The two women argued that the growing public interest in progressive education and the emergence throughout the United States of nursery schools for children as young as eighteen months of age meant that a sizeable market existed for the type of book they had in mind. Scott might therefore expect to earn a reasonable return for his efforts. He would not have far to go for publishable material. The Writers Laboratory produced a steady stream of manuscripts, some of them quite fine. Any manuscript that the firm was considering might first be tried out on Bank Street's nursery school children or on the older children at the affiliated City & Country School and the Little Red School House. A firm that specialized in child-tested books was bound to arouse the book-buying public's curiosity and establish its name rapidly.

Overwhelmed by Mitchell and Stanton's enthusiasm and sense of mission and by the simple logic of their idea, Scott agreed to the plan. With all the determination of a young Crusoe (except that he had had the freedom to choose the ground on which to prove his resourcefulness) Scott set up shop, partly in the projection closet made available to him at 69 Bank Street, partly in the dining room of his Greenwich Village townhouse, and partly at his farm in North Bennington, Vermont, where the barn became the company's warehouse and summer quarters.

Lucy Mitchell had been the inventor, instigator, and guiding spirit of the here-and-now movement in nursery literature. Because of other commitments and plans; she could not, she told Bill Scott, also serve as the fledgling firm's editor. She was pleased, however, to recommend a suitable substitute. Margaret was offered the job and accepted it gladly. Having emerged as the finest of the here-and-now writers, she would now, beginning in early 1938, also act as the new literature's chief impresario.

Margaret felt honored to have been entrusted with her new responsibilities, and she applied herself energetically to the search for authors and illustrators. In a letter to Louise Raymond she asked the editor to forward to her any interesting manuscripts found unsuitable for the Harper list. In the class notes section of the Hollins *Alumnae Quarterly,* she urged former schoolmates to send to her whatever children's stories they might be writing. New York bookshop managers made her acquaintance during the long sessions she spent scanning new juvenile titles on their shelves; Margaret invited them to give her name to any aspiring author or artist who came by seeking guidance about their careers. By these and other means, she soon gained a reputation as a highly accessible editor willing to consider projects that other publishers thought too offbeat or commercially risky.

In her dual role as editor and author, Margaret then and afterward "collected" illustrators, as Bill Scott later recalled.[43] While visiting a friend in Greenwich, Connecticut, for example, she became curious about the artist who had painted a series of whimsical semi-abstractions on the bathhouse ceiling. In one picture, a giant octopus held a huge tentacle over the head of an unsuspecting little fisherman. In another, a large, grinning shark was preparing to make short work of a hapless group of recreational swimmers. These paintings depicting the *Perils of the Sea* were the work of a young artist, recently returned from Paris, named Clement Hurd. Margaret asked to meet him.

The painter in question proved to be a tall, lanky man with a boyish, shy, patrician manner and a dry, off-tempo sense of humor. He earned his living, he told Margaret, by making decorative hooked rugs, painting murals like the ones she'd seen, and executing other such commissions for society clients, many of whom were school and family friends. He considered painting and scenic design his serious work. He had never thought about illustrating children's books, but was willing to have a try.

Born in New York City in 1908 to a family of considerable affluence (his father, Richard M. Hurd, was a mortgage banker, president of the Lawyers Mortgage Company and vice president of the Mortgage Bond Company), he had been educated at St. Paul's and Yale and had stayed on at Yale for a year of graduate studies in architecture. When his school days drew to a close in the spring of 1931, Hurd might easily have stepped into the comfortable role of gentleman banker that his family envisioned for him. Instead, he announced his intention to go to Paris to become an artist. Once persuaded that his son would not change his mind, Richard Hurd presented him with a parting gift that was a sardonic choice at best. The book that Clem (as friends knew him) received before sailing for Europe in the summer of 1931 was a bitter chronicle of Siberian exile, *The Road to Oblivion*.

Hurd's sojourn in Paris was liberating. It marked the first time in his sheltered life that he had refused to do what his parents expected of him, and he developed artistically as well. In Paris Hurd studied painting with Fernand Léger at the Académie Moderne, where for the equivalent of five dollars a month, the master—a thoughtful, patient teacher then in his fifties—critiqued his work twice weekly. From Léger, he learned important lessons in pictorial design, developing a graphic approach to form and color that was to serve him well as an illustrator.

Back in the United States in 1933 after his money ran out, Hurd renewed old friendships while becoming increasingly drawn into the cultural and social circle that columnists of the time referred to as the "streamlined intelligencia." In February of 1934 he was among the New York artists who chartered a railroad car to Hartford for the historic world premiere of Gertrude Stein's and Virgil Thomson's "Four Saints in Three Acts" at the Wadsworth Athenaeum. In New York, college friends took him along to sumptuous evenings at 10 Gracie Square, the Manhattan apartment of Wall Street lawyer Harrison Tweed and his celebrated wife, the socialite, actress, and poet (and former wife of John Barrymore), Michael Strange; Carl Van Vechten, James Montgomery

Flagg, and George Jean Nathan were among the vast and shifting cast of characters which would eventually include Margaret Brown.

Early in 1938 Margaret introduced Hurd to Bill Scott and John McCullough, and it was agreed that Clem should try his hand at illustrating a book for the new firm's list. Margaret presented him with a simply structured text composed of big-little comparisons ("Once upon a time/there was a great bumble bug/and a tiny little bumble bug/And there was a great big butterfly/and a little tiny butterfly . . ."). This manuscript, which she had written to order for Hurd, became their first collaboration, *Bumble Bugs and Elephants*.[44]

The artist soon learned that illustrating a picture book, at least a picture book for Scott, involved more than producing a sequence of paintings in one's studio. The art, like the text, had to be tested on actual children. Accustomed to submitting his work to the scrutiny of art directors, wealthy patrons, and his mentor, Léger, Hurd was thus understandably ill at ease as he arrived for his appointment at the Bank Street nursery school and was accosted by a swarm of clamoring critics who barely reached his knees.

The classroom teacher instructed the visitor to arrange his paintings on the floor and step back while the children examined them. The waiting period that followed was unnerving. When the children finally dispersed with what seemed like a killing indifference to the work laid before them, Hurd's heart sank. The teacher's cheerful verdict soon revived him. "Congratulations!" she said. "You held their attention for five minutes! I timed them with my watch."[45] Here was a novel measure of artistic achievement, one for which neither Yale nor Paris had prepared him. Hurd modestly accepted the accolade, collected his pictures and his hat, and strode out the door.

As work on *Bumble Bugs and Elephants* proceeded in this trial-and-error manner, more revisions were asked of him than he had perhaps originally bargained for. As Scott's inaugural fall catalog trumpeted, "In bringing this book to its final form, the artist discarded many finished pictures, keeping only those that had met with the children's 'complete approval.' "[46]

Hurd's illustrations for *Bumble Bugs and Elephants* were in any case splendid work. Compared to the *Perils of the Sea*, their style was more forthrightly representational; small children would have little trouble recognizing the familiar objects in each scene: a door, a window, a table. The artist's playful humor was everywhere in evidence. In one illustration, two well-behaved small dogs wait patiently while a large dog jumps up to inspect a tempting plate of food on the table. Pronouncing Hurd one of the most innovative young illustrators on the current scene, the critic Louise Seaman Bechtel would observe not long afterward that his art had a "flavor of recent French and Russian bookmaking in [his] use of flat color combined with bold spaces of black and white," and that there was a "verve" and a "toylike" quality about his simplified, graphic approach to image-making that children were bound to enjoy.[47] In his first picture book, Hurd had also demonstrated a sure grasp of young children's need for reassurance that the world they live in is a safe and secure place. His paintings depicted a fundamentally benign world, a sort of here-and-now peaceable kingdom with a sense of fun. Thereafter Margaret turned primarily to him to illustrate those manuscripts of hers that investigated the child's elemental feelings of attachment to home.

Small children, Margaret realized, did not place books in a special category of culturally exalted objects. They tore at, squeezed, and bit books just as they did their toys, their food, their parents. The very young experienced books as sensuous objects that might, for all one knew, be alive. Accordingly, *Bumble Bugs and Elephants,* as a book intended for the youngest ages, was printed not on ordinary paper but on durable cardboard stock strong enough to withstand the onslaught of toddlers' bites and tugs. For the same reason it was given an equally unconventional sturdy spiral binding. In all, the book's design was a remarkable innovation. Such experiments were the norm in the early days of Scott.

Margaret's written-to-order text was also experimental in form. The manuscript began with the familiar fairy tale invocation, "once upon a time," and proceeded as a litany of rapidly indicated contrasting images ("There were two little dogs and a great big dog") without ever developing a plot line. Instead, Margaret's text started over and over again, presenting image after comforting image of a small creature that had found its place in the world alongside a much larger one. *Bumble Bugs and Elephants* was not so much a story as a game patterned on an emotional reality of early childhood, a game that the very young might extend indefinitely by inventing big-little pairs of their own. Here was a book that did not end except in the reader's imagination. If it amounted to something less than Literature—Margaret narrowly credited herself as the author of the book's "word pattern" and gave Hurd top billing—the children on whom the book had been tested evidently did not care.

Among the artists who showed their portfolios to Margaret in the early months of 1938, while Scott was still preparing its first list, was a vivid young Russian Jewish emigré painter, Esphyr Slobodkina ("Slow-boat-*keen*-a," as she had long since become used to explaining to Americans).

Strong-willed, solidly built, and not easily impressed, she had come to the United States in the late 1920s with a firsthand knowledge of the heady Soviet Constructivist experiments that had become an important influence on American artists and designers by the 1930s. Her first impressions of her adopted country's artistic life, however, had aroused her deepest skepticism. A self-styled bohemian acquaintance had escorted Slobodkina to the Blue Horse Inn, a Greenwich Village hangout where the waiters dressed in silk shirts and berets and a singing parrot served as vocalist for the late-night dance band. All this had struck the serious-minded painter as merely "dingy." As she later recalled, she soon decided "not to fall in with the time-wasting, do-nothing . . . Greenwich Village crowd."[48]

In the spring of 1938, a friend to whom she confided her need to earn more money advised Slobodkina to see a certain "very beautiful, rich and clever girl who writes children's books" to learn how one went about becoming a juveniles illustrator.[49] He offered to introduce her to this dazzling acquaintance of his, whom she knew from parties around town, as soon as the artist prepared some sort of convincing portfolio.

For want of other ideas, Slobodkina started by making strings of paper dolls. With these repeating images as her building blocks, she experimented at composing complete pictorial scenes, which she pasted in place on a paper background. She then wrote a simple story to go with her designs. When the artist was done, she bedecked herself in a "chic outfit of moderately Bohemian swirling black cape and a beaded, crocheted skullcap over . . . invisibly snooded long hair" and arrived at 69 Bank Street to meet her fate "in the person of the twenty-eight-year-old, slightly chubby and short, but beautiful, blond and mercurial Margaret Wise Brown."[50]

The interview, conducted in Margaret's tiny office, was polite, a bit formal perhaps, and inconclusive as to the prospects for an assignment. During a rapid tour of the premises—Slobodkina had actually to run to keep up with her guide—an imposing older woman stepped into the corridor. This, Margaret announced, was Lucy Sprague Mitchell, who paused to offer a few words of friendly encouragement before disappearing, also in an unusual hurry, Slobodkina thought. As the artist and editor shook hands Margaret promised to examine her portfolio and telephone her in the next few days. This Margaret did, and on the strength of her highly favorable impression, she arranged for a second interview at Bill Scott's home where, in a gathering of Scotts and McCulloughs, Slobodkina encountered general praise—and certain reservations. It would be too costly, she was told, to reproduce her artwork well (Scott good-naturedly assured her this was not her fault, citing his own professional inexperience); the story she had written was a bit flimsy, and it lacked a satisfactory ending. Nonetheless, the publisher was determined to use her for some assignment. Margaret, she was told, would contact her again shortly, when a suitable manuscript had been found.

To the skeptical artist this sounded like a classic brushoff, but she soon discovered it had not been meant as such. As the others present at the meeting already knew, Margaret would simply write a book to order for her.

The Little Fireman, which Slobodkina illustrated and Scott published that fall (1938), was an elaborate variation on the big-little theme laid down in *Bumble Bugs and Elephants.* It could also be read as a sly comment on the pattern of Bank Street life itself, where little children and big teacher trainees learned in parallel by engaging in many of the same activities. It doubtless amused Margaret to equate Bank Street rushing-around with the putting out of fires.

"Once upon a time there was a great big tall fireman and once upon a time there was a little fireman."[51] The big fireman of Margaret's tale lives in a big firehouse, the little one in a little house. The big fellow fights fires of a suitable scale, the little one fights little fires. And so on. In alternating passages, parallel adventures energetically unfold, with a surprise reversal at the end—in bed at night, the big fireman dreams only a little dream, and the little fireman's dream is large. At Bank Street, Margaret had learned that the very young find humor in "reversals of observed relations"; in *The Little Fireman* she applied this principle somewhat mechanically at the end. Endings were always the most difficult part of a manuscript for her, though in her sequels, *The Little Farmer* (1948) and *The Little Cowboy* (1949), both illustrated by Slobodkina, Margaret crafted last-page surprises that seem less forced and so more nearly satisfying. As Margaret continued to develop as a writer, she increasingly modified Bank Street theory or set it aside altogether for her own literary purposes.

For *The Little Fireman* Slobodkina used the same cut-out-collage method as in her portfolio piece and thereby introduced a fertile new illustration technique to American picture book art. Her intensely hued, poster-like graphics were lavishly printed in five colors, with such a thickness of ink that the printer wondered aloud whether there was need of any paper.

Margaret was invited to share a house for the summer of 1938 on the island of Vinalhaven, off the Maine coast in Penobscot Bay. Mrs. Gertrude MacCormick, a Bank Street administrative assistant, had arranged to rent an old A-frame ocean-front cottage. Her teenage children, Jim and Joan, were also going, as was Margaret's good friend Jessica Gamble. They packed their bags with clothes and books and, because the house was situated at Long Cove, a remote part of the island inaccessible by road, with a month's supply of canned and packaged foods. Mrs. MacCormick, having taken to the cheerful notion of outfitting the isolated holiday retreat with a piano, made the necessary arrangements in Rockland, their point of embarkation. The upright was loaded onto an old green dragger. Then she, Margaret, and the others got aboard, and they were off. "The crazy MacCormicks" the local lobstermen called them, lumping the five together.[52]

The vacationers settled into their rough quarters, with Margaret and Jessica sharing an upstairs room under the eaves. More to their amusement than discomfort, their room was also inhabited by bats. The use of a fifteen-foot sailboat came with the house, which belonged to the poet Harry Vinal, whose ancestors had been early settlers of the island. Margaret named the boat "The Bat."

She had her own name for almost everything. She called the little island they rowed to for picnics "Starfish Island" for its distinctive shape, and nicknamed sixteen-year-old Jim, who years later remembered having had a secret crush on her, "Old Smoothy." (To millions of Americans, Bing Crosby was Old Smoothy; Margaret could hardly have paid the teenager a higher complement.) Margaret was a nester. As the summer wore on, she filled first her own room, then the house, with arrangements of pebbles, seashells, lobster traps, bits of driftwood, and feathers collected on walks. Her housemates might well have resented some of these nesting activities but for the fact that she brought them off so interestingly and with such good humor.

There was also fishing, swimming in the chill, phosphorescent water, and hiking in the deeply scented spruce forest. Because their cottage was situated on high ground along the granite rim of Long Cove, sounds emanating from the house echoed tremendously over the water. Margaret and Jessica eagerly took advantage of this natural phenomenon. On some evenings, the bellowing grunt-tones of what sounded like a gorilla—but was actually Jessica—shattered the Cove's arcadian stillness, and from their crank-up Victrola the jaunty strains of "Flat Foot Floogie" and Bing Crosby's plaintive "Don't Be That Way" piped out over the water.

A neighbor who doubtless heard these goings-on (and may have been their chief target) was William Gaston, a New York attorney who spent summers on his inherited Penobscot Bay property, Hurricane Island (just across from Vinalhaven) and the unfortunately named nearby Crotch Island, where he had built an extravagant house featuring a deck supported by a grand phalanx of antique ships' figureheads.

The grandson of a former governor of Massachusetts, Gaston, at forty-two, had numerous ties to the theater world and to East coast society. His former wives, Kay Francis and Rosamond Pinchot, had both been actresses, and Clare Booth, John Barrymore, and Michael Strange (Barrymore's wife from 1920 to 1928) were among the many celebrities who had made the trek north to be hosted by him. Gaston himself dabbled at playwriting and producing. Although heavy drinking had caused him to put on weight, he still had the dashing good looks of a leading man and (as the steady parade of female guests to and from the island testified) a well-deserved reputation as a womanizer.

At the time of Rosamond Pinchot's widely publicized suicide in late January of 1938, she and Gaston had been separated for years. Gaston was nonetheless deeply affected by the news of her death, and he was a man in urgent need of consolation when Margaret met him that summer. Their friendship soon became an affair.

The relationship went unremarked in a letter Margaret wrote over the summer to Marguerite Hearsey. As though to underscore her new-found professionalism, Margaret typed her communication, but the words sputtered out haltingly. That particular afternoon, she wrote, the air, by a trick of the weather typical of Maine, had suddenly turned cool, turbulent, autumnal; for a moment she had thought herself a Hollins student again, due back on campus. The thought of returning to Hollins pleased her, but she now had other, more pressing matters to attend to. The following day she was scheduled to fly to Vermont for a last-minute review of Scott's fall list. She would then be sailing on a pleasure cruise. Margaret was reading Steinbeck. "There is more tenderness and good writing in him than in all others," she declared. She was working on a new book for Harper, though "most of the ink poisoning impulse has gone away for the moment." She had spent most of the last several weeks generating . . . with friends, . . . generating to degenerate this winter. . . . It is wonderful just to know the importance of lying in the sun. . . . Life goes on in Transition. This summer it is better than it has been in a long time, and still [everything hangs] in the balance. . . . This is a silly letter. Maybe it is the typewriter. I'd better stop. Devotedly, Tim.[53]

A year earlier, when Harper agreed to publish *When the Wind Blew,* Margaret had written Marguerite Hearsey to say that at last, in the picture book genre, she had found a satisfying outlet for her literary ambitions. In books for young children, a field of "limitless" unexplored possibilities, it was possible to put the "wildest and best words into literature. . . . What a field it might have been for Ronald Firbank and V. Woolf and G. Stein and all the other playful writers and masters of imagery in our day."[54]

Now, as Scott's editor, she proposed to invite a number of such writers to author children's books for the firm. Over the summer of 1938, Margaret and John McCullough drafted a suitable letter and sent copies to Ernest Hemingway, Gertrude Stein, and John Steinbeck. As Bill Scott's partner, only McCullough signed the letters. He wagered Margaret what she referred to as a "box of Don Giovannis" (some good seats at the Metropolitan Opera) that no one would reply.[55]

Late in August, while Margaret was still travelling, a reply did come from Stein and it was an enthusiastic affirmative. Stein offhandedly reported that she was already well into a draft of the proposed book and wondered only how long it might run and still be appropriate for children. There were routine questions about royalty arrangements. Stein looked forward to the publisher's response. Elated, taken aback, out the price of a box at the Met, McCullough, having outlined the terms of Scott's standard contract, assured her, "I apologize if the decorous future conditional has sometimes slipped into future plu-perfect. The prospect of your story is enough to unhorse our decorum which is at best scarce a better rider than the White Knight."[56]

Stein had good reason to hope the project would succeed. She was then sixty-four and the last few years had been difficult ones for her creatively, the more so coming as they did on the heels of her triumphant American tour of 1934–35. Whereas her cunning memoir, *The Autobiography of Alice B. Toklas,* and her opera *Four Saints in Three Acts* had both been great popular successes of the early thirties, none of Stein's more recent work had fared half as well in the United States. When McCullough's letter arrived she was quite prepared to try her luck with a new publisher, a new genre, and new audience.

During the rapid exchange of cables and letters that followed, Stein, turning unaccountably testy at one point, demanded to know whether McCullough had meant to imply that he did not think her capable of writing a *long* work for young readers. (McCullough had made no such suggestion.) Did his letter constitute a formal agreement? Half concealing panic, Scott himself cabled a reply: "GREATLY DISAPPOINTED AT MUTUAL MISUNDERSTANDING. WE HAVE FAITH IN YOUR ABILITY TO WRITE FOR CHILDREN AT ANY LENGTH."[57] He would, however, need to see the completed book before making a formal offer. By October 24 friendly relations had been restored. "TERMS AGREEABLE," Scott flashed in response to a letter in which Stein had given details of the final plan of her work-in-progress.[58]

Throughout these exchanges Margaret felt ignored and cheated of an opportunity to become personally acquainted with a writer she greatly admired. When, however, on an unseasonably warm mid-November afternoon, the manuscript of *The World Is Round,* Gertrude Stein's first fantasy for children, arrived from France, all hands understood that the evening belonged to Margaret. Bill and John joined her at her apartment after work to read the book aloud, have a drink, and celebrate their good fortune.

In the happy confusion, everyone forgot about supper and Margaret had not thought to pick up refreshments. The only food in the house was an amusing cake in the shape of a boat, which she had ordered for a friend's going-away party and which the trio now appropriated in the name of experimental literature. They sat around the kitchen table and took turns reading the manuscript aloud: "Once upon a time the world was round and you could go on it around and around. Everywhere there was somewhere and everywhere there they were women children dogs cows wild pigs little rabbits cats and lizards and animals. This is the way it was."[59]

Suddenly the lights went out. Careless at times about her bill paying, Margaret had neglected the electric company. Candles were groped for, and the reading continued. "And everybody dogs cats sheep rabbits and lizards and children all wanted to tell everybody all about it . . ." There was a knock at the door that went unnoticed. It was Basil Rauch, come to return a borrowed vacuum cleaner. Letting himself in, he saw the three dimly-lit figures huddled absurdly around the cake, and listened—". . . and they wanted to tell all about themselves . . ."—and fled out the door.

Margaret and her guests stayed up well into the night, reading and laughing as Stein's young hero and heroine, Willie and Rose, pursued their adventures, each alone, before being happily reunited at the end. The following morning Bill Scott cabled France: "DELIGHTED WITH MANUSCRIPT. CONTRACT FOLLOWS,"[60] and Margaret made preparations for testing the book on the Bank Street nursery students and on older children at the nearby cooperating schools.

Each of the five books that Scott published in the fall of 1938 was a daring experiment. *Cottontails,* conceived by Ethel McCullough [Scott], illustrated by Sister Mary Veronica and printed on cloth, was, as Barbara Bader observes, "something new"—a "Tactile Book" with specially sewn-in novelty details for prereaders to touch.[61] On one page silkscreened rabbits had real cotton-ball tails, on another a lamb had a real toy bell around its neck. During the months prior to publication, Margaret and the Scotts had patiently done all the stitching themselves, an inefficient scheme at best, and *Cottontails* proved to be a book that one stacked in warehouses and sent through the mail at one's peril. "The spoilage," Scott later recalled with amusement, "was tremendous."[62] But the idea was sound. Two years later, Simon and Schuster published Dorothy Kunhardt's tactile book, *Pat the Bunny,* with resounding success.

For older children, *The Log of Christopher Columbus* provided the firsthand experience of reading about the explorer's adventures in his own words. Lucy Mitchell had long advocated this approach to teaching history, on the theory that the past might thus be brought to life with something of the immediacy of the here-and-now. Margaret adapted a translation of the original text without taking a title-page credit.

Posey Thacher had a book on the list, a picture-book satire for ages five to nine called *Hurry Hurry: A Tale of Calamity and Woe, Or, A Lesson in Leisure* with illustrations by Mary Pepperell Dana. The story concerns a babysitter who, by getting a bit ahead of herself, is always falling into man-holes and ditches and the like. Few picture books before had dared so pointedly to take the grown-up world to task for its capacity for childish self-importance. *The Little Fireman,* Margaret's collaboration with Esphyr Slobodkina, and *Bumble Bugs and Elephants,* her book with Clement Hurd, completed the list.

When copies of the books were ready, Bill Scott made an appointment to show them to Anne Carroll Moore at the New York Public Library. Both he and Margaret anticipated the meeting with wary expectancy. Moore's conspicuous silence at the time of *Another Here and Now Story Book*'s publication was hardly reassuring. Now the librarian would have a fresh opportunity to raise her voice for or against the "new kind of author for children."

Moore seemed to ignore Margaret as she looked up from the small heap of books ranged before her and prepared to deliver her verdict.

"Mr. Scott," she said with all deliberateness, "do you want to know what I think of these books?"

"Why yes, Miss Moore," he replied, sounding a note of forced optimism.

"Truck, Mr. Scott! They are truck!"[63]

The interview at an end, Scott and Margaret collected their things and shambled back downtown.

Later that fall, on assignment for the *New Republic,* Bruce Bliven, Jr., drove out to the Flushing Meadow landfill to size up the progress being made at the New York World's Fair construction site. The young writer arrived with an air of skepticism; four years earlier his father had denounced Manhattan's Rockefeller Center as a "piece of gargantuan exhibitionism . . . typical not only of the anarchy of modern capitalist society, but of America in particular."[64]

Much to his surprise, the younger Bliven found the "Trylon and Perisphere," the fair's monumental ball-and-spike trademark, was genuinely impressive. With rising curiosity, he observed that the avenues radiating like wheel spokes from the central hub formed by this two-part extravaganza had been color-coded (rather like the utility pipes at 69 Bank Street):

> From the warm off-white of the Theme Center the hues along each street will increase in intensity as one gets farther and farther from the central axis, and the buildings and murals and plants will all be in harmony. . . . A Fair visitor, confused by the bigness of it all, can approximate his distance from the center of things by a glance at the color of the nearest flower or building.[65]

Many of the public sculptures and murals flung up in all quarters of the fairgrounds struck the reporter as "dull and self-conscious in the Radio City style," with their "big circus women with round contours and no clothes, holding an assortment of lightning bolts or a plowshare and representing, according to the legend, The World of Tomorrow, Freedom of Speech or The Way to the Ladies' Room." But he found other artworks admirable, as was the theory underlying their thoughtful integration within the fair's overall scheme—that art could be fun, not just something to be "stared at with suspicious awe in galleries or public parks, but a comfortable, useful thing. . . . I shall be surprised . . . if this attitude as it is carried out here does not spill over into the building and decoration of tomorrow" (as in fact it did).

With a few months still to go before the official opening ceremony in the spring of 1939, the sprawling international and industrial pavilions remained largely empty, unfinished outlines of the fair's promised vision of "the World of Tomorrow." Still, Bliven wrote, one could tell that the exposition had been conceived with an overall purpose in mind, that of "sing[ing] the praises and underscoring the possibilities of the democratic form of government. . . . Dictatorship has developed to a fine point the technique of singing its own praises"—as anyone knew who had viewed recent newsreel footage from abroad or scanned *Life*'s pages lately. "In a sense," he concluded, with a prescient glance at things to come, "the World's Fair is an experiment in the same art but for democracy."

In anticipation of the World's Fair, New York public school children were being given a crash course in cross-cultural fellow-feeling. A story to this effect in the *Herald Tribune*—"Pupils to Learn Tolerance Here Twice a Month"—prompted the satirical poet Phyllis McGinley (afterwards also a Scott author) to marvel at the doubtful prospect of five- through eleven-year-olds quickly mastering an art and ethic that so consistently eluded their elders:

> To stretch their hands across the ocean;
> To open up their childish hearts
> And love their neighbor with devotion,
> As per the diagrams and charts;
>
> To call the foreigner their brother
> (Unless by chance he should endorse
> Some heretic opinion other
> Than that included in the Course). [66]

The fair as a whole was meant as an expression of faith in a future world in which technological progress and advances in international understanding would proceed hand in hand. But it was impossible to overlook the lack of participation of one of Europe's most powerful nations, Germany. Underlining the significance of Germany's absence were horrifying front-page headlines of early November, chronicling the Nazi regime's brutal Kristallnacht attacks on German Jewry after the assassination of a German diplomat in Paris.

November of 1938 marked the twentieth anniversary of the signing of the armistice ending the Great War, a fact recalled with foreboding by educators and child development specialists as they met at New York's Roosevelt Hotel and heard Yale psychologist Arnold Gesell assert that "only in a democracy can 'full respect' be given to the individuality of a child." [67] John Dewey had said as much a generation earlier, but set against the backdrop of the newly aggressive authoritarian regimes of Europe and the Far East, the idea carried renewed urgency. At a similar year-end conference held at Teachers College, Columbia University, education policy makers debated the proposition that the federal government, in order to assure an ample supply of talented national leaders for the dangerous times ahead, should establish a fund for the special education of children whose IQ scores indicated unusual promise.[68]

At Scott's office, meanwhile, work continued on Gertrude Stein's manuscript. At the Bank Street nursery and elsewhere, Margaret read bits of the text to children of different ages and recorded the children's comments in her sprawling longhand. A group of four-year-olds remarked:

"The world is going around all the time right now very fast."

"And cars are going on it and cars always go to a house somewhere don't they."

"Wild pigs are really bores [*sic*], wild bores."[69]

Children from three to thirteen accepted Stein's fantasy on some level, the younger ones eagerly mimicking "noises . . . they said kangaroos made, a roar for a lion and a barking growl for a canarie [*sic*]," while a thoughtful thirteen-year-old praised the author for her ability to offer readers the "freedom to escape" in her story, as in a dream. Evidently, *The World Is Round* could not be tidily age-graded; Margaret was deeply impressed by the fact that Stein's vibrant text resisted Bank Street categorization.[70]

When many samples of children's comments had been amassed, John McCullough, Bill Scott, and Margaret met to discuss possible revisions. McCullough, whose main roles in the company were those of financial overseer and congenial smoother of authors' ruffled feathers, ventured an occasional opinion, but the major editorial debates were joined by Scott and Margaret, who "fought, bled and died over a comma," as the latter recalled, in battles of wits and critical discernment that Margaret relished.[71]

Stein's punctuation, or (more often) the lack of it, was a particular concern. Children, it was agreed, needed more punctuation than did seasoned readers of the modernists. Margaret was assigned the task of reviewing the manuscript with this problem in mind, a turn of events she must have viewed with irony, considering her own undergraduate resistance to the comma, a literary rebellion Stein's own writings had inspired. Intent on keeping a tight rein on the company's dealings with Stein, it was McCullough, however, who wrote the author to ask whether she considered her punctuation final. Over the next several months, to Margaret's disappointment, McCullough continued to brief Stein on pre-publication developments.

Margaret's own reputation as an author continued to grow. Writing in the *Saturday Review of Literature* in the fall of 1938, Louise Seaman Bechtel heralded *The Streamlined Pig,* published by Harper with illustrations by Kurt Wiese, as "one of the few really American picture books I have seen that has any charm. . . . Miss Brown . . . is an author and an editor to be watched with interest."[72] Two of the five Scott books that appeared that season were also written by Margaret, and though these were perhaps less widely reviewed, they nonetheless stood as further proof of her own accomplishments.

Margaret's personal life remained a good deal less settled. Her brother Gratz came to New York in late October to be married and returned with his bride to Flint, Michigan, where he was employed as an engineer by the A-C Spark Plug Company. Professional success had come early to Gratz. While still in his early twenties, he co-invented a combination air-cleaner and silencer which was soon in use in most automobiles of the time. Like father, like son; his work kept him on the road a good part of the time. In any case, he and Margaret had little to do with one another.

The same was increasingly true of Margaret and Roberta. The two sisters had drifted apart since the time of their Swiss boarding-school days. Roberta's marriage seems to have accelerated the process, even if she, Basil, and Margaret still occasionally socialized.

The continuing decline of Robert and Maude Brown's marriage completed the portrait of a family in ever-widening disarray, a reality which filled Margaret with a sense of desolation. As Christmas approached she found herself alone and was greatly relieved when Dorothy Wagstaff, who was away at boarding school in Aiken, South Carolina, invited her to spend the holidays there. Traveling south by train, Margaret tried her best to put punctuation, family, and New York bustle out of her mind, at least for the moment.

CHAPTER FOUR

EVERYWHERE
AND
SOMEWHERE

Everywhere there was somewhere
and everywhere there they were
men women children dogs cows
wild pigs little rabbits cats lizards
and animals. That is the way it
was. And everybody dogs cats
sheep rabbits and lizards and
children all wanted to tell . . .
all about themselves.

GERTRUDE STEIN,
The World Is Round

The late 1930s, the time of Margaret's professional coming of age, was among the most dynamic periods in the history of American children's book publishing. The emergence of a small, feisty, independent-minded house like Scott was but one indication of the astonishing vitality of the field. Older firms, which had cut back or eliminated their juveniles departments during the first years of the Depression, had by the mid-1930s begun to show signs of renewed commitment. Children's departments that had proven their worth during the prosperous 1920s, in financial as well as literary and artistic terms, were once again in a position to do so. Moreover, the prejudice against "baby books" which wore so heavily at times on Margaret and others in the field now yielded unexpected dividends.

Because the executives in charge of the major houses had little or no interest in juveniles, they generally left their department heads to their own devices, to publish what they liked. Gifted editors, notably Viking's May Massee and (from 1940) Ursula Nordstrom at Harper, seized the initiative, publishing an astonishing array of books which were to last. The year 1939 alone saw the publication of Virginia Lee Burton's *Mike Mulligan and His Steam Shovel,* Hardie Gramatky's *Little Toot,* and Ludwig Bemelmans' *Madeline.* Artists like Gramatky, who had worked for Disney, and Bemelmans, who had come to New York from abroad, contributed to ·the exceptionally fertile creative environment within which Margaret was fast becoming a figure of importance. In 1938, children's book illustrators had even gotten their own award, the Caldecott Medal, given annually thereafter by the American Library Association for the most distinguished work of illustration first published in the United States within the past year. (The Newbery Medal, the ALA's prize for writers, had been established in 1921.) When Margaret returned to work after the long holidays in January of 1939, it was to an office and a corner of the book world overflowing with a sense of possibility.

Gertrude Stein, it turned out, had rather definite ideas about the illustration and design of her first fantasy for children; Scott and McCullough soon found themselves back in potentially treacherous waters. For one thing, Stein was eager to have a British artist protégé of hers, one Sir Francis Rose, as her illustrator, but Bill Scott, after seeing sample drawings by Rose, was unwilling to accept her choice. Conveying this news to Stein in a letter dated February 8, John McCullough offered an uncharacteristically garbled critique that betrayed his trepidation. The "rather studied decadence and sophistication" of Rose's style, he wrote, "though possessing qualities of its own strikes me as neither appealing to children nor particularly appropriate to the imaginative vitality of your writing."[1]

Sir Francis was to have been the book's "third rose"; Rose was the name of the story's heroine, and the author had specified that *The World Is Round* be printed on rose-colored paper with the text printed in blue, the imaginary girl's favorite color.

Problems posed by Stein's unorthodox color scheme were already putting Bill Scott's considerable ingenuity as a printer to the test. In the same letter to Stein, McCullough, finding his stride, noted, "We are having a terrific time locating a Rose colored paper that is possible. Next time we hope you will name your heroine Peach or preferably Snow White."

By early February several New York illustrators, having heard of the Stein manuscript, had applied for the assignment. As a courtesy to the author, McCullough sent samples of their work to France for her consideration. Whoever arranged for the shipping of the parcel failed to prepay the customs duty, as had been promised, and when Stein learned of this she insisted on inspecting the package's contents at the customs house before deciding whether or not to accept it. Accordingly, she examined the various sketches and then informed the clerk she did not wish to pay. Soon afterward, Stein wrote McCullough that she agreed to his first choice. Clement Hurd would illustrate *The World Is Round*. [2]

Among the other contenders for the job had been Leonard Weisgard, a tall, owlish-looking twenty-three-year-old commercial artist. When Margaret first met him for an interview, Weisgard, a former dancer and Macy's window dresser, had one published children's book to his credit and was much in demand as a magazine illustrator. The *New Yorker* cover for the week in which Stein's manuscript reached Scott's office the previous November had featured a Weisgard painting of a fashionable apartment interior superimposed on a page of real estate ads. The contemporary look of his designs, which owed something to Russian Constructivism, McKnight Kauffer's modernist graphics, and Stuart Davis's cubist phase, impressed Margaret as a welcome alternative to the wistful sentimentality of a great deal of children's book art—the "strawberries and cream school" of illustration, as she and Weisgard took to calling it. [3]

Margaret and the illustrator found that despite differences of background (Weisgard was a shopkeeper's son) they had much in common. His chief ambition, he confided to her, was to become a painter, a goal that paralleled Margaret's own dream of writing for adults. Like her, he had never been a good student; he had dropped out of Pratt Institute in order to paint on his own, and his commercial work was his means of support. But also like Margaret, he was a voracious reader with highly eclectic tastes; they had both, it turned out, read with great interest Julian Huxley's recent *Animal Language,* a study of animal sounds as communication. Margaret promised at their first meeting that whatever the outcome of the competition to illustrate *The World Is Round,* she would find some project for Weisgard at Scott. Following her well-established pattern, she proceeded in a few hours' time to produce for him the first draft of an ingenious piece of here-and-now-world-is-round mischief. Partly inspired by their shared enthusiasm for *Animal Language,* Margaret's first collaboration with Weisgard was *The Noisy Book.*

Published along with *The World Is Round* on Scott's fall 1939 list, *The Noisy Book* invited readers to imitate, as loudly as they wished, the sounds of horses, trucks, dogs, and jackhammers. Grown-ups could not recite the text without entering into the game—or else appearing stilted.

The story concerns a young dog named Muffin who, having gotten a cinder in his eye, has his eyes temporarily bandaged and is left to rely on his hearing:

> "Poor little Muffin," said the people in the street.
> "Muffin has a big white bandage over his eyes and can't see a thing."
> But Muffin could hear. . . .
> MEN HAMMERING
> Bang bang bang . . .
> Bzzzzzz bzzzzzz
> a bee . . . [4]

Another impetus for *The Noisy Book* was a Symbolist-related speculation of Weisgard's that sounds might be translated into visual equivalents through the colors and shapes of an illustration. Margaret had also remembered a Writers Laboratory experiment in which Lucy Mitchell had sent her and her colleagues outdoors to stand beside a city lamppost with their eyes closed, the better to listen to their environment with the clear-headed receptivity of toddlers. From Margaret, the ear-to-the-ground Bank Street researcher, had come Muffin, the "Noisy" dog.

Margaret, moreover, was no longer fearful of being over-whelmed by the influence of Gertrude Stein's voluble style. In *The Noisy Book* she took on some of the expatriate writer's rhetorical swagger.

> And then there was Rose.
> Rose was her name and would she have been Rose if her name had not been Rose. She used to think and then she used to think again.[5]

That was Stein in *The World Is Round*. And this was Margaret:

> Then the sun began to shine
> Could Muffin hear that . . .
>
> HORSES HOOFS
> Clop clop Clop clop
>
> Flippity flap flap flap
> an awning in the wind
>
> It began to snow
> But could Muffin hear that?

As Scott gave Margaret more or less free rein in the acquisition of manuscripts, she could afterwards say with little exaggeration, "I submitted it, and we"—Margaret again—"accepted it."[6]

Since Leonard Weisgard was to draw a dog, Margaret without consulting him presented the artist with a live model. The black mongrel pup was half Kerry Blue (the father was Smoke) and half standard poodle (the mother was a prize-winning dog belonging to Bill Gaston). Weisgard lived in midtown Manhattan in fairly sumptuous quarters at the Hotel Gotham, an elegant beaux-arts establishment known for its excellent dining room and European clientele. To placate (successfully) an elderly Irishwoman living across the hall from him, who might otherwise have insisted that the dog be removed, Weisgard named the puppy Finnegan. The artist's new charge proved a good bit less tractable, urinating on several *Noisy Book* paintings Weisgard had left out to dry. (Fortunately, he worked rapidly from already fully formed mental images and the illustrations were soon redone.)

Weisgard faced other difficulties. At Bank Street, the nursery

school children who previewed his illustrations balked at the artist's stylized way of rendering truck wheels—they complained
that eggs were oval, but wheels were round. Weisgard was obliged
to redo the wheels. Margaret came in for criticism as well. The
children told her that car horns did not go "honk honk," as she had
written in her first draft, but "awuurra awuurra." Margaret accepted this revision as the improvement that it was. She had considerably less respect, however, for the comments of a Bank Street
colleague to whom she also presented the manuscript. A staff
psychologist reported back that a story about a little male dog
whose eyes were completely bandaged over could suggest only one
thing—castration!—to a young male reader. The psychologist
urged the author to abandon the project. Bristling at criticism she
considered nonsensical, Margaret lost no time on account of it.

As part of his initiation into the Bank Street–Scott method of
testing books, Leonard Weisgard sometimes accompanied Margaret during the numerous trial readings she conducted of *The World
Is Round*. He was standing watch one day in the Bank Street nursery, serving as a second set of eyes and ears, as she read to a group of
eight seasoned three-year-olds seated in a circle in brightly colored
chairs. The children listened intently to the passage about Willie
and his pet lion: "Willie went with his father to a little place where
they sold wild animals. If the world is round can wild animals
come out of the ground."[7]

"No!" shouted the children as though (Margaret observed)
they thought the question addressed directly to them.[8] Many such
sessions were held with children of different ages. Passages that
provoked confused looks or restless behavior were duly noted, and
when the galleys went out to Stein on March 23, they were accompanied by forty single-spaced typed pages of "suggested" minor
revisions, most concerning the placement of commas. The lion's
share of the effort had been Margaret's, as she proudly reported to
the Hollins *Alumnae Quarterly*. She had, she wrote, lately been hard
at work "wrestling with Gertrude Stein's lack of punctuation and
Governor [William] Bradford's superflueity [*sic*] of punctuation in
his journal of the Pilgrim Landing." (The latter reference is to
Homes in the Wilderness, also published by Scott in the fall of 1939,
presenting original source material about life at Plymouth Col-

ony.) In her report, Margaret recounted the circumstances that had led up to her becoming the famed expatriate's editor, adding heartily, "I shouldn't be surprised but that we may have a wonderful book."[9]

Any publishing house would have considered it a great coup to have Gertrude Stein's first juvenile on their upcoming list, and at Scott anticipation was running high. The firm hired an advertising consultant, Joseph Ryle, to handle the publicity. Nursery wallpaper and decorative hooked rugs based on the book's illustrations were planned. There would be window displays along Fifth Avenue, and hundreds of review copies, far more than the usual number for Scott, were to be distributed to newspapers and magazines across the country. But if Margaret could take satisfaction in the dramatic events unfolding around her as a direct consequence of her editorial enterprise, her delight was marred by the fact that Stein herself remained virtually unaware of Margaret's pivotal role.

The note of recognition that did come Margaret's way that spring of 1939 was of an altogether different nature. On Sunday, April 16, her name and photograph appeared in the New York papers announcing her as the winner of a grueling cross-country footrace, the final event of her Long Island hunting club's spring season. Margaret took care to preserve the clippings—including one from the *Herald Tribune*'s society page ironically headlined "The Strenuous Life"—in a scrapbook that she showed proudly to friends. In honor of the occasion, John McCullough, with whom she remained on genial terms despite her frustrations over the Stein project, composed a commemorative poem that was also a parody of *The World Is Round*. Stein's book contained the passage: "I am Rose my eyes are blue / I am Rose and who are you / I am Rose and when I sing / I am Rose like anything."[10] This McCullough recast to read: "I am Margaret and my Wise are Brown / I am Margaret and how's your hown / I am Margaret and when I beagle / My picture gets into the *Brooklyn Eagle*."[11]

In May it was McCullough, not Margaret, who wrote Stein to say that steady progress had been made: "We are now working on a circular circular that should add to the rotundity of the world."[12] And in June, when the first proof pages came off the press, it was he who informed her that trouble had arisen at the printer: "My graphic minded partner [Scott] is in dark clouds of grief that there is quite a bit of color variation from page to page." Unable to find a suitable rose-colored paper, they had decided to tint standard white paper. "To my mind," he reassured Stein, "this variation is unexpectedly pleasing but I dare not express such heresy in his presence."[13] McCullough went on to relay a sampling of the comments gathered (if not by Margaret herself, under her supervision) from children. A twelve-year-old Long Island girl had said: "This would be an interesting story if written in everyday language. It could, to my mind, be built up to be a very good kind of story, perhaps if an entirely different story were used." Another young critic had faulted the author for her odd habit of repeating herself.

McCullough reported these comments for the author's amusement. The overwhelming response of children, McCullough wrote, had been exceedingly favorable. For his part, he had already declared *The World Is Round* a masterpiece. "We hope," he had written Stein the previous November, "that reaction to this book will tempt you to write us another."[14]

On June 24, 1939, just days before *The World Is Round* went to press, Edith Thacher and Clement Hurd were married on Cape Cod. Stein had written her collaborator to thank him for his efforts ("I am awfully really awfully pleased"), to which Hurd replied that her message had made "a delightful wedding present."[15] By July 12, the couple were back in New York so the artist could oversee the unusually difficult printing job Stein's book entailed. The newlyweds then returned north for a belated honeymoon at the North Ferrisburg, Vermont, farm where they planned to live for a part of each year.

Margaret spent the summer at Long Cove on Vinalhaven, in the same house as the year before. This time, however, she rented it alone. Much to her disappointment, Bill Gaston had remarried. Ensconced with his new bride on his private island just across the bay from Long Cove, he cavalierly dispatched his nine-year-old son Jimmy to run errands for her, while continuing to flirt with Margaret in a manner that left her in a state of turmoil. Illustrators from New York and other friends came and went over the summer as Margaret attempted to work and "regenerate," and was forcibly reminded once again of the painful confusion of her private life.

Back in New York the following fall, she took Leonard Weisgard increasingly into her confidence. Like Margaret, Weisgard was a good listener. He shared her enjoyment of extravagant living (and spending) and was generally willing to indulge her occasional patches of brooding self-absorption. On days when she "felt rich," as she would say, they might go for elaborate meals at La Crémaillère, an elegant rooftop restaurant with a view of Central Park, or to Aux Gais Penguins (another fashionable uptown French eatery) or downtown to Pappa Monetta's, at 32 Mulberry Street, a rustic establishment with fine northern Italian cuisine. 16

To feel rich, Weisgard needed only a slight upturn in his bank balance. But for Margaret, because she generally had enough of it, money had little to do with her notion of personal wealth. When she telephoned to say, "Leonard, I am so poor this week," what she usually meant was that she had not written a satisfactory story or poem in the last day or two, or that she was harboring again the recurring suspicion that writing for children was not serious work.

Margaret and Leonard often met for breakfast at Longchamps, a Greenwich Village restaurant and outdoor café with "smart" atmosphere, and they went for long walks through the city, wandering in and out of Third Avenue antique shops and Manhattan's sixty-odd art galleries, through flower and vegetable markets and Central Park. Both were restless, brisk walkers, but in midtown Manhattan they often slowed down to study the Fifth Avenue shop window displays, which during the late thirties burst with an exuberant artistry rivalling the most sophisticated design work in *Harper's Bazaar,* on Balasco's Broadway, or in the stark new galleries of the Museum of Modern Art.

Fifth Avenue—the "street of dreams" of Irwin Shaw's bittersweet *New Yorker* stories about lost and found romance in the imperial city—afforded passing glimpses of the good life. "Look at those dresses," a typical Shaw window-shopper sighed. "It's nice to know things like that exist."17 As though to resurrect, or at least refurbish, the American dream of prosperity after years of economic hard times, the city's fashion windows had become elaborately staged fantasy sets; larger-than-life mannequins, the unblinking stars of the drama, no longer stared down their haughty noses at passersby, as their forebears of the teens and twenties had done, but seemed to wink at them, inviting all to join the party.

Mannequins rode on ski lifts; mannequins sipped tall, cool drinks. At Saks Fifth Avenue, a mannequin-patient on an analyst's couch suffered from an obsession, visualized overhead, concerning a costly dress the store happened to be featuring. Perhaps, as Elsa Schiapparelli (whose extravagantly ticketed creations were achieving a high peak of fashionableness) said, life *was* "a-musing" in the fall of 1939, even if the Depression had not quite ended for everyone and England and France were at war with Germany. For Margaret and her collaborator, the elegant mid-town displays were like outsized picture books lining the avenue.

During their walks around town, Margaret often had occasion to greet some passing friend her companion had never seen before. Such occasions were forcible reminders to Weisgard that much remained hidden about the fascinating woman who so freely took him into her confidence at times. Once, in front of Rockefeller Center, a well-dressed bear of a man with short-cropped hair and a beefy complexion caught her eye, warmly embraced her, and chatted privately with her for a moment before continuing on his way.

"Oh, that was Irwin Shaw," she said remotely, leaving her ever-discreet friend to wonder how she happened to know Shaw (then the most lionized of New York's younger writers) and what the precise nature of their relationship might be. [18]

Margaret did introduce Weisgard to the Hurds, and the three liked each other from the start. Not long after their first meeting, the two illustrators enrolled together in an advanced design course taught by *Harper's Bazaar*'s renowned art director, Alexey Brodovich, at the New School. They also shared a serious interest as collectors of American folk art, the abstract and primitive qualities of which had come to represent to a small but expanding group within the art world of the twenties and thirties a sort of prologue to modernism, an historical precedent for expressing artistic truth outside the bounds of traditional realism.

In the way of New York friendships, Weisgard and the Hurds actually saw each other only occasionally. Their common thread was their connection to Margaret, and when she herself was not around her colorful doings and remarks provided inexhaustible material for conversation. They were all three deeply fond of her, and few people spent more time with her over the years, but one reason that Leonard, Clem, and Posey enjoyed getting together as a threesome was their unspoken mutual conviction that some member of the group—each assumed it was one of the others— must be the one person who really knew the elusive Margaret best.

Among the artists who called on Margaret at Scott in the fall of 1939 was Charles Shaw, a tall, robust, dapper man in his late forties. An accomplished polymath, Shaw was a writer, painter, collector, and man about town, a boyish enthusiast with a sizeable inheritance to bankroll his enthusiasms. A classmate of Cole Porter's at Yale, Shaw worked as a journalist for a time, contributing to the *Bookman, Town & Country,* the *New Yorker,* and *Vanity Fair.* A reserved but witty man, he not only belonged to the "smart set"—Dorothy Parker, F. Scott Fitzgerald, George Jean Nathan, and Monty Wooley were among his friends over the years—he wrote the book on the subject, *Nightlife: Vanity Fair's Intimate Guide to New York After Dark.*

While living for a few years in London and Paris, Charles Shaw had also begun to paint. Back in New York, in 1936 he became a charter member of the American Abstract Artists, the pioneering group of nonobjective painters that included Ilya Bolotowsky, Balcomb Greene, and Esphyr Slobodkina. Among the AAA's underlying convictions was the belief that because colors, shapes, and visual patterns are recognizable to all people, geometric abstraction held enormous potential as the basis for a new and highly accessible popular art. It was only a short step from that idea to thoughts of employing the lingua franca of abstract art in illustration for the young. [19]

Shaw was also a collector of Lewis Carroll first editions (as well as tarot cards, horse brasses, old English police truncheons, carved wooden tobacco figures, and scrimshaw). Always a figure of grand scope and ambition, he seems to have decided, some time in 1938 or 1939, to see whether he had it within himself to become a new Lewis Carroll or Edward Lear. Shaw composed some fantasy tales, began making the rounds of publishers, and after months of the usual rejections was directed to the firm of William R. Scott, Inc. It was suggested to him that Scott's editor might be interested in his type of work and that Scott had "lots of money behind them"— the implication being that even a book that seemed likely to lie dead in the water from a sales point of view might have a chance there if it had sufficient merit. [20]

Buoyed by this slender and, as it turned out, not altogether accurate bit of intelligence, Shaw, on a fine fall morning, dropped off one of his manuscripts for "Miss M. W. Brown" at her 69 Bank Street office. [21] The editor's initial response, by letter, was neither a definite yes or no, and on November 9, several notes and phone calls later, he and Margaret finally met for a talk which the artist, in his diary, judged "quite satisfactory." [22] The meeting inspired Shaw to write another story, "Jumble Pie," which Margaret told him fell into the crack between adult and children's fantasy and yet seemed "too good to turn down." [23] She continued to offer him a mixture of encouragement and direction which spurred Shaw on until she was at last able to accept a manuscript of his, *The Giant of Central Park,* the following spring of 1940.

Gradually, the formal manner of their early meetings gave way to a comfortable sort of mutual regard. A facile conversationalist with endless tales to tell of Gotham, "old London towne," and the art world, Shaw was also a deeply loyal and considerate friend. In time, he became one of Margaret's chief confidants.

That fall of 1939, the main focus of attention at Scott was on how *The World Is Round* would be received. Reviews began appearing in late September, and a great many of them were good, though there was hardly a critic in America, it seemed, who could resist putting an ironical twist on praise for the idiosyncratic expatriate's first work for juveniles.

Writing in the *New York Times Book Review,* Ellen Lewis Buell allowed that "for a skeptic who never quite finished the first paragraph of 'Tender Buttons' it is a pleasant duty to report that Miss Stein seems to have found her audience." Warming to her subject, she asserted:

Miss Stein has caught within this architectural structure of words which rhyme and rhyme again the essence of certain moods of childhood: the first exploration of one's own personality, the feeling of lostness in a world of night skies and mountain peaks, sudden unreasoning emotions and impulses, the preoccupation with vagrant impressions of little things filtering through the mind. . . . It will . . . probably be the most quotable book of the season. [24]

Writing in *Books,* another critic observed that while Stein's story was printed on paper of an "awful color, . . . every small child will think it lovely. It is the color once given toothpaste to induce children to brush their teeth, and it worked." [25] The *New Republic* ventured a cautious comparison with *Alice's Adventures in Wonderland.* In the *Horn Book,* Louise Seaman Bechtel unequivocally declared, "Here is a new book that is a new kind of book, and I like it very much." [26] Among the least admiring of Stein's reviewers, the *New Yorker*'s Katharine S. White, found the author's "flashes of wit" and "moments of poetry and imagination . . . so buried in tedious mannerisms and lumbering whimsy" that she doubted the excavation work required was worth the effort. [27] Others resorted to parody: "Gertrude Stein is writing is writing is writing a new Gertrude Stein a new book is writing is writing Gertrude a new a new a new . . ." [28]

Certainly the most surprising review was by Anne Carroll Moore, who a year earlier had summarily dismissed Scott's first list as subliterary. Writing in her "Three Owls" column in the *Horn Book,* Moore, after noting her "unfavorable reaction to the smell of the book," grudgingly conceded that *The World Is Round* was "genuine child stuff" that "holds joy for many readers. . . . We have need of gaiety and a return to childhood in these grave days." [29]

By the first of the year it was clear that *The World Is Round* had not been the financial success that both the publisher and author hoped for. Library sales were respectable, but retail demand fell far short of expectations. There were few takers for world-is-round decorative hooked rugs and wallpaper. Bill Scott consigned the unsold heap of rose-and-blue books to long-term storage in his Vermont barn.

Margaret and Leonard Weisgard's collaboration, *The Noisy Book,* had meanwhile become Scott's bestseller. Across the country, parents, progressive school teachers and presumably even some librarians were "tick-tick"-ing like clocks, "siss-sisssss"-ing like radiators and growling like empty stomachs, to the rapturous approval of three-, four-, and five-year-olds who, chiming in, "chirp-chirp"-ed like birds or were stopped short on being asked, "Then the sun began to shine. Could Muffin hear that?" By year's end, Margaret could contemplate her first large (by Scott's modest standards) popular success with the sanguine sense of having out-foxed everyone.

In January of 1940, having resolved to take certain matters into her own hands, Margaret wrote her first letter to Gertrude Stein: "It seems high time to come from behind the scenes and tell you how among all people I think I enjoy and delight in your book the most."[30] It was a lopsided declaration that doubtless betrayed her frustration at having been kept "behind the scenes" until then. Regaining her composure, Margaret recalled the young listeners who had also eagerly embraced Stein's fantasy, like the five-year-old who had told his grandmother, "I don't like it. Go on!" and refused to let her stop reading the book aloud.

In her letter, Margaret wove a starstruck tale of admiration for the author's innovative work, of having attended her Brooklyn Academy lecture and posted a bet with McCullough over their letter to her. "I never dreamed that you would really write the way things happen in children's heads. No one has ever remembered so well . . . before."

It is not known whether Stein replied to Margaret's overture. In all likelihood she did not, but Margaret longed for some contact with a mentor-like figure from the larger literary world. She had outgrown the genteel Miss Hearsey, and was close to having learned all she could from Lucy Mitchell.

Among Margaret's own writing projects just then was an outline for a magazine article that she hoped might gain her a foothold in the adult publishing world. "New York: The Melting Pot of Good Cuisine" was to consist of an international culinary guide to Manhattan, a sort of world tour for adventuresome diners. Margaret planned to have Leonard Weisgard design a festive map; she would supply pithy notations around the margins. She intended to present the idea to *Vogue* and *Harper's Bazaar*.

An early draft of the proposal proclaimed:

The Map of the World may change overnight and then change again next week. But the boundaries of good cuisine are more steadfast. . . . Dine every evening in a different country, the sound of foreign languages in your ears. Drink honey wines and mountain ash cordials from Poland, eat green salads from France, arroz con pollo from Spain, Scandinavian smorgasbord, Russian baclava, zabaglione from Italy, English mutton chops and ale, rose leaves from Turkey for dessert. . . . Down below Washington Square the water is boiling and they are about to throw three miles of spaghetti into a pot.[31]

The airy sophistication of high gloss fashion writing did not come easily to her, but the idea was engaging and *Vogue* expressed tentative interest. Margaret's timing, however, could not have been less fortunate. The worsening international situation lent a certain air of unreality to "The Melting Pot" and its incitements to eat, drink, and be merry. In the early weeks of 1940, with much of Europe at war and with the increasing likelihood that the conflict would spread worldwide, *Vogue* reconsidered and Margaret shelved the project.[32]

Meanwhile she and Scott quarreled over the terms of payment for her editorial services. Scott proposed to replace a generous earlier agreement to pay "editorial royalties" on books she oversaw with a more conventional annual flat fee to be set without regard to the profitability of the various titles. Suspecting she was being taken advantage of, Margaret accused Scott of trying to save money at her expense. For his part, the publisher insisted his motive was to establish the company's list on a sound financial basis. The incident was revealing of changes on both sides. Scott, who had run the firm in the beginning as a sort of elaborate family outing, was learning to manage his company in a more businesslike way. Margaret, who in the early days probably would have worked as a volunteer, was forming a clearer sense of her own professional worth. As both she and Scott viewed money in largely symbolic terms, they stubbornly refused to compromise. The publisher formalized his new offer in a letter to her dated April 22. In a moment of rage followed by a moment of something like calm reflection, Margaret tore the letter to shreds and then gathered up the pieces, placing them in an envelope marked "Broken Contract."[33] In one month and a day, she would turn thirty.

Except at William R. Scott, Inc., where John McCullough and Bill Scott took an active hand in editorial matters, virtually all American children's book editors of the 1930s and 1940s were women. At the larger houses, such editorships ranked at or very near the bottom of the ladder in power and prestige. Women accepted these posts partly because it was supposed that in some vaguely understood but important way, editing "juveniles" was a natural extension of a woman's role as mother. They also took these jobs, however, because they had little hope of advancing elsewhere in the profession. It was true that during the prosperous twenties, the juveniles editors at major firms like Macmillan and Doubleday had gained a measure of respect from management because they not only turned profits for their houses but also transformed their departments into unofficial laboratories of innovative book design and production. But even in the best of times, men had not wanted to edit "baby books." During the Depression and afterwards the pattern continued.

Most women who entered the field were "career women" who never married and who remained at their jobs for twenty or thirty years or more. Margaret's Harper editor, Louise Raymond, was atypical; for a time she had combined married life and work. Then, at the close of 1939, in anticipation of the birth of her first child, Raymond resigned, leaving her capable young assistant, Ursula Nordstrom, in charge. In their first face-to-face encounter, Anne Carroll Moore pointedly questioned the new Harper editor about her credentials; Nordstrom, who (as her interrogator meant to remind her) had never worked as a librarian, evenly replied; "I am a former child."[34] Margaret's and Nordstrom's mutual antipathy to Moore was one of the shared sentiments that got them off to a solid start.

Born in Manhattan in 1910, the daughter of the well-known Broadway stage actor Henry E. Dixie and actress Marie Nordstrom, Ursula Nordstrom spent her childhood at boarding schools, where she developed a keen sense of personal independence. As a young person she already possessed a strong capacity for empathizing with outsiders, and when the Depression dimmed her chances of going to college, she decided to look for a job as a social worker assigned to delinquent children. No opportunity of this kind materialized, however, and she eventually arrived at the offices of Harper and Brothers, "Publishers Since 1817," where she was hired as Louise Raymond's assistant.

An expansive, full-hearted, Hogarthian personality (years later, signing a note to one of her illustrators, she would claim that it was *she* who had been "Est. 1817"),[35] Nordstrom became Harper's editor just as Margaret's reputation as a writer was becoming secure. That Margaret herself continued to be plagued by periodic doubts as to the value of her work was another matter; it was among Nordstrom's chief assets as an editor that she generally had meaningful words of encouragement for Margaret, as she did for her other authors and artists, and she was able to make them all feel quite literally at home. Margaret rapidly accumulated a raft of Harper contracts. She and Nordstrom also happened to be neighbors, and they often met informally over breakfast at Longchamps, where Margaret typically arrived with Smoke on one hand and a manila envelope containing her current inventory of poems and stories in the other.

In the spring of 1940 Leonard Weisgard and the Hurds were also feeling their oats professionally. Weisgard, in addition to his magazine work, had lined up several picture book contracts and had begun to realize that he would always have as much illustration work as he wished. That same spring, Clement Hurd mounted his first one-man show of paintings in New York. The likely choice to illustrate any new children's manuscript that Gertrude Stein might have in the offing, Hurd had found, in Margaret and his own wife, two prolific long-term collaborators. The larger publishing houses, moreover, had begun to show interest in him and Posey. It was mostly out of a sense of personal loyalty that in early 1940 the illustrator submitted a new project to Scott, whose terms were bound to be less favorable than those offered elsewhere. *The Race* was the first book Hurd had written as well as illustrated. When Bill Scott offered to publish it only if the artist was willing to make substantial revisions, Hurd asked if he might try his luck with another firm. Scott, doubtless sensing that the first phase of his company's life, the ebullient time of inspired amateur-friends, was fast coming to a close, agreed to release the manuscript, which Random House promptly accepted in its original form.

Margaret, for her part, resumed outwardly friendly relations with Scott and continued to edit books for the company, though her disenchantment with her situation there steadily grew. From then onward, she offered fewer of her own manuscripts to Scott.

Margaret was known as "Brownie" to her colleagues at Scott, after the Bank Street pattern. But at Harper, Ursula Nordstrom teased (and flattered) her with "Miss Genius" and "My Favorite Author." Margaret in turn prodded John McCullough by referring to Nordstrom in conversation as her "Second Favorite Editor," leaving McCullough to wonder whether she considered him—or herself—her favorite.[36] The merest reference to Harper, which as a larger house was in a good position to win over Margaret's services from Scott, was not lost on him. Soon other publishers were also vying for her loyalty.

Among the growing circle of Margaret's acquaintances in 1940 was Bennett Cerf, president of Random House. A gregarious bachelor and inveterate party-goer, Cerf, then forty-two, was bound to meet an attractive writer like Margaret. They spent an occasional evening together with mutual friends (Bruce Bliven, Jr., among others) and in May arranged a luncheon meeting with Bill Scott and Random House's juveniles editor, Louise Bonino, to talk shop.

Scott's very small and specialized firm and Cerf's rapidly expanding general trade house epitomized opposite ends of the publishing spectrum. Cerf knew little about the juveniles side of publishing but clearly recognized its commercial potential. With Random House's purchase of Smith and Haas in 1936, he had acquired the American rights to Jean de Brunhoff's *Story of Babar*. The great popularity of the Random House edition of de Brunhoff's robust and very French picture book (and its sequels) piqued the publisher's curiosity about the field, though with only one other notable exception—the work of Theodor Geisel, "Dr. Seuss"—he left his firm's juveniles trade to others. Geisel's clever, jokey word play was close to Cerf's own sense of humor, but the publisher had little appreciation for the seemingly simple poetry of Margaret's type of writing. With more wit than tact he repeatedly poked fun at her by referring to her "baby books."[37]

Margaret and Cerf shared an interest in the work of Gertrude Stein—"Gerty" the latter called her. Random House and William R. Scott were just then Stein's most active American publishers, a fact not likely to have been overlooked at lunch, especially as the expatriate author had lately been contemplating a second lecture tour of the United States and had sought John McCullough's advice in the selection of a booking agent.

Stein hoped, she said, to be back in New York before the end of spring. As the publishers met, however, she remained in France, distracting herself from the alarming news of the German military advance by composing a second children's fantasy, "To do: a book of alphabets and birthdays."[38] Her travel plans were in suspension, and with the German invasion of France in June of 1940, all thoughts of a new tour would be abandoned.

It was most likely in the spring or early summer of 1940 that Margaret met Michael Strange, the flamboyant socialite, actress, and author who had achieved a certain celebrity during the 1920s as the wife of John Barrymore. (Michael Strange was her chosen pen and stage name; she was originally Blanche Oelrichs of Newport.) She had divorced Barrymore and was presently married to a prominent attorney, Harrison Tweed. It was Tweed, apparently, who first made Margaret's acquaintance at a party and invited her for cocktails at the couple's apartment at 10 Gracie Square, overlooking the East River.

The two women, it turned out, had several mutual friends. Bill Gaston had known Michael Strange since the twenties, when she and John Barrymore had visited Gaston's Maine island retreat. Charles Shaw, who had served in the Army Air Service with Strange's favorite cousin, Hermann Oelrichs, had written a *New Yorker* profile of her. Clement Hurd had known her eldest son, Leonard Thomas, Jr., first at Yale and then in Paris. (On Hurd's return to New York in 1933, it was Thomas who invited him to the gala evenings at 10 Gracie Square.) Joseph Ryle, the advertising consultant hired by Scott to promote *The World Is Round,* was another of the attractive young men that Michael Strange always had in attendance on such occasions, much to the exasperation, it may be assumed, of her husband. Members of the Buckram Beagles were, like her, also members of New York's exclusive Colony Club and were likely to cross paths with her during the year at any number of other society points of rendezvous in New York, Palm Beach, Bar Harbor, London, Biarritz, Paris, and elsewhere. It was all but inevitable that Margaret and Michael Strange would meet sooner or later.

Their relationship, as it evolved, was to become one of the most intense and eventually most painfully difficult experiences of Margaret's life. It began, however, with great expectations, as another of the many positive efforts she was making at the time to lift herself into the larger world of literary accomplishment and mature, impassioned living.

Margaret chronicled the beginnings of this friendship in a series of undated, unpublished short stories, including one called "The Scent," in which she recorded her first impressions of Michael Strange and suggested what each of the two might have meant to the other at the time of their first meeting. [39]

"The Scent" concerns a young woman named Carrie who looks up to a beautiful, glamorous friend twenty years older than herself. "If," Carrie considers, "to grow older were to become like this woman [Alison] her faith in growing old was restored." There is a sureness about Alison that is a matter not just of taste but of temperament: "The older woman had . . . what is most exciting in the same sex—Glamor. For Alison was famous and had lived a discreet and lusty life with her three husbands and her writing. And over all a discretion that made her a woman of her times rather than a mere bohemian."

When the two fictional friends get together—"at least twice a week which is very often in New York"—they talk about marriage, men, and about Alison's affairs. "You knew she had lovers and she would tell you about some of them. But she never mentioned any names. That was the difference between her own generation and Alison's Carrie thought. They went around as much as anyone but just had the sense to be discreet about it."

If to Carrie, Alison represents an ideal of modern womanhood and worldly sophistication, Alison sees in Carrie an uncanny reflection of herself at an earlier age: "So I sat with the same gravity, the same gayety [*sic*] when I laughed twenty years ago, the same anxious longing to live and not be too hurt by it." Carrie has "a quality of wonder about her, a way of brooding with her lips half parted" that also reminds Alison of "someone she had loved very much a long time ago in the wild loving days of her youth."

In writing "The Scent," Margaret made two significant departures from autobiographical fact. Each character is ten years younger, a change that highlights the supreme allure of the older friend while underlining (perhaps also justifying) the younger woman's contrasting lack of self-possession—a contrast that proved crucial to Margaret's relationship with Michael Strange.

Margaret also made both her protagonists married women. Although she had often expressed the wish to be married, in this story she seems to have come face to face with doubts as to the desirability of marriage. When Carrie returns from a vacation she has taken by herself, she is met by her husband at the station. "That night as Carrie sank back into her own bed and burried [*sic*] her head in the pillow waiting for Richard to come from his bath, she began to remember Alison. . . . She could even smell the scent Alison used, in the pillow. She could actually smell it, she thought." The next morning,

> when she woke slowly half dreaming she could still smell that scent of Alison's.
>
> After bathing she got back in bed to have breakfast. And there it was again. . . . She grabbed her pillow. . . . There was no mistaking it.
>
> The maid came in at that moment with the breakfast tray and telephone messages. There was one from Alison. She had called and would call back at noon.
>
> The maid was leaving the room.
>
> "If anyone calls today, tell them I am not at home," she said.

There Margaret thought to end the story with one portentous additional line: "She had to have time to think." This highly charged last scene, with its intimations—redolent of Poe's "Tell-Tale Heart"—of a troubled conscience, suggests the depth and disturbing nature of the passionate feelings that Michael Strange had unexpectedly aroused in her.

One of the chief and abiding facts of their long, erratic, and emotionally difficult relationship was that Margaret and Michael each seriously misjudged the extent of her own and the other's talent, and that both benefited from the misunderstanding in some important way. As in the two parallel worlds set out in *The Little Fireman,* Margaret and Michael Strange constructed between themselves a paired reality in which Margaret was the little poet writing little books for children while Michael was the big poet writing poetry and giving public recitations for the spiritual enlightenment of the world at large. For Margaret this was to prove a compelling emotional construct, a credible myth through which to explore both her most deep-seated self-doubts and her most ardent aspirations as a writer and a human being. Michael Strange, in turn, was all too willing to receive the younger woman's adulation and to feed her doubts.

"The way she laughed . . . and all the time those swift black eyes peering out even while she laughed never missing even the flicker of a shadow across another face."[40] All-seeing, elaborately self-assured, this was how Margaret characterized Michael in "Luncheon," another unpublished story set in the Cafe Lafayette, a fashionable room a few blocks from Margaret's Greenwich Village apartment where she often met friends for drinks or tea. Writing in the first person, Margaret dropped the pretense of disguising the other woman's identity, and had Michael address the narrator as "Goldie" (one of Michael's nicknames for Margaret).

The first to arrive, the story's narrator chooses a table and orders a Vermouth Cassis. Minutes later, Michael appears, "or rather . . . made her entrance. She stood in the doorway swirled in furs like a Cossac [*sic*] princess and looked all around the room and spoke to a waiter who rushed to her side. And then she saw me and came across the floor. . . . Then . . . we started to talk, and to watch each other."

Conversation centers mainly on men, in particular their mutual friend, Bill (an obvious reference to Bill Gaston). The narrator speaks of her "weekend and telaphone [*sic*] relationship" with him. (In the typescript Margaret struck the words "weekend and"; Gaston, after all, was married.) When the older woman inquires about her love life generally, the narrator describes it as a blank, "except as a waiting game waiting for someone like an old buzzard."

The conversation proceeds in this one-sided manner, with the older friend asking the questions and revealing little of herself, at least intentionally. But in another untitled story from this series, Michael Strange emerges as a woman in turmoil.[41] A small party of weekend guests, many of them strangers to each other, gather for Friday supper at a Long Island ocean-front retreat (unnamed but plainly Harry Tweed's house at Montauk). They include a sculptor, tall, quick-witted, the hostess's "ex-lover seventeen times removed," now an ailing, elderly man, and the artist's physician, an eminent gland specialist. Somehow the hostess has gotten the mistaken impression that the doctor is a psychoanalyst. On realizing her error, she is disappointed as she had hoped to have him serve as a foil for her own determined "resistance" to the "outrage" that psychoanalysis represents to the "human spirit." A young lawyer and his wife are also among the guests as is a "blonde girl," who "sat there laughing and watching and talking just enough not to appear silent and drinking a lot of white sautern [*sic*]. The same sautern they [the girl and the hostess] had drunk every evening during the past week when they had been alone down here on the coast together, writing and reading and with the endless exploratory talk that goes with getting to know someone." They had gone swimming together and had taken long walks in the rain, and "laughed a lot and read aloud together and both of them, she at the age of fifty and her new friend at the age of thirty had found a still questioning unlost youthfulness together. It had been an idyl all it's [*sic*] own."

The hostess's husband has come out from the city for the weekend. He sits in silence "like a great Irish Wolf-hound" across from her at the long table. All attention centers on the hostess, however, who is "outrageous" as she speaks in the "clear ringing voice" that brought her a measure of fame as a lecturer and radio personality if not as an actress:

> She kept talking about the house she wanted . . . and kept sketching a whole life that she wanted to live that completely left him out of the picture. And he sat there talking and watching . . . and the

currents shot like bullets between them. His silence bored into her . . . and she flung her dark head and ranted on never unconscious of him in her complete ignoring of him until a dark battle raged there unseen and unspoken between them.

In this story, Margaret theorized that the wealthy attorney had become an "infuriating symbol" to his wife of "something necessary to her existance [*sic*] . . . [a] security . . . she could return to after her necessary flights to the fantastic, . . . the haunting awareness of poets. For she was a poet"—even if the hostess's husband will not acknowledge this. He shuffles off to bed alone, preceded only by the ailing sculptor, leaving the two remaining male guests to their after-dinner conversation, a discussion of intellectual matters in which it is understood the women do not participate.

" 'I am the Poet, for God's sake why don't they ask me just once,' " the hostess sighs with only her younger friend to hear her as the men's discussion turns to the relationship between poetry and science in the modern world. "And the blonde girl told her to listen just once. And obediently she did for a few minutes and then impatient again the ladies went to the icebox, for such was the interminable length of the argument."

In her copy of Lytton Strachey's *Queen Victoria,* Michael Strange underlined the following passage: "The intensity of her [Victoria's] determination swept them [the British Cabinet] headlong down the stream of her desire."[42] This, doubtless, was life as she thought it should be lived. Strachey had dedicated *Queen Victoria* to Virginia Woolf. Michael Strange had come to view her own life as a classic example of the thwarted destiny of the woman writer as described by Woolf in *A Room of One's Own.*

It was plainly not, however, for lack of a room or of opportunity that Michael Strange had failed to achieve the artistic stature she considered her due. By 1940 she had published four books of verse and two versions of a play, *Claire de Lune.*[43] Early on in her gladiatorial marriage to John Barrymore (which lasted from 1920 to 1928) the celebrated actor had championed the play, arranging for a Broadway production, stepping into the principal role himself, and recruiting his sister Ethel to star opposite him. (Appar-

ently unmoved by the lines provided her, Ethel Barrymore petu-
lantly improvised her way through opening night.) When the bad
reviews began pouring in, Barrymore could barely be restrained
from responding publicly in his wife's defense during the second
evening's performance. "For the love of Mike," as Alexander
Woollcott commented.[44] Strange's various forays as a dramatic
actress had been met with similar if not even less favorable reaction. On stage she lacked the charismatic self-possession that she
effortlessly assumed in most other situations. The one role she excelled at playing was that of Michael Strange.

In his profile of her, which appeared in the December 3, 1927
issue of the *New Yorker*, Charles Shaw judged her a "marvelously
unkempt" woman of "extraordinary imagination" and original
taste who was "seldom without some new enterprise" to occupy
her.[45] Michael Strange, he wrote, never lacked for the precise
"trenchant simile" with which to seize the spotlight while leaving
a slower-witted companion in the dark and dust. She "allege[s],"
Shaw archly reported, to be a "great lover of classics." But he found
her "classical foundation," while "vivid," to be of the "sketchiest
texture." He continued with rising mockery,

> In her own opinion she is greatly influenced by the opinions of
> those she respects. . . . While outwardly a scoffer at superstition,
> she possesses a shadow of belief in many superstitions . . . [She is
> nonetheless] wholly unaware of the trivial. . . .
>
> Children divert her greatly and she wonders if it might not be
> possible to recapture somehow their unselfconsciousness and 'eter-
> nal spirit of picnic.' . . .
>
> Aesthetically she longs for simple emotion charmingly
> phrased. . . .
>
> Her style is completely her own.

The name Michael Strange had simply come to her one day "in
full . . . from nowhere," as she explained in her memoir *Who Tells
Me True,* which Scribner's published in the spring of 1940.[46] She
had been a young married society woman when in 1916 a publisher accepted a collection of her poetry. Well known on the social
circuit and hoping to establish a separate identity as a writer, she
had resolved to conceal her authorship behind the memorable

pseudonym by which she was thereafter known to friends and the public alike.

There had been three marriages in all. The first, to American career diplomat Leonard Thomas, produced two sons, Leonard, Jr. and Robin. The couple drifted apart as the young woman's literary aspirations drew her into a circle of friends within which there could plainly be no place for her rather proper husband. She and Thomas were still married when Michael met John Barrymore in April 1917. Their affair culminated in her first divorce and her marriage to the actor in 1920. The following year, their daughter, Diana Barrymore, was born. The stormy tenor of the couple's years together, their "incessant and endless arguments" (in the words of Barrymore biographer Hollis Alpert), quickly became public knowledge.[47] Shouting matches, self-dramatizing grand gestures, and even traded suicide threats were the norm of a shared life played out against the backdrop of the best hotels of London, Paris, and St. Moritz. "We are exactly alike in many respects," the actor concluded, looking back on the marriage. "Those respects separated us." Nearly thirty years later, their grown (and deeply troubled) daughter, Diana, offered much the same assessment:

> Their intense egos galled them: they were in competition with each other as artists, as lovers, as parents; each insisted on being the only focus of attention in the home, on the street, at parties; each had an uncontrollable temper—madly theatrical, they could explode in a rage at the turn of a word. Both seethed with jealousy; it was no secret that women shamelessly pursued Daddy or that there was hardly a gentleman acquaintance of Mother's who hadn't felt impelled to try his charms on her.[48]

As her second marriage came undone, Michael Strange had made new efforts to advance her career in the arts, appearing (to generally poor notices) on stage and later taking to the lecture circuit with a selfconsciously Whitmanesque talk on democracy and a somewhat less ponderous harangue on "The Stage as the Actress Sees It." In 1928 she married for the third time, opting for calmer but no less opulent circumstances as the wife of one of New York's most distinguished attorneys, Harrison Tweed. Her lectures, in the meantime, had evolved into recitals of poetry, her own as well as others', all painstakingly set by her to musical accompaniment. For a time during the thirties she gave regular performances of what she later called her "Great Words with Great Music" programs over the radio. A White House command performance for the Roosevelts came her way. By 1940 she had parted company with her producers, but was still often on the road, declaiming works by Shakespeare, T.S. Eliot, Poe, Dorothy Parker, Edna St. Vincent Millay, and of course, Michael Strange. (She noted in a promotional brochure, "It has seemed to me a good thing in such times for poets to shake themselves out of their habit of reciting only their own poetry, and to resume their ancient, their eternal role, that of the sayer.")[49]

All this she recounted in *Who Tells Me True,* an elaborate self-advertisement that afforded the public numerous glimpses of the artists, actors, literary lights, and other public figures, from Charlie Chaplin to Mrs. William Randolph Hearst, whom she had known. The book was above all a defense of herself as a poet—a plea, albeit a shrill and deeply contradictory one, to be judged not by her social pedigree (which she had, however, carefully mapped out in the book's early chapters) but by the strength of her art.

That her editor at Scribner's, Maxwell Perkins, seems genuinely to have thought well of the book was partly a measure of her moderate talent for characterization. However, it was doubtless also due to her far more considerable talent for charm and persuasion. (Perkins was smitten to the point of carrying her photograph in his wallet.)[50] She radiated an aura or allure that all but pulled down the distinction between willfulness and art in the relentless whirlwind of her activities. After years of presenting herself as a sort of high priestess of poetry, she had in fact become a celebrity.

Reviews of *Who Tells Me True* were mixed but far from entirely unsympathetic. The *New York Times Book Review,* which ran a substantial piece, declared:

> It has the faults one would expect, but it has also an interest which is not wholly casual. Its point of view is egotistic; its writing is pretentious and involved, more diligent in effort than objectively successful; its author's mind is apparently allergic to simplicity. Yet sincerity the book does possess, along with incident, its "tem-

perament" and its unquenchable springs of self-confident enterprise. . . . This is a glamour girl who sought something of wider
allurement than merely traditional glamour, and went after it in
her own individual way.[51]

By November 1940, sales of the memoir had proven disappointing, and Perkins found himself in the classic position of the
editor obliged to console an author over the public's modest response to a book. In October, Harrison Tweed had tried to inter-
vene on his wife's behalf, asking Perkins to consider investing
more money in advertising in time for the Christmas trade. Perkins had replied briskly that this was impossible, Scribner's had
already done all it could, but "for some reason which I cannot
explain the public were cool about the book."[52] An anonymous
New York Public Library cataloguer ventured a more caustic appraisal of Strange's memoir—in the space provided for "Subject"
on the catalog slip, "None" was entered.

In the late spring of 1940, Margaret was experiencing a new
period of agitated self-doubt. She wrote to Lucy Mitchell, who had
gone to Vermont for the summer, that she wanted to read for the
next six months and not do any writing at all, "feeling," she said,
"my ignorance instead of my oats, these days, or perhaps my five
year old literary existance [*sic*] is wearing down."[53]

Margaret had words of encouragement for Mitchell, with
whom she was then collaborating on a large and difficult project.
Apart from her participation in the Writers Laboratory, Margaret's
chief responsibility at Bank Street was her work as coauthor and
coeditor with Mitchell of a series of here-and-now-inspired "basal
readers," primers that they hoped might replace the monotonous
"I see the dog" books then in general use in schools. Margaret was
more or less dutiful about carrying out her assignment, which entailed, among other things, a tedious correspondence with the
publisher, D. C. Heath and Company. Margaret, knowing how
trying even her stoically self-disciplined former teacher was finding the whole affair, observed, "I supose [*sic*] that you as author,
editor, educator and geographer, are still bearing the brunt of

[Heath's] Doctor Byrle Parker's omnipotence. But if I can be of any help in writing revision or indignation, please let me know."[54]

For Margaret, vacationing on Vinalhaven had become an annual summer ritual. On July 1, just before leaving for Long Cove, she wrote Mitchell again with additional news of Heath and to say, "I feel clear about my decision to get . . . into another field. And this is the beginning."[55] In the meantime she would immerse herself in the peace and solitude of the "wild and deserted" islands off Rockland. "It is the best place left west of Ireland," she wrote from Maine. "I am healthy and happy as a cricket hauling rowboats and carrying buckets of water and painting pictures."[56] Margaret hoped that the Mitchells, whose own rustic summer quarters were in Greensboro, Vermont, might visit her at Long Cove. She promised to take Lucy out painting on the granite rocks overlooking the water. Mitchell declined the invitation, remarking that though Maine as Margaret described it sounded good, Vermont was good, too. "We are not wild but we are isolated (at least I am)."[57] She had once done a great deal of painting, she said, but the only kind she now allowed herself was furniture painting, and still there was too little time for work. She wished her young friend a happy summer.

Margaret, as she reported rather cryptically to the Hollins *Alumnae Quarterly,* spent part of the summer writing "other things under another name."[58] Random House had hired her to ghost-write a series of natural history picture books for famed African explorer Osa Johnson. *Pantaloons,* an adventure story featuring a young elephant, was the first of the series. In addition to a flat fee of $500 for each volume, she received a pair of leopard slacks. Margaret's reasons for having undertaken the project are unclear; she told friends that she simply wanted the leopard slacks. Perhaps writing books under another name also provided her with a way of keeping busy while she considered her future. By August, in any case, she had rededicated herself to writing and editing picture books, and was holding court as various collaborators made their way by seaplane or ferry to Long Cove.

The Hurds were the first to arrive. They had chosen the air route, and they had just enough time to snap a photo of Margaret rowing vigorously below them as they glided down to a landing by the black buoy that served as their point of rendezvous.

Once ashore, Margaret deposited her friends in the upstairs bedroom under the eaves, where (as she well knew) bats made their home. "Get me out of here!" Posey was heard to demand moments later, after Margaret had wandered off to give her guests time to unpack.[59] Bats notwithstanding, the Hurds stayed for several days, sailing, swimming, dining outdoors on lobster, and occasionally doing a bit of work. The couple had brought along a book they were collaborating on, and while they were "cutting pasting and typing at a dummy in the next room," Margaret sat down to write Lucy Mitchell. "We are having wonderful days with a few of those early fall days that creep into August and wring your heart with the poignancy of another season."[60]

When Esphyr Slobodkina arrived soon afterward, she seemed in a huff, as she often did to others associated with Scott. As she stepped from the seaplane into Margaret's boat she was carrying an armload of mailing tubes containing sample art for a book she was illustrating for Margaret, *Red Light Green Light*. While the others mainly lolled about, Slobodkina put in long hours of work each day, at one point remarking scornfully that *she* had to earn her living.[61]

Margaret had previously spoken to "Phyra" about Bill Gaston, describing him as the man she loved. But some hesitancy in Margaret's voice had impelled the artist to make further inquiries. Finally she asked Margaret directly, "Is he married or something?" Margaret had answered, "Yes, he is sort of married."[62] Slobodkina "raised a questioning eyebrow" in response. And here they all were together, with Gaston himself occasionally dropping by in his motor launch, sometimes accompanied by his wife, Lucille.

As this drama was unfolding, a letter from the Whitman Printing Company arrived for Margaret, proposing that she write a children's book about manners using Disney characters. "Hell said Donald Duck that aint [*sic*] polite," she joked as she reported the news in another letter to Lucy Mitchell, adding, "I think the idea has possibilities. I never could get progressive on manners. I think they are important as weapons if not graces and good props for shyness uncertainty and difficult situations and the more automatic they are the more effective. Is this herasy [*sic*]?"[63] Meanwhile, while they were out rowing one day, Phyra made some remark that caused Margaret to realize, apparently for the first time, that her companion was a Jew. To the artist's shock and dismay, this revelation seemed to irritate Margaret. "Why didn't you tell me that before?" she replied, as though her guest had somehow failed her in an obligation that might have spared her some trouble. [64] Margaret went on to insist that she disliked herself for harboring what she called a "Jewish prejudice," yet she had the prejudice all the same. Slobodkina soon left the island.

Margaret's attitude, however frankly acknowledged, was certainly one that Lucy Mitchell would never have condoned. When Margaret turned to Posey Hurd, who had gone rowing with them that day, to ask if she shared such sentiments, Posey responded indignantly, "Why, certainly not."[65] Anti-semitic feelings, however, were far from uncommon among Americans of the period, educated and otherwise. Margaret had thought twice about her own prejudice, but, alas, hardly more than twice.

When a friend on the staff of *Life* arrived at Long Cove with a copy of the magazine's September 16 issue, Margaret, slipping comfortably back into the role of teacher's helper, dashed off a letter to Mitchell to report on a photo essay in the magazine. The photographs, collected under the title "Flight Over America," amounted to an aerial national portrait, with views of farmlands, factories, and prairie plains as they had rarely been observed before. Here, Margaret declared, was a brand new visual tool for engaging school children's interest in geography.

Referring, for once, to the European war, Margaret added that the news from abroad had given the fine Maine weather an elegaic piquancy. "Don't you hate," she wrote, "to see this summer go. With the world in such a fireworks of horror, it seems like the last summer. I seem to cling to it as such and don't want to get back to New York where the radios and the newspapers seem more real."[66]

Margaret's ugly scene with Esphyr Slobodkina continued to trouble her. In an unpublished short story which seems intended as a coda of sorts to that incident, she described a meeting (possibly imaginary) with Slobodkina back in New York. In "Oh Gentle Jew," two women sit at one of the green-and-white tables at the Hotel Breevort's outdoor café. It is a beautiful October afternoon with the "first autumn leaves . . . drifting down on the sidewalk in the warm Indian Summer breeze."[67] They order drinks from the hovering French waiter and make small talk about the season just past. Margaret (unnamed in the story but described as "blonde, green eyed and wind blown") speaks of weeks of "fooling around in boats and thinking little thoughts that didn't bother me" and of seeing "a friend"—an obvious reference to Bill Gaston. Then the conversation takes a more serious turn as the blonde woman confirms that this friend of hers has a "Jewish prejudice." She proceeds to relate what she calls the "important dream" she had over the summer.

> It was a large courtroom. The courtroom was full and I could see every face in it and you [Slobodkina, identified in the story as the "dark, deep eyed" Jewess] were there and the Judge asked, "Who here has a Jewish Prejudice," and no one rose and I had to rise up in the witness box and stand there admitting it. It was like being a traitor, and yet it was the time to be honest. You looked amazed and hurt and I found your eyes . . .

The narrator's dream implies the rather shrill hope that she and the other woman might remain friends despite everything. To this suggestion the other woman replies ruefully: "Love the Jew and hate the Jews. I wonder if it is possible." The conversation then drifts in other directions.

As for *Red Light Green Light,* the book she and Margaret were then collaborating on, Slobodkina, by her own account, proceeded to botch the illustrations. (The project languished for a time, to be taken up and published in 1944 by Doubleday, with illustrations by Leonard Weisgard.)

Margaret's friendship with Slobodkina did not, however, come to an end. Over the next two years or so they saw each other occasionally in the company of their mutual friend, Charles Shaw, and as both Margaret's and Slobodkina's business relationships with Scott became increasingly antagonistic they turned to each other for comfort and support with greater frequency. Margaret and Phyra also admired each other's work, and well before the decade was out they were again collaborating on new projects. As the illustrator, never one to mince words, recalled:

> Margaret, whatever her personal faults might have been and there
> were quite a few from my point of view, was a superbly honest and
> dedicated worker . . . [who] possessed that rare quality of gener-
> osity and willingness to share her knowledge with those whom she
> befriended. . . . Greater tribute I cannot pay to anybody.[68]

Margaret had always been non-ideological, apolitical. Her quarrel in the summer and fall of 1940 with Esphyr Slobodkina was
more a reflection of the childish cruelty she was sometimes capable
of—of a certain pattern of lashing out while grasping for straws—
than of mature, deliberate conviction.

It was also in 1940 that Margaret entered psychoanalysis. She
hoped to sort through the pain and confusion occasioned by her
parents' failing marriage, her own frustrated attempts at love, and
her continued inability to write convincingly for her peers. Her
analyst, Dr. Robert C. Bak, was a respected young practitioner, a
Freudian and a future president of the New York Psychoanalytic
Institute and Society. Margaret approached her sessions with Dr.
Bak with a healthy skepticism considering the aura of cultish fascination that analysis had acquired in recent years in artistic and
fashionable circles.

Faith in Freudian treatment was not, however, universal, even
within Margaret's rarefied world. Painfully for her, Michael
Strange, whose judgment had come to mean so much to her in
other matters, was among the most relentless detractors. In *Who
Tells Me True* Strange had summarily condemned psychoanalysis's
"fussily obscene hands" for forever meddling in the work of the
"deep-eyed fates."[69] As to Margaret's earnest experiment, her hope
that analysis might help to free her from certain vexing old en-
cumbrances, Michael simply gave no ground.

William R. Scott, Inc. had grown modestly but well in its first
two years. The firm's initial list had consisted of five titles. In 1940
eight new books appeared. The 1940 offerings maintained Scott's
reputation for dash and daring. There were two new infant books
printed on washable cloth; a "modern fairy tale" called *The Tinker of
Turntable; Skinny Gets Fat,* an "eating is fun" book for finicky

eaters; Charles Shaw's "young mystery story," *The Giant of Central Park;* Margaret and Leonard Weisgard's *Country Noisy Book;* and a picture book that was to prove an enduring classic, Esphyr Slobodkina's *Caps for Sale.*

Completing the list, *The Comical Tragedy or Tragical Comedy of Punch & Judy,* written by Margaret and illustrated by Weisgard, was perhaps the most unconventional book of the lot. Everything about *Punch* was designed to involve readers actively. The dust jacket was printed on heavy stock and could be refolded and stood on its end to become a puppet theater. Paper cutout characters were provided so that children could stage their own Punch and Judy performances. Even the flap advertising had a mischievous slant: "Notorious Villain Captured: That gay, witty, and wicked rogue Punch, who for over three centuries has boisterously lived here and there abroad on the puppet stage and in the hearts of his admirers, has at last been captured alive and put into pictures and print."

To celebrate the book's publication, Scott gave a gala party at 69 Bank Street, complete with a puppet show and spaghetti dinner. Several Scott authors arrived in costume and mingled with book buyers. As an additional publicity stunt, McCullough arranged for a week of puppet performances at Bloomingdale's. Scott's decided flair for public relations did not, however, often translate into robust sales. Despite all the hoopla, *Punch* proved an even more short-lived experiment than *The World Is Round.*

Gertrude Stein's second children's book, "To do," had meanwhile arrived in manuscript at the firm's office, where it was not faring well. There was general agreement that the text was too abstract. Margaret in particular opposed talk of revision; "To do," she argued, was a completed work, only it happened not to be a book for children. Returning from a short trip to Maine in late November, she said as much in her second letter to Stein. The new manuscript afforded the immediate occasion for writing, but plainly Margaret still hoped to establish a personal exchange with her. She spoke offhandedly but awkwardly of her summer on Vinalhaven, of having tried to "break away from children's books" in order to write fiction. "The result," she confided with a nervous lunge at conviviality, was "twenty canvases of wild and wooly [*sic*] oil paintings"—who had said anything about her being a painter?—"which I enjoyed the manual labor of thoroughly, and a story about an old bum in Brooklyn which was really a story about Irland [*sic*]."[70]

She expressed her regret that no contemporary writer had yet produced stories worthy of the folk tales of ages past. She rambled on about this:

> I wish someone would do a book of modern folk or fairy tales—the world we know to-day and values in it, or if it's a fairy story with princes on tanks and forsaken mermen in a sea of submarines. Which is silly, perhaps because tanks and submarines are not yet symbols in the brain like white horses and dolphin's tails. Or are they? Anyway. Once there were folk tales about the world people lived in and now there arn't [*sic*]. But maybe this would be too hard a book for anyone to write now.

Perhaps, she suggested, Stein would feel challenged to do so herself.

She mentioned her own collection of Brer Rabbit stories, begun back in 1937, which Harper planned to publish in 1941. Perhaps Margaret herself would one day write the stories of which she now spoke, but "for the time being," she told Stein, "I know only one, about an old woman who lives on a barge and won't sell her pile of scrap iron for a river of gold." She ended her second, and apparently last, letter to Gertrude Stein with good wishes for the author's new dog, Basket II, and with news of the birth of eight puppies to her own Kerry Blue terrier, Smoke.

Stein responded with a postcard congratulating Margaret on the puppies while ignoring the more serious, literary portions of the letter, including, of course, the part critical of "To do." Margaret's criticism could hardly have been expected to put Stein in a particularly friendly or responsive mood; moreover, her flippant reference to military tanks could only have struck her correspondent as extraordinarily insensitive, as doubtless it was, given the depressing and terrifying facts of the European war. As Margaret read the papers only occasionally and seems almost to have prided herself on her ignorance of world events, she was not likely to have anticipated Stein's reaction.

In an undated story-memoir about this exchange, Margaret, referring to herself in the third person, wondered: "Why hadn't she written Gertrude Stine [*sic*] in answer to that terribly nice card of hers. . . . It was nice—No she had never liked that word 'nice.' "[71]

What name, then, *would* she attach to utter disappointment? Stein evidently had little in the way of friendship, wise counsel, or encouragement to offer her, unless one counts a passage from *The World Is Round,* in which Rose is "going up and up the green grass meadow that went right to the top" of a mountain: "It is hard to go on when you are nearly there but not near enough to hurry up to get there. That is where Rose was. And where was there. She almost said it she almost whispered it to herself."[72]

"There," for Margaret, was not Bank Street. It was not exclusively Scott's offices either. By the end of 1940 that much had become clear.

John Macrae, who as E. P. Dutton's president had published *Another Here and Now Story Book* and Margaret's book *The Fish with the Deep Sea Smile,* was delighted when he received a new manuscript from her in the first weeks of 1941. Over lunch Margaret spoke candidly to the publisher of her wish to quit the juveniles field and write fiction. Macrae was understanding; at the same time he offered to publish not only the story she had sent him, *The Poodle and the Sheep,* but also her next three children's books. Urging her to consider bringing all her future work to Dutton, he held out the prospect that her writing for adults would also be given a sympathetic reading there. It was an enticing offer, but Margaret had too deep a resistance to investing all her loyalties in any one publisher or person to accept. Writing Macrae on February 11 from Mont Tremblant, Quebec (where she had gone for a brief ski holiday), she declined, promising nonetheless to send him three more stories, "for I fear I will always write children's books by accident, even if I concentrate on other forms of writing." Touched by his generosity and good will, she added, "I will always remember with deepest gratitude, the vote of confidence you gave me as a young and comparatively unproved author."[73]

The oddly humorous, not very satisfactory *Poodle and the Sheep* was Margaret's first attempt at writing a moral tale. As such it represented a conscious departure from her Bank Street training. As she told Macrae in the letter from Mont Tremblant, it was he who had indirectly inspired the story, and that was why she had sent it to him:

> Do you remember that you once gave me a copy of *Careless Jane?* I liked that book because it amused me even while the voices of the people around me who make it their business to lay down the laws of what young children should have in books said "No morality for children." Then I watched children for awhile, and more and more my evidence and my instinct about what concerned children made me believe that a concern about right and wrong is of vital interest to them. The usual desire of little children to be good little children in the long run, seems most touching to me. And little dogs are not so unlike that either. So that when I spent an afternoon chasing a little poodle in Maine who was chasing sheep, and then, because the offence was so serious, I had to chastise the little poodle, much to his bewilderment and pain of heart, this incident began to grow in significance into a children's book.

In the class notes of the Hollins *Alumnae Quarterly* for spring 1941, Margaret listed six books due to be published that fall: *Young Animals, The Polite Penguin, Brer Rabbit Stories, The Seashore Noisy Book, Red Light Green Light,* and *The Poodle and the Sheep.* She was also, she reported, working on a play about the war in England. (Margaret's unfinished two-act drama, "The Earth Will Have Us," is an inconsequential romance about a group of young people, Europeans and Americans, who befriend each other at a youth hostel in Wales before the war, then meet again as enemies after the outbreak of hostilities.)[74] In contrast to her news, other classmates announced the births of their children. The class secretary, Leonora A. Orr, also commented, "Imagine my surprise when reading the March [8] issue of the *New Yorker* to discover in an article called 'Tallyho' that Tim Brown had inveigled the reporter [E. J. Kahn, Jr.] into accompanying her on an afternoon of beagling!"[75]

Kahn's piece about a certain friend named "Brownie" described with mild mockery the socially inbred atmosphere and physically daunting activities of the Buckram Beagles. A great many of Margaret's friends accompanied her at one time or another on these expeditions, though it was a rare friend who did so more than once. John McCullough was typical in his recollection of an exhausting afternoon of running through the woods with occasional time off for a sip of champagne.

As Kahn tells it, on the chilly, overcast afternoon of his outing (Bruce Bliven, Jr., was also along that day) "Brownie" proved herself a woman of extraordinary stamina, able to run for miles through underbrush and mud, over fence rails and hedgerows, without betraying the slightest hint of fatigue. Pressing ahead, she assured her less fit writer companions that there was "really nothing like fresh air." She also said that hares were in short supply on Long Island, that the Buckram Beagles actually knew by sight certain hares that had eluded them in the past. She told Kahn how one such hare, Flora, had at last been overtaken by the beagles and torn to shreds. A kill, on the rare occasions when one occurred, did not, she said, disturb her; her thoughts then were with the hounds, which reminded her at such moments of "the grooms in 'Macbeth.' " Here was a hair-raising analogy, especially, Kahn observed, from a writer of children's books with "quite a few sentimental references to . . . soft, cuddly bunnies."[76]

This last suggestion was, of course, in the Bennett Cerf "baby books" vein of casual abuse. But *The Noisy Book* and its sequels, Margaret's adaptation of the *Fables* of La Fontaine, *Punch and Judy,* and the soon-to-be-published *Brer Rabbit,* among others of her books, were all the work of a dry-eyed and cunning sensibility. If a friend could write so dismissively of her type of work in the *New Yorker,* it is not hard to see why Margaret's own doubts were so vexing, and so long-lived.

After Gertrude Stein, the writer whose work had meant the most to Margaret since college was Virginia Woolf. On April 3, 1941, she was shocked to read in the *New York Evening Post* that Woolf had committed suicide just a few days earlier. Margaret had bought the paper having glimpsed Woolf's name on the front page, with hopes of reading of some new literary triumph. With the somber realization of her death came memories of having walked shyly past the Woolfs' Bloomsbury residence in the late summer of 1937 and of having written the author a letter before leaving for Europe that summer, a letter she had never mailed. Now Margaret learned that the house she had surveyed from a distance that day had been destroyed in the wartime bombing raids. Still, she considered in a reminiscence prompted by the news, "what I went to see to remember I remember."[77] Margaret tried to imagine the author leaving a note for her husband and heading out the door of their country house for the river and "the last cold shocks of sensation . . . the last arrows of sensation." She recalled with a shudder a passage spoken by Bernard in Woolf's novel *The Waves:* "Sometimes indeed, when I pass a cottage with a light in the window where a child has been born, I could implore them not to squeeze a sponge over that new body."[78]

As Margaret typed her eulogy, the late night silence was broken by the clacking of horses' hooves as an old-fashioned Victorian hansom cab rolled past. She pulled the detail into her essay: "So the old horse returning to the darkly lighted stable is an obituary . . . the unknown driver thinking his own thoughts out in the night." Margaret, it would seem from remarks she made to the Hurds and to Leonard Weisgard, had hoped one day to meet Virginia Woolf, perhaps even to establish with her the sort of literary relationship that had failed to materialize with Gertrude Stein. But now those hopes, too, were at an end.

OTHER
HOUSES,
OTHER
WORLDS

I am of old and young, of the foolish
as much as the wise,
Regardless of others, ever
regardful of others,
Maternal as well as paternal,
a child as well as a man,
Stuff'd with the stuff that is coarse
and stuff'd with the stuff that
is fine, . . .
I resist any thing better than
my own diversity.

WALT WHITMAN,
"Song of Myself"

In the summer of 1941, Margaret re-
turned to her rented cottage at Long Cove, where as in previous
years she rested, painted, read, entertained friends, lost the weight
she had a tendency to gain when in New York, and pursued the
"hobby" that (on a publishers questionnaire) she called "Cat Life—
which means doing nothing and just watching."[1] As her professional commitments multiplied and the circle of her New York
friends continued to expand, the importance of these annual summer interludes increased correspondingly. As she later wrote Lucy
Mitchell:

> Isn't it strange what complete faith one can have in a place . . . I
> supose [*sic*] wisdom is to know ones [*sic*] necessities and not to live
> without them. And this huge silence, with the woods and the
> ocean together, and the air full of kelp and the sound of fish hawks

and seagulls and nothing else, seems to be something I perish and get parched without.[2]

Margaret hardly left her work behind when she went north to Maine, however. Clement Hurd once remarked that while one could not be sure just when Margaret actually worked on her books, it may well have been that she worked on them "all the time."[3] Writing, daydreaming, and "just watching" were never entirely unrelated activities for her.

A great deal of her Maine "Cat Life" found its way into the pages of her books, as in this passage from *The Little Island:* "Autumn came and the yellow pears dropped slowly to the ground . . . Winter came and the snow fell softly like a great quiet secret in the night, cold and still."[4]

Her work contains dozens of similar passages. Vinalhaven also provided the setting for a number of autobiographical stories. As Margaret reported later that summer to Lucy Mitchell, she had "finally discovered the obvious, again," and was writing a story a day about "things and people I know about instead of fictional themes, just batting them out without rereading trying to get over my shyness and blocks in front of writing older stories."[5] Almost as an afterthought she noted, "I have sheepishly written a few children's books too that the side of me that isn't hell bent to get into older writing is quite interested in."

One autobiographical piece from that summer concerned the visit of a writer friend, Preston Schoyer. Margaret had met "Pres," a novelist and journalist widely travelled in the Far East, in New York the previous April, at a costume party given by the Hurds. A charming, handsome man of about her age, Schoyer had come as Groucho Marx, Margaret as a blowsy blonde. They hit it off immediately, left together for Margaret's apartment, and spent the next two days there together in the first flush of romance. Two or three months passed without their seeing each other again; then Margaret asked Schoyer to visit her in Maine.

Her account of his arrival at Carvers Harbor is a study in self-doubt and a curiously detached kind of longing:

> Walking by his unfamiliar side she heard her own voice chatting along, overchatting in order to sound at ease. And she wondered

why he seemed such a stranger to her when he had been in her mind so long. . . .

. . . They picked up old threads, he told her more about China. They talked of publishers and unconsciously they vied with each other so that in retrospect they found themselves boasting of contacts with publishers, using a few first names quoting remarks— like two little kids boasting nervously and boring themselves by the act. [6]

The story continues in this vein, its tone an accurate reflection of the emotional confusion, desperation even, that had given rise to it. Aptly, Margaret left the piece unfinished. Friends later recalled having heard that Margaret had wanted to marry Schoyer but that he had not been interested. To his sister, Polly Brooks, who had been Posey Hurd's best friend at Radcliffe, he confided, "She's too mystical for me." [7] When Schoyer's book, *The Foreigners,* was published the following spring, the author inscribed a copy:

For dear Margaret

from a foreigner who never feels foreign in 21 W. 10th.

Always the best,
Your old China hand,
Pres,
who will always remember
the house in the fog and the
long still rocks which look
Westward to the Sun. [8]

After Schoyer left Vinalhaven that summer of 1941, Margaret turned her attention to work. A letter to Lucy Mitchell in late August said nothing of the romance but was full of news about her many current projects. She enclosed a draft manuscript that she described as the "skeleton beginning" of a picture book, scribbled down that same morning. *SHHhhhh . . . BANG,* she said jauntily, was to be her revenge on librarians: "Can't you see children in the hushed atmosphere of a library tiptoeing up to a librarian and asking for it—*Sshhhhhhh B A N G!* [sic]"[9] Margaret had printed out the title by hand in letters of contrasting size that made their mischievous point with the expressive force of an Apollinairian *calligramme.*

Among the other books she worked on while in Maine was one begun the previous summer, *The Runaway Bunny*. Margaret had come across a medieval Provençal love ballad, the "beautiful pattern" of which, she had written Lucy Mitchell, might "be applied . . . to our ends" as the basis for a picture book. [10]

In the ballads (known to Chaucer) of the Provençal troubadours, love was the moving force behind all of humankind's noblest undertakings. The song Margaret had found was a love story recast as a hunt involving magical transformations:

> If you pursue me I shall become a fish in the water
> > And I shall escape you
> If you become a fish I shall become an eel
>
> If you become an eel I shall become a fox
> > And I shall escape you
> If you become a fox I shall become a hunter
> > And I shall hunt you . . .

"I may use it for a picture book," Margaret had warned her teacher with a sporting flourish. "So, beat me to it and use it toward a more serious end."

In *The Runaway Bunny*, Margaret changed one type of hunt for another. Working with the structure of the original ballad, she transformed the story of a lover's pursuit of his beloved into a fable of childish adventuring and maternal devotion and strength. Margaret's text is a stirring evocation of the universal need of two- and three-year-olds to test the world beyond the mother's protection in such a way as to be assured that the mother will always be there should something go wrong:

" 'If you run away,' said his mother, 'I will run after you. For you are my little bunny.'

" 'If you run after me,' said the little bunny, 'I will become a fish in a trout stream and I will swim away from you.'

" 'If you become a fish in a trout stream,' said his mother, 'I will become a fisherman and I will fish for you.' "[11]

For the young reader, the mother emerges as a reassuring bridge between the real and imaginary worlds, for while the bunny child escapes into a succession of other-than-human guises—as a fish, a flower, a bird—his mother nearly always overtakes him by adopting a familiar human form, as a mountain climber, a tight-rope walker, a gardener seeking "a crocus in a hidden garden."

In the final exchange the bunny child, as though tired out at the end of a long day, vows to become a human child and "run into a house," which of course is no escape at all from a child's point of view. The young hero has come to the end of his tether and, tellingly, what he is left with there is the here-and-now world of real little boys and girls, their houses and other mundane realities. The rabbit mother replies, " 'If you become a little boy and run into a house . . . I will become your mother and catch you in my arms and hug you.' " The bunny child thinks better of this.

" 'Shucks,' said the bunny, 'I might as well stay where I am and be your bunny.' And so he did."

Margaret thought to end the story here. She sent the manuscript to Ursula Nordstrom, who had bought the book for Harper on the strength of an earlier draft. The editor found the revised version extraordinary, except for the ending; the bunny child's resignation, followed by the last few throw-away words, seemed to Nordstrom to end the piece too abruptly—a touch of whimsy was needed to release the powerful emotions built up in the exchanges between mother and child. She cabled Margaret in Maine (there were no telephones at Long Cove), asking her to come up with something appropriate.

" 'HAVE A CARROT,' SAID THE MOTHER BUNNY," Margaret wired back. Nordstrom was delighted.

Margaret, however, was reluctant to let go of the manuscript. In October of 1941, while spending a few days at the Hurds' Vermont farm, new doubts began to plague her. (Margaret had recommended Clement Hurd to illustrate *The Runaway Bunny* and Nordstrom had agreed to the choice.) Curiously, it was not to Nordstrom but to Lucy Mitchell that she turned for help, writing from North Ferrisburg,

> I wallow in uncertainty about punctuation, wording, and form. Whether I should use *If you become I will become,* or *If you are I will be* or mix them both up so that the rythm [*sic*] gets broken from page to page and isn't too soporific, or what is consistancy [*sic*] and what makes the best poetry. . . . Which is stronger the sense of a line or the meaning. [12]

Perhaps Margaret needed to include Mitchell in the writing of the book which more clearly than any other until that time marked the withdrawal of her deepest loyalties from the Bank Street founder and her ideas. Margaret would continue to write sequels to the original *Noisy Book* and many other works that plainly bore the mark of her Bank Street training—the clear and memorable patterning of *The Runaway Bunny,* though adapted from an old chanson, was a device that Mitchell had taught her to use—but the bunny child's rejection of the here-and-now was a telling clue to the private meaning the book had for its author. Mitchell's empiricism had begun to pale for Margaret, who was increasingly preoccupied with the insights to be gleaned from dreams, from memory, and from the "child that is within all of us . . . perhaps the one laboratory that we all share."[13] In writing *The Runaway Bunny,* it is as though Margaret had set out, like the wayward bunny child, to see how far astray she might go and still remain within her teacher's protective ken.

As for the unruly *SHHhhhh . . . BANG,* Margaret had reminded Lucy Mitchell on sending her the manuscript that summer, that "even a here and now story can be a dream and you have written plenty of them yourself which your litteral [*sic*] heavy footed followers have failed to notice—Anne Carrol [*sic*] Moore has retired."[14] Except for the last reference, which must have amused her greatly, it is hard to imagine Mitchell reading Margaret's comment without a slight shudder, for here was a rather faint-hearted attempt to recast her in an image more compatible with Margaret's own changing aesthetic. The real significance of the gesture lay in its lack of conviction.

In December of 1941, Margaret received word that her mother had suffered a serious stroke. On December 7, the day Japan attacked Pearl Harbor, Margaret, Roberta, and Gratz (who now lived in Michigan) gathered in Great Neck for a rare family reunion, shuttling back and forth on roads where military guards had been hastily posted between the Brown family home and their mother's hospital bedside in Garden City.

Maude, whose health had been in decline for some time, made

a partial recovery, becoming well enough to come into Manhattan for Theosophical Society meetings and occasionally to see Margaret for dinner, but little happiness lay in her future. She and her husband had been steadily growing apart for years, and at the time of her stroke Robert Brown was living at his yacht club in nearby Port Washington. Work had always satisfied him in a way that home life seems not to have done. With two children married and the third well launched on a career, still less had remained to keep the couple together. In late 1942 or in early 1943, he moved out of the family home permanently, taking up residence in a new house of his own in Port Washington. After presiding over the closing of the house at 8 Ridge Drive, Maude Brown lived alone for a time in a Manhattan hotel before moving to Ann Arbor to stay with Gratz.

A few years earlier, as a Bank Street student, Margaret had written a note to herself under the heading "What is Focus."[15] She was always, it seemed, making lists of one kind or another; this was another in the order-and-self-discipline genre. "Intellectually," the prescription began, to have focus meant "to discover and explore; to do this in some way through writing; to contribute something new. Emotionally, [it consisted of] marriage, leisure and children. Combined—To know always the excitement . . . in mere living. To somehow justifie [*sic*] my place on earth."

Margaret, like countless young women of her own and earlier generations, had been raised to equate married life with the promise of personal fulfillment. How desperately—recalling the broken engagement with George Armistead, the ill-fated affair with Bill Gaston, and most recently, the forced romance with Preston Schoyer—she must have wanted to bring the matter right. And now her parents' separation must have seemed a stern caveat issued against whatever hope still remained to her, at more than thirty, that such a future might be hers. Some years later, Margaret's Bank Street friend, Rosie Bliven, told Lucy Mitchell that the effect of Maude and Robert Brown's separation on "Brownie" had been devastating, and that the intense relationship that developed between Margaret and Michael Strange could be understood in terms of Margaret's need for a mothering figure to replace, in some sense, Maude Brown.[16] There can be little doubt the separation (which coincided with the break-up of Michael Strange's third marriage) caused Margaret to question where, if it was to be had at all, love might be found.

Margaret's work seems not to have suffered as a result of the turmoil of her family life. Perhaps, on the contrary, her manuscripts served as safe harbors in which tumultuous feelings could be calmly examined and transformed. She published five books in 1941: *The Poodle and the Sheep,* with illustrations by Leonard Weisgard (Dutton); *The Polite Penguin,* illustrated by H. A. Rey (Harper); *Baby Animals,* illustrated by Mary Cameron (Random House); *The Seashore Noisy Book,* with art by Leonard Weisgard (Scott); and *Brer Rabbit,* with adaptations of the illustrations by A. B. Frost (Harper). There would be four new books in 1942, five in 1943, eight in 1944, and three the following year.

The war likewise had little impact on the overall pattern of Margaret's activities as a writer. Certain collaborations were interrupted, but others were begun, continued, or renewed. Some projects were delayed or scaled back due to wartime shortages, especially of paper. (The juveniles departments at the major publishing houses, which had approximately 25 percent less paper at their disposal than before the war, generally dealt with the problem by foregoing marginal projects while printing somewhat larger editions of their best authors' and illustrators' new work.) But Margaret's reputation was such that she was not likely to have had trouble placing the lion's share of her manuscripts, even in a time of narrowing possibilities.

The major interruption caused by the war for Margaret was occasioned by Clement Hurd's departure for military service. Both Clem and Posey had always considered themselves pacifists. Recent events, however, had convinced them of the absolute necessity of fighting Hitler. In early 1942 the illustrator enlisted in the U. S. Army and was commissioned a second lieutenant. It seemed likely he would be stationed in San Francisco, where Posey had taken a job as a researcher in the Office of War Information.

That spring, while Clem awaited his orders, *The Runaway Bunny* was published to strong reviews. The *Horn Book* ignored the book, as did the New York Public Library in its annual holiday list issued later that year; but the *Herald Tribune*'s May Lamberton Becker summed up the views of many critics when, after commenting on *The Runaway Bunny*'s "rich" folkloric background, she declared it an "up-to-date, affectionate picture book" in which "pictures and text are in complete collaboration. Brilliant, in color, the large scenes show the dreams, while realistic black-and-whites show that this is really a mother-play."[17]

Clem did the cover illustration for the April issue of *Town & Country*, a pitch for War Bonds and a plum assignment. Two picture books by the artist and his wife, *The Annie Moran* and *Speedy, the Hook and Ladder Truck*, were due to be published by Lothrop within the year and Posey's first juvenile novel, *The Wreck of the Wild Wave*, was expected from the Oxford University Press. Then in May a telegram arrived instructing the illustrator to report for temporary duty to Jefferson Barracks, Missouri; on November 1 he sailed from San Francisco Bay for the Pacific theater. Ten years earlier, as an aspiring artist heading for France, Clem had passed the time on shipboard reading *The Road to Oblivion*. Now, feeling hopelessly unprepared and bound for points unknown a half a world away, he read his three-volume Everyman edition of *War and Peace*.

Leonard Weisgard, who failed his Army physical, illustrated books throughout the war, rising to the top of his profession. One day Margaret, who always had some project in the works with him, approached him with a sporting challenge. During the war years, one way that publishers economized was by limiting the extent of color printing in their illustrated titles. Margaret invited Leonard to collaborate on a picture book to be done entirely in black-and-white, a book in which the restricted palette—here was the trick—would be revealed as the best choice in terms of its suitability for the story. The text of *Night and Day* is a somewhat slight and precious fantasy about two cats, one of which (the black one) loves the night while the other (a white cat) must overcome his fear of the dark in order to feel fully at home in the world. Margaret and Leonard were determined to make *Night and Day* the "most beautiful book" they had "ever done."[18] Weisgard's illustrations were in fact quite good. In the end, however, Harper refused to print the book by the relatively costly gravure process, which yields a creamy, richly layered, almost tactile kind of black, and the subtlety of the experiment, such as it was, was thereby lost.

Leonard Weisgard was every bit as prolific as Margaret. As much to serve notice that publishers ought not to take their work for granted as to keep their output appearing without delay, they both continued to add new publishers to the list of those with whom they worked. Margaret had opened the door for Weisgard at Scott and at Harper. Early in 1942 he returned the favor, introducing her to his Doubleday editor, Margaret Lesser.

Like Harper and Brothers, Doubleday, Doran and Company (as the house was then known) was among the industry's most profitable firms. The publisher of such distinguished picture books as A. B. Frost's *Carlo* (1913) and C. B. Fall's *ABC Book* (1923), and of Rudyard Kipling's *Just So Stories* (1902), Doubleday had been among the first American houses to establish a juveniles department. May Massee, one of the field's most respected figures, had been the department's original editor. More recently, under Margaret Lesser, Doubleday had become known for the kind of cautious, mainstream approach with which librarians generally felt quite comfortable. While caution was hardly the watchword of Margaret's aesthetic, Lesser was a valuable new ally with a far better chance than Scott, certainly, of placing her books in the nation's public libraries.

A former newspaper reporter, the editor had become curious about the here-and-now style of writing for young children, and was not averse to considering manuscripts in this vein. Moreover, Lesser seemed disinclined to fuss with a text once she had accepted it for publication. Almost to the extent that she had done at Scott, Margaret could edit herself, an arrangement made the more enticing by the understanding that Weisgard would illustrate all her Doubleday titles. Partly to celebrate and partly to keep the market from appearing glutted with her work, she chose a pen name— Golden MacDonald (the name of an elderly Maine handyman of her acquaintance)—under which all her books for Lesser would appear.

No one within the juveniles publishing world doubted for a moment who Golden MacDonald really was—least of all Ursula Nordstrom, Bill Scott, and John McCullough. But most people, it is fair to assume, never thought to link the two authors. For her own part, Margaret seems rather to have enjoyed concealing her identity from her readers. She was convinced, for one thing, that children are generally oblivious to authorship. As she recalled once of her own favorite childhood books, "It did not seem important then that any one [*sic*] wrote [them] . . . they were true.[19] She also savored the quixotic theater of assuming different literary identities and the idea that she wrote differently under each of her names. Whether or not she actually did is far from clear, but the mere belief that she did may have been as important to her creative work as the Runaway Bunny's quick change act is to his expanding sense of self. The power to change oneself, to be a part of the ceaseless changefulness of life, was always for Margaret a transcendent ideal.

The most interesting of the Golden MacDonald war years books was *Red Light Green Light* (1944), a jazzy, percussive improvisation—not so much a story as an "interlude," as Margaret called such fusions of poetry and prose:

> Red Light
> they can't go.
> Green Light
> they can go. . . .
> The horse came out of the horse's house
> *a barn* . . .
> And a mouse came out of the house of the mouse
> *a hole.*[20]

A striking feature of *Red Light Green Light* is the piece's plaintive, abstract, modernist atmosphere: "And they all went down their own roads . . . / Dog roads, / Cat roads / And mouse roads through / the / grass." It was as though, Margaret implied, being oneself required one to live in terrible isolation from one's fellows.

The wish to rise above such feelings of isolation reverberates through an undated letter written to Michael Strange some time early in 1942.[21] Margaret and Michael had continued the friendship begun in 1940, but in recent months they had seen little of each other. Michael was preoccupied with the fate of her marriage, the brittle nature of which had been apparent to Margaret during her stay at Montauk. The marriage was at last in its final phase. (By July 1942, documents providing for the division of the couple's property would be signed; the divorce took effect that November.) Margaret's letter was in part an apology for a recent quarrel the two women had had on meeting for the first time after Michael had moved out of 10 Gracie Square.

Over the last weeks, Margaret explained, her psychoanalysis had caused her to feel "completely abandoned" in life. It was not usually the case, she said, that such emotions, however strong, "spill[ed] over" into her relations outside the doctor's office, but in this instance "that desolation . . . did spill over in spite of all I would wish . . . and I hung onto you so that you had to in all decency brush me off." Caught up in the emotional turmoil surrounding her impending divorce, Michael could hardly be expected, Margaret now realized, to have deep reserves of comfort and reassurance to offer her.

Margaret proceeded to defend her decision to remain in analysis despite Michael Strange's scornful protestations. She explained that she had resolved to put "my trust and my energies" into psychoanalysis only as a "temporary treatment." She considered the process to be a sort of "operation," an "uncovering of forgotten desolations and traps in a forgotten past." She recalled having once, in a conversation with Michael, characterized psychoanalysis as an "obscene process." (Curiously, she seems to have forgotten that Michael Strange herself, in her memoir *Who Tells Me True,* had called Freudian analysis obscene.) By this Margaret said she had meant only to suggest that "from the outside and from the pleasure, excitement and hook-line-and-sinker absorption in it of most of the devotes [*sic*] of analysis I have met, it seemed obscene to me. It still does, as a whole." But the "real experience" of analysis, she insisted, might be otherwise:

> To go in to that hour feeling suddenly alone on the rock itself with no one. Every one you love is lost. You may blame your own childishness and stupid loving or not. This is an experience of desolation curses and prayers and terrible tears. They say that if you relive this desolation and face it, as you once met it and couldn't face it then

you are free of it. Perhaps, that is what one hopes. You don't even have to know what incidents caused the pain you are facing, as long as you do feel it again and stand it.

She granted that there was a danger in this: "It is certainly far from the intellect—this frightful purging of the emotions. And all for the hope of a greater clarity. That hope you must respect, however misguided you may think it." She did not view her own analysis as obscene because it was a "treatment for a purpose," not a self-indulgence.

> I suffer it but do not revel in it and don't think much about it outside the hour. In fact it leaves you freer not to think about yourself when it is working properly, which isn't all the time by a long shot. I too am filled with a horror of something behind all this . . . but the horror is real.

Sessions with the doctor, she argued, might be useful to one's work. Her writing, Margaret said, was a "big angry issue" in her analysis. She did not elaborate on this point, but doubtless this was a reference to her often expressed, long frustrated wish to be able to write for adults.

Psychotherapy, Margaret wrote, had helped her realize that ever since childhood she had been drifting "deeper and deeper into the aloofness of a lonely illusion—the illusion that one is separate and so far away from others that only by playing a part . . . could one meet one's fellows. No wonder it *hasn't worked.* Fortunately this has never deceived a few people." Here she might have been thinking of Marguerite Hearsey, Lucy Mitchell, Dr. Bak, and not least of all, Michael herself. "And perhaps too much lack of coherence has been forgiven in me. And a long habit of mixing words and deserting my own thought for other thoughts in the middle of a sentence [*sic*]." How humbled by Michael Strange's extraordinary facility as a conversationalist and dramatic reader Margaret must have felt. She had, she said,

> a frightening hopeless feeling every time I open my mouth. That is why someday I will have to write and write honestly since to speak simply and honestly from the core that is me is difficult. . . . The first great wonder at the world is big in me. That is the real reason that I write.

She hoped, in any case, that through her work she would eventually prove herself worthy of the faith and fellowship that Michael had extended to her and for which she remained ever grateful.

> Michael I have listened to you harder than to anyone in the world and I have heard you. I still listen and I still hear you. And if my life ever makes any sense *who you are* even more than what you say will not be lost in me or in what I write. I believe in you. And I see you too, being greedy child and pristine child, ruthless pig and generous by your quickness as few could be. I have seen your self-confidence the size of a mouse and the size of an elephant and I have seen you *in between* apart from all fluctuations of confidence love or hate. For Michael is greater than Michael.

This last declaration clearly suggests the high reverence Margaret felt for her friend; it seems she was utterly determined to believe that Michael was indeed the figure of boldness, originality, and strength she claimed to be. Such adulation notwithstanding, Michael Strange's disapproval of Margaret's analysis remained unqualified.

In early July of 1942, Margaret, having not yet left for Maine and feeling unusually tired, went to see her doctor. The examination revealed a growth on her left breast; he advised her to have the growth removed immediately. It proved to be benign, and after a terrifying week in the hospital and another week spent "wilting about New York" and trying (unsuccessfully) to find a friend interested in "braving the wilds" of Vinalhaven with her, she left unaccompanied for Long Cove. [22]

"At present," she wrote Lucy Mitchell from Maine, "I am so relieved and grateful for my returning strength that I feel like offering myself as a propitiation to Life itself and starting a brand new life at twice the reality." [23]

She had gotten an "old fisherwoman" to cook for her and to "act as a left arm" because her own was to remain out of service for another few days. "I carry one bucket of water up from the stream instead of two and if I want to row the boat I have to row with one arm in an endless circle. But fortunately or unfortunately readers

get written with the right arm so I will tackle them this afternoon."

The massive basal reader project, begun in 1940 and still in
preparation, had become the chief remaining link between Margaret and her former teacher, but the two women rarely saw each
other. Margaret expressed the wish to meet Mitchell for lunch one
day, "free of readers," the following fall.

> I am in transition, one never knows towards what until we get
> there. But am trying to read and not write for a while, only it is
> hard to sit still as long as it takes to read, sound by sound and
> image by image and word by word with an echoe [*sic*] if I like it.
> All very progressive.

"Please remember me warmly to Mr. Mitchell," Margaret
added in formal farewell, "and to yourself, aways"; then, suddenly
flush with a mischievous impulse, she signed her name "Brown-
ies—They get more and more plural."

Margaret and Bill Scott's disastrous interview with Anne Carroll Moore in the fall of 1938 had far-reaching consequences for
public library sales. Between then and August of 1942, when Scott
paid a courtesy call on Moore's successor, sales of Scott books to
libraries had suffered not just in New York but nationally.

Having resolved to try his luck with the new regime of Frances
Clarke Sayers, Bill Scott adopted the gingerly attitude of a relative
newcomer eager for the advice of more seasoned professionals. He
arrived at Sayers' office alone and with no books in hand. He had
come, he explained, with a simple question: Why had the New
York Public Library taken so little interest in the work of his small
publishing house?

"He is an extremely fine person—young, idealistic, and sincere," the new chief librarian wrote Bertha E. Mahony at the *Horn
Book;* they had had an "interesting conference . . . about books
for little children."[24] When Scott had asked her why his company's books failed to meet with the library's approval, she had
replied, "Because the books have nothing in them but some words,
some color and sometimes a very thin shadow of an idea."

"Mr. Scott, as you know," the letter continued, "was apparently 'born and bred in the briar patch' of Nursery School Progressive Education. . . . He has an open mind, however, and he said upon leaving, 'you only confirm what I'm beginning to feel myself.' "

Of Margaret's new collaborations during the war years, the most memorable was certainly the one begun at Scott with the French and Mexican artist Jean Charlot. Charlot was a distinguished printmaker, muralist, and authority on pre-Columbian art. During the 1920s he had been a member of the group of Mexican populist artists that included Rivera, Orozco, and Merida. By the time he taught at Bank Street for a brief stint during the mid-thirties, he had also made several brilliant forays into book illustration. Among these was a picture book compilation of Toltec, Aztec, and Spanish legends retold by Amelia Martinez del Rio, *The Sun, the Moon and a Rabbit*.

Charlot shunned all attempts by critics to distinguish between "high" and "low" art. Making books for children, he asserted, was no less serious and dignified an activity than fresco painting. "A painter accustomed to run the gauntlet of grown-up criticism," he would later write, "should not expect an easing of the ordeal as he switches to children as his onlookers. . . . Shorn as they are by nature of their parents' pretense, children do meet by instinct the artist's exacting requirements as regards picture books."[25]

John McCullough met Charlot through the writer Anita Brenner, whose collection of Mexican folk stories, *The Boy Who Could Do Anything,* Scott published with pen-and-ink drawings by Charlot in 1942. Anita Brenner had a distinctly low opinion of the here-and-now style of books for the young, which she called the "Beep beep crunch crunch" school of children's literature.[26] (Scott's decision to publish folklore books for older children did not in itself mark a departure from Bank Street orthodoxy, though it came at a time when Lucy Mitchell and her colleagues were themselves showing greater flexibility in their views on fantasy literature.)

Charlot agreed to Scott's invitation to illustrate a new manuscript of Margaret's, a bedtime lyric called *A Child's Good Night Book,* in which animals go to sleep one by one in the way natural to each: "The little fish in the darkened sea sleep with their eyes wide open. Sleepy fish. The sheep in the fields huddle together in a great warm blanket of wool. . . . Sleepy sheep . . . "[27] The spare, telegrammatic text offers comfort by calming the listener with repeated sounds and phrases and by conferring dignity on the mere fact of being at home at the end of the day: "And the cars and trucks and airplanes are all put in their houses—in dark garages and hangars. Their engines stop. Quiet engines." Careful not to refer to inanimate machines as sleepers, Margaret, in the best Bank Street way, achieved an uncomplicated poetry for the very young which intensifies reality without contradicting known facts.

Margaret's manuscript had come to Scott in the casual way that the old friends still did business; she had simply telephoned John McCullough one day and announced that she needed a hundred dollars—would he please "come by and see what you would like to buy" of her current stock of unpublished work.[28] The text of *A Child's Good Night Book* was scribbled on the back of an envelope. McCullough, having made his selection, presented the author with a hundred-dollar bill. The next day he sent Margaret a contract indicating that the money tendered was to be considered as an advance against royalties.

Charlot was then living in Athens, Georgia, where he was teaching art at the state university. He and Margaret were not in touch while he worked on his prints for the book—twelve lithographs, completed during April and May of 1943, which he drew (in four colors) directly on the plates. Charlot's terse diary entries for the period—"pm: litho book" (April 7th); "Scott . . . satisfied" (May 29th)—give no hint of the difficulties he wrestled with before arriving at his finished designs.[29] Years later he would tell an interviewer of his exasperation on contemplating the line of text which reads "Night is coming. Everything is going to sleep." How was he to depict "everything" (Margaret had intended this to mean all the animals in creation) in a single image? "I was a little mad at the author," Charlot recalled, "for that particular page."[30]

More than any other of her collaborators, Charlot shared Margaret's commitment to an aesthetic that merged the elemental pith and candor of folk art with modernist verve. Childhood was the theme of several of Charlot's most evocative prints; the image of the child represented for him, as it did for Picasso, Klee, and others, pure possibility and creative renewal. His powerful totemic figures and electric pastel colorwork expressed a joy-in-being that seemed well attuned to what Margaret, in a biographical note written for Harper, called the "young child's most excessive awareness."[31] As a poet of the primitive, Charlot was an illustrator with few peers in the picture book realm.

When Margaret returned to Vinalhaven that following summer of 1943, she went for the first time not to her old quarters at Long Cove but to an abandoned quarrymaster's house that she had been gradually making over for herself and would soon buy. The Only House, as she called it, was the only home Margaret ever owned. It was not, of course, the only house on the island (the population of Vinalhaven when she purchased the property in the mid-forties was just over 1,600) and some islanders were said to have been a bit irked by the name she chose for her summer haven. Describing it to the Hurds, Margaret managed to convince them that it occupied a separate island unconnected to Vinalhaven. "Later," Clem remarked, "I found it wasn't true."[32]

The native islanders, in turn, had their fun with her. Passing Margaret out on the water one day, a lobsterman tossed a scrawny fish into her boat and shouted across to her, "Well, Maaagrit, there's your supper."[33]

Her neighbors soon learned, however, to respect her for her tenacity and physical stamina, two qualities required of them by local conditions but which they did not as a rule look for in "summer people." Islanders were touched by a certain fearless vulnerability in Margaret that led her, at times literally, to venture into turbulent waters. On fogged-in days, some fisherman always took care to go by her house to make certain all was well there. Mr. Ames delivered her firewood. Others kept up her supply of fresh lobster. Margaret herself made sure that her larder was well stocked with champagne, fresh cream, imported cheeses, and other such necessities. "Comforts aren't for me," she told a visitor, "luxuries are."[34] No one would have called the Only House comfortable, but it was an extravagance from end to end—the world made over in its chief occupant's ineffable image.

Dozens of friends visited the Only House over the years. Most came by the Rockland ferry. From the boat landing to the house itself was a brief walk along a path in the woods. A white rabbit—a cast-iron Victorian doorstop—stood watch by the Only House's entrance, which opened onto a narrow pantry-lined stairway leading upward to the main rooms.

The house was a small pearl-gray clapboard affair with white trim, perched on high ground so as to afford its original occupant, the quarrymaster of the Bodwell Granite Company, an unobstructed view of the loading dock that was now Margaret's private pier.

There were three compact floors in all: the ground level, over the crawlspace, with a workshop and comfortably furnished guest room; the middle floor, where Margaret had her bedroom, a living room—study and kitchen; and under the eaves, the attic, which served as another guest room.

Homey and extravagant touches were mixed unpredictably throughout the house: an orange satin fin de siècle divan in one corner, an old-fashioned crank victrola in another. The narrow, low, wood interiors suggested a ship's quarters—or a "coffin," as Leonard Weisgard thought.[35] (He spent weeks at a time there, sometimes by himself.) The Only House was not wired for telephone service or electricity, and when a fog moved in, completely enveloping the house, one might feel quite convincingly in a world of one's own.

Few details at the Only House had been left completely to chance or the elements. Rainwater for bathing was collected in a large tin basin on the roof. The well doubled as a refrigerator, with various ropes leading down into it tagged "Butter," "Milk," and so on. One pulled the rope for the thing one wanted and, with luck, up it came.

Bottles of wine could sometimes also be pulled from this remarkable well, and Margaret liked to surprise visitors on picnic hikes through the woods by absently reaching down into the running stream beside them to fish up a properly chilled bottle just as thoughts were turning to lunch. When wine was wanted at the Only House, she might also send a guest outdoors with certain instructions: "Go past the big black rock. Turn left and walk about eight paces. Look down and you'll see a stone that looks like it might be loose. It is. Lift it up . . . "[36]

There were three outhouses on Margaret's property, each positioned for the sake of the view. As the Only House had no indoor plumbing, a mirror had been nailed to one of the apple trees in the yard, and a pitcher and basin were left out on a battered Victorian washstand. First-time visitors would be surprised on opening the drawers to find the freshly laid supply of scented soaps and toiletries of Margaret's "Boudoir."

Margaret kept her typewriter in the living room by a window looking out on the sea, with a view of the small outcropping of granite and spruce that she would write about as "The Little Island." Beside the window was a door that opened onto a sheer fifty-foot drop (a gale having long ago blown away the original wooden stairway) to the rocky shore below. There was a Hitchcockian hint of menace about the door that opened onto nowhere, which Margaret called "the Witch's Wink" and above which she had posted a sign reading "Mind the View." From inside, the door framed a breathtaking scene with yachts, herring boat fleets, and seal herds all passing in a kaleidoscopic procession.

On a section of wall directly opposite the Witch's Wink Margaret had hung a collection of small mirrors, each differently framed and made flush with its neighbors, so that when the door was open each mirror reflected a different image of the sea to produce endlessly shifting effects of multiple perspective and light. To step before the wall was to glimpse oneself as fragmentary, ever-changing, harlequinesque—"plural," in Margaret's own word.[37] It was as characteristic a work of Margaret's protean imagination as was the Only House itself.

In Maine Margaret pursued a life of pure sensation. Mornings, she plunged in the buff into the icy waters off her granite pier, an exercise for which few guests shared her enthusiasm. On some such occasions local fishermen would wander by in their boats, calling out, "Maaagrit, can you use some lobsters today?"—hoping, of course, to catch a glimpse of their tantalizing neighbor.[38]

Margaret picked rosemary to hang over her windows and sweet fern to use for scenting the Only House's mattresses, and she enjoyed showing off her knowledge of local woodlore for friends. There were troublesome spots in that knowledge, however. A root tea she prepared one day for Dorothy Warren, her first caretaker's wife, had a horribly acrid taste. Another time, during a walk in the woods, Margaret mistook poisonous dogberries for blueberries. Dorothy Warren's castor oil and care may have saved her life.

Although Margaret found the island's calmer pace of life deeply restorative, quite a few of her New York friends became restless sitting for hours in silence on the Only House's porch with her lobsterman neighbors, waiting for the few words the local men might utter concerning the condition of their boats or the weather. Margaret took mischievous delight in observing her guests' attempts at coping with Maine living. If there was childishness in this, there was also comic theater. Few visitors looked back at their misadventures on Vinalhaven without a grin. Charles Shaw, who was glad to leave the Only House after a few days, was perhaps typical in his reaction: "M.W.B.'s house and land has really [*sic*] beauty and true nature unadulterated. I fear for me, I miss plumbing and hot water. Also the early morning noises [the groaners, screeching gulls and the like] are, alas! too much for me."[39] Other clamorous sounds disturbed the Arcadian calm as well. During the war years, the Navy took gunnery practice in the waters off Vinalhaven and Margaret's island refuge periodically resounded with the rumble of cannonfire.

From her college days onward, Margaret had never been without the wise counsel and comforting assurances of some older woman mentor. With hindsight, it seems plain that these significant friendships formed a progression, that each corresponded to a new phase in Margaret's bravely exploratory, ever-widening efforts to make contact with the most basic parts of her being. It had become Margaret's pattern to learn all she could from each woman in turn (it was certainly no coincidence that all three were old enough to be her mother) and move on.

From Marguerite Hearsey, Margaret had acquired the funda-
mentals of intellectual self-confidence and received her first real
encouragement as a writer. There was, however, a certain aloofness
about Miss Hearsey, a ladylike diffidence that gradually rendered
her a model or mentor of distinct limitations. The gentle teasing
that Margaret engaged in with her was symptomatic of the lack she
sensed. How was it possible, as Margaret had obliquely suggested
in class, to fully appreciate Chaucer (or for that matter literature
generally, or life itself) if one was embarrassed by the poet's lusty
humor, his earthy embrace of sensuality?

In Lucy Mitchell she had found a teacher who had squarely
faced the severe restrictions that Victorian morality imposed on
artistic and emotional expression, particularly in women, and who
had dedicated her life to helping to free new generations of children, teachers, and writers from all such debilitating restraints.
Mitchell provided Margaret with the inspiring example of an accomplished woman who had tried quite literally to reinvent herself, to integrate a highly developed intellectual capacity with a
long-suppressed life of the senses.

Margaret learned from her the importance of discipline in creative endeavor, a love of craft, and a certain faith in direct observation as a richly useful tool of understanding. It was also Lucy
Mitchell, of course, who had introduced Margaret to her vocation
as a writer for the very young.

But once set on her path as a writer, Margaret had matured so
rapidly that she was soon keenly aware of serious limitations inherent in here-and-now-style writing, strictures that reflected Mitchell's own limitations both as a writer and as a self-made woman.
Self-consciousness marred Lucy Mitchell's forays into the sensory
realm, thwarting the realization of her goal of a childlike spontaneity in perception. Mitchell was, when it came down to it,
temperamentally unsuited to the task she had set for herself. She
remained ever fearful of the unconscious as a wellspring of creativity. No wonder she had made a better mapmaker than poet.

Margaret met Michael Strange at a time when Mitchell's influence over her was in decline, when the prospects for a literary correspondence with Gertrude Stein had come to seem very remote

indeed, and when her personal life, both with regard to her parents and men, was in a shambles. Michael's brio and sophistication, her self-proclaimed allegiance to the emotionally liberating poetics of Whitman and contemporary writers like the late Thomas Wolfe (with whom she was rumored to have had an affair), and her famous past all, one suspects, had their appeal for Margaret. Michael Strange was indisputably a woman of the world and Margaret was certain she had much to learn from her.

Their friendship had thus begun as one of non-equals, and as their relationship took an increasingly emotional and passionate turn, the imbalance between them grew more complex. Just how, and when, that relationship became a sexual one as well is not clear. Michael Strange may well have had sexual liasons with women in the past.[40] As far as can be known, Margaret had shown no such interest before, but given her loneliness and her frustrated attempts at love in recent months and years, she probably stood open to the possibility as a worthy experiment in living—just as she had approached painting and writing for children, playwriting, and analysis.

In the spring of 1943, in any case, Margaret was giving her address as 10 Gracie Square, where Michael Strange was staying temporarily while making other arrangements following her divorce from Harrison Tweed.[41] Whether Michael visited Margaret in Maine over the summer is not known, but that October, Margaret gave up her Greenwich Village apartment and moved uptown into a railroad flat across the hall from Michael Strange's new quarters, just around the corner from Gracie Square, in the brownstone at 186 East End Avenue. Although their relationship was to remain riddled with Runaway Bunny–like, catch-me-if-you-can evasions and ambiguities, they were now living together for all intents and purposes.

Margaret's move uptown also marked a farewell to Bank Street and to day-to-day work as Scott's editor, and the beginning of a new, more independent life of working only for herself.

She had anticipated her departure from the school earlier in the year, making Bank Street a gift of her rights to three books she had written under Lucy Mitchell's mentorship, the popular *Noisy Book, The Little Fireman,* and *Bumble Bugs and Elephants.* Mitchell's personal fortune notwithstanding, the school staff was periodically left to grapple with financial crises of one dimension or another. Margaret's gift, which amounted to an annual contribution in the hundreds of dollars, represented more than a token gesture and was gratefully accepted as such. On November 19, she made a second parting gesture, appearing with Bill Scott on "The Baby Institute," a weekday-morning radio show hosted by Bank Street nursery school director Jessie Stanton. Reading from a script prepared by Lucy Mitchell and Margaret's Writers Laboratory colleague Irma Black, the threesome sketched out the basic outlines of the here-and-now philosophy:

SCOTT: A publisher's hardest problem is to persuade adults
            that books which are simple enough for a small child
            are not *too* simple.

STANTON: Possibly that's because adults forget that the every day
            things they take for granted are brand new to these
            children. Things like the taste of a baked potato—the
            color of the sky—the sound and smell of sizzling
            bacon—the feel of rain.

BROWN: And tables and chairs, plates and telephones, animals
            they know. Children love to find the "here and now"
            world they know in the heightened experience of a
            story. Because, as you say, Miss Stanton, this is a
            wildly exciting new world to them.[42]

For listeners well versed in Bank Street theory, the one surprise of the morning came when the panelists agreed that fairy tales were not necessarily unsuitable for the very young, that contrary to what Margaret herself had been taught a few years earlier, some five-year-olds might be ready for such incredible tales after all. (This depended not so much on the child's chronological age as on his or her individual backlog of experience.)

Margaret, one suspects, had always known this. She now hoped, in any case, that her career as a writer for children was about to end. Time would tell whether she would succeed in her new work, poetry and fiction writing. In this, as in much else, she trusted that the influence of Michael Strange would be a boon to her, that her revered friend would serve her as an inspiration and a shining example.

From the front room of her new East End Avenue apartment, Margaret had a direct view of Gracie Mansion, the Mayor's residence, and more particularly of the mansion's kitchen. Late at night, she teased friends, she watched Mayor LaGuardia raiding the ice box. Looking past Gracie Mansion, she could see the East River. Wishing to watch the river traffic from bed, Margaret put her bed in the front room; her commodious turned-wood Victorian four-poster nearly filled the small parlor. (Leonard Weisgard remembered the bed as a "room within a room.")[43] First-time visitors were taken aback; one felt as though one had entered the apartment by the wrong door and somehow landed in a more private quarter of the premises than one had planned.

If Margaret was pleased by the hint of a scandalous life that this arrangement suggested, she also hoped that her new home would afford her fresh opportunities for reflection and renewal. She made the apartment over into a sunlit haven where it would always be summertime. "Yellow curtains looped their rare brightness of yellow organdie over the two wide windows that looked out on the grey day and the darker grey river flowing by," she wrote in an unfinished story-memoir, "Room and a River."[44] The walls were "all white and yellow with pictures of other summers . . . Renoir's table laid . . . with fruits and wines and surrounded by the warm rosy flesh he loved so well . . . and more quietly . . . Van Gogh's apple blossoms . . . incredibly white and pink on the barren bough."

Privacy was not to be the primary feature of life at 186 East End Avenue. The doors separating the two facing apartments were generally left unlocked, and as Michael Strange was rarely without visitors, neither was Margaret. Michael may have divorced Harrison Tweed—or convinced herself that she had done so—in order to have the requisite time to herself to realize her literary ambitions, but even in solitude Michael Strange required an audience. And although no longer able to entertain on a grand scale, she kept up the pace of her social activities, both in New York and at her new weekend country home, Under the Hill, in Easton, Connecticut, which had been purchased as part of the divorce settlement. She now even boasted about her reduced circumstances, as though proof were to be found therein of her superiority to the conventions of the merely wealthy. Proud as she was that her china was the best Rockingham, she once announced to a group of guests that every piece she owned was chipped. "I have taken the things that were always kept under glass," she declared, "and am using them all!"[45]

Shuffling about the premises during the day and for evening entertainments were Michael Strange's longtime butler, Pietro Ricchi—also called "Pierre" in Margaret's shifting parlance— who divided his time between looking after the domestic needs of "Miss Brown and Miss Strange," and Mrs. Ethel Malcolm, an elderly woman who cooked and cleaned for them both.

Pietro was a tall, gauntly elegant silver-haired man. In his youth a member of the Carabinieri, the crack Italian national police, he was a figure of dignified reserve, a man for whom duty and discretion were all. Once, just as the two women were about to drive off for a short trip to Nova Scotia, Michael casually remarked that she hoped Margaret had gone to the bank because she had not remembered to do so. Why no, Margaret said, she had not gone to the bank either. At this, Pietro, who was standing solemnly by, reached into his pocket and produced a roll of bills "thick enough to have choked a horse," as a friend who was present recalled.[46]

"And how much money do you think you'll need, Miss Strange?" he asked in measured tones. He peeled off a number of bills equal to the amount specified and handed them over to her. Then he turned to Margaret with the same question.

"Well, I think I'll need a little more than that," she said, naming a sizeable figure. Pietro gave her the money without comment and off the travelers went.

Pietro was also an excellent cook, and when he took charge of the kitchen for special dinners, his reserves of patience were apt to be tested. On such evenings drinks were usually served in Michael Strange's apartment, followed by dinner across the hall. Pietro's delicately prepared northern Italian dishes, however, were more than occasionally ruined when Michael, on a jag of dazzling conversation with some guest, held up the entire party until, when the guests finally crossed over to Margaret's rooms, the food was cold.

Unschooled and irrepressibly talkative, Ethel Malcolm, Michael Strange's longtime housekeeper, could hardly have been more different from Pietro. She spoke an ungrammatical, broken kind of English but was never reluctant to answer back to her imperious employer, who doubtless enjoyed their duels in part because her own verbal superiority was assured. But Michael Strange also plainly admired Malcolm's feisty spirit—a quality which alone might have been enough to earn her a permanent place in Michael's household entourage. At times the self-styled high priestess of poetry turned to the elderly working-class woman for practical advice.

Old theater and society friends were always stopping by. The "incredible Mr. Ted Peckham" (as the *Herald Tribune*'s society columnist, Lucius Beebe, called him) was a familiar presence.[47] The son of a Cleveland industrialist who had lost his fortune in the Depression, Peckham was a born salesman. He had come to New York as a feverishly ambitious young man and through a series of brassy business ventures had installed himself as a conspicuous figure in "smart" society. Peckham ran a widely publicized society escort service, bought and sold fine furs and jewels, and occasionally even wrote a book. But he spent most of his time, it seemed, at parties, sometimes attending a half dozen in a single night, all, as he was quick to confess with a raffish glint in his eye, for the sake of "contacts, contacts!"[48]

There were a Russian prince, a French count, and assorted theater people, most of them well turned out younger men of the kind that Michael Strange had always surrounded herself with. Joseph Ryle, the advertising consultant Scott had hired to publicize *The World Is Round,* contributed a jaunty expression to the circle's private lexicon: "the noon balloon" came to mean "the latest fashionable thing" and afterwards became the title of one of Margaret's picture books.[49] To Michael Strange and these friends, Margaret became known as "Bunny." Michael was "Rabbit."

Michael Strange's children all lived in or near New York. Of the three of them, Leonard Thomas, Jr., her eldest son, had by far the simplest relationship with her. By nature a business-minded man like his father, Thomas had become a lawyer, had married and had generally fashioned a solid and independent existence. The tattered remnants of Michael Strange's glamorous Barrymore days seem not to have interested him at all, and he was less than impressed by his mother's dramatic abilities. On the one occasion when he attended a recital of hers in New York he became bored enough to attempt to coax his wife into leaving early.

In her memoir *Too Much, Too Soon,* Diana Barrymore recalled that

> Mother had made a new life for herself after her divorce [from Harrison Tweed]. She had bought a house in Easton, Connecticut, where she lived with a companion, Margaret Wise Brown, a well-known writer of children's books. Mother still lectured, but now she toured the country giving readings from the Bible, to a harp accompaniment. Though she had a career, Robin [her younger son] was the core of her existence. She literally lived for him.[50]

The passage is revealing on several counts, not least for Diana's having mistaken her often distant mother's weekend house for her principal residence. More significant is the simple acknowledgment, however oblique, of Margaret's importance in her mother's life. At the same time there was a complicated sort of truth to the assertion that Michael Strange "lived for" Robin. She had always doted on him with what friends recalled as an almost cultish fervor. It is as though she had resolved, Pygmalion-like, to make a masterpiece of her younger son. She had imagined (perhaps "projected" is the better word) a brilliant career for him in the arts. But Robin rebelled, removing himself first to Vienna, then London, and eventually to a house of his own near New Milford, Connecticut, where, his stepsister wrote,

> he was living in a fashion that can only be compared to that of Henry VIII. He was the master of the manor: guests were entertained day and night, weekdays and week ends. . . . Mother was unhappy about him. . . . His shining career . . . had never materialized. His friend Tyrone Power had gone on to great things, but Robin had become an eccentric country squire, trying to live a fifteenth-century life in the twentieth century.[51]

Margaret, one suspects, was asked to endure many reminders of Robin Thomas's prior claims on his mother's affections. Even when considered merely as a promising "work," she would never fully eclipse Robin in Michael Strange's eyes.

Margaret and Diana Barrymore seem to have maintained a respectful distance from each other, with Margaret genuinely wish-

ing the best for the volatile, troubled young actress. In the letters
to Michael Strange in which Diana's name appears, Margaret always had a kind word to say about her. [52] As for how Margaret may
have been perceived by Diana and her stepbrothers, a recollection
of Leonard Thomas, Jr.'s widow, Yvonne, who attended many of
their parties, is something of a clue. Yvonne Thomas could recall
Margaret only as a shadowy presence within the group. [53] As a
daughter-in-law whose relationship with Michael Strange turned
cordial only by stages, she may well have had her own reasons for
not being more attentive to Margaret's contributions on such occasions. But it was also plain that Margaret felt out of her depth
in the company of Newport-bred Oelrichs, and of Thomases and
Barrymores, and tended to listen more than to put herself forward.
The more frenetic the social whirl, the more isolated Margaret was
apt to feel in its midst.

Having given up her office at 69 Bank Street, which had never
amounted to much more than a desk, Margaret now worked at
home. Not surprisingly, this arrangement proved problematic.
Once, for instance, when an editorial assistant from Doubleday
came by to review a set of page proofs with Margaret, Michael
Strange suddenly burst into the room and in deeply theatrical tones
announced, "Diana is coming!"[54] The young publishing aide was
suitably impressed by her brush with celebrity. Margaret, for her
part, soon realized she would need a separate work place. Accordingly, with the help of her Bank Street friend Jessica Gamble, she
found a quiet (and characteristically idiosyncratic) writing studio a
mile or so from her apartment. Cobble Court, as the curious structure was already known, was an early nineteenth-century wooden
farm cottage, incongruously left standing in a hidden courtyard behind the rowhouse block at York Avenue between 71st and 72nd
streets. [55]

Evenings, Jessica used the two cramped upper-floor rooms she
had rented there as a workshop where she made finely crafted children's toys—wooden tugboats and the like. Margaret rented the
equally compact ground floor rooms, which had waxed brick floors
and, as her only heat source, an open hearth. As Margaret worked

by day and Jessica by night, the two friends rarely saw each other, which on the whole was probably just as well. What Margaret most needed was a place in which to be alone from time to time. At Cobble Court, where even city street noise ceased to exist, she had found at least that much solitude. (After about two years, in late 1945, Jessica became engaged and made plans to move to Connecticut, and Margaret took over the whole of the little house.)

Her intentions notwithstanding, Margaret continued to write children's books and to do so at an extraordinary rate. Many of her new manuscripts—Noisy book sequels, *Horses* (for which she devised the pen name Timothy Hay), and others—still displayed the direct influence of Lucy Mitchell's ideas about patterned language and direct observation. At the same time, however, Michael Strange's forceful personality was bound to effect Margaret's work and her view of her work in a variety of ways. Unfortunately, much of the toweringly willful woman's impact was to prove damaging. Henceforward, when Margaret experienced her periods of professional self-doubt, Michael stepped into the breach to confirm her sense of the smallness and insignificance—compared to the true poet's art—of writing stories and poems for small children.

It was not that Michael Strange questioned Margaret's talent—only the uses to which she put her abilities. Had not the older woman, through her poetry recitals, set out to bring the high traditions of literature and music to the people of a troubled world? Michael regarded herself as a sort of latter-day Joan of Arc. She had once recited from *Saint Joan* for Shaw himself, had written a play, *Forever Young,* about her, ("to me . . . the most sacredly enigmatic personage in all history"), and had even considered naming her daughter after the martyred saint.[56] Placed beside a mission like Michael's, Margaret's own work might well have seemed a bit undersized. If Margaret benefited from the weight of her friend's criticism and reservations, as she doubtless did at times, it was by being driven to write more searchingly and more clearly.

There were unmistakable signs, however, that Margaret had begun to pay dearly for the other woman's double-edged admonishments to excellence. At Harper, some new manuscripts were drawing an unaccustomed level of criticism from Nordstrom's staff. In one internal report a reader commented that Miss Brown's recent stories had become overly "symbolical," that in striving for double planes of meaning, the author seemed to have lost touch with the imaginative impulses that gave her best work its extraordinary vitality. [57]

One such story, "War in the Woods," was intended as a patriotic fable of democratic values. The bears who inhabit the forest of this tale have just won a war against their fellow creatures and promptly issue a decree that all animals must live like bears. When this leads to food shortages, the bears order the others to live like any animal *but* themselves or bears. When this policy results in chaos, they tell the animals to go back to being themselves again and shuffle off for their winter hibernation. "As a lesson in democracy," Harper's reader commented, this was a "very sad and inconclusive thing." [58]

Margaret could not have escaped feeling the war's threat and sadness, and this might well have been enough to prompt her to attempt such stories, but she had never been comfortable in the teacher's role. Now, however, under Michael Strange's informal tutelege, she felt a growing obligation to make some contribution to the greater good. Asked on a publisher's questionnaire to indicate her wartime service, she replied in earnest "writer of children's books." [59]

The most original of her "war efforts" was a picture book project that did not get much beyond the rough draft stage, primarily, one suspects, because it violated so completely the juvenile book world's unwritten taboo against openly presenting wartime concerns to toddlers. Margaret's proposal for "The Bomb Proof Bunnies," a book on civil defense for preschoolers, displays her characteristic alertness to the small child's point of view:

> One of the most frightening things an adult can do about air raids for a child, it seems to me, is to evade the issue or keep a strange silence about it all. So a child, quick to sense adult fear and nervousness, is terrified again by the unknown or an evasive unrealistic answer. This book would hope to provoke much practical discussion between parents and their children under five. And because it is once removed to a world of carrots and beets and bunnies and mice, it might be less terrifying and equally practical as it would be to read them the standard air raid precautions. [60]

At about this time, Margaret decided to revive an old manuscript that Louise Raymond, Ursula Nordstrom's predecessor at
Harper, had rejected years earlier, a lyrical allegory of the creative
process called *The Dark Wood of the Golden Birds*. A Writers Laboratory colleague had dismissed the piece in its original incarnation
as "an overripe tomato," and Margaret herself had once described
the story as an uncertain experiment "toward a new direction" in
her work.[61] Resubmitting *The Dark Wood* to Harper in the first
weeks of 1944, Margaret added an epigraph taken from Michael
Strange's poem *Resurrecting Life:* "Somewhere was a white bird
once / And singing upon a golden bough—"[62] She had begun to
view the book as an homage to her friend. As such, it now assumed
still greater significance for her.

Nordstrom's staff reader, however, in a report dated February
29, proved to be no more enthusiastic about the piece than Raymond had been. "I'm sorry that Miss Brown is so attached to this
ms," the reader stated, "because I don't think it is good"; the author was doubtless "terribly sincere . . . but that is one of the big-
gest dangers of terrible sincerity. . . . Your thought becomes so
personal that you can no longer know what it would mean to an
outsider."[63] Margaret, it was noted respectfully, was a writer who
had inspired many imitators; it was a pity in this instance to find
her imitating herself.

None of this was communicated directly to the author. Nordstrom decided to override the staff recommendation to reject *The
Dark Wood* because Margaret had made it clear that her future
relations with Harper might stand or fall on the manuscript's fate.
The editor made a notation for her files that "MWB is revising
drastically"; she hoped, in vain as it turned out, that her favorite
author would be distracted by other projects and redirect her energies elsewhere.[64]

By early March of 1944, Margaret was feeling secure enough
in her new life to give a small dinner party for the purpose of
introducing Michael Strange to some old colleagues and friends.[65]
Lucy Mitchell and Rosie Bliven (and to a lesser extent their husbands) had been among the constants of her Bank Street days, but
Margaret had seen little of them since moving to East End Avenue.
Her former teacher must have appreciated the evening's laboratory

aspect, the experiment of bringing together representatives of such different sides of Margaret's world. All the same, it is difficult to imagine what the first here-and-now author and the author of *Who Tells Me True* might have had to talk about—what feelings, apart from skepticism, mutual suspicion, and proud disdain, could have passed between them.

The following month, Michael Strange's younger son, Robin Thomas, died. Robin, who was twenty-nine, had been distraught following the suicide of a man he had been romantically involved with, Billy Rambo. While languishing in his Connecticut home, Robin had taken a fatal dose of alcohol and pills.[66]

Apparently, in fashioning her idealized fantasy of Robin, Michael Strange had left him little room for an independent sexual identity. On the contrary, she had meddled in his relationships, by some accounts even seducing his male lovers. With Robin's death, her deeply distorted feelings for him seem only to have intensified. With the real Robin no longer around to interfere as it were, Michael Strange was now free to refine her fantasy version of him to cultish perfection. As Diana Barrymore recalled,

> Mother . . . brought Robin's furniture to her home in Easton. She . . . reconstructed his bedroom and study there and made a shrine of them, keeping everything exactly as it had been when Robin was alive—his paintings, his antiques, his books and music. Even his desk remained as it had been the morning he was found dead. Mother had made only one change. She took Robin's bed into her bedroom and placed hers in his—and for the rest of her life she slept in Robin's bed. She still wept when she talked of him.[67]

Margaret dutifully accompanied Michael to Indianapolis, where Robin was buried in accordance with his wishes in the Rambo family plot. The part of comforter and consoler had once again fallen to Margaret, as it had when she first met Bill Gaston, and for all the emotional upset this must have entailed, the role still suited her. Yet for all the kindness and concern that Margaret was so capable of and so ready to offer, the death of Robin almost certainly marked the beginning of the slow unraveling of the affectionate bond between Michael and herself.

1. *(left)* Margaret, circa 1917.
Courtesy of Westerly (R.I.) Public Library.

2. *(below)* Margaret with her sister Roberta *(left)*, the Brown family collie, Bruce, and other pets.
Courtesy of Westerly (R.I.) Public Library.

3. *(right)* "Tim" *(seated, front row, pointing to basket)* and Dana Hall School classmates, 1928.

Courtesy of Marion Ristine Bowes.

4. *(above)* Margaret riding at Hollins College.

Courtesy of Susanna P. Turner.

5. *(right)* Margaret in May Day Court costume, Hollins College, 1932.

Courtesy of Susanna P. Turner.

6. Graduation portrait, Hollins College, 1932.
Courtesy of Fishburn Library, Hollins College.

7. Marguerite Capen Hearsey.
Courtesy of Fishburn Library, Hollins College.

8. Lucy Sprague Mitchell.

Lucy Sprague Mitchell Papers, Rare Book and Manuscript
Library, Columbia University.

9. Children at the City &
Country School in
Greenwich Village playing
with the blond wood unit
blocks developed by Lucy
Sprague Mitchell's colleague
Caroline Pratt, spring 1937.

Courtesy of the City & Country
School, New York.

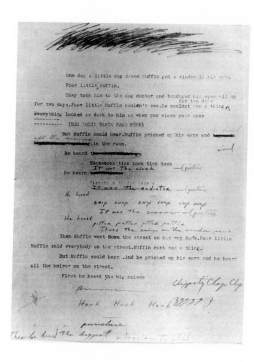

10. Revised typescript page for *The Noisy Book.*

11. From *The Noisy Book* by Margaret Wise Brown.

12. *(right)* Leonard Weisgard.
Lotte Jacobi Archives, University of New Hampshire.

13. *(below)* Charles Green Shaw at home with one of his collection of tobacco figures.
Charles Green Shaw Papers, Archives of American Art, Smithsonian Institution.

14. *(right)* Esphyr Slobodkina.
Photograph by Ted Tessler, courtesy of Esphyr Slobodkina.

15. *(left)* Michael Strange during the period of her marriage to John Barrymore.
Photograph by Hugh Cecil; Charles Green Shaw Papers, Archives of American Art, Smithsonian Institution.

16. *(below)* Publicity photograph of Michael Strange, 1948.
Culver Pictures, Inc.

17. Illustration by Leonard Weisgard from *The Little Island*. The island pictured closely resembles one which could be viewed directly from The Only House.

18. Ursula Nordstrom.

19. Garth Williams.

20. *(above)* The Only
House.

Photograph by Consuelo Kanaga
(1894-1978). *Untitled.* Negative 2⅝
x 2½ inches. The Brooklyn
Museum 82.65.1820. Gift of the
Estate of Consuelo Kanaga
through the Lerner Heller Gallery.

21. *(right) Margaret Wise's*
Boudoir.

Photograph by Consuelo Kanaga
(1894–1978). Negative 2¼ x 2¼
inches. The Brooklyn Museum
82.65.1277. Gift of the Estate of
Consuelo Kanaga through the
Lerner Heller Gallery.

22. Jean Charlot, 1951.
Courtesy of the Estate of Jean Charlot.

23. From *Little Fur Family* by Margaret Wise Brown.
Illustrated by Garth Williams; copyright 1946 by HarperCollins Publishers, reissued 1984; reprinted by permission of HarperCollins Publishers.

24. Clement, Thacher, and Edith Thacher Hurd in Vermont.
Courtesy of Thacher Hurd.

25. The "great green room."

Crispin's Crispian lived in a two-story doghouse in
a garden. And in his two-story doghouse, he had a
little fur living room with a warm fire that crackled
all winter and went out in the summer.

His house was always warm. His house had a chimney
for the smoke to go out. And upstairs there was
a little bedroom with a bed in it and a place for his leash
and a pillow under which he hid his bones.

And there was plenty of room in his house for the boy
to live there with him.

NO CATS

No Dogs

26. In his illustrations for *Mister Dog*, Garth Williams modeled
Crispin's Crispian's house on Margaret's own Cobble Court.

Reprinted by permission from *Mister Dog* by Margaret Wise Brown © 1969 by Western
Publishing Company, Inc.

27. Margaret with Crispin's Crispian.

Photograph by Consuelo Kanaga (1894–1978). *Margaret Wise Brown K.* Negative 2½ x 2½
inches. The Brooklyn Museum 82.65.1833. Gift of the Estate of Consuelo Kanaga through
the Lerner Heller Gallery.

During 1944 Margaret published eight new books: *Big Fur Secret,* with illustrations by a French architect and friend, Robert de Veyrac (Harper); *Black and White,* illustrated by Charles Shaw (Harper); *Horses* (Harper), published under the pseudonym Timothy Hay, with illustrations by "Wag" (Margaret's friend Dorothy Wagstaff); *Red Light Green Light,* a Golden MacDonald book, with illustrations by Leonard Weisgard (Doubleday); *Willie's Walk to Grandmama,* with illustrations by a young artist named Lucienne Bloch (Scott); two of the Heath readers that she and Lucy Mitchell had labored over together, *Animals, Plants and Machines* and *Farm and City;* and, most interesting of all, *They All Saw It,* with photographs by the well-known wildlife photographer and adventuress, Ylla.

Ursula Nordstrom was always eager for unusual new material to publish. One day a friend of hers, Leo Lerman of Condé Nast, brought by a parcel of photographs of animals viewed up close, all taken in the crisp, clear, subtly ironical style for which Ylla had come to be known. Ylla, born Camilla Koffler, was a photographer of animal portraits whose work appeared in *Colliers'* and the *Saturday Evening Post.* She had a remarkable knack for capturing her subjects in moments of heightened attention, with something very much like human expressions on their faces. Lerman deposited the photos on Nordstrom's desk, suggesting that she find a way to make a book of them. For six months the resourceful editor had been stumped. Then Margaret, come to talk with her about other business, inquired about the photographs, and on hearing of Nordstrom's dilemma, volunteered to see what she could devise.[68] The result was a brilliantly silly bit of manic nonsense, in which the reader is given to understand that each of the various animals in Ylla's images has been witness to *something*—the mysterious "It" of the title. Margaret, of course, left it for the very last page to reveal the object of fascination.

In February of 1945 Margaret and Michael Strange toured California together. From Los Angeles they traveled north to San Francisco, where after staying together for a time at the Mark Hopkins Hotel, with its fine views of the city from high atop Nob Hill, they made the spectacular two-hour drive south along the coastal road to the storybook town of Carmel-by-the-Sea. In Carmel they stopped at the Cypress Point Club for a "whirl" of socializing, as Margaret wrote Ursula Nordstrom, and met "everyone" from the local tycoons and priests to the poet Robinson Jeffers. [69]

Margaret paid the northern California coastline her highest compliment, declaring it "the wildest and most beautiful and haunted [setting] west of the west of Ireland."

A priest at the Carmel Mission asked her, "My daughter—what are you in love with?"

"The Fabulous, Father; I'm in love with the Fabulous," she replied.

"And so am I, my child," he said, "and have been all my life." [70]

Among the books that Margaret brought along on the trip were two with green dust jackets: Catherine Drinker Bowen's biography of Oliver Wendell Holmes, *Yankee from Olympus,* and Joseph Campbell's and Henry Morton Robinson's *Skeleton Key to Finnegans Wake,* both published within the last year. Margaret folded the two covers into an envelope and sent them to Ursula Nordstrom with a note indicating that the enclosures were printed in the precise shade of green she wanted for the jacket of her forthcoming picture book, *The First Story.* [71]

Another letter written to Nordstrom from San Francisco likewise illustrates the care with which Margaret attended to every detail of the design and illustration of her books. The editor had just mailed her sample proofs of a picture book due to be published that fall, *The House of a Hundred Windows.* This book, Margaret's highly innovative young children's introduction to art appreciation, was to be illustrated with lithographs in two colors by Robert de Veyrac.

> The sheets for *The House* came and I have looked at them a Hundred times. I think the color is wonderful—It is more than a two color book—[it has] the very quality of stone. . . . I will be glad to see the end sheets with it and the whole thing bound in a bright red, I hope or yellow. I only wish the Title Page had been a reverse plate. A little of this unbleached paper goes a long way. Also I don't like

that copyright stuck outside the square. Couldn't it have been printed on the edge of the window-sill. And I wish the title had been placed with more skill—It all sprawls like a country newspaper add [*sic*] for a patent medicine. . . . And on the title page and in future copy for adds [*sic*] and jacket flaps, try and keep the The in the title in small caps as it makes the title too long and hard and as a word has no importance in the title.[72]

While in San Francisco, Michael and Margaret had another of their rather routine and predictable quarrels. Margaret, sent packing by her companion, went to stay with Posey Hurd, who was still in the city doing wartime service.[73]

Posey had an apartment on Scott Street, with a view of San Francisco Bay. It did Margaret a world of good to see her old friend and to know again Posey's accepting, even-tempered camaraderie. Before long they were collaborating on a book.

In honor of the occasion, Margaret proposed a joint pen name, Juniper Sage. She explained that this was a variation on Junipero Serra, the eighteenth-century Franciscan friar responsible for establishing the California mission system, including, of course, the mission at Carmel that Margaret had lately visited. Posey was to be considered as the "Sage" of the team. Margaret would be "Juniper."

"Sage" did the legwork for *Five Little Firemen,* stopping by a local firehouse to inspect the equipment and question the men about their duties—all in the best Bank Street way. Margaret, in contrast, simply disappeared for hours at a time, once returning to the Scott Street flat with a taxi crammed with wild mimosa. On another occasion, just as Posey was sitting down for a work session, Margaret decided to take a bath. Posey, understandably irked, declared that she would start without her. From behind the closed bathroom door Margaret would shout an occasional line that "belonged" in the book. It was for "Sage" to determine just where in the book the line belonged. More often than not, Margaret's contributions were in fact worthwhile additions—witty, brilliant touches. In this way, *Five Little Firemen,* which Simon and Schuster published under its Little Golden Books imprint in 1948 (under the coauthors' actual names), got written that spring.[74]

Margaret was back in New York in May in time for her thirty-fifth birthday, which she marked by joining the Authors League. This, too, was a part of her personal "war effort." Henceforth she became increasingly involved in efforts to demand fair treatment from publishers for herself and the many artists with whom she worked.

That summer Michael Strange pleased Margaret greatly by offering to give her a new Kerry Blue terrier pup.[75] But trouble soon arose; on a visit to the kennel, Margaret found herself drawn to a pup that Michael immediately sized up as having an unusually wild and contrary temperament, even for a Kerry. She proceeded to tell Margaret in no uncertain terms that she simply would not agree to buy her that particular dog—she must choose another one. Margaret, standing her ground, replied that it was to be that dog or none at all, that if her friend was unwilling to pay for the animal, she was quite prepared to do so. Whoever won this latest test of wills, Margaret left the kennel with the Kerry she had wanted from the first. She gave him an extravagant name recalled from Shakespeare's *Henry V,* Crispin's Crispian.[76]

Often a canny judge of character, Michael Strange had been quite right about Crispian. Several of Margaret's friends eventually caught a bit of the dog's fury on the trouser leg, and Crispian put her to considerable expense, tearing up upholstery and generating veterinarian's bills for the repair of other dogs he periodically attacked in the street. Crispian was a terror—and this, doubtless, was what Margaret liked about him. He was the wildness of small children, hers at times to rein in, at other times hers only to keep pace with. One day on Park Avenue, Crispian broke his leash and tore down the street. Racing after him, Margaret herself became—as Leonard Weisgard, who witnessed the scene, thought—somehow "not human," transformed, as she closed in, with absolute certainty and quickness and ease, on her quarry.[77]

CHAPTER SIX

IN THE
GREAT
GREEN
ROOM

There is a loving way with words
and an unloving way. And it is
only with the loving way that the
simplicity of language becomes
beautiful.

MARGARET WISE BROWN

For Clement Hurd, as for many others
in the American armed forces, the war wound down slowly, with
months of delay following Japan's surrender on September 2, 1945
before the return trip home. By the time Hurd steamed into San
Francisco Bay, rejoined Posey, and boarded a train for New York,
it was almost Christmas. Margaret, eager for the couple's company, had contacted Posey about the welcome she was preparing
for them; she sent specific instructions. On their arrival at Grand
Central Terminal, the Hurds went directly to Cobble Court.

When their train finally pulled in at one o'clock in the morning, it was fifteen hours late. The city had just received a light
dusting of snow, and the midtown streets, at that hour nearly deserted, had taken on the dim, brownish cast of an old daguerre-
otype. It was an ethereal, wonderland setting, or so the couple

might have thought but for their grueling cross-country trek. The new arrivals climbed into the back of a cab and were duly deposited at 1335 York Avenue. After passing through an unlocked door, they made their way precariously through the dark, damp, narrow hallway they had been told to expect, and which smelled of newly washed laundry. Bone tired, they shared a little gasp of amazement when at last they reached the open courtyard within and came face to face with Margaret's implausible wooden cottage. The front door had been left unlocked, and once inside they found a fire ablaze in the sitting room hearth, fresh flowers in profusion, fur rugs, fur coverlets, and fur blankets scattered everywhere, and a warm bed for the night.

Margaret herself was nowhere in evidence. She left the travelers to themselves, to get what rest they could after their long journey. Late the next morning, she appeared at the door to rouse and greet them, and to show them how to survive in the antiquated house. She then gave them the keys and invited them to consider Cobble Court their own for as long as they wished.

Posey Hurd had continued to write intermittently during the war. But for Clem, the war had meant a complete disruption of his career just at a time when his reputation as an illustrator was being solidified with the publication of *The Runaway Bunny* and the Hurds' own early collaborations. Like many another returning soldier, he worried about the difficult task of picking up where he had left off professionally. Margaret had provided for this, too. Early in the new year, on her instructions, Harper mailed Hurd the spiral notebook she had submitted to Ursula Nordstrom—the manuscript of *Goodnight Moon*.

Margaret had written the text one morning upon waking and had telephoned Harper's editor for a first impression, which had been quite positive. On the notebook's title page, Margaret gave the author as "Memory Ambrose"—a name Hurd recognized as that of a friend's housekeeper. Beneath the pseudonym she had written "With pictures by Hurricane Jones"—the name of a character in *Five Little Firemen* (the yet unpublished story that Margaret and Posey had worked on in San Francisco the previous spring). Hurd understood that "Hurricane" was meant to indicate himself. [1] In the letter that accompanied the notebook, Nordstrom asked him to make a sample drawing and send it on to her as quickly as possible.[2]

Margaret began the new year of 1946 resolved to straighten out her increasingly complex business affairs. As a first step, she wrote Evelyn Burkey at the Authors League requesting advice concerning her "involved situation," as she called it, "of being an over prolific author with several publishers."[3] She was, she said, about to sign a raft of new contracts with Simon and Schuster and wanted to be certain not to "cross wires" with her various other houses by unnecessarily limiting her right to publish with whomever she pleased.

Margaret had come down with a bad cold and was not taking care of herself. When Ursula Nordstrom phoned her only to find that Margaret had blithely stepped out for the afternoon despite her urgings, Nordstrom dictated a few double-barreled words of motherly and businesslike concern: "I must ask you to take better care of your health, at least until you have a satisfactory text for the LITTLE FUR FAMILY."[4]

The book to which Nordstrom referred was not an ordinary production. Margaret's nearly full-size mock-up of the book was less than three inches tall. The editor had agreed to this unusual format as well as to Margaret's still more extravagant proposal that *Little Fur Family,* which concerned the adventures of an animal child in a wild but fundamentally safe and secure world, be bound in real rabbit's fur.

Harper's editor had a particularly strong motive just then for trying to accommodate Margaret's most ambitious flights of fancy. Far and away the most significant development in American children's book publishing during the last half dozen years had been Simon and Schuster's establishment of its Golden Books imprint. Starting in 1942, in the midst of wartime, the firm had introduced a series of full-color picture books that sold for substantially less than other children's titles then on the market (a mere twenty-five cents as compared to an average of a dollar seventy-five) and were every bit as good in quality.

A relatively young, maverick firm during the forties, Simon

and Schuster had already pioneered in the mass-market paperback field with its immensely successful Pocket Books. It now applied similar methods to the sale of unprecedented quantities of juveniles; it aimed to print and sell several hundreds of thousands of copies of each of its titles per year (as against the very few thousands that the older houses considered a respectable showing). The idea was to market books in heavily trafficked, nontraditional locales, like five-and-ten-cent stores and drugstores. Greater sales volume made unusually large press runs feasible; this in turn led to economies of scale that lowered the overall production costs and justified the low retail price of the books. Nordstrom was not alone among editors at the older mainstream houses in fearing that talented authors and illustrators would be lured away by the advantageous terms that Simon and Schuster was able to offer. The contracts that Margaret had recently signed with the firm were as good an indication as any that Nordstrom's fears were well founded.

At the same time there were compelling reasons for Margaret to maintain her relationship with Harper. Ursula Nordstrom was without question the most creative juveniles editor of her day, a figure within her often rather undervalued field of Maxwell Perkins' stature in the literary world of Hemingway and Fitzgerald. Like Margaret, she approached her work in a spirit of adventure and was continually energized by the prospect of publishing genuinely innovative material. If a book struck a blow at the emotional squeamishness that characterized a great deal of what passed for children's reading matter, then so much the better. When Anne Carroll Moore attempted to suppress the publication of E. B. White's first juvenile fantasy, *Stuart Little,* on the grounds that a story about a normal American mother giving birth to a mouse was indecent, Nordstrom would have none of it and proceeded as planned.[5]

Nordstrom was a very demanding but equally fairminded editor. A marginal notation from her of "N. G. E. F. Y."—not good enough for you—had put a momentary chill in many a heart, but the end result was quite often a better book than the author in question had thought possible. A voluble, emotionally complicated person, Nordstrom thrived on turmoil and generally saw to it that some lively joke—or argument—was always floating about

the Harper "Tot Department." ("Somebody answer it," she liked
to say when the telephone rang. "That could be the next Mark
Twain!")[6] However, once she decided to commit herself to an
author or illustrator—as she had committed herself to Margaret
from the start—there were few lengths of patience, dedication,
and friendly concern to which she would not go. Margaret was
hardly alone in making a trusted confidant of Nordstrom, one of
the very few people to whom she told her troubles. This almost
familial level of trust carried over constructively into the writing
and illustration of any number of the books Nordstrom published.
Her authors and artists wanted passionately to please her, to re-
ward her faith in them. It was not by chance that Harper published
Margaret's two most deeply felt and fully realized picture books,
The Runaway Bunny and *Goodnight Moon.*

A little elegy and a small child's evening prayer, *Goodnight
Moon* is a supremely comforting evocation of the companionable
objects of the daylight world. It is also a ritual preparation for a
journey beyond that world, a leave-taking of the known for the
unknown world of darkness and dreams. It is spoken in part in the
voice of the provider, the good parent or guardian who can summon forth a secure, whole existence simply by naming its particulars: "In the great green room / There was a telephone / And a red
balloon / And a picture of— / The cow jumping over the
moon."[7] And it is partly spoken in the voice of the child, who takes
possession of that world by naming its particulars all over again,
addressing them directly, one by one, as though each were alive,
and bidding each goodnight. Nursery rhyme reality and here-and-
now reality seamlessly merge, as in a small child's own thoughts.
Odd fellows are joined and familiar pairs are bound together with
unexpected poignancy. The nameless, imponderable "nobody" is
bid goodnight, along with the homeliest of everyday things,
mush. The sense of an ending descends gradually, like sleep.

The book's haunting immediacy arises from the authority with
which it fixes an irreducible type of human experience. In Mark
Twain's *Adventures of Huckleberry Finn,* an older child catalogs his
provisions as he prepares to set out alone on his river journey. For

Huck, as Alfred Kazin has said, it is as though the very act of naming his belongings has the power to drive out loneliness and fear:

> I took the sack of corn meal, and took it to where the canoe was hid and then I done the same with the side of bacon, then the whiskey-jug. I took all the coffee and sugar there was and all the ammunition; I took the wadding; I took blankets and the skillet and the coffeepot. I took fish-lines and matches and other things—the gun and now I was done. [8]

The full-grown "veteran Nick Adams" of Hemingway's leanly carved psychological stories shows the same "compulsion," as Kazin calls it, to "say about certain things—*only this is real, this is real, and my emotion connects them.*"[9]

Margaret herself was given to similar compulsions, a certain habit, for example, of squinting intently at the flower market as though to extract the last measure of enjoyment from the beautiful things she beheld. At home, whether in New York or Maine, she often had some small brass object or other in her hand to polish as she chatted with a visitor. At the Only House she saved her cooking grease and rubbed it into the floorboards and furniture. Polishing an object, as the philosopher Gaston Bachelard observed, can, like naming it, become an act of praise:

> When a poet rubs a piece of furniture—even vicariously—when he puts a little fragrant wax on his table with the woolen cloth that lends warmth to everything it touches, he creates a new object; he increases the object's dignity; he registers this object officially as a member of the human household. [10]

To mix the fat of the animal one has eaten with the table one has eaten it on; to be the hunter becoming the hare; to merge subject with object, the actor with the acted upon, each element with its corresponding opposite—this, again, was Margaret, through her robust imagination, struggling to make contact with the world beyond the self. *Goodnight Moon* is a here-and-now story, but one so supercharged with emotion, with so freewheeling a sense of the fantastic as an aspect of the everyday, as to render it a cunning transparency of Bank Street ideas and their opposites. Margaret's simple-sounding bedtime story was her most incisive response to the old Fairy Tale War.

After two refreshing weeks at Cobble Court, Clem and Posey Hurd moved to the country, to rented quarters in West Cornwall, Connecticut. All March and for the rest of the spring, the artist worked on the illustrations for *Goodnight Moon.*

Margaret had not given the illustrator many suggestions for the art, as she sometimes did. She simply scribbled a few brief notes and, along with them, offered inspiration in the form of a small color reproduction of Goya's dashing *Boy in Red,* which she pasted onto the notebook's front cover. At the top of the first manuscript page, Ursula Nordstrom had written, "Interior of room—fabulous room . . . Little Boy Bunny in bed." To which Margaret added, "Show both pictures on the wall that are to be enlarged on the following pages." [11] (These were the pictures of the Cow Jumping Over the Moon and the Three Little Bears.)

The first sample drawings of the great green room met with disapproval on various counts; so did the second ones. In March, Hurd submitted a third set of sketches, noting that the room had been restored to its "original hugeness" and that "the bunny is young and the old lady is loveable if not 'fairy story.' "[12] One reason, he explained, that he could not make the woman in the rocking chair look more like a fairy-tale character was that he thought of all such women as witches, which he was sure was not what Nordstrom had in mind. If, the artist suggested, Nordstrom did not yet feel the bigness of the room, it was probably for technical reasons, which would be cleared away with the laying in of colors. He, for one, thought the book was "shaping up well."

Much remained to be done, but by then certain key elements of the design had been established. There would be a sequence of full-color views of the great green room. These would grow progressively darker and would alternate with smaller spot drawings in line and gray wash. As the work progressed, Hurd seemed to summon up everything he had thus far done as an artist. The child's room, rendered in flattened perspective, has the airy, floating quality of a stage set. The shafts of light cast by the child's lamp give the heightened emphasis of theater spotlights. The festive color scheme and distilled, geometric approach to image making owed something to the influence of Hurd's former teacher, Fernand Léger. At the same time, the unstudied candor of the illustrations suggests the manner of the American primitives. And when one looks closely at the book on the rabbit child's shelf, one can see that it is a copy of *The Runaway Bunny*.

One evening in March, Margaret, the Hurds, and Doubleday's editor, Margaret Lesser, boarded a train in New York for Danbury, Connecticut, for the dinner party Leonard Weisgard was giving to celebrate his and Margaret's new book about Maine, *The Little Island*. Weisgard had just completed his paintings for the book, which Doubleday planned to publish that fall.

Dressed in a favorite old brown corduroy jacket, Weisgard met his guests on the station platform and drove them out past the town to the Victorian house set back from the road against a backdrop of tall maples, which he had purchased during the war.

It was an evening of small recognitions. When the Hurds had last seen him, almost four years earlier, Leonard still lived in Manhattan. Their friend had evidently taken well to country life; his house, which the visitors investigated while dinner was cooking, was a treasure trove of ingenious oddments, the illustrator's burgeoning collection of American folk art and other beautiful things. There seemed to be antiques everywhere, the well-worn, homey kinds of objects they all enjoyed rooting around for in New England jumble shops; often, however, the piece inquired about proved of startlingly recent vintage. Weisgard, it seemed, had taken up a second hobby besides collecting—that of "making . . . new antiques."[13] Clem and Posey were delighted by the idea (Clem would one day fabricate a series of bogus Hurd ancestral portraits).

After a hearty roast turkey dinner, Weisgard led his guests into his small studio, where the paintings for *The Little Island* hung in a row along the wall. Clem, Posey, and Margaret Lesser had all visited Margaret in Maine at one time or another and had seen for themselves the curiously carved bit of granite and greenery in Penobscot Bay that she had once named Starfish Island. Here again, in Leonard's richly toned images, was that island haven with its wildflowers, massed rock formations, sea birds, seals, and changing light.

Her fullest attempt at capturing in words her love of the Maine coastal islands, *The Little Island* was a special book for Margaret. Although the text falters in its plot line, it is in other respects a poised and exquisite piece of work, a poet's notations of seasonal change: "One day . . . the seals came barking down from the north . . . And the kingfishers came from the South to build nests . . . And the gulls laid their eggs . . . And wild strawberries turned red. Summer had come to the little Island."[14]

Ample, delicate, vividly imaged, *The Little Island* points to a sense of the world as a vast and various place in which one need never feel dwarfed or overshadowed: "And it was good to be a little Island. A part of the world and a world of its own all surrounded by the bright blue sea." Here in this passage is another of Margaret's searching attempts at a definition of selfhood, a definition framed in her characteristic mode of paradox, but a paradox from which all fear of loneliness has been safely removed. There is none of the muted desolation of *Red Light Green Light*. *The Little Island* reveals Margaret at her most comforting, accepting, and resolute.

In the middle section of the text, however, she turns impatient, apparently confused as to her own intentions, and the beautifully crafted hymn to the natural order, merging the Romantic sensibility with here-and-now fidelity to observed fact, breaks down. The island itself speaks, becoming involved in a portentous dialogue with a naive and rather skeptical kitten. The kitten cannot believe that the island, which appears to stand all on its own, is actually a part of the larger world. A talking fish assures him that the island is, in fact, connected to earth and that in life some matters are to be taken on faith even though they cannot be verified by observation. As philosophy, and more particularly as a rebuff to lessons learned at Bank Street about the supreme value of direct experience, *The Little Island* is a murky affair, mixing geography pell-mell with fantasy and metaphysics. Once again, Margaret's conscious striving for a big statement had not worked; grandiose gestures simply did not become her as a writer.

On Saturday morning, April 13, Charles Shaw took a mid-morning train to Westport, Connecticut, where Michael Strange and Margaret were waiting for him, their weekend guest. They made the short drive to Under the Hill. The house seemed cold and a fire was lit as the three friends sat down to an early lunch. They passed a pleasant afternoon in animated conversation spurred on by rounds of drinks. After a lull for napping and reading, they had cocktails, and then dinner at the long library table in the main room. At one end of the table, as always, stood a dramatic four-foot carved wooden Virgin Mary; at the opposite end were massed banks of Madonna lilies. Later that evening Shaw wrote in his diary: "Immediately after dinner M. S. attacks M. W. B. in most violent and abusive terms. M. W. B. leaves the room and building. Talk with M. S.—standing in front of fire—for about three hours. We then say good-night to M. W. B. who had gone to bed in small house. Turn in 12:30."[15]

At noon the next day Margaret and Michael appeared outdoors together, joining Shaw, who had been painting and sketching in the brilliant sunlit morning. The three friends found a shady spot on the grass and took a leisurely breakfast of eggs and coffee. What remained of the day was given over to long walks and violet picking, cocktails, and supper. A little after nine o'clock Margaret and Michael dropped Shaw off at the Westport station, then returned together to Under the Hill.

Such eruptions of verbal cruelty as Shaw had witnessed were evidently a common occurrence between the two women, with Margaret, always on the receiving end, generally all too ready to accept Michael's harsh judgments of her as the clear-eyed if painful insights of a more knowing woman.

Not long after this episode, with its nearly instant reconciliation, Margaret decided the time had finally come for her to present Michael with a copy of the manuscript she had dedicated to her, *The Dark Wood of the Golden Birds*. At Harper, Ursula Nordstrom (whose own opinion of the book had not changed) entertained no illusions as to the extreme importance Margaret attached to this project; she was also well aware of the cruel cuts that her now more than occasionally tearful author periodically received from the book's dedicatee. Perhaps, however, it was only an innocent mix-up when Harper dispatched the wrong typescript. [16] Margaret had wanted her gift to arrive as a surprise by May 23, her own birthday, but instead of *The Dark Wood of the Golden Birds,* Michael Strange was sent a copy of the rejected "War in the Woods."

On July 2, before leaving for the Only House, Margaret attended the wedding of Dorothy Wagstaff, the friend she had tutored long ago. Dorothy had been a child then; she was now twenty-four. Her groom, Louis Ripley, was a businessman from a prominent Connecticut family. A dozen or more years earlier, Margaret had watched as her schoolmates married; now the wheel had begun to turn for the generation of her younger friends. Margaret, who was Dorothy's maid of honor, was happy for her, but if a note sent to the Hollins *Alumnae Quarterly* a year earlier is any indication, she may have been feeling a bit unnerved as well. "How many children have you?" she had teased her classmates, with a shrillness and an edge that for once betrayed her insecurity. "I have 50 books." [17]

Alone for much of the summer of 1946 on Vinalhaven, Margaret decided the Only House needed a paint job and hired a local jack-of-all-trades, auspiciously named Billy Brown, for the job. Approaching the project with the same ironclad determination she applied to her books, she explained to the unsuspecting young handyman that she had a certain luminous shade of gray in mind for the exterior walls.

The mixing of paint, as overseen by her, proved to be an arduous business. In the end, however, Billy Brown would reach much the same conclusion about Margaret that her illustrators did—that she was as purposeful a manager and muse as she was demanding. Billy, like many another habitually skeptical islander, took a keen liking to her. And when Margaret gave him his next assignment—to cut off at the halfway mark the legs of all her furniture—he proceeded unquestioningly, however odd the idea would have sounded coming from anyone else. When the work was done, the Only House's previously cluttered small rooms had been transformed into calmer and airier places of unexpected intimacy.

The Little Island had long since gone to the printer; Margaret would see the first bound copies on her return to the city in early fall. In the meantime, she had Starfish Island to herself, clearly visible from her writing desk window, and the cat (named Bobby because he bobbed his head) that she had made into the book's hero.

In August, she wrote Ursula Nordstrom, "How is my great fur editor? I am a hermit not working at all." (By now Nordstrom knew not to take such declarations literally.) "You will be relieved to hear that I have written no more stories [that is, short stories for adults]. I don't think I ever will again."[18] That Margaret had shown her "serious" fiction to Nordstrom suggests, again, the full extent to which Margaret had let Nordstrom into her confidence.

"It is so damned beautiful up here," she went on, "that existence and just watching seem enough. I have a sailboat and I can't sail, but I sail anyway. I have lots of old fisherman friends—in their 70s and 80s and I like them." She closed her ramble by inquiring if the editor had succeeded in her search for a house in the country.

Nordstrom, who had been on vacation for most of August, found Margaret's loosely scrawled communication in the heap of paperwork that had accumulated in her absence. "I love to think of you sailing," she wrote back warmly, "and wish we could have a publicity picture of our Little Golden Little Fur author at the tiller."[19] Nordstrom did not miss the opportunity to make a gently pointed reference to Margaret's activities under contract with Simon and Schuster. Although there was little that she could do to counter that development directly, she might at least take comfort in the knowledge that Margaret was not likely to sign an exclusive contract with any one publishing house.

The first copies of the fur-bound *Little Fur Family* were due to arrive at Harper's offices, she reported, in less than a week. She would immediately rush a copy to Maine. The printer had not done as good a job as had been hoped for, but everyone, she said, was finding the book irresistible. The advance sale was expected to run to at least fifty thousand copies, an enormous figure—by all but Golden Books standards. Nordstrom was not taking the competition for her favorite author's services lightly.

Never had Ursula Nordstrom's inspired editorial instincts revealed themselves more clearly than in her choice of Garth Williams to illustrate *Little Fur Family*. Williams had made an auspicious debut in the children's book field as the illustrator of *Stuart Little*. Prior to that, he had been a sculptor and had done some work for the *New Yorker*, where his bravura comic drawings had caught the attention of E. B. White.

Like Margaret, Williams was quick-witted and independent—a dedicated artist full of mischief and beans. When he and Margaret got together, new book ideas flew back and forth so freely that they soon adopted the joking precaution of "copyrighting" their more promising utterances in mid-sentence.[20] As the illustrator of *Little Fur Family*, Williams understood perfectly Margaret's technique of abstracting characters to the point where only the reader can say precisely who or what they really are. As painted by him, the book's family of creatures might be part bear, part puppy, part human. With no exact real-world counterparts, the members of the little fur family are all the more liberating as springboards to fantasy.

In 1945 the most widely publicized birth in America—Stuart Little's—was an imaginary one. But an unprecedented rise in the nation's annual birth rate was itself fast becoming one of the most conspicuous facts of postwar American life. Since the turn of the century, the number of live births recorded in the United States had remained fairly constant, at approximately 3 million per year. But between 1945 and 1946 more than 3.4 million live births were counted. The following year the figure jumped to 3.8 million, and the numbers continued to rise for some time.

The postwar baby boom was bound to have great significance for the children's book world. One small evidence of this awaited Margaret on her return to New York in September of 1946. Bruce Bliven, Jr., had interested *Life* magazine in a feature-length celebrity profile of her. The widespread popularity of Margaret's many books was certain now to increase still further; the public, *Life*'s editors had evidently concluded, would be eager to know about the woman who was capable of writing so knowingly for their preschoolers and even for their babies.

Over the early fall, Bliven and Margaret met for a series of informal interviews.[21] Characteristically evasive about her family, she was amusing about most other matters—her idiosyncratic homes, her practice of writing first drafts on the backs of shopping lists and other odd scraps of paper, her delight in playing mischievous tricks on her friends.

A high point of the behind-the-scenes work came when Philippe Halsman, the *Life* photographer, appeared at Cobble Court. Halsman arrived on a brisk autumn day with a princely entourage of attendants bearing his lighting equipment and tripods in elegant camel-colored leather golf bags slung over their shoulders. The photographer stood back from the fray as his well-trained technicians executed his orders. When all was in readiness, he stepped casually up to the camera and recorded image after image of his agreeable subject.

Margaret and the photographer took to each other immediately. Between poses there was much laughter as Halsman received the full impact of Cobble Court, which Margaret had decked out in its furriest. She told her visitor that she sometimes wrote with a quill pen, that she preferred swan's plumes but at the moment had only a blue heron feather on hand, that she often wrote in bed. He photographed her scribbling on a legal pad by a favorite student lamp given her by Leonard Weisgard and by the telephone she sometimes used to phone in a book she had "dreamt" the night before. She mentioned having published fifty-three books in her ten years as an author. Duly impressed, the photographer asked to see some of the books, arranged them face up on the floor and persuaded her to lie down to be photographed in the middle of her work. The new fur-covered *Little Fur Family* merited a photograph all its own. Margaret paused to be photographed in the crooked entranceway to Cobble Court as she opened the door for Crispin's Crispian.

Accompanying Margaret to one of the final *Goodnight Moon* editorial meetings, Bliven was bemused by the cryptic exchanges between the author and her colleagues.

"I like the rabbit," someone ventured. "He has real sleepiness."

"Yes, but I'm worried about the yarn; it loses personality and softness."

Such impressionistic "doubletalk," Bliven wrote, was "essential, probably" to a medium in which visual images had to be precisely matched in mood and intention to the author's words.

In these last meetings several minor changes and one major revision were considered. A framed map on one of the great green room's walls was replaced by a scene from *The Runaway Bunny*—a whimsical self-advertisement and, apart from that, an amusing idea. On Nordstrom's instructions, the udder of the Cow Jumping Over the Moon was reduced to an anatomical blur so as not to disarrange the fragile sensibilities of some librarians—the "Important Ladies," as she called them. By far the most contentious discussions centered on the question of whether the child in the paintings (and presumably the old lady as well) ought to be depicted as a rabbit or more straightforwardly in human form. Hurd, it was decided, was better at drawing rabbits—and so rabbits it was. [22]

In Margaret's dealings with publishers, there had always been occasional minor flare-ups of impatience and temper. But such incidents occurred more frequently now and were more likely than before to leave residues of disappointment and injured pride. Michael Strange's self-serving exhortations to higher standards doubtless fueled Margaret's dissatisfaction. At the same time, however, Margaret was learning to use her considerable power within her field to safeguard the artistic integrity of her projects from mishandling by others less skilled and less sensitive. There had been a literal level of emotional truth to Margaret's flip remark to the effect that her books were her children. She was more determined than ever that every detail of her work be handled with proper care.

A new contentiousness was particularly evident in her relations with William R. Scott, Inc. Others besides Margaret had detected, and doubtless also contributed to, the changed atmosphere at Scott. As Clement Hurd recalled, in the early days everyone there "worked together closely, so it was difficult to say who contributed what to which book. Later, when we all had more confidence and were beginning to feel successful, it was more difficult to collaborate." [23]

William R. Scott, Inc. was still a small publishing house by

New York standards. In 1946 the firm published nine titles as compared to two or three times that number of juveniles brought out by older companies like Dutton and Doubleday. But Scott had long since ceased to be a casual family operation within which a privileged few—Margaret first among them—had been elevated to the status of honorary members of the clan. Late in the war years, before he and John McCullough entered the service, Bill Scott hired someone from outside the family, Lillian Lustig, as the firm's new president. Lustig had previously worked for Pocket Books, Simon and Schuster's mass-market paperback division. To continue growing, Bill Scott realized, his firm would have to move closer, in a business way, to the publishing mainstream.

Now, when Margaret phoned Scott's office, she as often as not found herself on the line with a stranger. Worse than that, when she received the first copies of *The Little Fisherman* (a 1945 title), her most recent book with Scott, she discovered to her dismay that four lines of text had been dropped from her manuscript and others changed—all without her knowledge. Thus it was with considerable apprehension that she telephoned Scott on returning to New York from Maine in early September, 1946 for assurances that a similar surprise was not in the offing with her next project. The editorial assistant who answered the phone sounded unconcerned; after all, she said, the changes made in *The Little Fisherman* had been of "no importance since the book was selling."[24]

"Of course I hit the ceiling," Margaret wrote Lillian Lustig,

> and had every right to a second bounce on the phone [with Lustig herself] the other evening. If it ever happens again, and it never has happened with any other publisher but Scott, that will naturally be the end. In spite of certain pretentions in your catalogue—which by the way I called up to tell you I thought by and large superb—a writer still writes the story and an artist draws the pictures and I am too old a hand to be told in your letter "The type must go with the pictures and must fit the page size." . . . Obviously. . . .
>
> I didn't mean to go into all this because I am in perfectly good spirits about it all. [Obviously.] So let's have lunch some time.[25]

Her relationship with Harper remained good, so good in fact that Margaret routinely showed Ursula Nordstrom her new work before submitting it elsewhere. However, she was also determined not to let Harper take her services for granted, and to keep Nordstrom on the run. And Margaret knew that to do so she had only to make an occasional reference to Simon and Schuster. Thus, in a sporting mood she and Garth Williams telegrammed Harper on October 26 with an ultimatum which, though obviously meant as a joke, still served her purpose:

> HAVE OFFER FROM SIMON AND SCHUSTER TO TAKE ON IMME-
> DIATE PRODUCTION OF 250,000 COPIES OF LITTLE FUR FAMILY
> IF YOU ARE NOT ABLE TO FILL IMMINENT INCREASED DEMAND
> FOR COPIES DUE TO LIFE'S SIX PAGE FEATURE ARTICLE ON
> BOOK APPEARING NOVEMBER 10TH. WIRE REPLY IMMEDIATELY.
> APRIL FOOL BUT WITH INTENT.[26]

Nordstrom, who had little trouble recognizing this particular bolt from the blue for what it was, scribbled in the margin "very funny,"[27] but she also ordered her staff to determine whether *Life* had in fact scheduled the piece. The magazine, it turned out, had not yet done so. Margaret having made her point and Nordstrom having effectively stood her ground, the two friends were soon back on the best of terms. Before long they would share a good laugh over a report from a mother whose little boy had held open his fur-bound copy of *Little Fur Family* at dinnertime and tried to feed the book his supper.

Children's Book Week, celebrated with posters and special events at libraries and bookstores around the country, came in mid-November. This was the week when the New York Public Library announced its annual list of recommended children's books. In the fall of 1946, anticipating her exclusion from the list (only one book by her, *A Child's Good Night Book,* illustrated by Jean Charlot, had received this important endorsement), Margaret wrote a caustic note to Ursula Nordstrom from Under the Hill. The Book Week poster slogan for 1946 was "Books Are Bridges," a catch phrase meant to suggest the power of books to help unify a world so recently torn apart by war. Margaret insisted, however,

> if I were a child, and saw [on posters] "Books are Bridges" I'd go
> out and make channels of diverted water from a stream through the

sand and stretch the Books across the little streams for my imaginary armies to march across. . . . If I were a child and read "Books
are Bullets" I and other children would throw them at each other.
If I were a child and read "Books Around the World" I would wish
that I had gone myself— If I read "Friendship Through Books" I
would have wished the Book weren't there between us. Therefore
for next year I propose "Books are Books" for the Book Week slogan. A fact any child would recognize with relief.[28]

As a literary document, Margaret's letter was an impromptu
display of her astonishing facility for generating variations on a
theme without end; as an emotional artifact, it was an amply justified exercise in the venting of spleen. Margaret's association with
the progressive education movement, through her work at Bank
Street and for Scott, had long since rendered virtually all her books
suspect in the eyes of Anne Carroll Moore, her successor, Frances
Clarke Sayers, and others in the New York library establishment.
Their suspicions had proven remarkably durable and as Margaret
well understood, her newly forged association with Simon and
Schuster was likely only to make matters worse. The librarians
bitterly attacked Golden Books as an ominous intrusion of commercial values and practices into the uniquely important and gentle-spirited realm that they themselves had long labored to hold
above crassness. Although these critics correctly understood the
potential for mediocrity on a massive scale that a publisher like
Golden Books represented, they had closed their minds to the possibility that the new publishing imprint might produce some
books of lasting merit.

One reason for their rigid outlook doubtless boiled down to a
question of power. The traditional publishers of juveniles relied on
public library purchases for as much as a half (or even more than
half) of their total annual sales; hence the extreme importance of an
endorsement of a given book by a librarian like Moore. But by
marketing its lists directly to parents, to the customers of drugstores and five-and-dimes, Simon and Schuster had for all intents
and purposes factored the librarians out of the system. From the
librarians' standpoint, where culture had flourished anarchy might
soon reign.

The *Life* piece by Bruce Bliven, Jr., which appeared in the magazine's December 2 issue, provided Margaret with another opportunity to reach over the heads of "the Important Ladies." Whether or not her books were chosen for the library lists, millions of parents were now certain to know about them. (*Life*'s cover that week featured Ingrid Bergman as the valiant Joan of Lorraine; Margaret, having fought a few battles of her own lately, probably considered herself in good company.)

Bliven's article presented a portrait of an attractive, sophisticated, unpredictable young woman who led a charmed, fairy-tale existence while racking up publication credits on an Olympian scale. As of that fall, the journalist estimated, at least 835,000 copies of her various books had been sold. In October alone three new titles had appeared: *The Little Island, Little Fur Family,* and *The Man in the Manhole and the Fix-It Men* (the last a collaboration with Posey Hurd under the joint pseudonym Juniper Sage)—each published under a different name and by a different house. For the curious book buying public, Bliven offered appealing snapshot impressions of the eccentric "Miss Brown" sporting "some startling accessory . . . a live cat in a wicker basket or a hat made out of live flowers."[29] Readers may also have been surprised by Bliven's assertion that the apparent simplicity of Margaret's books was not evidence of a literary deficiency—that, on the contrary, simplicity was the very hallmark of her wonderfully distilled poetic writings for the very young.

The most startling portion of the piece for most readers, however, was undoubtedly Bliven's tongue-in-cheek account of the author's rabbit hunting activities, which he juxtaposed with Margaret's thoughts about small children:

> Whenever anybody points out that beagling is an odd hobby for a girl who lives by writing books about the hopes and aspirations of small furry creatures, Miss Brown is likely to counter with: "Well, I don't especially like children, either. At least not as a group. I won't let anybody get away with anything just because he is little."[30]

Intended primarily as a defiant swipe at the librarian-critics who deprecated her work and whose own more sentimental view of childhood Margaret scorned, these remarks had evidently been weighed carefully. On October 7, while the article was still in manuscript, Margaret sent Evelyn Burkey a copy at the Authors League, with a request that she look the piece over: "I would like your opinion and so would he [Bliven] on the advisability of it. It seems a little risky to me."[31] No sooner did the profile appear, in early December, than the predictable uproar began.

"Did you see the article on Margaret Wise Brown in *Life?*" Louise Seaman Bechtel (critic and former Macmillan editor) wondered in a letter to Bertha E. Mahony at the *Horn Book.* "Surely 'everyone' saw that!"[32] Bechtel, who had been an early and steadfast champion of Margaret's career, ventured no further comment except to say that she did not ordinarily read *Life* herself; three friends had clipped the piece and sent it to her. Bechtel had been preparing an essay of her own about Margaret for the *Horn Book,* but, she added, sounding a bit put out, "no need to finish mine now."

Mahony, for her part, made no bones about her own view of the *Life* piece: "Such an article, I suppose, is meant as a caricature. I think it's horrible. Plain destructive for an author of picture story books for little children."[33] The *Horn Book's* editor had long since become an admirer, albeit a somewhat cautious one, of Margaret's work. One can only imagine in what caustic terms Anne Carroll Moore (who had retired from the Central Children's Room but was still a regular presence there) and Frances Clarke Sayers must have dealt with the profile.

Throughout the forties Margaret continued to have little to do with her family; such was the impact of the article in *Life,* however, that the reactions of at least two family members are recalled. Having learned from the piece that Margaret was earning ten thousand dollars a year from her books, Basil Rauch is said to have toted up the number of words in a typical annual output, divided the number into ten thousand, and concluded from the result that Margaret did indeed have a serious vocation. Her father, Robert Brown, was evidently just as impressed by the size of her income. His reaction, according to family legend, was to announce that he planned to stop giving Margaret her annual allowance. Whether he actually did so is not known. If he had, however, Margaret would almost certainly have understood the gesture for what it was, a genuine if oddly circumspect show of paternal affection—Robert Brown's brusque way of acknowledging that she had at last become her own person. Margaret spent large sums of money each year on fresh cut flowers for Cobble Court and her East End Avenue apartment. During one of her very occasional conversations with her father, he had advised her that as a writer she was clearly entitled to claim her florists' bills—were not flowers a writer's inspiration?—as a business expense on her tax returns. The remark was a bit of mischief worthy of Margaret herself. She accepted the suggestion, with mixed astonishment and gratitude, as a precious gift.

Whether Margaret's mother read the *Life* article is not known. By then Maude was living with Gratz and his wife in Ann Arbor, Michigan. She was ill much of the time. In early January of 1947, word reached Margaret in New York that Maude Brown had died.

Margaret arrived by train for the funeral in Ann Arbor, where Roberta and Gratz, whom she hadn't seen in years, met her at the station. Stepping showily, her brother thought, onto the platform, Margaret, dressed in mourning, was holding a Madonna lily.[34] It was a stubbornly Wildean gesture, the aesthete on parade, though she proceeded to conduct herself with appropriate dignity. In her conversations with Bruce Bliven, Jr., Margaret had spoken with pride of her mother's old Virginia family without mentioning her father's far more notable background of governors, senators, and judges. Perhaps, in her curiously limited way, this had been a last attempt at honoring Maude Brown, at righting the balance between her mother and her father. In any case, much was left unresolved between Margaret and Maude.

Back in New York a few days later, she found the jacket copy for *Goodnight Moon* awaiting her approval. In late March she flew down to Florida for a brief vacation and returned to the city at the wheel of a spanking new, honey-colored Chrysler Town & Country convertible. New cars were still scarce commodities in the postwar industrial northeast; she had purchased the deluxe Chrysler in St. Augustine for the princely sum of thirty-six hundred dollars. Margaret timed the trip so as to be down south for the onset of spring, and back in New York in time to see spring arrive all over again.

In San Francisco that summer, Leonard Weisgard attended the

American Library Association's first annual meeting since the war. There, on Wednesday evening, July 2, he accepted the Caldecott Medal for *The Little Island*. Weisgard had not only won the coveted prize but had also emerged in the voting as first runner-up for another picture book called *Rain Drop Splash,* written by Alvin Tresselt.

Such a double success would have been a remarkable achievement for any illustrator. Nonetheless, Weisgard's mood in San Francisco was decidely grim. For one thing, he dreaded having to make a public acceptance speech. Even casual conversation had always been a nerve-wracking experience for him. Margaret had once surprised him by remarking, accurately he thought, that when he talked he sounded "like someone translating from a foreign language."[35] Lately, he had also begun to question the validity, within the larger scheme of things, of his artwork. Had he not originally intended to paint and to design for the ballet? With bittersweet irony, the attainment of the highest recognition in his field now served to fuel his misgivings.

In his address to the American Library Association, Weisgard gracefully submerged his private doubts in a public meditation on the role of children's literature in an uncertain world. Wondering aloud whether books for the young ought to concentrate on presenting honest reflections of the world as it is, or whether they ought instead to venture beyond the bounds of realism, Weisgard asked:

> Should we think of the world as we would like to make it? Should we wish it were better, so that we could all sit back, marvel at it and at little children looking at us, all safe and secure? . . .
>
> Our adult reality is a world of precarious balance. Some of us enjoy all the ingenious complexity of today's machinery. . . . Some of us . . . yearn for the basic truth of the primitive.
>
> But those original realists, the children to whom primitive mysteries are plain and natural, are for me the most exciting examples of the curious balance that swings the world.[36]

Years later Weisgard remarked that he had learned to illustrate children's books by "learning to dance, living, breathing, being with children, with people, being alone, reading, writing, traveling, brooding, dreaming, beachcombing, wondering, and, mostly, listening to Margaret Wise Brown."[37] As a thoughtful reconciliation of the conflicting ideals of Romanticism and here-and-now realism, Weisgard's Caldecott address might almost have been written by Margaret herself.

In a touching tribute published in the *Horn Book,* the Hurds sounded a valedictory note as they speculated about their "unusually sensitive" and "restless" friend's future plans. Would he continue to illustrate, they wondered, or would he instead venture into some other phase of art or design, or simply stay at home in the manner of Voltaire's Candide and make more "new antiques for another old house?"[38]

To celebrate Leonard's success, Margaret presented her collaborator with a pocket watch, a resplendent platinum Gübelin special edition, on the reverse side of which she had had engraved the following:

Leonard Weisgard
from
Margaret Wise Brown
To keep time with
"And many a green isle still must be
In this sea of misery."[39]

The quotation, from Shelley's "Lines Written Amongst the Euganean," was an affirmation that sounded distressingly like an epitaph. At issue for both Weisgard in his broodingly intellectualized way and Margaret in her more intuitive way was the survival, in an age of mass conformity and atomic destruction, of the wild green nature of Romantic solitude that *The Little Island* celebrated.

Margaret's gift had been solemn and formal. Putting self-doubt momentarily to one side, Weisgard responded in a playful mood, presenting her with a boxful of the impressive-looking gold foil Caldecott medallions that would henceforth adorn the dust jackets of copies of their book. Delighted by her new treasure, Margaret made good use of the seals, pasting them (occasionally more than one) on the dummies of her works in progress.[40]

Later that summer, Michael Strange gave Margaret a copy of

Kathleen Hoagland's *One Thousand Years of Irish Poetry,* and a gold wishbone small enough to fit in the palm of one's hand, a good luck charm for travelers. And in mid-August Margaret flew by herself to Ireland, green isle and great green room, where she had not visited since before the war.

Arriving at Shannon Airport on Saturday, August 16, she rented a car and drove southwest with plans to spend the night in Tralee. The flight over had been comfortable and had seemed surprisingly short, though "something invisable [*sic*] in it," she wrote Michael the next day, had crept up on her, and had left her feeling exhausted two hours after landing.[41] She had pulled off the road at Listowel, taken a room at the Listowel Arms and gone to sleep in mid-afternoon. Next morning, awakened by the sound of "little donkeys [*sic*] feet bringing the milk across the square and hidious [*sic*] shrieks as some of them howled at the hot weather," Margaret inhaled the "smoky sweet smell of burning peat" and began to feel herself again. As she dressed, she watched from her window as women in black shawls and a man leading a pair of greyhounds passed in the square. After a good breakfast she drove off toward her final destination, Dingle, County Kerry, a sleepy coastal village in the oldest inhabited part of the island.

In Dingle, a village of fifteen hundred inhabitants and a different pub for each week of the year, Margaret took up lodging at Benner's Hotel, a hospitable old house frequented by the more adventurous sort of well-heeled traveler from England, the United States, and Ireland itself. Guests stayed long and returned often to the gracious small establishment, with its well-run dining room and well-kept garden, and with the ever-attentive Mrs. Benner herself always ready to minister to one's needs. From this snug haven, Margaret ventured forth each day by foot, bicycle, or car into the "wildest" landscape (as she said) that she had ever known.

"This is a world wilder than my own fantasy and that is one reason I love it so," Margaret wrote Michael from Dingle on Monday.[42] That same day, she bicycled on the coast road around the Ring of Kerry and had her first look at the mysterious, ancient "beehive" stone huts and fortifications and the Gallarus Oratory, all built without mortar and perfectly preserved from early Christian times.

Halfway to the fisherman's landing at Dunquin, Margaret saw a massed array of low-slung islands in Dingle Bay. These were the Blaskets, sparsely inhabited by a handful of stout fishermen and their families, who made the mile-and-a-half journey between the mainland and their exposed and forbidding homes in curraghs, tar-black "skin boats" of ancient design which were easy rowing in calm weather and completely useless in a storm. Margaret decided to see the Blaskets for herself, and on Thursday, August 21, left from Dunquin for a day of exploration. Landing on the largest island, she spent the afternoon hiking in the hills, which were (as it happened) overrun with wild rabbits. By day, there were spectacular views of the rugged mainland; in the evening, local storytellers held forth as of old by a peat fire in the island village.

Margaret's sojourn in Ireland had a compelling private meaning for her. Historians traced back to Kerry the earliest origins of the Irish people. To identify herself with this place was to reach beyond her immediate family heritage—problematic in some respects as that was—for a more elemental kind of belonging. It was a subordination of the personal to the archetypal, the mythic. And identify Margaret did, as is apparent from a letter written to Michael Strange a few months before her trip:

> Anyway Rab, the Bun will try to be very steady and clear headed and orderly and chic and maybe some day some one will love it for its shiny shoes and its tender heart and forgive the mercuric change of mood which is more Celtic than me and is born out of climates and races and oceans that are older than memory and that can no more change than the varying rhythms of the sea.[43]

Whether by chance or design, she had also come to a part of the world where certain place names might be imagined to have had a private significance for her. The smallest of the Blasket Islands was called Beginish, or Little Island. Twenty miles to the south, in the Atlantic off Bolus Head, a monumental rock mass rose like a tower more than seven hundred feet above sea level. Carved into the rock (by what means no one had been able to determine), a staircase led up most of that height to an ancient Celtic monastery, whose ascetic inhabitants had lived in constant exposure to savage winds. Nothing was known of the fate of these monks; they had disappeared without a trace, probably in the fourteenth century. The name of their heroic island-monastery was Skellig Michael, or Michael's Rock.

Dingle and the surrounding countryside were also full of the sort of charming incongruities that Margaret appreciated. There was a river that ran directly under a row of houses on its way through town to the sea; another river flowed gently *over* the narrow stone bridge that had been built to span it. On Upper Main Street, a flat rock nearly as long and wide as a car had been left undisturbed in its ancient resting place and the road built around it.

At Ventry, a short car drive from Dingle, Margaret walked on the beach and swam in chill water reminiscent of the waters off Vinalhaven. Grass and turf swept down to the water's edge, and one afternoon when she arrived for a swim, the cows in the near field all followed behind her in procession, ambling into the surf to cool themselves in the ninety-degree weather.

Margaret had planned to stay in Dingle for a week, but by the third day she decided to remain at least a week longer in the "enchanted friendly spot" she had found. "There are so many creatures in this town," she wrote Michael Strange, "it is certain that they would puncture the tires that would try to roll me out of it."[44]

As Margaret lingered on in Ireland, the first bound copies of *Goodnight Moon* arrived in New York.

In the meantime, Michael Strange had left for England on a recital tour. She and Margaret did not arrange to meet in the British Isles, however, and when Margaret returned to New York in late September, Michael was still abroad, with plans to remain out of the country until late November. Throughout the period of her absence, Margaret was troubled by an acute loneliness. Once, in October, she made a pilgrimage of sorts to Greenwich Village, returning to the scene of their first, relatively untroubled years as friends. In a letter to Michael begun later that day, she wrote:

You might as well know . . . what I saw on the streets—You walking down lower Fifth Avenue in the late afternoon seen to meet me. You and I walking down Tenth St. towards Fifth Ave. in the Blackout. You and I in my apartment—and Smoke—among the memories of eight years there. . . . If only somewhere there was a way to sustain this dream—the only reality I have ever known.[45]

The next evening Margaret reread this melodramatic fragment and, evidently wishing to put a happier face on things, added, "At which point MacConachie gave me a quick and real kick and reminded me that I was very sleepy and off I went." (MacConachie was one of several jester-like imaginary "creatures" who occasionally ventured an opinion or odd bit of advice in their letters.) The weather in New York was beautiful just then. It was Indian summer. While Michael Strange was away, Margaret was living full-time at Cobble Court. Earlier that day she had put Crispian into the open Chrysler and driven past 186 East End Avenue, on a second pilgrimage; without stopping to go inside, she had circled back to Cobble Court along the East River.

The next morning she attended a children's concert at Town Hall during which a story of hers, *The Little Brass Band,* was read with an orchestral setting by Walter Hendl, who conducted members of the New York Philharmonic. The performance was a success, though Margaret complained in a letter to the Authors League that only Hendl was properly credited in the program and associated publicity.[46] Back at Cobble Court, she had lunch alone except for Crispian, and was about to take a nap when Pietro burst into the house bent over with an armload of gladiolas, roses, and chrysanthemums. A neighbor of hers, he explained, had died, and the family (before leaving for the country following the funeral) had thought of her and wanted her to have the flowers.

That evening, when Charles Shaw came to dinner, Margaret served a favorite root soup of Michael Strange's. Inquisitive as always about Michael's activities, he spoke as well of Hermann Oelrich's failing health, hoping to pass word through Margaret that a visit from Michael, who had been feuding with her cousin Hermann for some time, would now be welcomed. Margaret, for her part ever the bounteous provider to worthy friends, had a new manuscript for Shaw to illustrate. The remainder of the evening, as she wrote Michael around midnight, was consumed in talk about "a pleasant lot of nothing."[47]

Nothingness—absence—was much in her thoughts as she wrote, "Nothing is new with the Bun, and No one is new with the Bun except that it leads its own funny little life more peacefully and doesn't go out of its own life into things that mean nothing quite so often. And always loves its Rabbit[.] And is your Bun . . . "[48]

Margaret had meanwhile gotten back into the social whirl of Michael Strange's circle of family and friends. Despite a bad cold, she attended a party given by Diana Barrymore. Over the last weeks, Margaret wrote in another letter,[49] she had been working very hard on "books and records and order," and on a film version of *The Noisy Book* (a project that in the end did not materialize). She had overstrained herself and come down with a fever. Still, the company of friends, or the friends of her friend, seemed preferable to the recurring bouts of loneliness that now plagued her.

Diana, wearing a dramatic huckleberry velvet dress, looked "cunning and pretty and young," Margaret thought. Gypsy Rose Lee, parading showily back and forth, had just put up the outsize revers of her coat when Diana, suddenly returning from the next room, took the measure of her guest and remarked dryly, "For your chins, dear," leaving the other woman speechless.

Margaret, once the silent observer at gatherings of this kind, had evidently learned a thing or two about acid repartee. When another guest, a young woman who was planning to spend time in Paris, repeatedly pressed a more experienced traveler to recommend her to some "good French family" with whom she might stay, Margaret exploded, "Vraiment you pretentious jeune fille of thirty je-ne-sais-quoi. Fuck off."

This was the sort of arrow that Michael Strange was so extraordinarily adept at finding her mark with. It was as though for a moment Margaret had become her friend; at other moments during the long, chatty evening, she had, as she wrote, "kept walking up and down pointing to where Michael should have been and saying Who is that prominent space with the flowing hair and the dark wild eyes, and . . . kept roaring with laughter and when people asked . . . why . . . said The Hero would have just said something brilliant and clever to make me laugh."

Despite her cold, Margaret stayed on until one-thirty in the morning. The next day, upstairs at Cobble Court, she made herself some chicken lima bean soup, a scrambled egg, and an Old Fashioned, read the papers, and wrote her letter to Michael Strange, to be sent care of the Savoy in London. (Michael had not left an itinerary but was bound to turn up at the Savoy sooner or later.) Margaret urged her to stop on her way back to New York at Benner's, in Dingle, for a respite. She told again of having savored her own recent stay there, the more so—so she said—for having been there alone.

Barely over her fever a day or two later, she was feeling restless and had begun making plans to visit the Only House for a few days, probably by herself even though in early November the wind-whipped island would be a far from hospitable refuge. A passage from Michael Strange's last letter had made her unhappy, in need either of escape or reassurance.

Michael had asserted that Margaret had good reason to know that Michael loved her. Margaret wrote back on October 29,

> I don't know that Rab. You only told me once in the past year. . . . And ten days later—Crash—you said you didn't any-more. . . . There was a time I felt well loved by you and it was the warmest happiest time in my life. And I remember it. And that is all I can honestly say. Since coming back to America I have felt lonlier [sic] than I have ever felt in my life and you might as well know the truth—terribly raw and exposed. That is why I stay alone more and more—And that is why I can't rest more in a relationship that has lost the certainty it once had. I can rest in my love for you sometime. And I do. It is the center I come back to and revolve about. But loving the unknown becomes lonely some-times. . . . It is very simple. I do not know that you love me any more.[50]

That afternoon Margaret had gone downtown to see an exhibition of paintings by Albert Ryder, whose dark, mystic canvasses she had found "so pure, and so true to the halflights of the dream, and the moonlight, and the sea." Ryder, she wrote, had gone unrecognized as an artist during his lifetime and yet had remained devoted to "his dream."

"So in my love for you, Michael, I have the dream that is you and I guard it in my heart for you to come back to.—When you will." What a few lines earlier she had termed "very simple" was in reality not simple at all; Margaret had gone round in these very circles of dejection and wishful longing before.

Listlessly, she put the letter aside, took a Midol tablet, made an Irish coffee for herself, and poured a glass of soda water for a chaser. Then, returning to her letter, she easily escaped into third-person fantasy: "The Bun has disappeared into a small Irish smoke—and flown out the window and only you can find it and bring it back." And with that she fell asleep.

The next morning, feeling (or so she thought) less frazzled and vulnerable, Margaret set out in her open car for lunch at the Cafe Lafayette with a friend. However, Michael Strange's indifference toward her continued to gnaw at her, and when she found her path blocked by a crowd gathering in Union Square—traditional rallying ground of union workers, the unemployed, and other political protesters—her own powerlessness and frustration flared up in arrogant rage. Leaning out from behind the windshield, she shouted in a gravelly, muffled, belligerent voice, "Make way for the rich!" and drove on through to her luncheon appointment.[51]

Margaret amended her latest letter to Michael yet again, this time with a request for a few small luxury items which Michael would be able to purchase at a certain shop on the Boulevard St. Germaine. Then, sealing the envelope but still reluctant to let go of this only link to her friend, she scribbled a last request on the envelope: "Will you bring me a white swans feather from the Thames?" She was, she explained, putting words to Prokofiev's *Ugly Duckling* and working on a book called "The Wild Whistling Swan." She would use the feather for a pen and as her good luck.

In the meantime, Margaret's efforts at fashioning a text for Prokofiev's score proceeded haltingly. "Not only can't I read a note," she wrote Michael in her next letter, mindful of her friend's self-proclaimed talent for pairing great music with great words, "but the brain balks at it as at arithmetic. . . . The Bun's ears are drooping over it."[52] She had put aside plans for a trip to Maine. She was too tired for travel.

But when Margaret continued this latest letter, she was again resolved to appear more cheerful, more in command of herself. "The Old Bun," she declared had "gone to Newfoundland to rest its fevered head on an iceberg." A "New Bun" had appeared who was a fatalist of sorts—who knew how to "slow down and laugh" as the world rushed by.

The first weeks of November were taken up with intensive work and more socializing, including another party given by Diana Barrymore, attended by James Montgomery Flagg and Carl Van Vechten among other old friends of Michael's. "It all looked a little like the 10 Gracie Square parties," Margaret wrote Michael of the evening, "only . . . the Bun left early."[53]

Margaret reported impromptu visits with Diana (who was just then preparing to go on tour as well); a private reception for Pola Negri; an evening at the ballet to see Agnes DeMille's "Allegro" ("a bum cheap rehash . . . with Our Town Weddings Funerals and Remnants and all the old American wistful stabilities"); a few days in the country with Dorothy and Louis Ripley at their home in Litchfield, Connecticut, with a brief stopover at Under the Hill; and a noisy, glutted night on the town at El Morocco. And more letters were sent to Michael Strange care of the Hotel Savoy, London.

"I started to call you this morning," Margaret wrote late at night on Sunday, November 9, after returning to Cobble Court. "But then there was an hours [*sic*] delay so I didn't and as Shoe-button [like MacConachie, one of the imaginary "creatures"] said—leave the Hero alone in the Foreign Country. You aren't suposed [*sic*] to telephone foreign countries across Oceans, and it only disturbed last time."[54]

Margaret still belonged to the Buckram Beagles and often joined the group on their Sunday outings when she was not spending the weekend at Under the Hill. But on this particular Sunday her loneliness was such that she had thought better of venturing out with friends: "Stayed in all day and worked. I am so afraid of most people in this lonesome state of mind. Why inflict it on *everyone*."

She had nonetheless dropped in at Diana's, where another guest of the moment asked her to dinner. Although it was a Sunday night, the city streets were jammed with traffic, a circumstance that left her feeling more alone than ever. "The whole world," she wrote, "is so crazily over detailed. . . . So many big shiny cars and no reall [*sic*] gaiety—Like people singing with their own voices. . . . Rabbit—you alone seem alive in all this darkness."

A letter arrived from Michael Strange, written on board a train bound for Paris.[55] Too tired to thread her way to the dining car, Michael had made a picnic of some sandwiches that Margaret had had sent over specially. She urged Margaret to calm down and allow herself to feel strengthened and comforted by her love. A marvel of ambiguities, the letter included comments attributed to several of the "creatures," with news reported by the Baby, someone called Surly, and by Michael Strange, referring to herself in the third person as the Cricket looked on.

At one moment she urged Margaret in a worldly wise, motherly way to be responsive to the overtures of suitable men, even if the gentlemen in question were a bit dull. Earlier she had made a provocative reference to the soft back of her younger friend's neck. Periodic talk of Margaret's eventually marrying was yet another facet of their complicated, fundamentally evasive relationship. Michael Strange would one day startle Leonard Weisgard by taking him aside and with a sigh of exasperation suggesting, "Why don't *you* marry Margaret, and take her off my hands?"[56]

Early the following week, Margaret ate lunch by herself in Central Park while "looking into the bright eyes of a sparrow in the chrysanthemum boxes."[57] It was a beautiful brisk late-autumn morning with the few remaining leaves on the trees seeming somehow "primordial" to her. "The sparrow," she wrote Michael back, "kept looking at me and looking for messages." Then she appended the following poem, which she began in quotation marks as though to indicate the words were quoted from someone else (one of the "creatures" perhaps?) but which she ended without closing the quotes, either out of carelessness or because she wished the sentiment to be thought of as her own after all:

"And send me words
By little birds
To comfort me
And Oh my darling
Oh my pet
Whatever else you may forget
In yonder land
Beyond the sea
Don't forget
Oh don't forget
You married me—

To which Margaret added, as a hasty afterthought or disclaimer, "The sparrow must be crazy."

By midweek, a cable had arrived with the news that Michael Strange was feeling ill. Margaret wrote back with words of comfort and encouragment, promising to send over a "tonic of chicken and rice and butter."[58] It was now her turn to adopt a mothering tone. Michael's brother, Charles Oelrichs, was traveling with her. Urging Michael to "give him my best," Margaret added,

> and tell him to fatten you up a little. . . . I know why, now, parents keep telling their children to keep warm and get fat and not to get wet. It is all they can say to express something poor devils. And yet the Rabbit poet in me has always longed for another language before it is too late—a more fearless baldness of the heart to say the things we never say and the other never knows. Sometimes we ourselves know only too late what we wanted to say. But now I know only by indirectness by writing it into the crystal of the dream in a story or somewhere can it be said where all excess feeling comes to rest. I believe in the excess. The bird who flies too high in the light and whose heart breaks in his song to break again Spring after Spring. I never loved the autumn or the Summer as I love that excess of the Spring. And it is Spring fever I have.

In the fall of 1947, reviews of *Goodnight Moon* were generally favorable, but the *Horn Book* overlooked it and the New York Public Library did not include it on its list. In a harshly worded internal review, the library dismissed the book as an unbearably sentimental piece of work.[59] A more dispassionate and typical response, however, was that of Rosemary C. Benét, who in the December 6 issue of the *New Yorker* described *Goodnight Moon* as a "hypnotic bedtime litany."[60] The *Christian Science Monitor* declared that "in these days of hurry and strain, a book for little children which creates an atmosphere of peace and calm is something for which to be thankful. Such a book is *Goodnight Moon.*"[61] The *New York Times* and *Herald Tribune* were equally laudatory, while *Kirkus Reviews,* a journal widely consulted by booksellers, praised the book as a "really fresh idea."[62]

Sales of *Goodnight Moon* were strong in the first season, but hardly the phenomenon they were to become in later years. Just over 6,000 copies were sold in the fall of 1947—1,000 copies more than the collaborators' next book, *My World* (1949), sold in a comparable period, and 1,000 copies less than *Hello Peter* (1948), a picture book written by a relative newcomer, Morrell Gipson, and illustrated by Hurd.

Demand for the future classic declined markedly in its second year (following the usual pattern as the new season's titles move to the forefront) and leveled off at an annual rate of 1,500 or so copies until 1953, the year in which the book's gradual, steady, and eventually astonishing ascent began. There may be no specific explanation for what ensued—4,000 copies sold in 1955, 8,000 in 1960, nearly 20,000 in 1970, and onward and upward—other than that parents who knew *Goodnight Moon* and found it memorable recommended it to their friends.

In 1973, the New York Public Library, having concluded in effect that since children loved the book it must be good, reversed its original decision and placed its first order. By the time the second significant postwar rise in the American birthrate began in the late 1970s, the first generation of *Goodnight Moon*'s young listeners were fully grown and ready to read it to their children. In the 1980s, the advent of book club and paperback editions greatly accelerated the rate of increase of annual sales. By 1990 the total U.S. sale of the book stood at nearly 4 million.[63]

Margaret, alas, would live to see none of this. But for sheer numbers her many Golden Books furnished spectacle enough from the moment of publication. *Five Little Firemen,* the picture book she and Posey had written in San Francisco, sold 170,000 copies in its first year and nearly 1 million copies the following year, and remained perennially popular thereafter. Three sizeable editions of the coauthors' *Two Little Miners* were exhausted within a mere twelve months.[64] Several of Margaret's Golden Books became more quickly popular than *Goodnight Moon,* if not as widely remembered.

Goodnight Moon was one of eighteen titles on Harper's fall 1947 juveniles list. Of these, three were books written by Margaret and two were by authors whose work she had helped call to Ursula Nordstrom's attention. *It Looked Like Spilt Milk,* a clever visual counterpart to Margaret's Noisy series, was by Charles Shaw. *The Growing Tree* was by Ruth Krauss, a young poet who had passed through the Bank Street Writers Laboratory.

Also on the list was *The Sleepy Little Lion,* a bedtime book with Margaret's "running" text (as she called it) about a lion cub so drowsy that he could barely keep his eyes open. As with *They All Saw It,* she had produced the story to order around a bundle of photographs by Ylla. For the French edition, Jacques Prévert composed a completely different text for the same pictures. It was doubtless through Ylla that Margaret and Prévert later met in France. As to the last of her new Harper titles, Margaret, writing to the Hollins *Alumnae Quarterly* just after returning from Ireland, was prepared to call it "the book I care more about than all my other books put together."[65] Elliptically "dedicated to the Moon," *The First Story* had languished in manuscript for a number of years. A self-conscious attempt at imagining, as the *New Yorker*'s guardedly favorable review said, "just how things might have been after the Creation,"[66] it boiled down, one suspects, to another of Margaret's forced efforts at emulating Michael Strange's grandiosity, a "little" creation story to parallel Michael's "big" recitations from the Bible.

When most of the review media ignored *The First Story* altogether, Ursula Nordstrom wrote consolingly to Marc Simont, the accomplished young artist whom Margaret had handpicked to illustrate the book and whose services the editor was eager to retain for the future. Nordstrom snarled at the foolishness of the critics, one of whom had sarcastically summarized the plot as "Adam and

Eve as a boy and girl." Another reviewer had complained that the story had "no basis in fact whatsoever."

Nordstrom dismissed these appraisals with an exasperated "Ho hum."[67] Privately, however, her own opinion of the text could hardly have been much more favorable. Together with the as yet unpublished *Dark Wood of the Golden Birds,* Margaret had placed *The First Story* in a special category of projects that she simply demanded be published. Nordstrom had bowed under pressure and to her considerable discomfort had further agreed to assign Marc Simont to the *Dark Wood* manuscript. (Simont would not be the last illustrator to attempt to scale that particular glass mountain.)

The Harper editor was out of the office for much of November with pneumonia. Margaret celebrated her return with a surprise gift. Delighted by the gesture and grateful to be back at her old stand, Nordstrom typed out an ebullient letter of thanks:

> Ten o'clock, a.m.
> December 2, 1947
>
> Dear Margaret:
>
> The prescription from Bendel's has just arrived and I am deeply touched and very appreciative. The box created quite a riot in the Tot Department and now everyone wants to go home with me tonight and take baths in my apartment. I feel that this prescription will mean a great deal to me in the days ahead and that now anything can happen. I'll certainly have to meet a whole new group of people. No one I know at present is nearly elegant enough to go with this addition to my life, except you, of course, and *perhaps* one or two librarians.
>
> Thank you very much, dear friend and author.
>
> > I beg to remain,
> > yours sincerely,
> >
> > Ursula Nordstrom
> > who is about to
> > smell *divinely.*[68]

Later that same morning, hurrying to make the noon mail, the editor composed a hasty letter to Marc Simont, asking that they meet soon to discuss *The Dark Wood of the Golden Birds.*[69]

Margaret once again had Nordstrom on the run, no small achievement, and she remained as determined as ever to please Michael Strange. But when Michael returned from England in late November, she was preoccupied with the failure of her daughter Diana's latest marriage, her continual obsession with Robin (some of her letters to Margaret had been written on Robin's pale blue stationery), her upcoming recitals, and—for the first time—her own health. Diana, who was touring in the lead role in Maxwell Anderson's *Joan of Lorraine,* recalled this as the period when her mother's "incredible vitality" first began to wane, rendering Michael "even more irritable than before" toward her and presumably toward Margaret as well. [70] Ironically for the author of poignant, tender-hearted books like *Little Fur Family* and *Goodnight Moon,* the prospects for a secure and comforting love and a satisfying home life were, as the eventful year of 1947 drew to a close, more remote than ever.

CHAPTER SEVEN

"GRAVER CADENCES"

The beauty of the world has
two edges, one of laughter, one
of anguish, cutting the heart
asunder.

VIRGINIA WOOLF,
A Room of One's Own

Margaret Cousins, in early 1948 *Good
Housekeeping* magazine's newly appointed managing editor, cared
little for children's books and knew little about the people who
wrote and illustrated them. Cousins had heard of Dr. Seuss, but
everyone had heard of Dr. Seuss. Because her literary agent friends
had no dealings with juveniles authors, they could offer her no help
when *Good Housekeeping*'s editor in chief, Herbert R. Mayes, sent
down word to find someone capable of producing a monthly page
for the young children of the magazine's more than three million
readers.

Mayes wanted nothing in the comic book or Disney vein. He
wanted *literature,* the work of (say) another Kenneth Grahame or
Lewis Carroll, for which he was prepared to pay accordingly.
Cousins wandered off to the "moppet departments" of Brentano's

and Scribner's book stores to survey the terrain. Partly because so many of her books turned up on the shelves of both stores and partly because Cousins herself found the books "curiously irresistible," the editor decided to contact Margaret with the magazine's offer. [1]

If Cousins had read the *Life* article about Margaret published less than two years earlier, she no longer remembered it. It was without prior expectations that she telephoned the author at home and introduced herself to the elderly lady (or so Margaret sounded to her) who came on the line and spoke in a "whimsical, faraway" voice that seemed to "come and go" oddly as they talked. Cousins wondered if she had stumbled onto some sort of "retired librarian or leprechaun." (Evidently she had certain preconceptions about juveniles authors in general.) Doubtful though she was that they could do business, she made a luncheon appointment to talk over the assignment.

The editor was thus hardly prepared when Margaret arrived for their meeting a few days later all elegantly turned out, and whirled into the restaurant looking (Cousins thought) "like a fashion model."

Noting her bewildered expression, Margaret spoke up reassuringly. The home magazines had generally ignored children's needs in the past, she observed; *Good Housekeeping*'s idea was both timely and sound. Having seized the initiative, she then proceeded to outline her terms. She would submit a list of story ideas to Cousins. For those the magazine approved, Margaret would work directly with the illustrator, the text and art to be delivered well ahead of deadline to allow ample time for any problems to be resolved. She indicated her eagerness to have Garth Williams as her collaborator for all the pieces. Cousins replied noncommittally that she supposed that that could be arranged. Margaret responded that it would *have* to be.

Cousins was relieved to realize that Margaret knew so exactly what she was about. By the end of lunch they were getting on quite well. Margaret's first piece for *Good Housekeeping,* a brief story about an adventuresome kitten, titled "One Eye Open," appeared in the magazine's April 1948 issue, with illustrations by Williams. [2] She remained a regular contributor for a year and a half, keeping precisely to her original plan except that other illustrators besides Garth Williams were sometimes used or considered. Throughout their association, Cousins found Margaret to be as dependable a writer as she had ever known. Margaret in turn saw the work as a gratifying new challange. "Their big problem," she told Clement Hurd in a letter offering him one of the assignments, "is that they never know what is coming on the page opposite. . . . They want something big and simple and striking to knock the eye out of an Armour's ham add [*sic*]."[3] As for her share of the work, "the fewer words I find the better they like it but they don't want it to look like poetry"—evidently literature was to be carried only so far.

Margaret had reserved the right to collect the pieces later in book form. In the mean time, the monthly fees that she and her collaborators received were themselves comparable to a standard royalty advance for an entire picture book. "I love this *Good House-keeping* chance," she wrote Hurd. Of course it was nice to be well paid, but more important to her than the money was the fact that in her first professional relationship with the adult publishing world, she had been well treated.

In marked contrast, Margaret's dissatisfaction with Scott was at the crisis stage. On April 5, 1948, fearful that a project she had particularly high hopes for was about to be bungled, Margaret abruptly withdrew *The Important Book* from the publisher. Scott had been working on the manuscript with her for months. Because the firm had not yet signed a contract for *The Important Book* (aptly named considering the heated exchanges that were to follow), Margaret was within her rights. The ethics of her action were less cut and dried, given the time and effort the publisher had already expended and the advanced state of their contract negotiations in early April.

Bill Scott had not helped the situation when he retreated from his promise concerning the extent of expensive color printing for the illustrations. Margaret saw a potentially first-rate book in danger of being reduced to something dull-looking and ordinary. She had watched this happen before, with Scott's later editions of her *Little Fireman,* for example, which had originally been printed in five glorious colors, but then in various subsequent editions brought down to as few as two colors with far less satisfactory results. Esphyr Slobodkina eventually threatened to sue to have her name removed from the book because she no longer considered the once-splendid artwork her own.[4] With *The Important Book,* Margaret was determined to make her stand.

The next day she received an urgent letter from John McCullough setting forth the firm's formal bill of grievances in the language of an old friend betrayed. She had withdrawn the book, he said, after having led Scott to believe that only a few details remained before a contract could be signed. (Scott, as she well knew, had already made plans to feature the book at the head of its fall list.) The publisher would now be hard pressed to find a suitable replacement. He reviewed the prickly nature of their negotiations. It had been to hold down the retail price to a competitive dollar-fifty that the firm had proposed to pay only half the usual royalty (a total of 5 percent to be divided between author and illustrator) for as many copies as it would take to recoup their production costs (Scott had estimated this figure at 7,500 copies). A standard 10 percent royalty was to be paid thereafter. But on her copy of an early draft contract, Margaret had simply struck out 7,500 and replaced the figure with 2,500. McCullough wished, he said, that he had the same power to rewrite the facts at will.[5] And so the letter continued.

Margaret, however, had not acted capriciously. For some time she had felt that Scott's contracts were unfairly weighted against the firm's authors and artists. "I crossed off as ruthlessly as they seemed to ruthlessly reduce it [the royalty]," she wrote Evelyn Burkey at the Authors League. "It is too good a book to waste on nonsense."[6]

At a time when illustrators were often paid a flat fee for their services and authors received all the royalties from a book, Margaret routinely insisted on equal payment for her collaborators. It was partly for similarly noble reasons that she consulted at length with her illustrator for the project, Charles Shaw, in the days just prior to her withdrawal of *The Important Book* from Scott. In this instance, however, Margaret's benevolent impulses were overpowered by her concern that the book be removed, as it were, to a better home. Asked to dinner at Shaw's apartment on April 4, she brought Crispin's Crispian with her. Shaw in his diary noted this as unusual; Crispian would have added a desired touch of menace to the scene as Margaret, preparing for battle, made certain of her friends.[7] She took the further precaution that evening of leaving Shaw's place with his sketches for *The Important Book* securely under her arm. On April 10, having not quite calmed down from McCullough's letter, Margaret wrote Evelyn Burkey with the latest developments: "I wired him I would shoot him . . . if I were a man and that his point of view and distortion of facts I would not accept."[8]

There was a certain irony—apart from its title—in the fact of *The Important Book*'s having become the momentary focus of the growing conflict between Margaret and Bill Scott's firm. Both sides insisted on the correctness of their own positions; *The Important Book,* meanwhile, was a playful nod to the subjectivity of individual experience.

"The important thing about rain," Margaret had written, "is that it is wet." "It falls out of the sky, and it sounds like rain, and makes things shiny, and it does not taste like anything, and is the color of air. But the important thing about rain is that it is wet."[9] The manuscript was a collection of such vivid declarations, all tantalizingly arguable, which was their real point.

The crisis continued to build. In 1948, William R. Scott, Inc. was celebrating its tenth anniversary. To mark the occasion *Publishers' Weekly,* in its April 4 issue, ran a long adulatory piece reviewing the maverick small firm's brief history and many accomplishments.[10] Conspicuously absent from the article was any reference to Margaret's pivotal role as the house's first editor and as a vital link to Bank Street philosophy. Margaret was mentioned two or three times as the author of this or that Scott publication (the original *Noisy Book,* it was noted, had sold thirty-four thousand copies and was the firm's bestseller), but that was all.

When Margaret learned of this she became enraged all over again, assuming (as was plausible) that the omission had been intentional on Scott's part. Even allowing for the vagaries of magazine reporting and editing, Scott's interviewer was unlikely to have come away unimpressed by Margaret's essential contribution unless the publisher had wanted it that way. The article had gone to press well before the business about *The Important Book* boiled over; hard feelings between the author and publisher had been brewing for some time.

Margaret meanwhile brought *The Important Book* to Ursula Nordstrom, and she was promptly offered a contract that provided for the standard 10 percent royalty. Nordstrom was delighted to have the book, one of Margaret's most spirited and inventive works. She was also doubtless pleased to be the beneficiary of her favorite author's falling-out with a rival house. She moved swiftly to consolidate the advantage thus presented her.

The editor, it soon became clear, was not satisfied with Charles Shaw's illustrations. Nordstrom was personally fond of Shaw and was working with him on other projects. She was determined, however, to make *The Important Book* a major success. Accordingly, she replaced Shaw with Leonard Weisgard, who had recently won the prestigious Caldecott Medal for illustration. As part of the book's special promotional campaign, Harper printed up sheets of Important-Book commemorative stamps bearing the images of the author and illustrator. Nordstrom clearly hoped to cement Margaret's loyalty to Harper once and for all.

Once Weisgard was on the project, Nordstrom showed him a copy of a curious memo that Margaret had sent his predecessor. Shaw, while experimenting with page layouts, had altered some of the author's original line breaks. Upset to have her manuscript treated so casually, Margaret had written:

> The important thing about the break in typesetting is
> > That you break here
> > It is true that you might want to break els[e]where
> > And breaking elsewhere makes a pretty picture
> > And that you for[g]et the break is for the reader
> > And that the break is to make a pause
> > In which the child will chime in
> > And that that is the purpose of the book
> > So that the important thing about the break is—
> > That you break here. [11]

Nordstrom told Weisgard that Margaret had written several more pages of stanzas than could be fitted into a standard thirty-two-page picture book and had suggested that the three of them meet to make the final selection together.

On May 1, Margaret telephoned her Hollins friend Adeleide Dana—now Mrs. J. Gilbert Parker—and sang with her, as they did each year, their May Day class song: "We are the best of friends / Everyone agrees / Little nixie pixie folk / Helping to paint the trees!"[12] On May 23, her thirty-eighth birthday, she wrote Bill Scott declaring an end, apart from the two books then under contract with his firm, to their business relations. [13]

Considering herself free to exclude Scott from her future plans, Margaret showed Harper an outline for "The Ridiculous Noisy Book," which was to be the next in the popular Noisy series that Scott had published in the past. Here, Nordstrom thought, was a still bigger coup, assuming that Margaret actually had the legal right to change publishers in the special case of a series already closely identified with another house.

Margaret's previous contracts for the Noisy series seem to have clearly indicated otherwise. It was standard practice for publishers to protect their interests by limiting, by means of a variety of restrictive clauses, an author's right to publish related works with a competing firm. While Margaret had regularly resisted her various publishers' exhortations to offer all her work to a single house, she had always agreed to these restrictions on "similar" manuscripts. Books belonging to the same series were clearly similar.

Wishful thinking on Nordstrom's part, an overeagerness to assume that Margaret had effectively severed all obligations to Scott, may have accounted for Nordstrom's apparently hasty offer of a contract for the proposed "Ridiculous" work. A highly competitive businessperson, Nordstrom may also have seen good sport in the situation. She set aside an unusually generous advance for both Margaret and Leonard Weisgard (who was to illustrate the book) and told them that she hoped the project would bring the three of them "closer together."[14] Margaret had yet to write the book; for the time being it fell by the wayside.

Margaret had rarely been able to persuade Michael Strange to join her during her long summer stays on Vinalhaven. When Michael Strange went to Maine, it was more often to relax amid the creature comforts and high society of Bar Harbor, forty miles to the northeast, where cottages were mansions and one did not draw one's water from a well.

Margaret's spirits were high in July of 1948 when Michael Strange arrived at the Only House with plans to stay the week, but the visit proved to be an unmitigated disaster. Garth Williams and his wife were also staying with Margaret, and when all her guests were gathered together and the illustrator took out his guitar time passed pleasantly enough, but in private Margaret confided to Michael that she had been thinking a good deal lately about her mother and was wracked with guilt over not having done more to help Maude Brown during her final years.

Margaret's words aroused little sympathy; instead Michael Strange replied with impatience to confessions of remorse which, to judge from the diary she kept in a ledgerbook that summer, she had heard Margaret express many times before. Margaret, she said, had from childhood been unwilling or unable to accept her fair share of responsibility in life; she had always sought out someone to lean heavily on when the going got rough. Michael accused Margaret of having resorted to psychoanalysis out of just such an impulse to escape responsibility. In her diary she pounded away at the bombast and prattle of psychoanalysis.[15] Michael was not about to allow Margaret to use her as a crutch. She left the island early.

Margaret was still at the Only House in mid-August when she wrote Ursula Nordstrom to thank her for the sizable advances she had lately received. She reported that she was using the money to build a granite house on her property. This second house (as she did not explain to Nordstrom) was intended as a gift for Michael. Margaret had always been better at places than at people, more skilled at remaking her surroundings in conformity with her wishes and needs than at reaching a meaningful parity with others. Now she hoped, surely against all hope, that a grand gesture of this kind would suffice to induce her friend to return to Vinalhaven the following summer. To Nordstrom Margaret boasted that she had hauled "seven pink rocks 10 × 20 square"—all before breakfast. "Quite an exercise. Develops criminal muscles. . . . The wind is blowing a Hurricane—the way I like it."[16] She invited Nordstrom to visit her in September, giving detailed travel instructions that made the exhausting journey to her remote island sound easy. Replying by telegram a week later, Nordstrom declined:

SORRY CANNOT ACCEPT GRACIOUS INVITATION. WISH I COULD. HAVE IMPORTANT DATE WITH IMPORTANT LIBRARIAN ABOUT IMPORTANT BOOK. WILL WRITE WHEN I AM LESS IMPORTANT
—*Love, Ursula.*[17]

Just as Margaret was inviting Harper's editor to Maine, her Golden Books editor, Dorothy Bennett, arrived there. A hearty, capable, small woman, Bennett had at one time commuted to her Manhattan office from a houseboat. She was a skilled brick mason and carpenter. On a previous visit she had noticed that the Only House had no fireplace and decided that it needed one; she now came prepared to build the fireplace herself, aided only by an illustrator, J.P. Miller, whom she had brought along ostensibly to discuss new projects.

In Rockland Bennett purchased bags of cement, a thousand bricks, and a trowel. She and Miller soon got down to business, first by piling granite rocks in the crawl space under the ground-level floor boards to support the weight of the construction. When Margaret was not sailing serenely offshore by herself, she observed the proceedings, now and again voicing a vague concern that her house would soon collapse from the visitors' efforts. As usual, however, Bennett knew precisely what she was about and managed to put the last brick in place on August 31. She and her artist companion had done a first-rate job and Margaret mustered all her considerable graciousness to express her appreciation. "You have given this house," she said in her halting, gravelly voice, a voice that might have been coming from the next room, "a heart."[18]

Of the five books Margaret published in 1948, three were Golden Books and one each was published by Scott and Harper. The Scott book, *The Little Farmer,* appeared in the spring and marked the revival of Margaret's collaboration with Esphyr Slobodkina. Despite their past differences, the two women had come to regard each other as comrades in arms in their various disputes with Scott. As work proceeded on *The Little Farmer,* the second sequel to *The Little Fireman* (the first sequel, *The Little Fisherman,* had been drably illustrated by Dahlov Ipcar), Margaret assumed her usual role as her illustrator's protector and demanding muse.

As the artist recalled:

> Anytime I seemed to stray from the narrow path of strict honesty and complete integrity, [Margaret] raised loud, bitter objections. When I failed to draw the pigs from nature and, instead, relied on some children's books [*sic*] illustrations, she returned the drawings with a cutting remark to the effect that why didn't I leave the cutie-cutie junk to Walt Disney and do my own, honest-to-goodness stuff.
>
> That remark was gratefully accepted and guided me . . . in all my subsequent work. She fought the introduction of [human] facial features in our books to the extent that, once, when alarmed that I might succumb to people's blandishments, she sent me an urgent telegram to stand pat while she was away . . . and unable to defend the integrity of my style. [19]

The end result was a splendidly illustrated picture book— "your masterpiece," Margaret wrote her collaborator in a congratulatory letter. [20] The full brilliance of Margaret's wit shone through in the text, except in the ending, which was somewhat flat. Margaret could turn endless fresh variations on an imaginative theme; here as elsewhere in her work, letting go of the impulse proved more difficult.

The background of *Wait Till the Moon Is Full,* which Harper published in the fall of 1948, was in some respects more tumultuous. Garth Williams, who illustrated the book, had been hired only after Margaret dismissed Clement Hurd from the project. [21]

A reviewer for the *Library Journal* had predicted that *The Runaway Bunny* might "well become a very-small-child's classic." [22] Since then Margaret and Clem had half-jokingly referred to their Harper collaborations as their "classic series." *Wait Till the Moon Is Full* was to be the next installment. Margaret's "dark night book," as she called it in her letter to Hurd which accompanied the manuscript, had originally been a tale about rabbits, not (as it later became) about raccoons. [23]

In the same letter to Hurd, Margaret had provided a detailed sketch of the double-page illustration she wanted him to prepare as a sample. Her drawing showed a nocturnal forest landscape with moon and clouds and a cutaway view of the subterranean world where a rabbit family had their home, with its "warm glow warm lit interior and security." Hurd proceeded to do the painting and was very pleased with the result. (Years later he described it as his finest single piece of illustration work.) But during a walk in Central Park Margaret told him that she did not like the picture and that she wanted Garth Williams to illustrate the book.

This was a cruel stroke and one which is not easily explained on the basis of artistic merit alone. The fact was that Garth Williams took a positive view of Michael Strange and the Hurds did not. Williams had gotten on well with Michael from their first meeting, when he mentioned being distantly related to the Barrymores; he came to believe that Michael had helped Margaret break out of the conventional mold of her family upbringing. Both Clem and Posey Hurd, on the other hand, were more alert to Michael's assorted pretensions and destructive impulses. They never forgot the comment of one of their Vermont neighbors, who after the briefest of encounters with Michael Strange had pronounced her an "educated damned fool."[24] Nor had Clem and Posey ever tried to conceal their intense dislike of her. In the present instance Margaret had evidently decided to use her considerable power in such a way as to let Clem feel her displeasure.

In *Wait Till the Moon Is Full,* Margaret returned to the compelling theme she had previously explored in *Goodnight Moon* and *The Runaway Bunny*—the small child's gradual development from a condition of absolute dependence to one of increasing self-possession. The animal child of *Wait Till the Moon Is Full* has outgrown the Runaway Bunny's ambivalence about the desirability of venturing out into the world. His impatience is real: "This little raccoon wanted to see the night. He had seen the day. . . . But his mother said, 'Wait. Wait till the moon is full.' "[25] The mother of the piece is knowing, patient, sensible, and true to her word. When the night sky is at last illuminated by a full moon and the world thus made safer for small travelers, she lets her son leave. The text lacks the emotional intensity of the two earlier books. The cumulative structure of the narrative becomes cumbersome; the mother's songs are self-conscious attempts at verse. Williams' drawings are wonderfully accomplished works, mixing whimsy with tenderness, but the book as a whole lacks the overall integrity of *Goodnight Moon* and *The Runaway Bunny*. Like the small hero of the story, it addresses questions of self-sufficiency that Margaret herself was only just ready to consider.

That fall of 1948, Michael Strange kept to an extremely demanding schedule as she toured with her "Great Words With Great Music" program. Margaret had purchased a wire recording machine (a precursor of tape recorders), and when Michael was home in New York she helped her prepare for the stage by recording her rehearsals and playing them back. Audiences were proving to be less than enthusiastic, and Margaret (to the extent that the other woman would allow her to do so) increasingly took it upon herself to help Michael polish her performance. In the meantime, to bolster lagging ticket sales, Margaret secretly bought up blocks of seats and distributed tickets to friends in the vain hope of packing the house.

It was also at about this time that Margaret persuaded Michael to try her hand at writing a children's fantasy. Michael worked fitfully at the project, with guarded encouragement (which one assumes was completely forced) from Ursula Nordstrom, and found the going unexpectedly difficult. But whether this experience caused her to realize that Margaret's type of writing was neither obvious nor easy is not known. Other concerns, in any case, crowded in on her attention. Until recently an extraordinarily vigorous woman, she now found that performances left her unaccountably weak. She went to see the doctor. By year's end it was clear that she was gravely ill with leukemia.

She had scheduled a series of recitals at Manhattan's Times Hall for January of 1949 and Michael resolved to keep the commitment regardless of her health. She had always prided herself on her fiery disregard for conventional wisdom. As she put herself on special dietary regimes and (with Margaret's help) searched for doctors willing to hold out any promise of a cure, she felt increasingly certain of the importance of her work. It was her destiny to bring a measure of spiritual solace to a troubled world, and she would not be stopped.

Michael's illness only deepened the fracture in her declining relationship with Margaret. Her diffuse rage (and doubtless the jealousy she felt in respect to her younger, more accomplished, and healthier friend) found a particularly insidious new focus in cruel suggestions that Margaret was somehow responsible for her illness. The accusations were of such an extreme nature that even Margaret, vulnerable as she was, does not seem to have believed that they could be true. She was, however, left feeling terribly hurt and confused, and in the first weeks of the new year of 1949 she cast about listlessly for some temporary way of escape.

During the years just after the war, Margaret had continued to see little of her sister and brother, and she seems to have visited her father only occasionally. In recent months, however, she had formed a new friendship with Judith Thorne, a younger cousin of hers from her father's side of the family. "Little Judy" was the daughter of Robert Brown's younger sister Judith, whom Margaret's family had visited from time to time when the children were growing up. But it was only now that Judy had graduated from college and come to live in Manhattan that she and Margaret became acquainted. They soon developed a sort of big-sister–little-sister relationship, a friendship predicated—as so many of Margaret's were—on distinct differences of age and experience. Margaret could be a wonderfully good listener and sympathetic adviser; she found it deeply satisfying to assume that role. On February 11 she and her cousin flew to Switzerland for a ski holiday at St. Moritz.

They stayed at Suvretta House, a deluxe hotel where Don Juan, the pretender to the Spanish throne, was also a guest during their visit. Margaret met the king-in-exile and a brief flirtation passed between them—"that flashing laughing moment," as Margaret called it in the diary notes she kept for those few days, in which she also jotted down dream fragments and scattered reflections on what was in fact a most precarious time for her. [26]

"Michael and a big bottle of Port—didn't offer me any. . . . Rearranging furniture in mother's house to get sofas in front of the fire. But said she wouldn't like it." Here were unsettling images of love, warmth, pleasure, and home comfort denied. "Michael's always telling me that I have killed her and that's what is wrong— Nuts!"

For the moment at least, Margaret recognized the unfairness of Michael Strange's abusive accusations. "Wake up with courage to look at myself." She thought herself overweight, tired- and sad-looking, and she was overtaken once again by the recurring, painful sense of having "no attachment" to the people and things around her. She felt like a "small unattached particle sitting on the rocks on the crest of a very beautiful world. The mountains frighten me. They are so much the upper edge of the world, above which there is no connection with the earth."

How at variance this was with the buoyant immediacies of *The Important Book:*

> It is true that it is blue,
> and high, and full of clouds,
> and made of air.
> But the important thing about
> the sky is that it is always there.

In Margaret's book, the sky is one of the great constants of experience, a godlike or parental presence, a source of encouragement and calm. In contrast to all this, Margaret in Switzerland now counselled herself in a radical skepticism: "Must be careful not to ever depend or count too much again [on anyone or anything]. Change the need."

She had dreamed of being back in New York and unable to find her way home. Arriving at last at the correct address (186 East End Avenue), she discovered that in her absence the building had burned to the ground. Searching through the rubble, she found a single room still intact. Curiously, it did not belong there—it was one of the rooms of her old West Tenth Street apartment. She sensed right away that she could no longer live in that room. Looking on nearby, Michael Strange now spoke up to remind her of Cobble Court—she was not without a place of her own in the city.

In another dream, Margaret's first dog, Smoke, was hit by a truck; her first impulse was to run to the dog to try to save him, but she was momentarily distracted by a domestic-minded friend who wanted help in relining her kitchen pantries. Margaret obliged her friend for a time, then left to minister to her ailing dog, recognizing at last the more urgent need.

"Of course," Margaret wrote, venturing her own analysis, "Smoke is Michael's lucimia [*sic*]." The absurd distraction of the pantry shelves was "Michael's nonsense," her rantings and accusations. Margaret was apparently girding herself for fresh abuse as she resolved to be of what assistance she could to the dying woman. As the earlier of the two dreams suggested, she was also coming to realize that at some future time she would be able to live on her own.

While at Suvretta House, Margaret telephoned Michael Strange in New York, but Michael refused her call. "I knew it was for myself I called," she rebuked herself in her makeshift diary,

> but she was sick and I wanted to show her how near I was. My conclusion is that she wants to feel deserted and hurt by me. Love turned to hate—Rage raging out to hurt—Anyway—This is the last time I will ever call her and the first time she has ever refused to speak to me. So I must accept that there is no more love coming from Michael till it comes like a wild bird of its own free will and finds me. Sickness and Death be damned. It is Life that is important and the way to obliterate Life is to keep trying to prove there is no death.

Michael had become increasingly preoccupied with speculations about rebirth and resurrection, but Margaret clearly had little sympathy for such ideas. The following morning she wrote in her diary that she felt "better . . . more in than out of life. It is that out of life feeling that is hard to bear." She wondered whether it was better to live alone, or to suffer the abuse of another person's hurtful behavior, adding cryptically, "Contact—even negative contact. That is the worse danger. Mother's isolation—Is there a final quick to which one can be cut."

In her own separation from Michael Strange, in the latter's rejection of her, she had found a flash point of identification with

Maude Brown, a glimpse of her mother's painful experience reflected in her own: "I think I was cut to the heart last night. And yet I dreamt of M making a futile love to me and then the great Mother child love that I wanted—Michael being taken to hospital. Comes back to find and cherish me, make room for me in her house."

From Switzerland Margaret and her cousin travelled by train to Paris, where they stayed for half of March. Leaving behind the costly elegances of the Suvretta House, they entered the outré Left Bank realm of the Hôtel du Danube on the rue Jacob, as different from their previous lodgings as Cobble Court was from 10 Gracie Square.

This was a regenerative if restless time, when Margaret's capacity for living in the moment served her well. On a trip to the flower market, she bought as many flowers as could be fitted into a taxi and brought them back to her hotel, to the bemusement of the concierge. There were visits to the Grand Guignol shows in the Luxembourg Gardens and an appointment at Schapparelli, where Margaret met the House's chief designer, Hubert de Givenchy, and ordered an evening dress, yellow and black in broad horizontal stripes, that made her look, her cousin thought, "like a bumblebee."[27] At an antique shop she purchased as a gift for Charles Shaw an eighteenth-century painting of a monkey and a dog playing cards, with the legend in French "I will kill you if you win." She also brought back a set of copper pots and pans. Wishing to avoid paying duty on these, she tied them together with little pieces of string and hung them like an outlandish boa around her neck, so that when she stepped off the plane in New York and passed through customs, she might claim to be wearing them.

While Margaret was vacationing abroad, Clement Hurd was home in Vermont illustrating a new project of theirs for Harper, *My World*. Their friendship had easily withstood the unpleasantness surrounding *Wait Till the Moon Is Full*. The artist recalled philosophically years later, "Working with Margaret was difficult but at the same time stimulating and satisfying."[28] She had left the manuscript in particularly rough form, and in late February the illustrator wrote Ursula Nordstrom with various questions and dry remarks.

"Our bird in the gilded cage claims that she will be back by mid-March so I guess she will have time to write this fine book." Margaret had supplied him with a sheaf of miniscule handwritten notes indicating the approach he might want to take; in the sample artwork he was sending Nordstrom, he had "followed partly the so called text and partly what Margaret suggested on one of her multitude of cards. 'Let's see how it grows and let it grow out of itself.' So it did, sometimes a little to my surprise."[29]

A question of propriety had arisen. Room by room, *My World* detailed the domestic life of a typical modern family (a family that happened to consist of rabbits). The author had not neglected to mention the bathroom. Hurd was aware that Leonard Weisgard had once been obliged to redraw a *New Yorker* cover illustration of a beach scene in which he had indiscreetly included an outhouse, and he recalled the trouble he himself had experienced over the cow udder in *Goodnight Moon.* What, then, might children's librarians think of *My World?* With tongue in cheek, Hurd sought Nordstrom's guidance: "Is it proper to have the whole family in the bathroom at once in a book published by the House of Harper?? (and Papa in the tub, too?) . . . or do I go too far?"[30]

The Hurds were expecting their first baby. "We are waiting for a blizzard," he explained, "for things to start." In March word came from Vermont of the birth of John Thacher Hurd; and a few weeks after that, along with the news that work on *My World* was proceeding rapidly and well, the artist wrote to remind Nordstrom of the payment due him: "This is a plea that even though the baby can't walk he needs a new pair of shoes! Get the idea—Best regards, Clem."[31]

The artist promised to deliver the finished paintings in person in early May. Nordstrom put through a check for his advance and said she looked forward to seeing him then—and no later: "This is going to be a wonderful book. . . . So take care of yourself and don't break a finger—at least not on your right hand! Yours, Ursula."[32]

That spring of 1949, Harper published *The Important Book* to excellent reviews. Critics were quick to recognize it as the innovative, intellectually challenging and playful book that it was. Margaret, however, felt listless, not triumphant. She spent a fretful first part of the summer in New York and then went to Maine, where in a frenzy of organizational activity she put Billy Brown to work completing Michael Strange's cottage. Margaret "supervised" while the young lobsterman, who had never built a house, constructed a stone hearth, fitted the center beam, and installed the cottage's most original feature, a "Picture Window" made from an ornate picture frame Margaret had found in a Rockland antique shop.[33] From inside the house, the Picture Window framed a splendid view of the magnificent spruce forest that covered portions of Margaret's property. By a typically witty paradox, Margaret had made nature appear to imitate art. It was the sort of visual joke that Michael Strange was certain to find amusing—if, that is, she could be induced to visit the house at all.

Margaret's manuscript for "The Ridiculous Noisy Book" was to remain unfinished. Among the many projects she was then actively working on, however, were a handful of other Noisy titles. In November Bill Scott was both shocked and angered to read in *Publishers' Weekly* that Harper planned to bring out Margaret's *Quiet Noisy Book,* with illustrations by Leonard Weisgard, that spring.

Margaret had not felt obliged to inform him about this in advance. Scott now found himself in a highly embarrassing position. His office was receiving phone calls from people in the trade wanting to know if it was true that his company had sold off its most popular series to Harper. Ethel Scott accepted the delicate assignment of writing Margaret to express the firm's consternation. A coolly legalistic first draft metamorphosed into a more or less cordial invitation to dinner.[34] The company, she said, viewed the situation as grave. She trusted, however, that by sitting down together they might yet sort matters out amicably.

When Margaret withdrew *The Important Book,* the Scotts had been forced to acknowledge their powerlessness to stop her. But the new situation was of a different order. The "similar manuscripts" clause clearly applied. Determining what constituted a "similar" work might be an obscure business some of the time. There had in fact been several recent instances in which the firm might conceivably have invoked the clause in respect to books that Margaret had published elsewhere, but had chosen not to do so. In the case of the Noisy series, however, an unambiguous definition of similarity had been agreed to. Two distinct elements had been determined to comprise the irreducible essence of a Noisy work: the use of "Noisy Book" in the title and Muffin as the hero's name. It was obvious from Harper's ad that the new book satisfied both requirements as to similarity. The Scotts thus had every reason to think themselves on solid legal ground as they awaited Margaret's reply.

Margaret, however, had left town to go horseback riding on the ranch of some friends, Josephine and Richard Reeve, near Tucson, Arizona. Finding the Scotts' invitation on her return in mid-December, she replied by letter that she would be happy to meet with them but that as far as she was concerned the matter had long been put to rest: "It's almost two years now, I think, since I wrote Bill that I didn't see how we could do any more books together when there were so many complications about the contract and for all the other reasons I went into at that time."[35] Leonard Weisgard, she noted, had likewise decided that he no longer wanted to illustrate another Noisy Book for Scott. This being the case, it was "only logical" that they should continue the series elsewhere.

Friends can choose to adopt whatever course of action seems only logical to them, but parties to a contract may have prior obligations. What had broken down was the informal, at times almost familial, way in which Margaret and Scott had done business over the years.

"Believe me," Margaret wrote, "I am as sorry and as pulled apart by our particular parting as evidently you seem to be at this late date." She signed the letter in the cordial manner of their early collaborative days, "Sincerely and affectionately," but, as was obvious to all, their differences were beyond settling over a meal. Accordingly, shortly after the first of the year, Scott's attorney,

Michael Halperin, drafted a letter advising Harper and Brothers that Margaret was in breach of contract and that Scott intended to press its claim by all means necessary.

Harper's lawyer, now also Margaret's, was Morris Ernst, the famed civil libertarian who had won the *Ulysses* censorship case on behalf of Random House and James Joyce. Ernst responded to Halperin's accusations with a terse note stating the opinion that Scott had no valid claim against his clients. That same day, however, he wrote Frank S. McGregor at Harper to say that he had recently spoken with Margaret and believed her to be in serious trouble from a legal standpoint.[36] His letter to Scott's attorney, he confided, had been a bluff aimed at drawing the Noisy Books' publisher into an out-of-court settlement.

Shortly after the New Year of 1950, Michael Strange flew to Switzerland to undergo treatment for leukemia. She was accompanied by Ted Peckham, the enterprising socialite jack-of-all-trades who was among the most loyal members of her entourage. A witty, prankish man, Peckham was always good company. They stopped for a respite in the grand style at the Hôtel Royal in Lausanne before continuing on to the Hirslanden Clinic in Zurich, where Michael Strange registered as "Mrs. John Barrymore."[37] Over the holidays she had had another falling-out with Margaret and had told her that she did not want Margaret to visit her in Switzerland. This rejection, like others in the past, hurt Margaret deeply.

Michael Strange's medical condition was not promising. As her doctor at the clinic said, she had come to him not at the eleventh hour or at midnight but at "ten past twelve"; still, he told her, there was reason to hope that she might live a few years longer.[38] Her fierce determination to live would help her fight the disease.

On January 26, Margaret wrote from New York;

> Dearest Michael—the Michael I used to know from the self I used
> to be. How bewildering all these people are—I walk among them
> not of them making a broken voiced effort at pretend. You were

born a good actress to act for people. I act—an actress for myself
and so many actresses for so many selves. But to-night I am so
sober like the quiet person I have always been. And I am writing to
the you I used to know who was quietly you beyond all those people who came and went.[39]

On February 1, she wrote again to express her anguish about
the "terrible division of pride and impulse" that left her uncertain
how, if at all, to respond to Michael Strange's repeated rebuffs.
Yet, she said, "forgetting everything" she still wished to come to
Switzerland to care for Michael "while there is time. . . . It isn't
the ocean that separates us. And yet nothing that separates us holds
us apart."[40]

A reassuring letter from Michael arrived soon afterward and
was followed by Margaret's eager reply, including details of her
flight plan and other news delivered in the name of one or another
of their imaginary creatures—the Hero, Miss Bambino, Carpe
Diem.

Inspired by Michael's poetry recitations to musical accompaniment, Margaret reported, she was writing song lyrics—an experiment begun about two years earlier with *The Little Brass Band,* the
never-completed "Ugly Duckling," and several other projects. She
had recently met Oscar Hammerstein, Jr., who offered his encouragement; she was now at work on some lyrics for the "light Music
Department" of the Manhattan radio station WQXR: "Miss Bambino [Margaret] hides the hero [Michael Strange] in the songs the
way she used to disguise him in her books as a rabbit."[41] She would
bring her friend the year's first yellow primroses.

But on February 11, in a letter that stung Margaret all over
again, Michael wrote saying that her physician, Dr. Rohr, had
expressly forbidden a visit. He had asked her whether the prospect
of seeing Margaret made her anxious and Michael had replied affirmatively. She told Margaret this even while assuring her, without
a nod to irony, that a visit from her would be as welcome as one
from a guardian spirit.[42] For the present, however, she urged Margaret not to make any sign or gesture toward her but rather, quite
simply, to leave her alone.

On February 28, Margaret flew to London. The following

morning, as previously planned, she made a connecting flight to Zurich, where she had arranged to attend to some business on her own and Harper and Brothers' behalf. At the publishing house of Guggenbuhl and Huber, she discussed the possibility of a Swiss edition of *Little Fur Family*. Whether she also attempted to contact Michael Strange while in Zurich is not known. After her meeting, she left immediately for the Hotel Mont Cervil, at Zurmatt, for a month of skiing.

Toward the end of her stay at the luxurious Zurmatt resort, Margaret cabled her bank in New York for a fresh infusion of cash, but was declined for lack of sufficient funds. She then sent Ursula Nordstrom an urgent airmail plea (in those days, transatlantic air letters were delivered overnight): "Dear Ursula, S. O. S. The Government seems to have taken my money and I turn out to have minus 670 (six hundred seventy) dollars in the bank."[43]

She asked if she might have an advance for any one of a long list of pending projects, "or on a couple of them." She requested that her next royalty check be deposited as soon as possible in her account in the city.

> I came out of the snowdrifts to-day to find this situation. It must have been the Income Tax people. I haven't my check book with me.
>
>   Anyway if you can keep me out of jail AGAIN, please do.
>
> > Love from,
> > Your Favorite Jailbird."

Nordstrom replied that she had put through Margaret's royalty check, which came to $1,300. She wondered if that amount would be enough to tide her over. "Your S. O. S.," she noted a bit irritably, "was not clear on this point."[44] She looked forward to seeing Margaret again and to getting down to work with her. She recalled a manuscript titled "The Fathers Are Coming Home" that had fallen by the wayside. "I find myself wanting to get back to 'The Fathers,' " Nordstrom said. "That could be such a lovely book." She would ask Clement Hurd to join them for a "good long session" as soon as Margaret returned home, which she hoped would be before long: "I really miss you."

Nordstrom had one other piece of news: "I've just met a young artist—pretty good I think—who might be a possibility for some M. W. B. books. . . . You'd make an interesting looking couple on book programs." Nordstrom, like Margaret, was always on the lookout for new talent. Her judgment in general was extraordinarily keen. Certainly, it had been on this occasion. The artist Nordstrom had just discovered was Maurice Sendak.

From Switzerland Margaret headed by train for Rome, where Garth Williams and his family were spending the year. She had taken her seat aboard the Rome Express in a compartment opposite a man who was puffing heavily on a cigar. When the narrow compartment, occupied by just the two of them, filled up with smoke, the man had lunged at her and administered a whiff of chloroform that rendered her unconscious. When she came to at the Rome station, her assailant had long since disappeared with her valuables. (She had, however, been left the suitcase loaded with manuscripts for Williams's consideration.) Margaret was understandably shaken when she telephoned her friend from the station. But she soon recovered her composure well enough to joke with Williams about the experience, an episode straight out of an Agatha Christie whodunit. Margaret embellished the incident for her friend, suggesting with forced good cheer that for all she knew she had been raped as well, that in nine months time she and the artist would have to meet again to celebrate the birth of her child—a boy, she said, whom she would name Espresso.

From Rome she travelled by train to Paris, arriving there on April 13. She checked into her favorite room at the Hôtel du Danube. "The Captain's Cabin," as she called it, was hung with red satin in such a way as to remind one of a high-toned bordello, or so Margaret liked to tell friends. From her windows she had a particularly fine view of a stand of trees in the small park below.

Throughout her stay an uneasy peace prevailed between Margaret and the hotel's proprietress. Mme Legrand tolerated some of her guest's outlandish attempts at interior decoration, notably the carting up of several ornamental orange trees to her quarters. Live birds proved another matter. A frequenter of the open-air bird market, Margaret returned one day with a pair of *oiseaux d'île* which she released in her room so as to be able to enjoy the sight of them flying up into the curtains. Mme Legrand, in the tradition of the ever-vigilant French concierge, soon got wind of this and protested to Margaret, conjuring the spectre of the mice which birds were bound to attract.

Margaret generally travelled alone, meeting friends at various points along her itinerary. Among those she had arranged to see in Paris was Virginia Mathews, an American in her twenties whom she had known since the war. Mathews until recently had managed Brentano's children's book department. She was already a great admirer of Margaret's work when they met, and was soon equally impressed by her generosity of spirit. Another writer might have foraged the shelves with a jealous eye to finding chinks in the armor of her competition; Margaret never seemed to begrudge another person his or her success, but appeared genuinely glad to see others advancing.

She enjoyed her talks with Mathews, taking a particular interest in her family history. (Mathews, in contrast, learned very little about Margaret's family.) Virginia's mother had attended Margaret's Swiss boarding school, the Château Brillantmont. Her father, a full-blood Osage Indian, was the tribe's historian. In 1945 John Joseph Mathews published a book of Osage nature lore, *Talking to the Moon,* which Margaret had soon read. Its title alone might well have struck a responsive chord in the writer who later that year would awaken one morning to compose the text of *Goodnight Moon.*

The two friends made several excursions around the city. At the Louvre, Margaret had certain paintings in mind, those by Jacques-Louis David in particular, that she wished to study. The monumental works of the Emperor Napoleon's court painter were an improbable choice for her—but for the fact that Margaret knew the paintings appealed to Michael Strange. Margaret's Paris stay included many such allusions, conscious or unconscious, to the woman she missed.

There were trips to the Musée Carnivet, with its luminous Impressionist canvasses, and to the Musée de Cluny, where the author of *The Runaway Bunny* surveyed the famed Unicorn tapestries, the fifteenth-century allegorical hunting scenes that filled an entire gallery like a picture book writ large. On their way out of the Cluny, Margaret purchased a set of postcards of the tapestries. "Wouldn't it be interesting," she said to her companion, "to make up a new story to go along with the pictures?"[45] She wanted to reorder the scenes, she explained, in such a way that the unicorn might elude his captors. At a nearby stationer that Margaret knew, she bought a parchment album. Returning to her hotel, they began arranging the cards.

In time they had their story, and after inscribing it on the album's leaves Margaret said that it "would certainly be interesting to have the album bound in red leather." She knew a bookbinder in the neighborhood, a M. Esperon in the rue Visconti, and before long they had deposited the album with him. Then Margaret thought of having a small medallion inset on the cover. They wandered off to a local flea market where she found just the right bronze medallion with the image of a hunting horn emblazoned on it. They brought this to the binder. Margaret, it seemed, knew precisely where to find virtually anything she wanted in Paris, usually without having to venture more than a few blocks from her hotel.

She stopped briefly in London on her way back to New York in early May. Among her purchases while abroad were a dartboard for herself and an elaborate service of old English pewter flatware with pistol-design handles as a gift for Leonard Weisgard. She also brought home a brace of eighteenth-century dueling pistols. She told Weisgard she planned to challenge John McCullough to a duel. Margaret's gift for Michael Strange had been in preparation in New York while she was away.

Earlier that year, Ursula Nordstrom had at last scheduled *The Dark Wood of the Golden Birds* for publication. Michael was dying; time was growing short. Two illustrators had been dropped from the project, presumably because Margaret had not found their sketches suitable, and Leonard Weisgard had reluctantly agreed to complete the perilous assignment. By the late spring of 1950, the book was at last done. *The Dark Wood* was due out in July.

The Dark Wood of the Golden Birds is a haunting, albeit vexingly elliptical allegory of the artist's heroic struggle against the dark forces that constitute the wellsprings of creativity. In it, Margaret achieved a somber grandeur of expression that is unmatched in all her work. The text, however, is overly obscure—certainly for a children's picture book. It is like a locked secret compartment: fascinating to contemplate but ultimately beyond one's grasp. Margaret may have come closer to realizing the piece's true potential when she proposed it as the subject of a ballet. At John McCullough's suggestion in the spring of 1947, she sent the manuscript to Lincoln Kirstein of the Ballet Society; he respectfully declined.

Margaret described the story as that of a boy who

> goes into the dark woods in search of the song of the golden birds. . . . He eludes madness and destruction only because he has gone not for himself but for some one in the world who has become sick through denying the voice of the golden birds. And because he goes into the wood from which there is no return, not for himself, but to bring back and to give away to the old man he loves the song that alone can restore balance to his understanding, he can come back. For in all dark intensity in all dark woods lies both the power of life and the power of death, the powers of good and of evil, and the magic of the golden birds is the song bursting forever new out of the dark warring forces of the wood.
>
> The boy is the Artist.
>
> And the golden feather that pierces his heart [not killing him but presumably extracting a price for his heroic defiance] is the symbol of his difference. [46]

Does the "boy" represent Michael Strange, whom Margaret in letters had often called "the hero," "the boy?" Does the boy's journey into the woods stand for Michael's exertions as a poet and public lecturer or "sayer," whose "Great Words With Great Music" performances were aimed at bringing spiritual renewal to the world? Is the "lady," mentioned early on in the text—the woman who went into the woods "just a little way" but then came back speaking "in words that none of the other people could understand"—meant to suggest Margaret's mother, who had once aspired to a creative artist's life but abandoned her ambitions? Is the "golden feather" Michael Strange's illness, the tragic personal cost of having undertaken so selfless and godlike an enterprise?

Leonard Weisgard was convinced that the book held a key to its author's innermost makeup. Ironically, although he illustrated *The Dark Wood of the Golden Birds,* he never felt he understood the allegory. Whatever Michael Strange may have thought of the book is not known.

During Margaret's absence her dispute with Scott (now also Harper's dispute) became the focus of intensive legal negotiations. An out-of-court settlement was deemed in the best interests of all, and considering the bruised feelings that the episode had caused, the accommodation that was finally reached showed admirable resilience all round. Harper agreed to purchase outright the entire Noisy series, including all five titles already published by Scott. Instructed in her obligations under the law, Margaret agreed thereafter to clear her potentially "similar" projects with Scott in a timely way.

"It was pretty straight shooting there for a while," Margaret, sounding relieved, told Evelyn Burkey at the Authors League.[47] (The dueling pistols had, however, remained in their case.) That summer she wrote John McCullough that Simon and Schuster would be sending Scott her manuscript for a Little Golden Book to be called *The Train to Timbuctoo.* As Scott had published her *Two Little Trains* (illustrated by Jean Charlot) the previous year, she wanted to make certain that the new book's title posed no problem. She described the book as a "poor old Mike O'Finnigan Begin again pattern with onomatoepoetic sounds . . . and my big little device thrown in." A second manuscript based on the same device, *Little Indian,* was also in the mail from Simon and Schuster to Scott. "I trust," she said, allowing some irritation to show through,

> you will find no objection to these and will write me your reaction. As you know I used the pattern in *Big Dog Little Dog,* you used it to some extent in *A Very Little Dog* [a book McCullough himself had written] and Ylla used it years ago in *Grands et Petits.* . . . Anyway I'd go crazy if everything I wrote had to be held up legally. One idea evolves out of another as in music adding something new

and carrying along something old. And each of us alas plays only one or two themes many times in what we write and act in infinite variation. I wish it were not so.[48]

She warmly thanked McCullough for his recent letter concerning the enthusiastic critical response to *Two Little Trains*. Even the New York Public Library was championing the book. *That* was something that she and John could laugh about together—and be gratified by.

The spring and summer of 1950 was a time of seeking reconciliation and renewal wherever such could be found. On June 15, Margaret drove to Harlem to attend a party at the Countee Cullen branch of the New York Public Library. It was there, years earlier, that she had gone to scout out prospects for Lucy Mitchell's Writers Laboratory. The present occasion was a gathering to mark the birthday of the late James Weldon Johnson, in whose memory the children's room at the library had been renamed. Among the two hundred guests were many authors and illustrators whose works were represented on the library's shelves: William Pène du Bois, Fritz Eichenberg, Marie Hall Ets, Harold Courlander, and Margaret's old friend Ellen Tarry, who had gone on from the Writers Laboratory to publish a number of picture books.

Since the time of Margaret's first visit to the library in 1937, modest progress had been made toward the goal of providing black children with books about their own experiences. The evening was also a celebration of achievements in that vein. When Margaret pulled up in her car, Lucy Mitchell, who had been one of the first people outside the black community to encourage the publication of such books, was seated beside her. It had been a half dozen years since they had last gotten together for a talk.

That summer of 1950, for the first time in two years, Margaret dispatched a note to her Hollins class secretary, reporting the diverting if not very current news of her Swiss ski holiday. "Those Alps," she wrote, "look awfully high when you're on top of them looking down with two sticks tied to your feet."[49] That was the old "Tim": athletic, supremely good-spirited, unflappable. And just before leaving for the Only House, she made a quick trip to Glens Falls, New York, to call on another old acquaintance.

Montgomery Hare, a college friend of Clement Hurd's and a regular at Michael Strange's evenings at 10 Gracie Square, was in Glens Falls directing the Barter Theater, a romantically conceived traveling stock company which operated on a shoestring, as its name implied. Margaret, who had not seen Hare in years, had decided to lend the actors a hand and had gone to the trouble (and considerable expense) of purchasing at Hammacher Schlemmer a shiny new aluminum cookstand, an elegant version of the sort of cart that hotdog vendors operated around town. As she pulled up in her massive Chrysler, the cookstand in tow, Hare was delighted as well as more than a little taken aback by her sudden appearance. Over the next few days she presided over her refreshment stand, crooning jolly songs to attract customers. Margaret's show was easily the equal of the one being presented under the tent. Her departure, days later, was just as unexpected as her arrival. Margaret needed little diversions, temporary escapes from the inexorable fact of Michael Strange's imminent death, and there was no end, it seemed, to what her imagination could devise.

Determined against all odds to resume her recital work, Michael Strange had returned to New York from Zurich by late May. She stayed at East End Avenue for a time, but as climbing steps became too taxing for her, she made the Plaza Hotel her second home when in town. Margaret remained as eager as ever to help her, and there is little reason to doubt that their old pattern of flare-ups and reconciliations continued as before, with Margaret falling in and out of favor at the other woman's whim, and all the while pursuing the full range of her projects.

No recognition that Margaret received for her work seems to have pleased her more than the commission that came her way from *The Book of Knowledge* for an essay on the theme "Creative Writing for Very Young Children," for the encyclopedia's 1951 *Annual*. She worked on the piece over August and September in Maine. Michael had decided once again to vacation in Bar Harbor—not at the house Margaret had specially built for her on Vinalhaven. Margaret shuttled back and forth between one retreat and the other.

Writing the essay gave her a chance to take stock of her accomplishments, and the finished piece suggests that she had begun to emerge from the shadow of Michael Strange's influence and to know that she was not such a "little" poet after all. A new steadiness and certitude were sounded in the article, her fullest accounting till then of her career: "Children are keen as wild animals and also as timorous. So you can't be 'too funny' or 'too scary' or 'too many worded.' All these are things not as easy as they sound for grown people. There is always that old problem of learning how to write. We speak naturally but spend all our lives trying to write naturally."[50]

She compared the poetry of Chaucer, who had lived "when the English language was young, when it was a joy to name all the things about him," to the delight young children routinely take "in murmuring the names of the things in the world." In writing for the very young, the end result was bound to seem simple, but the art required to achieve that end was no less demanding than any other.

Writing was like carpentry: "One must humbly learn and serve the craft." To write honestly and well for children, one had also to look inward to the "child that is within all of us always— perhaps the one laboratory that we all share." It was to this inner laboratory, rather than to the Bank Street–style tryouts of manuscripts, that Margaret herself had increasingly turned for inspiration and guidance: "A child's own story is a dream, but a good story is a dream that is true for more than one child."

She recalled the origins of several of her innovative works. Her very first picture book, *When the Wind Blew,* had been inspired by a Chekhov short story about "a very sad and bitter man trying to drown a fly in an ink blob and then suddenly deciding to save its life and by that one small gesture feeling better." She had wanted to write a sad story for children, "believing," she said, paraphrasing Lewis Carroll, "that many of the graver cadences of life are there at any age."

The Runaway Bunny "was an attempt to put the bold, tender, repeated cadence of an ancient French love song into the loving world of a child." In *Bumble Bugs and Elephants, A Child's Good Night Book,* and *Little Fur Family,* she had "merely dared to be very simple." Elsewhere she had given the very young child a "form to put his own observations into—as in the 'Noisy' books and *The Important Book* published by Harper." (Margaret gave Scott no such free publicity.)

She noted with amusement her own childhood habit of citing *The Book of Knowledge* as her source for the outlandish stories she told her sister and friends. "Story teller," Margaret recalled, was "a polite word in our family for . . . liar." What a delicious irony to find herself now actually writing for that same *Book of Knowledge* which had once stood her in such good stead. She offered this summing-up:

> A book should try to accomplish something more than just to repeat a child's own experiences. One would hope rather to make a child laugh or feel clear and happy-headed as he follows a simple rhythm to its logical end, to jog him with the unexpected and comfort him with the familiar; and perhaps to lift him for a few moments from his own problems of shoe laces that won't tie and busy parents and mysterious clock time into the world of a bug or a bear or a bee or a boy living in the timeless world of story.

Michael Strange was in and out of hospitals for much of the summer. On July 8, she was discharged from New York's Memorial Hospital and checked into the Plaza. On the twelfth, she returned to 186 East End Avenue, but within days was readmitted to the hospital, where her cousin by marriage, the society bandleader Eddy Duchin, was also a cancer patient. Glad for each other's company, the two ailing celebrities amused themselves by racing their wheelchairs through the corridors. From her hospital bed Michael telephoned Charles Shaw, already vacationing in Bar Harbor, to say that she would join him there soon. Shaw, in his diary entry for that day, July 27, commented, "I doubt it very much."[51] But on July 28, she boarded the Bar Harbor Express for the strenuous thirteen-and-a-half-hour ride north.

While in Maine, Michael took another turn for the worse. On October 8, she was admitted to Boston's Massachusetts General Hospital.

Margaret, who had returned to New York from Maine in late September, now took a room in Boston's Hotel Eliot, where she tried to work between visits to Michael's bedside. Golden Books had asked her for excerpts from the letters she received from children. Most letters, she replied, "30 or 40 at a time," were essentially form letters, "writing exercises in Block Letters and Neatness copied from a blackboard {and} written by a teacher. I love children but distrust teachers, librarians, and policemen."[52] When children wrote on their own, however, she was delighted, "touched in the heart," and made a point of responding, "especially if the child is perceptive enough to challenge me on some naturalistic phenomenon that I have made a mistake in or that he thinks I have." One young correspondent, she reported, had been disturbed because in *The Country Noisy Book* she had written, "The stars came out." "He said the stars were always there. And I wrote that he was right and I would change it next time." It was for such moments of insight that she had always found it worthwhile to test her unpublished work on groups of children. "All children's letters end, please write another story. That is perhaps more important to them than answering every dear unnatural grubby little letter."

During her Bank Street years, Margaret had worked closely with a great many children. In the years since then she had never been without a few child acquaintances, mostly the children of friends and neighbors. But such day-to-day contact with the very young, she insisted, was not the real key to her type of work. To be a children's writer, she said, "one has to love not children but what children love." Margaret's favorite letter concerning her work had come from "a little rich boys [*sic*] father in Chicago." He said that after reading *Five Little Firemen* his child had tried to set the house on fire. "My answer was, 'Dear Sir, I am glad you caught your son in time.'"

Michael Strange died in Boston on November 5, 1950, with Margaret, their housekeeper Ethel Malcolm, Ted Peckham, and a few others at her side. Extravagant to the end, at the time of her death she was wearing a massive double strand of pearls that countless people had admired over the years. How odd it must have seemed to those present to realize, on top of their grief, that Michael Strange, poet and actress, sayer and celebrity, was suddenly no longer there to fend for herself; how very unlike her it all was. When someone finally spoke up, it was the ever-pragmatic Ethel Malcolm, who said of the pearls, "We'd better take [them] off her—before someone else does."[53]

CHAPTER EIGHT

"THE FIDGET WHEELS OF TIME"

And pluck till time and times
  are done
The silver apples of the moon,
The golden apples of the sun.

WILLIAM BUTLER YEATS,
"The Song of the Wandering Aengus"

In death, Michael Strange was recalled much as she had presented herself to the world. In the many obituaries which appeared in newspapers around the United States and abroad, she was eulogized as a rebellious Newport socialite turned actress and poet, as one of the most strikingly beautiful women of her day, and as the former Mrs. John Barrymore.[1] None of the articles noting her passing made reference to her attachment to Margaret. With the help of friends, Margaret amassed a collection of the obituaries and saved them along with what remained of their correspondence.

Michael had left no detail of her funeral arrangements to chance. In accordance with her instructions, her body was dressed in the white-and-gold pleated robe she had worn for her poetry recitals and lay in state in the cavernous living room at Under the

Hill, where a recording of Wagner's *Parsifal* played continuously as friends and relatives came to pay their respects. The Catholic funeral mass was conducted at the house and followed by burial at Woodlawn Cemetery in the Bronx, in a grave beside that of her son Robin. (Robin had originally been buried in Indianapolis, but soon after Michael Strange realized the seriousness of her illness, she had decided—her son's own express wishes notwithstanding—to remove his body to Woodlawn.) She had ordered twin headstones. On the one reserved for herself, Michael Strange had engraved part of a passage from the Song of Songs: "For, lo, the winter is past, the rain is over and gone." On Robin's headstone was the passage's refrain: "Arise my love, my fair one, and come away."[2]

For Margaret, Michael's passing was the end of a relationship that had remained as baroquely complex as it had been intense. When Virginia Mathews, the former bookstore manager whom Margaret had last seen in Paris, spent an afternoon with her shortly after her return from Boston, she left with the impression that Margaret was as relieved by her long-time companion's death as saddened by it.

The ever-loyal Charles Shaw was another friend who was a particular comfort to Margaret. They went for long walks in Carl Schurz Park, in the shadow of the house where Michael had first admitted Margaret into her rarefied social world. They met for dinner often over the next several weeks, and on December 21 it was Margaret who delivered a Christmas tree to his door. They spent a quiet Christmas eve together at Cobble Court, drinking Old Fashioneds.

Michael's death also meant the end of an apprenticeship. If the older woman had played "big poet" to her "little poet," Margaret now would assume the larger role herself. "We are no longer amateurs," she wrote Alvin Tresselt, one of the younger writer friends whose work she was championing.[3]

Margaret continued to live at East End Avenue, where to keep her company various friends came to stay in Michael's rooms across the hall. She kept Cobble Court as well, and Pietro stayed on as her butler and cook, arriving each morning in time to bring her her "orange juice and crust."[4] Pietro spent his days polishing and dusting, making runs to the florist, and preparing the elegant small lunches and dinners she still gave for friends.

Under the terms of Michael Strange's will, Margaret inherited Michael's poetry library and one highly dramatic piece of jewelry, an outsized fleur-de-lis diamond brooch designed by John Barrymore. The brooch was so massive that Margaret hesitated to wear it in public for fear of attracting thieves. She asked Lucille Ogle, one of Golden Books' executives, what she should do with the piece. "Wear it," Ogle replied. "No one will ever guess that the diamonds are real."[5]

Margaret was also made coexecutor of Michael Strange's literary estate. Among the papers put in her care were the various sketches for children's books she had coaxed Michael into writing. Margaret attempted to interest Ursula Nordstrom in these, but without success. As for the other manuscripts, she apparently decided to let matters rest.

The death of Michael Strange caused Margaret to concentrate her energies with unprecedented intensity. She resolved, in whatever ways lay open to her, to put her house in order. There were pressing money worries to address. Simon and Schuster, nowadays her principal source of income, had sold out the most recent printings of all her Golden Books titles and was not planning to go back to press with them for at least another year. Earnings she had counted on would thus be much delayed.

Just as Margaret learned of this, she received more bad news from Ursula Nordstrom, who had been doing some housekeeping of her own. In the wake of the Noisy Book settlement, as part of which Harper made a substantial cash payment to Scott and incurred heavy legal fees, Nordstrom was under extraordinary pressure to keep a tight rein on her budget. The editor reminded Margaret of an advance Harper had paid her years earlier for a book never published and suggested she should be willing to consider that money as her advance for their next new project together, *The Summer Noisy Book.*[6] Nordstrom's proposal would have been a reasonable one unless, as Margaret insisted was the case in a letter dated March 16, she had in fact submitted a satisfactory manuscript for her "Little Fat Cat Book" and it had been Nordstrom who had held up the project for six full years. Margaret proceeded to enumerate a handful of other projects which but for delays for which the publisher was responsible would doubtless have earned both her and the house a good profit. To Margaret's further consternation, Nordstrom had recently declared that she could "see no future market" for the *Little Fur Family*, the sale and distribution of which had been complicated by an invasion of moths into the Harper warehouse, among other problems. To this Margaret replied that since her "Fur Book" was so "very near to my heart" she was prepared to do whatever was necessary to keep it in print, "even if I have to form my own publishing scheme," have copies printed in Japan, and "import and distribute them myself."[7]

She asked for an immediate clarification of Nordstrom's thoughts on these and other matters, a request to which the editor responded with such tact and friendly, respectful regard that within two weeks' time Margaret was assuring her that the "mutual honorable assumptions" between them had not only been "clarified" by their recent skirmishes, "but strengthened."[8]

In late March Margaret spent a nostalgic evening with Lucy Sprague Mitchell. Mitchell had lost her beloved husband Robin little more than two years earlier and she was starting to feel her age. Writing afterwards to thank "Brownie" for the visit, she praised her former student: "Your things—all of them, the verse books & Heath readers—have a magic power that words *can* have but so seldom do. I sometimes wonder—now that my chance has passed—whether I could have made words magical if my civic conscience had been less domineering?"[9]

Mitchell was writing her memoirs, a project she had planned, unconventionally, as half autobiography and half the biography of her late husband—a sort of valedictory exercise in relationship thinking. Despite a severe cold, she was forging ahead with the manuscript of *Two Lives*. But apart from that effort, she confided, she was having a hard time finding it within herself to work: "I am learning the art of procrastination for the first time in my life and I don't really enjoy it." She asked Margaret to visit her over the summer in Vermont ("*if* I go") and to read her manuscript and tell her what she thought of it. "Somewhere, some time, at any rate," she concluded, "let's meet again."

In mid-May Margaret drove up to see the Hurds in Vermont, hoping to rekindle their old friendship, and had a glorious time. A few days later she wrote Clem and Posey from New York. "Our Spring Trillium Magnum binge is becoming dearer and dearer to my heart. Do you supose [*sic*] when we are all old and white (not grey) Thacher will explain to his college friends that—They get this way every year about the time the trilliums come in bloom."[10] She hoped they would allow her to return the favor by joining her at the Only House in August. Margaret then left for a short trip to Maine, and was back in New York again in time for her forty-first birthday. She had lent Cobble Court to a theater friend of Michael's, Luther Greene, who organized a surprise party for her. It poured on May 23; the dozen or so invited guests, including Charles Shaw, Margaret's cousin Judy, and Leonard Weisgard, had to press inside Margaret's wonderland cottage to toast her health.

For Margaret, a common thread linking the work of Lucy Sprague Mitchell, Gertrude Stein, and Michael Strange was the emphasis they all placed on the musical element in language and literature. In a second essay commissioned by *The Book of Knowledge Annual* (for 1952), called "Stories to Be Sung and Songs to Be Told," she made the theme her own as she speculated on the elemental nature of music making within the overall scheme of human activity and argued that her own type of work was simply a contemporary expression of that very basic urge: "In the natural impulse to amuse and to delight and comfort very young children the song came first. . . . The picture book is but a recent development of those early songs that told a story."[11]

She proposed this jaunty maxim: "A good picture book . . . can almost be whistled. . . . 'The Three Bears,' 'The Three Billy Goats Gruff,' *Millions of Cats* . . . all have their own melodies behind the storytelling. When such stories are told well, really told, their cadence and rhythm are a large part of their meaning." Margaret had once tested this proposition by reading from a French book to a group of small children who did not know the language. "They couldn't understand a word," she told a friend. "They loved every syllable."[12]

She explained to *Book of Knowledge* readers that the songs she wrote for children were meant to be "silly simple" lyrics that "might make any child feel that he could do just as well himself." She offered as an example "The Secret Song," which begins, "Who saw the petals / drop from the rose / I, said the spider / But nobody knows." Margaret's lyric continues in this light vein for four more stanzas about fog and sunsets, night owls and foxes.

She did not disparage the new medium of television out of hand. "Maybe," Margaret wrote, "television will bring back the ballad singer." But "most of all," she declared, "how wonderful it would be to walk along the street and hear children putting their own thoughts to music, making up their own songs."

What Margaret recalled as the "saddest thing I have heard for a long time"—a remark of one of her Maine lobsterman friends— found its way into the article. "What a pity it is," he had said, "to never hear anymore a woman singing at her work."

The advent of radio, Margaret argued, with its steady hum of music and chatter, and more lately of television, rendered urgent the need to encourage the very young to continue their own music making. "I should like," she said, "to see strolling ballad singers go into nursery schools, to show up suddenly at Story Time."

Burl Ives had recently recorded *Two Little Trains* for Columbia Records and was planning to record *The Runaway Bunny*. In August the popular folk singer wrote Margaret to express his pleasure over this. "I am sure there is a dimension in children's books," Ives said, "especially your books, which must delight any adult with imagination."[13]

"The cradle, the rocking chair, the crooning mother holding her baby or comforting him through those endless griefs and joys of babyhood before he can communicate in that later rhythm called speech, the father jogging his children on his knee, the child swinging through endless years of rhythmic reflection in his swing"—all these, Margaret said, were instances of musicality in everyday experience. Traditional Mother Goose rhymes echoed these rhythms and were the more memorable for it. So too, she might have added, were *Goodnight Moon* and a great many of her other books.

Margaret's essay surpassed the previous year's article in insight and eloquence. She was proud of it, and in a touching gesture made the more poignant by the apparent unexpectedness of it all, she sent a copy of the manuscript to her father. Robert Brown had remarried and was living in Clinton, New Jersey, where Margaret seems to have seen him occasionally. One suspects that this small gift, her symbolic offering to him, did them both a world of good. The essay was clearly voiced and self-assured, the well-considered summing-up of a master. But in venturing to show the manuscript to her father, Margaret reverted to a half-embarrassed shyness that she had otherwise largely outgrown. She hoped, she wrote him, that the piece would "give him a good laugh."[14]

While in Maine Margaret received a letter from Louise Seaman Bechtel that was full of praise for her work. Writing back to express her thanks, she invited the critic to visit the Only House whenever she wished and used the occasion for a sort of stock-taking:

> For the past two weeks I have been more or less alone. It is quite an experience. Yet I seem to do it every year, serve my hermitage. Everything is so astonishingly wild and beautiful here and I have developed the ears of a rabbit and the eyes of an eagle. There is little silence in the wildernesse [*sic*]. Michael used to say that only a great saint or a beast could live alone and I seem to have described the beast.[15]

Bechtel did not go to the Only House that summer, but the Hurds accepted Margaret's invitation, sending word of their expected arrival on July 31, with plans to stay a week. Clem and Posey had last visited her in Maine at her old Long Cove house before the war. If they hoped for an easier time making their way to her new place, they were soon to be disappointed. "If you telephone Billy Brown at Vinalhaven," she assured Clem, "he'll meet your boat at the black buoy in the narrows. Unless you want to fly over."[16] Flying was more expensive but, she suggested a bit cryptically, in good weather the extra seven dollars per passenger was worth "the experience." She signed this missive "Love from, Esmeralda, Your father's Fancy Lady."

The Hurds chose to come by ferry. With Thacher (then little more than two) along, they were more than willing to forego an unspecified experience in return for an added measure of dependability and safety. The sea route proved perilous enough as the ferry did not actually stop at the buoy in the narrows, but merely slowed down beside it, forcing the Hurds to make a hastier transfer of themselves, their belongings, and their son into Billy Brown's boat than they might have wished.

Margaret had gone to great lengths to prepare a "Little Fur Room" for Thacher with fur pillows, fur blankets, and a leopard-skin rug set out on the floor complete with the head preserved, teeth displayed, and glass eyes glaring. To her evident disappointment the toddler showed no appreciation for her efforts. On the contrary, at the sight of the rug he screamed in terror. Smarting from the experience, Margaret observed, "Perhaps it's better for small children to stay in their usual environment."[17]

A bowl of soup she made for Thacher from a favorite recipe did not appeal to him either. A potato his mother put in the oven for his lunch went unattended as everyone left for a walk in the woods. As they headed back, Margaret and the others could see smoke billowing skyward in the distance. Fortunately, only the potato, not the house, had been reduced to ashes.

And so it went all week. There were the usual wine and lobster picnics, early morning swims and afternoons spent lazing by the water. But all in all, these were not quite the good old times they remembered.

Margaret spent much of the fall of 1951 working on new Noisy books and having quiet dinners with friends. The much-needed calm of this period abruptly ended, however, on October 25, when the electric icebox in her East End Avenue apartment exploded, filling the entire lower portion of her building with noxious ammonia gas. For forty-five minutes, while she waited for the police emergency squad to arrive, Margaret lay on her stomach by an open window, straining for air "with a large dog under one arm," as she reported in a long, indignant letter to "Captain [Vincent] Astor," her landlord. The fireproof staircase had also filled with gas, rendering it impassable. She had only gotten out, she said, "by the aid of the tenants on the next top floor—an English lady . . . who had been through the Blitz in London, who opened the door onto the roof and whose husband came through the gas with wet towels." For weeks afterward she suffered from an aggravated bronchial condition. Submitting a bill to Astor for some minor property damage she had also sustained, she insisted that "as a rational and responsible individual" it was her "humane duty to point out a danger that has such a simple remedy—one ladder"— a fire ladder, that is, to be left in the hall. [18]

Harriet Pilpel, the attorney at Greenbaum, Wolff and Ernst who was now handling Margaret's legal affairs, pressed her client's claims in a lawyerly follow-up letter. Margaret confided to Pilpel her amusement at "such petty crooks" as landlords generally proved to be. "Why," she said, "are they so boringly evasive. Who do they think they are—a writer?" [19]

Another unwelcome surprise befell her two weeks later on a visit to the New York Public Library during Children's Book Week. When Margaret and Ursula Nordstrom arrived for the annual celebratory tea, they were met at the door by a staff member checking for invitations. When Margaret was unable to produce hers after searching through her purse, the librarian decorously informed her that she would not be allowed to enter the room until everyone with an invitation had been seated.

As there was no reason to doubt that Margaret had been sent one, the door-keeper's adamancy was ludicrous in the extreme. Harper's editor, her invitation in hand, retorted that she simply refused to attend the event except in the company of her illustrious companion, and that rather than be subjected to an unnecessary wait the two of them would hold a Book Week meeting of their own out front on the Fifth Avenue steps, between the library lions. This they did, and Margaret took the occasion to promise Nordstrom a gift of three stuffed owls to hang over her office desk so that she could thenceforward be just "like the important ladies." [20]

The Hurds asked Margaret to join them in Vermont for Thanksgiving, but "an old-fashioned cold and a new-fangled flu"—the still-lingering effects of the icebox explosion—kept her home in bed. She was sorry, she wrote them afterward, to have "missed a good fire and a snowstorm with you." She had momentarily lost her usually robust appetite, if not the impulse to be a little shocking: "I didn't even touch a sparrow that day."[21]

Eager, perhaps, for additional rest in a warmer climate, Margaret flew out west to spend the Christmas holiday with her friends the Reeves near Tucson. As more guests were expected than could fit in the house, her hosts had rented a trailor as a temporary spare bedroom. The children were delighted to learn that this was to be set aside for them and that Margaret intended to decorate it. The Reeve girls idolized the glamorous writer from New York who always had time for long big-sister–little-sister talks with them. For her part, Margaret had evidently learned a lesson in life from her experience with young Thacher Hurd over the summer. There was no fur in the Reeve children's holiday house, just holly and juniper cuttings, strings of cranberries, and tinsel.

Early in the new year of 1952, Margaret sat for an interview at Cobble Court with a reporter from the Richmond *News Leader*. The occasion was one for nostalgia mixed with old-fashioned story-telling and self-promotion.

She had decked out the tiny, low-ceilinged parlor with gracious Southern touches: a table arrangement of white dogwood blossoms, a large urn of magnolia leaves. Recalling with pride her Virginia school and family ties, Margaret suggested that one reason she had wanted to live in Cobble Court was that it reminded her of an old Charlottesville house she had stayed in one summer. Gratified by her visitor's predictable astonishment at her improbable quarters—"miraculously located," as the reporter was to write, "in the heart of Gotham"—she offered a second, more cryptic account of the cottage's appeal for her.[22] "I used to come by to look at this house to make sure I hadn't dreamed it," Margaret said. Satisfied as to its existence, she had finally gotten Cobble Court for herself, "thinking they would be less apt to tear it down if I was in it." Her explanation for one of the house's most extravagant features sounded oddly like common sense; she had covered the parlor sofa in leopard skin and scattered polar bear rugs on the floor because "insulation is something of a problem."

She was eager to discuss her burgeoning career as a songwriter. She had, she said, written about one hundred songs, several of which had already been recorded or published, and she had more such projects in the works. One of her musical collaborators, Elizabeth Randolph, was a concert pianist and composer from Norfolk, Virginia. Margaret spoke proudly of her fledgling association with Burl Ives. She also made mention of her many illustrators, noting with delight that her most frequent collaborator, Leonard Weisgard, had won the Caldecott Medal for *The Little Island* and that more recently *Two Little Trains,* with illustrations by Jean Charlot, had been chosen by the *New York Times* as one of the ten most distinguished picture books of the past fifty years.

Leaving her visitor momentarily, Margaret disappeared upstairs, returning with a tea tray and hot cross buns for toasting in the hearth. Crispian, who had been napping all through the interview on the leopard-skin sofa, was roused to consciousness by the smell of the buns just as the conversation turned to him.

"Crispian," Margaret said, "has a book of his own, called 'The Dog Who Belonged to Himself,' which will come out in October."

"At the mention of his literary prowess," the *New Leader* later reported, "the dog jumped off the sofa and, in a jealous rage, knocked four of Miss Brown's books from the butler's table." In the "ensuing scramble," Crispian "retrieved a hot cross bun."

A small comic masterpiece, *Mister Dog; The Dog Who Belonged to Himself* revealed Margaret at the height of her powers. Her most fully realized tale of self-possession, it was also the work of a creative artist gathering up the tag ends of an immensely productive period of writing in preparation for new things to come.

The winsome tone of the piece is set in the subtitle, which is also, of course, a gloss on Margaret's own rather dauntless dog's name. The fictional Crispian is a more agreeable if no less adventuresome pup who one day meets a similarly self-possessed little boy. Recognizing each other as equals, they decide to live together as friend and friend. In *Wait Till the Moon Is Full* Margaret underscored the gradual nature of the process by which an emerging self becomes ready for an independent life. In *Mister Dog,* she carried her account of the process an important step further, showing that with self-possession comes the possibility of friendship—perhaps even of love—based on mutuality.

Mister Dog was a happy synthesis and recapitulation of old concerns, the elemental wish for a safe and secure home that Margaret had already expressed in *Goodnight Moon* and other books. Like *Goodnight Moon,* the new book was a stock taking and inventory, another of the author's lists. "Crispian was a *conservative.* He liked everything at the right time—dinner at dinnertime, lunch at lunchtime, breakfast in time for breakfast, and sunrise at sunrise, and sunset at sunset."[23] Aptly, for Crispian's "two-story dog house in a garden," Garth Williams painted an only slightly modified version of Cobble Court in his illustrations for the book. For it was Margaret's new-found self-possession, as well as the reader's, that the carefree *Mister Dog* heralded.

In April Margaret left for a week's vacation on Cumberland Island, Georgia. An old school friend had invited her to see this tranquil spot northeast of Jacksonville, a portion of which was set aside as a wildlife preserve stocked with deer, wild horses, and an astonishing variety of rare sea birds. There were marshlands, forests of wild dogwood and oak, and a pristine eighteen-mile beach. Margaret found natural beauty there to rival anything she had encountered in the Ring of Kerry, at Carmel-by-the-Sea, or in Maine. There was also fascinating evidence of the island's many-layered history of human habitation: the grass burial mounds of Cumberland's original inhabitants, the Timucuran Indians; the gravesite of Revolutionary War hero Light-Horse Harry Lee, who died on the island in 1818; the burnt-out brick chimney remains of Cumberland's antebellum slave quarters. There were ruins of a fantastically turreted Scottish-style castle built by the turn-of-the-century robber-baron Carnegies, an intact second Carnegie estate that was now an inn, and the summer cottages of other famous families, notably the Rockefellers.

At a crowded party one evening, Margaret traded glances with an animated younger man, who was introduced to her as "Pebble." At twenty-six, James Stillman Rockefeller, Jr., was a gentle-spirited romantic and sailing enthusiast. A descendent of both

Andrew Carnegie and the branch of the Rockefeller family which controlled the First National City Bank of New York, he had recently graduated from Yale following two and a half years of service in the Army Air Force. He was now, he told Margaret, well into the planning of a transpacific crossing in his sloop *Mandalay*. Pebble's easygoing boyish manner and lack of pretense appealed to Margaret greatly. As he later recalled, theirs had been a case of love at first sight.

The next morning at dawn they went for a walk along the beach. Rockefeller, who was almost as many years younger than Margaret as Michael Strange had been older, asked her if she had ever been married. "Oh no, I'm too busy and too selfish to get married," she replied.[24] Margaret then spoke with schoolgirlish pride of her accomplishments. She had, she said, published seventy-two children's books. Queen Mary of England kept a copy of the *Little Fur Family* by the royal bedside. (This may or may not have been true, but the mother of Britain's reigning monarch, George VI, is known to have purchased a copy of *The Sleepy Little Lion*.)

Margaret was playing delightfully with her new friend—even a Rockefeller would have to be impressed by a writer in demand with a queen. Then, however, her self-confidence abruptly ebbed away. "Someday," she said, "I will write something serious." Yet this too was a part of the flirtation. She had already decided that she could let down her guard with Pebble to an extent she had done with few people in the past. She cherished this about him. She talked to him about her hectic New York routine and how the "fidget wheels of time" were "forever getting in the way." Cobble Court stilled the "fidget wheels."[25]

Soon afterward, Margaret left for New York, promising to return to Cumberland Island the following month. On April 17 she telephoned Charles Shaw to ask him to dinner at Cobble Court and to say that she had fallen in love.

Margaret and Posey Hurd had always been candid collaborators able to speak their minds as they worked toward a finished manuscript acceptable to them both. But in the early months of

1952, a new Golden Books project in the here-and-now vein, "The Early Milkman," became a battleground on which some of the tensions of the previous summer resurfaced in exchanges that reached the heated intensity of family strife.

With the Hurds living in Vermont, collaboration had to be carried on by mail, except for the occasions when Margaret drove up to their farm for a visit. She felt put upon by this arrangement, she now said, and asked—demanded rather, with a child's irritability—to know why they could not come down to New York more often.

Margaret proceeded to send Posey a nearly completed draft of their book in which four pages—a fraction of the whole—had been left blank, ostensibly for her collaborator to fill in as she saw fit. This high-handed gesture aroused her usually mild-mannered friend's indignation. With unrestrained sarcasm, Posey thanked Margaret for having created the conditions for such a "complete collaboration," and returned the manuscript with some fairly piquant marginal notations.[26] To these Margaret added notes of her own.

Margaret's draft of May 8, the focus of all their commentary, began, "Shhhrrrrr (italics) — — — (complete line) The milkman's rubber tired truck sounded soft and hushed in the still, pale darkness before dawn." To the left of these lines, Posey commented, "About as dull a beginning for a children's book as I have yet read." To which Margaret replied, "Thoroughly disagree! . . . The quietness of milkmen is their wonder! and consequently their drama for children." She proposed that they leave this point for the editor to resolve.

Further along, Margaret suggested that a passage of Posey's be deleted: "Let pictures carry the burden of the information." Posey rebutted with an impatient "Why bother to write anything?" Margaret replied, "To Hell with you!" Later in the piece, Margaret referred to a "wagon" which she had previously called a truck. Posey pointed out the inconsistency and Margaret responded, "Quite right Professor." And so the collaboration was left for the moment, to be continued over the next weeks and months.

In the past, Margaret and Posey had been rather good at catching themselves in the act of their critical excesses and quickly restoring their friendship to an even keel. Along with her latest round of comments, Margaret sent a note calling, perhaps only halfheartedly, for a truce:

> Listen Pose—Maybe we are talking like children's writers—a penny a dozen—What you call my arrogant high horse is what I call saying quickly what I believe and what else can I say. What else can you say. . . .
>
> Here is my rewrite which I expect you to rewrite which I expect to rewrite which I expect you to rewrite which I expect S & S to rewrite which I expect us to rewrite and so go the pains of collaboration . . . which we are both obviously fed up with.

Margaret registered a raft of other complaints before finally calming down: "All this is silly between us and I hope you will think so to [*sic*]. Lets [*sic*] go to work. Love, Old Horror."

As part of her campaign for a more ordered, less frenetic life, Margaret had concluded by the spring of 1952 that Simon and Schuster, of all her publishers, offered her the best possibility of stabilizing her wildly fluctuating financial situation. Accordingly, she informed Georges Duplaix, the founder and principal figure in the Golden Books operation, that she might be willing to sign a long-term contract binding her to write a specified number of new Golden titles each year—provided the agreement was not an exclusive one. The Golden Books management had made a policy of attempting to commit their authors and artists to working full time for them. Margaret, for one, had resisted any such suggestion. Confident as she was in her continued productivity, she had little fear, however, of entering into the type of agreement she proposed. On receiving word from her, Duplaix and his associates eagerly commenced negotiations.

The ensuing confusion might have been predicted from the peculiarly divided nature of the firm's chain of command. Duplaix, having hired a staff and gotten the Golden Books imprint started, had become an absentee director. As he had told his editor in chief, Dorothy Bennett, from the outset, he had "an orderly mind only for painting" and intended to spend as little time as possible in the office and to continue living in Europe. [27] During the months each year when he was away, even Mssrs. Simon and Schuster were not to be allowed to disturb his concentration. Once when Max Schuster telephoned Bennett to ask how Duplaix could be reached, she firmly replied that she and her staff were not at liberty to give out that information.

Bennett's office and Duplaix's studio were two centers of power of the Golden Books operation. There was also a third—the office of Lucille Ogle, who managed the production end of the business from her desk at the Western Printing Company in Rockefeller Center. Ogle initiated a great many Golden Books projects as well, and as one of the chief operating officers she took part in deciding which books from previous lists were to be dropped on account of disappointing sales. Such prunings of the list amounted to another form of editing, and a high pitch of tension generally prevailed between Ogle's and Bennett's sides of the business.

Duplaix seems to have served as the final arbitor in disputes in which authors and illustrators often found themselves caught uncomfortably in the cross fire. Margaret was not the only Golden Books author to turn to legal counsel for help in sorting out her knotty affairs with the firm.

It was with Georges Duplaix himself (in New York on a brief business trip) that Margaret first discussed the outlines of a long-term contract. Duplaix's offer appeared to be generous, but in a follow-up conversation with Ogle, Margaret found that a number of key provisions had changed. Duplaix, meanwhile, had returned to Paris. Demanding clarification, Margaret angrily wrote him there:

> What on earth am I dealing with? And with whom? Lucille has completely reneged and gone back on your proposition to me over the telephone. . . . There is an emotional destructiveness in this kind of dealing with artists that you as an artist should be the first to recognize and which I am damned if I can understand. I lost my temper last night and sent Lucille the enclosed telegram which, on sober reflection, I would like to send her again. . . . Be glad that the ocean is there. If you don't make good your word to me I will be over to shoot you with a bow and arrow in August. Love, Margaret Wise Brown. [28]

The telegram to Lucille Ogle that she had referred to, dated May 15, was equally firm:

LUCY, THIS AFTERNOON'S MEETING HAS SHOCKED ME TO THE END. IF YOU AND GEORGES AND DOROTHY OR WHOEVER IS IN AUTHORITY IN YOUR COMPANY CANNOT AGREE TO ONE JOINT PROPOSITION SUCH AS GEORGES PROPOSED TO ME SUCH AS LEVANTALL [*sic*] AND SHIMKIN ARE ALSO AWARE OF I CAN SEE NO POSSIBLE WAY IN WHICH HUMAN LOGIC AND MY DIGNITY AS AN ARTIST CAN DEAL WITH YOU. I WILL BE IN NEW YORK ONE MORE WEEK.[29]

Her attorney, Harriet Pilpel, followed up on the matter, reporting afterward, "As is usual, I found that your confusion simply reflected theirs."[30] Margaret's irritation had been amply justified. Discussions with Golden Books continued, however, and the final agreement appeared to be highly satisfactory to her, although she told Pilpel she did not yet think the time had come to lower her guard. From that year forward, Margaret was to receive from the firm a guaranteed annual general advance of six thousand dollars—a handsome sum in 1952—in addition to her standard advance for each manuscript they bought from her and whatever royalties she earned. Margaret retained the absolute right to publish other work elsewhere. Money would most likely not be a problem for her again for the foreseeable future.

Shortly before departing for Cumberland Island, and in the same spirit of putting her affairs in order, Margaret sent Harriet Pilpel the general outlines of a new will. "I am going off in the car for another 2,000 miles," she told her lawyer, "and again it occurs to me that it wouldn't be a bad idea to have a Will to sign . . . so that the rapacious State of New York cannot take one-third of my horse brasses and Crispian."[31] She expected to be back in the city around the start of summer and looked forward, she said, to "that remote day outside a telephone booth in late June" when the two of them might meet, cloak-and-dagger-style, to "discuss those unsuspected obscurities of legal language" of which wills and contracts were made.

Once back on Cumberland Island, Margaret put most thoughts of work out of her mind. She and James Rockefeller were very much in love. She was happier in his company than she had been in years.

Exploring the island also gave her great pleasure. In a letter to her Doubleday editor, Margaret Lesser, she reported that she was "too busy watching to take pictures or notes or write."[32] Besides, she said, art did not "work that way" for her—as a matter of willed attention. "Years from now a great sea turtle will crawl out of the sea and over the page to lay its eggs in the sand at night"—that is, she would write a new picture book or poem or short story— "and I'll wonder where it came from." Crispian, she said, had gotten into an altercation the previous day with some wild hogs. "I jumped into a palmutta [sic] bush and pulled him off and the only two casualties were the pigs [sic] ear and me."

One business matter seemed pressing enough to warrant a gingerly tug at the editor's sleeve. A new collaboration with Leonard Weisgard, *Little Frightened Tiger,* had been much delayed. Margaret inquired, "Tiger Tiger burning bright—What goes on there?"

It was great fun, she said,

being here in a household of men [James Rockefeller and his comrades] about to sail arround [sic] the world. I mend the holes in their pants and we cook up out of Jim Beards [sic] cook-book shark meat, venison, and turtle eggs, and paint the boat and roam the beaches. They are all writers—as well—and no one gets any quarter.

She was considering flying down to the Virgin Islands from New York in October (there were to be several variations on her plan) to rejoin them there. "Will you send me a copy of *Kon Tiki*— author's discount—to Maine. I want to see what's ahead."

Margaret also had a message for her editor's young daughter: "Tell Kiki I hope she grows a big red beard. That would surprise her." (Pebble had already grown a black one.)

Margaret had brought along copies of two books she had edited in the early days at Scott. One of these, chosen most likely in anticipation of new travel adventures of her own, was *The Log of Christopher Columbus.* The other was Posey Hurd's *Hurry Hurry.*

Margaret regretted having never reestablished friendly relations with Bill Scott following their legal troubles over the Noisy Books. From Cumberland, she wrote Scott reminding him of the voluminous subtitle of Posey's book: *Hurry Hurry: A Tale of Calamity and Woe; or, A Lesson in Leisure, Relating the dire mishaps which befell a certain nurse who went too fast, together with a faithful account of her Reform, the whole comprising a powerful Lesson.*

Did Margaret now believe she had been too quick to mistrust Scott in her dealings with his firm? Had she, too, learned some unspecified "powerful Lesson?" She let these suggestions hang in the air as she waxed nostalgic: "We will never be as right again as we were instinctively in that first rebellion we all created to-gether in Children's Books,—or have as much fun."[33] Brushing formality aside, she added, "This is just a friendly letter and why not after all these hectic over busy years. Again I'm trying to step out of it. The insane rush." Perhaps for the first time in her life Margaret no longer felt the need to prove herself. She was on Cumberland, she wrote, visiting "four fellows who are about to take three years to sail arround [sic] the world to see for themselves if people are really so different anywhere in it or on it." She hoped to accompany them for at least part of their journey. In the meantime she wondered if the Scotts would join her one evening that fall for dinner at Cobble Court.

Scott thanked her for her "good letter and for the spirit which prompted . . . it" and said he would be happy to see her again.[34] He preferred, however, not to view the past with nostalgia. "No one and no thing that lives stands still," he reminded her in a mild rebuke that sounded vaguely like a cross between a Bank Street geography lesson and a sermon. "Even the earth and seas and mountains slowly change. It's up to us to see that the change is constructive."

Lofty analogies were hardly needed to drive home the point that the lives of many in their initial little group had changed dramatically since the time they first began making books together in the late thirties. Bill Scott had recently seen Leonard Weisgard on a city bus. A flustered, gangling odd-man-out when he had first met him, Weisgard now looked self-assured sitting beside his wife and their baby daughter.

Margaret made no effort to conceal her age from the much younger James Rockefeller. She joked about it, telling him that her age "kept changing" and so could not easily be guessed. Whether she was more concerned about their difference in years than she acknowledged is less clear. She dated a note from Cumberland to Ursula Nordstrom "May 23, 1952—20 yrs old."[35] Perhaps this was just a reminder of her birthday should the editor be in a gift-giving mood, but Margaret, of course, had not turned twenty but forty-two.

Arriving in New York in mid-June, she telephoned Luther Greene to say she had brought someone back with her from Cumberland who had nothing to wear but a T-shirt, shorts, and sandals. She wondered if Luther might possibly lend the young man some clothes. When Greene learned that Margaret's ill-clad companion was a Rockefeller, he was delighted. He took an immediate liking to Pebble, and afterwards thought that the time Margaret spent with him must have been the happiest period of her life. After a brief stop in Connecticut, where she introduced Pebble to her now-married friend Jessica Gamble Dunham, the couple continued on to the Only House where they stayed for the rest of the summer. By then, Margaret and James Rockefeller had decided to marry.

"Here I go—out to sea with my fog horn," Margaret wrote from Maine to Alvin Tresselt, the editor of a soon-to-be-inaugurated children's magazine, *Humpty Dumpty*.[36] She had promised to compose a poem about the magazine's namesake for the premiere issue and was having trouble coming up with a version that Tresselt liked. "I'll tie up at the black buoy," she vowed, "and write you some more verses." Endlessly reworked nonsense stanzas shuttled back and forth between New York and the Only House all summer. But nothing Margaret did pleased the editor and in exasperation she finally gave up. She had pulled order out of chaos many times in the last several months, but apparently even she could not put Humpty Dumpty back together.

Keeping an eye on her other business affairs, she wrote Harriet Pilpel to ask whether her new contract with Golden Books, over

which the fur had so recently flown, would soon be ready as promised for her signature. In late August she and Pebble were back in
New York for a few hectic weeks of socializing.

As Margaret contemplated married life, she reconsidered the
details of her new will. In a note to her executors she expressed the
wish to be buried in the Brown family plot in Oakhill Cemetery in
Kirkwood, Missouri. Evidently she wanted to be certain that this
conciliatory gesture toward her family would not be mistaken for a
renunciation of the years she had spent with Michael Strange:

> for a tombstone, I would like the square block of granite which
> forms at this moment the second step from the top as you come out
> of the left-hand front door towards the sea of the new house I built
> for Michael Strange in Maine. This piece of granite has a hole in it
> and I would like on it the following inscription:
>
>
>
> MARGARET WISE BROWN
>
> Born   Died
>
> Writer of Songs and Nonsense
>
>
>
> It is my desire that this stone be left in the rough. [37]

Just a day later, however, she changed her mind, and an attorney with the firm of Greenbaum, Wolff and Ernst wrote to the
United States Coast Guard's New York headquarters on her behalf
to inquire whether their client's wish to be buried at sea by the
Coast Guard could possibly be satisfied. "In our many years of
experience," the lawyer continued, barely concealing his amusement, "we have never heard of such an arrangement and we would
like to have further particulars on this." [38] The Coast Guard's Legal
Section was quick to respond to this "rather unique proposal" with
a diplomatic no. [39]

One evening Margaret gave a small party for her fiancé in the
garden at Cobble Court. A few days later she and Pebble and
Charles Shaw drove down to Chinatown for dinner. ("Alas!, as I
feared," Shaw wrote in his diary, "This type of thing is no longer
my cup of tea.")[40] From New York, Rockefeller intended to rejoin
his crewmates in Miami and to sail from there to the Virgin Islands
on the first leg of the great adventure. Margaret, before rendez-
vousing with him, wanted to spend some time resting up for the

rough-and-tumble journey in more luxurious surroundings. On Tuesday, September 23, James Rockefeller, Dorothy Ripley, and a few others saw her off as she set sail on the cruise ship *Vulcania* for Cannes.

The off-season ocean crossing proved to be restful indeed. Her cabin had a private balcony. The food was excellent. Even Crispian was well provided for. "Crispin's [*sic*] dinner," she wrote Dorothy from on shipboard, "is small cubed beef and meats with finely chopped vegetables that a steward brings him . . . at six."[41] The boat was uncrowded. Among her fellow passengers were the director of the cruise line, the Italian consul general, several doctors, an "attractive Italian couple—Conte and Contessa Hypolite or some such name and some darling young nuns from Ohio who are going to Rome to take charge of 60 little 5 yr olds."

The relaxed pace of the voyage gave Margaret a chance to reflect on recent events and contemplate the future. "I can see," she told Dorothy, "why Pebble says the sea is unconfused and uncomplicated. . . . You know your adversaries and its [*sic*] a clean fight." Before leaving, Margaret had given away to friends many of the books in her library. Some of the recipients had thought this odd, but she was only house cleaning, preparing to start over fresh: "This is more than just a trip. I don't think I'll ever live the old life I led in New York again. I've left the city. High time. It was like living in a telephone booth."

The *Vulcania* dropped anchor in Cannes on October 2. From there Margaret headed by train for a brief visit to Italy, then returned to the south of France, reaching the secluded medieval coastal village of Eze by October 12. An old friend of Michael's, Walter Varney, had taken up residence there as the manager of the Château Barlow, a hotel cradled high in the hills, with splendid views of the Mediterranean directly below.

With the attentive, elderly Monsieur Varney—Margaret called him the "Wizard of Eze"—at her beck and call, and with all the privacy she could want, she settled in behind thick stone walls, in a room that opened onto an interior courtyard.[42]

Her new Golden Book, *Mister Dog,* had already been published in a French-language edition, and Margaret brought some copies with her to present to the town's children. The original

"Monsieur Chien," Crispian, promptly got himself into a brawl with one of the local dogs by the village fountain and for once suffered a complete rout. Margaret lamented his stunning reversal of fortune in a little poem:

> *The Crispian Blues*
>
> Bitten on the bottom
> In my first fight in France
> Why did I not
> Wear a pair of pants?
> Zut
> Et crotte
> Zis
> Ees
> Not cricket. [43]

Troubled by her own recent battle of words with Posey Hurd, Margaret scribbled a conciliatory postcard to her. Their relations over the last several months had been such that she had not yet gotten around to telling Posey and Clem that she planned to marry.

"Dearest Pose—A long way from home in The Town of Pretend. Then heading for the Caribbean and even across the Pacific. I fell in love with a sailor."[44] Of their latest collaboration she wrote:

> Have given one final and vast struggle to pull our flippent [*sic*] and overserious efforts together. I loved your continuation of my nonsense and I think for all its foolishness it gave the book a push in the right direction. You take it on from here. . . . Hail and Farewell. Love, Juniper.

Margaret made the short drive to Saint-Paul-de-Vence to visit Jacques Prévert and thank him for having quoted from her picture book *Les Chatons barbouilleurs* (*The Color Kittens*) in his own poetry collection, *Spectacles*.

On an impulse, she decided to make a second trip to Florence, borrowing the equivalent of three hundred dollars for this purpose from a friend of Walter Varney's. (Her bank account was for the moment once again overdrawn.) Her plans changed suddenly, however, when on Thursday, October 30, she was stricken with an acute abdominal pain and rushed to the nearest hospital, the Clinique des Dames Augustines in Nice.

During the postwar years, French hospitals were generally considered inferior to those in the United States. As a sensible travel precaution, Margaret was carrying an identity card with instructions to take her to the American Hospital in Paris in the event of an emergency. In the present circumstances, however, travel was clearly inadvisable.

The next day she went into surgery. The exploratory phase of the operation revealed an ovarian cyst, which the surgeon removed. As a precaution, her appendix was also removed. She stood the operation well and was expected to make a full recovery.

Writing in longhand on her Cobble Court stationery, Margaret drafted a codicil to her will while awaiting surgery. In this document, she reaffirmed her love for James Rockefeller and settled what she considered an outstanding debt to Walter Varney. To Varney, who had lately been a help to her and had in the past been a good friend to Michael Strange, she made a bequest of two thousand dollars—and Crispian, if he wanted the dog. She asked that the two family members who were named in her will, Roberta and her cousin Judy, allow Pebble to "have anything of mine he wants since he is closest to me" and to have the use of her East End Avenue apartment and Cobble Court.[45] "He has the keys and I consider these places to be his home as well as my own." Her body was to be cremated, the ashes to be given to him to be scattered in the Atlantic. At the bottom of the page Margaret wrote, "witnesses October 30, 1952" and beside this added the numerals 1, 2, and 3 in a column and the formula "My own handwriting is my witness."

Under French law, this method of witnessing the codicil was legal and binding. How Margaret knew this is not known; plainly, however, she took care to handle the matter properly.

While recovering from her surgery, Margaret had plenty of time for letter writing. In a lighthearted missive to Garth Williams, she compared the winged white caps of the hospital nurses to the sails of ships gliding effortlessly in and out of port.[46] As she wrote this to Williams, her thoughts were no doubt racing toward her sailor friend, James Rockefeller. In a letter to him, she was rather less guarded: "I've never been in a situation like this before, a big helpless creature becoming younger and younger."[47]

Before Margaret took ill, Ursula Nordstrom had written her at Eze, remarking that with the first anniversary of their Book Week meeting between the library lions fast approaching she thought it "mighty strange" that she had still not received her promised gift of three stuffed owls.[48] Margaret replied from the hospital that she had rounded up two of the owls and would now "have to shoot a third or catch it alive." She claimed she and Crispian had recently "travelled in a compartment at night with six hunters and an owl in a train to Pisa from Florence. They were going to shoot larks in the morning. . . . The hunters shoot the little birds and cook them on a spit with their eyes still glaring."[49] Having done her best to give the editor a little shock, Margaret continued in a lighter vein. The hunters, she said, "passed me the basket and when I looked inside I looked deep into the eyes of an owl. (Nearer than I ever got in the library.) . . . I take Crispin [*sic*] around with me the way Ike takes Mamie."

Kind nuns attended her, she wrote Leonard Weisgard. "[They] reach deep in their pockets like big rabbits and pull out pills, trying not to laugh to [*sic*] much."[50] Except for the first three days, she had been enjoying the experience. "Everyone is so human. The old rattlebag chambermaid sings musichall songs and closes the window so 'her little rabbit' won't catch cold and I have a wonderful time with one of the younger ones"—the attendant with whom Margaret said she had gone a few rounds at boxing. "The room is full of flowers that Walter brings in and everyone is here but Crispin [*sic*]. I send him a sandwich every day."

Weisgard had recently been commissioned to design a West Coast production of the *Nutcracker* ballet. Cheering him on, Margaret expressed her delight that her old friend had at last gotten a chance to realize one of his longstanding ambitions. She was beginning to see some of her own long-term goals come into view. She thought, for one thing, that her analysis was proving to be ever more helpful to her. "I seem to feel increasing freedom to act," Margaret said, "and to censor my imediate [*sic*] mistakes."

Margaret had never taken for granted her talent as a writer. As she wrote Weisgard, she no more took love for granted now:

> I had great chance in meeting Pebble. Someone who[m] all my
> hearts can love and who[m] my deepest one admires and knows. I
> have never known such tenderness. No more separations! And my
> one hope is that I will always be able to make him happy. We are
> rarely given that chance in life and it is a big thing.

According to one plan under consideration, Margaret was to meet her fiancé in Panama, where they would marry and set sail on the transpacific leg of the voyage. For the moment she intended to rest and get well. "How like a child getting younger and younger it is," she wrote, "to lie up here in a big blue hospital room. My doctor is old fashioned and doesn't believe in jumping up right away." (The routine practice in American hospitals was to get a patient ambulatory within a day or two of surgery.)

"LaMere—the chief nun on this floor is so strongly sensitive and otherworldly. I send word to her that there are devils in my room so she will come and tell me good-night. It is all so unlike the big white efficiency box of an American Institution."

She needed a bit of discreet scavenging work from Leonard:

"Could you call a taxidermist and find three old owls for Ursula. And we can tie them up by their legs or find a funny old cage for her to hang them in her office. There's a taxidermist on the corner of 11th or 12th and Sixth Ave—I think." Margaret was rarely at a loss for such information. "She wants her owls. And having threatened to give her three owls for Christmas I've got to make good."

Margaret's doctor brought her good Bordeaux from his own cellar to drink with her meals. By Wednesday, November 12, when she wrote a long letter to her cousin Judy, she was thinking in some detail about her social calendar:

"Here I sit in a Big Blue Room in a sort of Ba Ba [sic] the elephant hospital—As George [a mutual friend] would say We always do end up in a swarm of Nuns. . . . I've really enjoyed this odd French hospital."[51] Her appendix, she explained, was presently "sitting in a bottle" in her room. "It nearly exploded. And Pebble is so glad it's out he's jumping up and down on his ship between the Bahammas [sic] and the Virgin Islands." She expected to be discharged soon. After a brief stopover in London, she intended to fly back to New York around November 25 and would see her cousin then. By December 1 she hoped to rejoin her fiancé. "Peb and I are never going to be apart again and I will probably cross the Pacific with him."

Judy had recently given birth to her first child, a boy. "I came staggering out of Italy," Margaret reported, "with a huge blue basket of a cradle on my head and some little white rabbit slippers" as gifts for the baby. "How big are Jame's [*sic*] feet?" she wanted to know. "What do you call your little man child?" There was a sense of shared triumph in Margaret's congratulations for her cousin and in her happy report of her own plans. They both had reason to feel proud. "Lots of love and warm hugs to prove we aren't like the rest of that cold breed of Browns. Your letter came the fourth or third day of my operation and it did me so much good."

On Thursday, November 13, Margaret was nearly recovered and about to be released for further rest at the Château Barlow. She was in a jaunty mood as she greeted her nurse just before ten o'clock in the morning. Lying in bed, Margaret kicked one leg high over her head, can-can style, as much as to say, "See how well I'm doing!"[52] Then suddenly she blacked out. It was later found that an embolism which had formed in her leg had at that instant dislodged and travelled the short distance to her brain. Margaret regained a groggy sort of consciousness a moment later, but only for a moment. Then she was dead.

Word of Margaret's death spread rapidly from friend to friend over the next twenty-four hours. Charles Shaw, on hearing the news over the phone from Bruce Bliven, Jr., gasped for breath, sounding briefly as if he might be having a heart attack. He spent much of the rest of the day calling other friends and colleagues of hers: Bill Scott, Ursula Nordstrom, Esphyr Slobodkina. When he lay down for his afternoon nap, sleep eluded him. As the day came to an end, he wrote in his diary, "I am more shocked and saddened than I can say. . . . Her absence will be a large gap in my life."[53]

Bruce Bliven, Jr., telephoned Garth Williams to tell him what was known about her death. Mustering a tone of mock exasperation that Margaret herself would doubtless have appreciated, Bliven sighed into the phone, "This is the dirtiest trick Margaret ever played on us."[54] As the obituaries appeared in newspapers and magazines throughout the country, the last of the letters she had written to friends arrived from France.

In accordance with her wishes, Margaret's body was cremated in Marseille on Friday, November 21. In a communiqué dated November 24, the American Consul General stationed in Nice, Quincy F. Roberts, wrote Roberta to confirm the circumstances of her sister's death and to express his sympathy. Leonard Weisgard, who had previously arranged to meet Margaret at Idlewild Airport on her return to the city, instead retrieved her ashes early on the morning of November 28. As had been provided for in the codicil to her will, he gave these to James Rockefeller, who took the ashes to Maine and scattered them in the waters off Vinalhaven.

As provided for in her will, Rockefeller also took title to the Only House and its surrounding property, but he renounced his claim to her other personal property and effects. Rockefeller proceeded with his planned sail, which lasted three years and eventually took him around the world. On his return, he moved out of his family home in Greenwich, Connecticut and established his residence in a Maine town on Penobscot Bay in close proximity to the Only House. In a grassy clearing on the island property, he erected a simple stone marker as a monument to Margaret.[55]

Early on in *Man and His Island,* Rockefeller's memoir of his round-the-world journey, he recounts a friendly parting with one of his original sailing companions, a young fellow who like himself had fallen in love during the time of their final preparations. When the friend decided to drop out of the crew, he apologized for leaving "Peb" short-handed, to which Rockefeller replied, "Go ahead and grab happiness when you see it. You may never get a second chance."[56]

The Hurds were in California at the time of Margaret's death. When they got back to Vermont they found her last postcard to Posey perched on the mantelpiece where they'd left it. The final words of the message, Margaret's footloose "Hail and farewell," now sounded darkly premonitory as, keeping to an old theme, they wondered if Margaret's untimely death was not in some obscure way the final legacy of Michael Strange's destructiveness.

In the weeks and months following Margaret's death, Ursula Nordstrom caught herself repeatedly in the impulse to telephone her favorite author to ask her advice about this or that publishing matter, only to realize with undiminished force that it was no longer possible.

In January of 1953 Lucy Sprague Mitchell, writing in the first issue of the 69 *Bank Street* newsletter, eulogized "Brownie" as "an experimenter, a kind of scientist." She was, Margaret's former teacher declared, "as experimental as anyone I have ever known."[57]

There was a groping, oddly second-hand quality to portions of the piece, for which Mitchell had plainly relied on published sources (the *Life* article and others) for a number of details. Her own recollections of Margaret's "experimental" temperament were perhaps too emotionally charged to set down in specific terms. She was struggling there and then, it seems, to resolve her unease over Margaret's relationship with Michael Strange. In an oblique reference to Michael, she acknowledged that while the Bank Street community had always called Margaret "Brownie" there had also been "some friends" who called her by other names. Poignantly, Mitchell recalled that

> for years [Margaret] had told me that she wished to stop writing for children. She wanted to write for grown-ups. And I always had the feeling that some time she would. But not until she herself had fully grown up. In the last few years, which were full of human suffering for her, I felt that time was approaching. . . . Given a few more years of living, of experimenting, where might that gleam of hers have led her?

In the days immediately following her death, her friends had tried to decide what might constitute a suitable memorial to Margaret. A traditional service had been quickly ruled out on the grounds that Margaret surely would not have wanted one. Instead, a party was planned, to be held at Cobble Court on what would have been her forty-third birthday. The gathering took place in the late afternoon of Thursday, May 21—two days early. Present in Margaret's garden for the bittersweet occasion were Garth Williams, Leonard Weisgard, Bruce Bliven, Jr., Charles Shaw, Judith

Stanton, and a dozen others. Shaw, in his diary entry for that day, noted that the champagne served at the "little party in memory of MWB" had been "very good."[58] Margaret's cousin recalled years later, "We all got drunk. That's what Margaret would have liked."[59] But Garth Williams's impression of the event was perhaps the most telling. At Margaret's many intimate dinner parties and garden gatherings over the years, there had always been an atmosphere of convivial banter and festivity, but with Margaret herself not present to set the tone, her friends appeared to have little to say to each other.[60]

That spring of 1953, Harper published *The Duck,* another of Margaret's collaborations with Ylla. On the dustjacket of the book, in place of the usual author's biography, there appeared this eulogy, probably written by Ursula Nordstrom:

> Margaret Wise Brown's recent death brought a tragic and untimely end to a brilliant career. She was the author of more than a hundred books for the very young. . . . The wisdom and beauty and tenderness of her writing, which approaches true poetry, finds unending response in the little children for whom she wrote and whose love for her books is a real and lasting tribute to her genius.[61]

A far less expected tribute was published in the June 1953 issue of the *Horn Book* magazine, in Anne Carroll Moore's "Three Owls' Notebook" column. After reaffirming her admiration for the illustrator Jean Charlot (several of whose books Margaret had written), Moore turned to a consideration of Ylla's picture books. "I feel very strongly," she wrote, "about the treatment of animals, as mere properties in books for children. Respect for animals . . . is well served by so beautiful a book as *The Duck.* . . . Of Margaret Wise Brown's many stories for little children this is to me one of the best: it is so natural."[62]

As a critical appraisal of Margaret's merry fantasy, which in tone and substance has rather more in common with the Marx Brothers' *Duck Soup* than with a Roger Tory Peterson field guide, Moore's praise was notably misdirected. More striking than that, however, was the mere fact that the librarian had written affirmatively about her work at all.

In accordance with the provisions of Margaret's will, Roberta Rauch and Bruce Bliven, Jr., were appointed coexecutors of her estate. Margaret had not consulted either her sister or her friend about this in advance. The responsibilities which now fell to them entailed a five-year labor of sorting through voluminous stacks of unpublished manuscripts, disposing of a nettlesome challenge to the will initiated by Walter Varney, and seeing into print a substantial number of additional works, some already under contract, many others not.

Varney's challenge concerned the disposition of the rights to Margaret's Doubleday books, which she had rather mischievously tied to the custody of Crispian. The August 28 will provided that if Margaret's sister was prepared to take custody of her difficult dog she could also have the Doubleday income. The October 30 codicil, however, offered Varney the dog ("if he wants him") without making reference to the book royalties previously linked to Crispian. Varney, who at the time of Margaret's death already had Crispian in his care, decided to press his claim. The matter was not laid to rest for five more years, when it was finally decided that Varney was welcome to keep Margaret's Kerry Blue and Roberta was entitled to the income.

It had widely been assumed by Margaret's friends, and by publishing associates who knew of her frequent travels, assorted homes, and extravagant gift-giving, that she was the lifelong beneficiary of a sizeable inheritance. This was not so. Her only inherited wealth consisted of a modest amount of stock left to her by one of the Brown aunts. Her father had continued to give her an annual allowance at least through 1946 (and possibly afterward), but this sum, whatever it was, appears not to have been large. Far and away the lion's share of her annual income, which during the last years of her life averaged around $15,000 (or about $80,000 in 1990 dollars), derived from her earnings as a writer.[63]

Margaret had never been very careful about financial record-keeping and bill-paying. (She once told a friend that she often remembered to pay her bills while strapped into her seat on an airport runway during the moments before take-off.) At the time of her death, her bank account was at a low ebb: there was no money whatsoever with which to pay her miscellaneous creditors, the lawyers' fees, and the bequests to her heirs.

Margaret had always viewed will making as an opportunity to repay past kindnesses and to commit herself by word and deed to what mattered most to her in life at the moment. For years her friend Bruce Bliven, Jr., had talked of breaking away from journalism to become a novelist, a frustrated ambition that Margaret could well understand. Under the terms of an earlier will dated December 22, 1949, she had bequeathed him the Only House, "hoping," as she wrote then, "he'll find it a good place to write in some day."[64] In the document in force at the time of her death, the Only House had become a token of her love for James Rockefeller, "my first of kin and closest."

By far the most surprising provision of the will concerned the disposition of the majority of Margaret's royalties. All future earnings from books published during her lifetime, excluding only the Doubleday titles, went to an eight-year-old boy who lived in the York Avenue tenement one passed through on the way to Cobble Court. Albert Clarke III was the son of Joan MacCormick Clarke, whom Margaret had known since the late thirties, when Joan, her brother Jim, their mother, and Jessica Gamble had shared a summer house on Vinalhaven. Joan had been a teenager then. She was now the wife of a struggling musician and mother of three boys. (It was Margaret, most likely, who had helped the young family find their apartment by her studio.)

Albert, like Margaret, was a middle child. He was a beautiful, blond, cherubic boy. Years later Jessica Gamble Dunham would wonder whether Margaret had chosen him as her principal heir because he looked so much like the kind of child she herself might have had. Margaret's obvious heir, in the sense that she considered him her "first of kin," plainly did not need the money. It would appear she had determined to put her wealth into the hands of someone to whom it might mean a great deal.

Margaret had already made some provision for the Clarkes' eldest son, Austin. Among the books due to be published around the time of her death was *The Sailor Dog,* a Golden Book. Under the terms of the contract insisted upon by Margaret, young Austin was to share equally with her in the royalties and in the author credits. (The boy's name did appear in the first edition but was subsequently dropped by the publisher.)

"In his precise, little-boy way," Margaret told her interviewer from the Richmond *News Leader* months before her death, Austin had explained to her how the hero of the story, a sailor who also happened to be a dog, "lived near the dock, and had a hook for his hat, and a hook for his coat, a hook for his handkerchief."[65] She had shaped and revised the manuscript into its final form, but was entirely serious about considering Austin Clarke her coauthor and partner in creation.

In the spring and summer of 1952, when she drafted the will that named Albert as her principal heir, Margaret had no reason to think she might die any time soon. In all likelihood, had she lived she would have changed matters around again in another year or two, as she had done in the past. Just as Margaret, by her own account, had written her children's books through a "happy accident," Albert Clarke III had the great good luck to become her heir.

Immense caches of unpublished manuscripts, in varying states of completion and of widely varying quality, were found at Cobble Court, 186 East End Avenue, and the Only House. It became the large and laborious task of Roberta Rauch and Bruce Bliven, Jr. to determine the copyright status of each of these works and decide which of them might be publishable. It was agreed at the outset that publishers should not be permitted to revise the manuscripts in any appreciable way, that it was preferable to forego publication rather than allow a book to appear in a form Margaret herself might not have sanctioned. Even with this commendable restriction in force, more than twenty books were issued posthumously. While none of these rank with her very best work, several are quite fine: the evocative *Wheel on the Chimney*, with watercolor paintings by Tibor Gergeley, which chronicled the annual transcontinental migration of storks and was a Caldecott Honor Book for 1954; *Three Little Animals*, with illustrations by Garth Williams, which Margaret had originally conceived as a sequel to *Little Fur Family;* and *Four Fur Feet*, illustrated by Remy Charlip, a buoyant lark of a ballad about a fur-clad hero's farflung travels and dreams:

> And as he slept
> he dreamed a dream,
> dreamed a dream,
> dreamed a dream.
> And as he slept
> he dreamed a dream
> that all the world was round—O.[66]

In addition to the manuscripts that were eventually published, there were scores of others that had been left in an unfinished or not quite finished state. Among these were stories called "The Little Iceberg," "The Little Wind," "The Little River," and one called "The Little Golden Tugboat Book," which Margaret had subtitled "The *Annie Moran,* or That Old Tug at My Heart."[67] "The Number Bears: Count to 10 and Count to 10 Again" was planned as a sequel to *The Color Kittens: A Child's First Book About Colors.* Margaret had made notes for two sequels to her innovative picture book of art appreciation, *The House of a Hundred Windows.* "The House of a Hundred Children" was to have been an album of historic art works in which children figured as subjects. In "Here Comes the Sun: A Weather Book," the paintings were all to have been ones that happened to illustrate different weather conditions.

"The Green Wind" was to have been a major verse collection. With Posey Hurd, Margaret had been at work on a folk tale anthology to be called "Rich Man, Poor Man, Beggar Man, Thief," a sampler of traditional stories about heroes from all walks of life, honorable and otherwise. Also left unfinished was their hotly disputed collaboration, "The Early Milkman."

There were drafts of at least four new Noisy books, including one called "The Smelly Noisy Book," for which Margaret had investigated the possibility of impregnating the book's pages with a variety of scents. Had she lived long enough, each of the five senses would doubtless have been equally well provided for.

There were unfinished attempts at manners books and notes for a great many "social studies" books in the Bank Street here-and-now vein; a story-poetry-recipe anthology to be called "The Potato: A Root"; a set of travel books about various European cities and towns, including one about her beloved Dingle in Ireland, called "The Town that Climbs a Hill"; a collection of equine songs and verses called "A Horse of Course"; and a book titled "How Now Owl? A Book of Children's Questions, Answered by an Owl, Translated from the Owl by Margaret Wise Brown."

Taking a leaf from the popular turn-of-the-century novelty books of Peter Newell, Margaret had made a dummy for "The Cardboard Egg," whose hero was determined to escape from the book's pages—whether by "scrambling" or by other means—to become a "real egg." Margaret had punched egg-shaped holes in each page of her cardboard mock-up to indicate the hero's escape route.

Perhaps the most notable experiment in book design to turn up among Margaret's papers was "North South East West," a "story in all directions." Square pages had been cut along their diagonals to form sets of four triangles, one triangle for each point of the compass. Spiral bindings on all four sides of the square held the triangular sections down to a common backing, and each section could be opened and read separately in any order, in a kind of Dutch-door arrangement. Margaret's story concerned a young bird eager to learn what lay beyond his home in each of the world's four corners, an array of possibilities that her four-part design ingeniously mirrored.

Margaret's musical interests had taken her in a great many directions as well. At the time of her death, she was well along in her plans to have several Golden Books set to music for release in record form. On her return from her Pacific crossing, Burl Ives was to have visited her at the Only House to discuss various projects of this kind. She had also sketched the outlines for two song books, "Singing Stories: Stories to Be Sung and Songs to Be Told," which was to have consisted of traditional and original lullabies and ballads; and a second such collection to be called "The Youngest Singing Stories." In her notes for these treasuries, Margaret had also raised the possibility of designing radio and television programming based on the books.

She had made notes for television versions of a number of her published titles, including *Wait Till the Moon Is Full* and *The House of a Hundred Windows*. Margaret's idea for adapting her books to the new medium was essentially to exploit the interactive possibilities of the text to their fullest, replacing straight narrative whenever possible with direct questions for the viewer to wonder about and answer.

In a television series for preschoolers called "The Monkey Man and His Monkey," for which Margaret had written a proposal, a hurdy-gurdy man was to have told stories and entertained his simian companion. The running joke of the show was to have been that the man "assumes as he tells [his monkey] stories and sings his songs, that the two of them are broadcasting to young monkeys all over the world." Margaret wrote, "I am sure that children would be very amused by all this secret joking with them and that each child would think it . . . his own joke with the Hurdy-Gurdy man."[68]

There had also been plans for a dramatization of *Two Little Trains* for small children to perform at school (detailed notes had been prepared for this). Margaret had made scattered notes for a musical comedy, "The Life of the Dream." Also among her papers was her treatment for a ballet version of *The Dark Wood of the Golden Birds,* a project she had apparently abandoned by the time of Michael Strange's death.

In addition to her unpublished short fiction for adults, scores of unpublished poems were found. Most were lyrics, many were on the themes of love and the fleeting nature of time. In more than a few, rhyme was used selfconsciously to the point of overpowering the content. Among the best of these poems was one with a title borrowed from Tennyson, "The Unquiet Heart":

> Bind the winds, o bind them
> And still this heart of mine
> Drain the seas, o drain them
> And still this heart of mine
> But the seas and the winds you cannot bind
> And it will not be still, this heart of mine.[69]

On November 29, 1956, the Margaret Wise Brown Collection, consisting of a nearly complete set of her published works and files of assorted personal papers, manuscripts, book dummies, and related material, was dedicated at the Memorial and Library Association of Westerly (Rhode Island). The Westerly library had been chosen at the suggestion of Margaret's friend, Jessica Gamble Dunham, who knew it to be well endowed and who, as a resident of nearby Old Mystic, Connecticut, would be available to watch over the collection. At the dedication ceremony, Louise Seaman Bechtel gave the principal address, making use of her notes for the *Horn Book* article she had abandoned when the *Life* profile of Margaret appeared. She offered the assembled gathering an affectionate but canny appraisal of her late colleague and friend.

"I suspect," suggested Bechtel, "she enjoyed that wide arena of her publishing world in the same sporting spirit as that which took her off to hunt with the Buckram Beagles."[70] Margaret, she said, "enjoyed any contest of wits." The critic took sharp exception to the "rather fantastic picture" of Margaret "concocted" by *Life* and proceeded to relate her own impressions of this "laureate of the nursery" and "engaging friend" who, though "adult and sophisticated in many ways," had "never lost . . . a present sense of the real and the dream worlds of her childhood."

"Once she said to me," Bechtel recalled, " 'In the back of my head, I keep busy; in the front of my head, I am slow and stupid.' " She had once received a list of current projects from Margaret headed "Books Under Construction."

Over the years Bechtel had become aware of Margaret's unfulfilled literary ambitions and, like Lucy Mitchell, believed that at the time of her death Margaret may have been close to a turning point in that and other aspects of her life. "I love to think of her at Eze," she said, "seeping in impressions of that beautiful old world and the sea spread out below, wondering whether she would now, in a new life at home, turn at last to writing for adults."

Such speculation was perhaps inevitable in the case of a creative artist who died so young, was charismatically beautiful, and had already accomplished so very much. Margaret herself had proceeded through life ever wary and aware of "mysterious clock time," the relentless running of the clock, but she had also tried to remain philosophical about the future. Late in her career, in her first *Book of Knowledge* essay, she observed, "Writing for children is for me a happy accident. I still don't mean to and I always mean to stop when it is natural for me to do so. But I am grateful to the world of children's books for remaining one of the purest and freest fields for experimental writing today."[71]

Margaret was being modest. It was she as much as anyone who had *made* the children's book world a vital creative enterprise in her time. But claiming credit for herself had rarely been an overriding concern of hers. With Margaret, the book came first—the picture book as experiment. Everyone who worked with her came to appreciate this, and there was much truth in Clement Hurd's remark that "all Margaret's main illustrators did their best work in her books."[72] She had always needed to include others in her own fascinating game. As "Laureate of the Nursery," "Child's Best-Seller," and "Writer of Songs and Nonsense," Margaret made collaborators of old friends and chance acquaintances alike. Time and again with them and by the dazzling reach of her own brave and buoyant art, she made timeless books about the simple things that children love.

Notes

INTRODUCTION

1. Margaret Wise Brown (hereafter abbreviated MWB), "Creative Writing for Very Young Children," *The Book of Knowledge 1951 Annual,* ed. E. V. McLoughlin (New York and Toronto: The Grolier Society, 1951), 77.

2. Barbara Bader, *American Picturebooks from Noah's Ark to the Beast Within* (New York: Macmillan, 1976), 252.

3. MWB, "Stories to Be Sung and Songs to Be Told," *The Book of Knowledge 1952 Annual,* ed. E. V. McLoughlin (New York and Toronto: The Grolier Society, 1952), 166.

4. MWB, *The Train to Timbuctoo,* illustrated by Art Seiden (New York: Simon and Schuster, 1951); MWB, *Mister Dog; The Dog Who Belonged to Himself,* illustrated by Garth Williams (New York: Simon & Schuster, 1952).

5. Virginia Mathews, interview with author, Hamden, Conn., 18 July 1984; Ursula Nordstrom, interview with author, Southbury, Conn., 7 March 1981; Joseph D. Ryle, interview with author, New York, N.Y., 27 October 1983; Lucy Sprague Mitchell, "Margaret Wise Brown, 1910–1952," 69 *Bank Street* (1953): 19; Bruce Bliven, Jr., interview with author, New York, N.Y., 7 August 1984; Colette Richardson, interview with author, New York, N.Y., 17 January 1983; Clement Hurd, "Remembering Margaret Wise Brown," *Horn Book* (October 1983): 554.

CHAPTER ONE   "A Wild and Private Place"

1. MWB, "Publishers' Biographical Material," written for Harper & Brothers, undated, Margaret Wise Brown Collection, Memorial and Library Association of Westerly, R.I. (collection hereafter cited as Westerly).

2. *The Book of Knowledge* (1952), 167.

3. *The Book of Knowledge* (1951), 78.

4. William L. Felter, *Historic Green Point* (Brooklyn, N.Y.: Green Point Savings Bank, 1918), 58.

5. Norma L. Peterson, *Freedom and Franchise: The Political Career of B. Gratz Brown* (Columbia, Mo.: University of Missouri Press, 1956), preface.

6. Roberta Brown Rauch, interview with author, Jamaica, Vt., 20 September 1982.

7. See note on Brown family history prepared by Margretta Mason Brown (sister of B. Gratz Brown) at Liberty Hall, Frankfort, Ky. Among the notable Browns in America were: Rev. John Brown (1728–1803), who was born in Londonderry, Ireland of English and Scottish Presbyterian descent and became rector of Augusta Academy, near Staunton, Va. (later Washington and Lee University); Hon. John Brown (1757–1837), Revolutionary War veteran, United States representative and senator from Kentucky, president pro tem of the United States Senate; Judge Mason Brown (1799–1867), circuit judge and secretary of state of Kentucky, coauthor of *Digest of the Statute Laws of Kentucky.* B. Gratz Brown (1826–1885), Margaret's paternal grandfather, was editor of the *Missouri Democrat,* colonel of a Missouri volunteer regiment during the early days of the Civil War, United States senator from Missouri (1863–67), governor of Missouri (1871–73), and vice presidential candidate on the Liberal Republican and Democratic tickets headed by Horace Greeley (1872).

8. Maude Johnson's student records are in the archives of the Fishburn Library, Hollins College (archives hereafter cited as Fishburn).

9. MWB, handwritten verses on back of an Only House envelope, collection of James Stillman Rockefeller, Jr. (collection hereafter cited as Rockefeller).

10. Peter J. Schmitt, *Back to Nature: The Arcadian Myth in Urban America* (New York: Oxford University Press, 1969), 20–32, 125–40.

11. Jane Thurston Shepard to author, 28 April 1986.

12. Roberta Brown Rauch, 20 September 1982.

13. Roberta Brown Rauch, telephone interview with author, 14 March 1987.

14. MWB, "Writing for Children," *Hollins Alumnae Magazine* (Winter 1949): 1.

15. Roberta Brown Rauch, 20 September 1982.

16. *The Book of Knowledge* (1951), 79.

17. Jane Thurston Shepard, interview with author, San Diego, Calif., 9 July 1987.

18. B. Gratz Brown, Jr., interview with author, Jamaica, Vt., 20 September 1982.

19. Roberta Brown Rauch, 20 September 1982.

20. MWB, "Publishers' Biographical Material," Westerly.

21. Roberta Brown Rauch, 20 September 1982.

22. Ibid.

23. Roberta Brown Rauch, telephone interview with author, 31 May 1987.

24. Margaret Wise Brown, "The Dead Bird," *The Fish With the Deep Sea Smile* (New York: E. P. Dutton, 1938), 62–63. The story was adapted to the picture book format as *The Dead Bird,* illustrated by Remy Charlip (New York: Scott, 1958).

25. MWB, "Discovery," unpublished typescript, undated, Rockefeller.

26. MWB, *Little Fur Family,* illustrated by Garth Williams (New York: Harper & Brothers, 1946).

27. Roberta Brown Rauch, telephone interview with author, 19 January 1985.

28. MWB, *The Little Fir Tree,* illustrated by Barbara Cooney (New York: Crowell, 1954).

29. MWB, *The Golden Sleepy Book,* illustrated by Garth Williams (New York: Simon and Schuster, 1948).

30. Roberta Brown Rauch, 14 March 1987.

31. Roberta Brown Rauch, telephone interviews with author, 28 July 1984, 15 February 1987.

32. Winifred Lowry Post, *Purpose and Personality: The Story of Dana Hall* (Wellesley, Mass.: Dana Hall School, 1978), 32.

33. Dorothy R. Luke, interview with author, New York, N.Y., 22 December 1982.

34. Dana Hall Class of 1928 yearbook (Wellesley, Mass.: Dana Hall School, 1928), 106.

35. MWB's application, dated 2 April 1928, Fishburn.

36. Marguerite C. Hearsey, "Columns," *Spinster* (Hollins, Va.: Hollins College, 1932), 17. Marguerite Capen Hearsey (1892–1990) received her B.A. from Hollins College, her M.A. from Radcliffe, and her Ph.D. from Yale, where she was a Sterling Fellow. After teaching English at Bryn Mawr and Wellesley, she joined Hollins College's faculty in 1929, where she later served as acting dean (1934–35). In 1936, she became the principal of Abbot Academy, Andover, Mass., a girls' preparatory school which has since merged with Phillips Academy. She remained in that post until 1955.

37. Jane D. Sutherland, telephone interview with author, 9 July 1984.

38. Margaret P. Scott, telephone interview with author, 5 July 1984.

39. "Dr. McBride Delivers Interesting Lectures," *Hollins Student Life*, 16 March 1929.

40. MWB's handwritten copy of Margretta Mason Brown's note on Brown family history is in collection of Roberta Brown Rauch.

41. "Hollins 'Listens In' on Edison Golden Jubilee," *Hollins Student Life*, 26 October 1929.

42. "Mr. Neibuhr Gives Series of Lectures at Hollins," *Hollins Student Life*, 9 November 1929.

43. "Hollins Alumna Speaks on 'The Modern Girl,' " *Hollins Student Life*, 23 November 1929.

44. MWB became a frequent contributor to the class notes section of the *Hollins Alumnae Quarterly*, renamed the *Hollins Alumnae Magazine* in 1946.

45. Julia Lamar Parish to author, 30 June 1983.

46. Marjorie Forte, "A Review of 'The Lamp and the Bell,' " *Hollins Student Life*, 13 April 1929.

47. "Christmas Pageant Presented Sunday," *Hollins Student Life*, 17 December 1930.

48. Martha Huguley Naftel to author, undated (postmarked 22 July 1982); 12 August 1982; 30 August 1982.

49. Martha Huguley Naftel, calendar, June 1931, collection of James A. Naftel.

50. MWB to Fanona Knox, undated (summer 1931), Fishburn.

51. MWB to M. Estes Cocke, undated (summer 1931), Fishburn.

52. MWB, "Chaucerian Kindliness," *Cargoes* (February 1932): 60.

53. MWB to Marguerite C. Hearsey, inscription in a copy of *When the Wind Blew*, Fishburn.

54. Marguerite C. Hearsey, telephone interview with author, 18 June 1984.

55. MWB to Martha Huguley (telegram), 27 March 1932, collection of James A. Naftel.

56. Martha Huguley Naftel to author, 30 August 1982.

57. "Senior Plans for Next Year," *Hollins Student Life*, 28 May 1932.

CHAPTER TWO   New York Here and Now

1. Martha Huguley Naftel to author, 30 August 1982.

2. MWB to Marguerite C. Hearsey, undated (summer 1934), Letter 3, Fishburn.

3. MWB, "The Meeting," unpublished manuscript, undated, Rockefeller.

4. Leonard Weisgard, interviews with author, Traelløse, Denmark, 26 October–5 November 1982.

5. MWB, "Running/Running to Hounds," unpublished typescript, undated, Westerly.

6. MWB to Marguerite C. Hearsey, undated (summer 1934), Letter 3, Fishburn.

7. MWB to Marguerite C. Hearsey, undated (fall 1934), Letter 4, Fishburn.

8. MWB to Marguerite C. Hearsey, undated (fall 1934), Letter 7, Fishburn.

9. MWB paraphrased in Bruce Bliven, Jr., "Child's Best Seller," *Life,* 2 December 1946, 60.

10. MWB, "In Ten Years," unpublished typescript, undated, Rockefeller.

11. Handwritten notation by MWB's instructor, Helen Hull, Rockefeller.

12. Inez Camprubi Mabon, interview with author, Greenwich, Conn., 29 January 1985.

13. MWB to Marguerite C. Hearsey, undated (fall 1934), Letter 4, Fishburn.

14. MWB to Marguerite C. Hearsey, 31 December 1934, Letter 15, Fishburn. The quotation from Chaucer is from E. T. Donaldson, ed., *Chaucer's Poetry: An Anthology for the Modern Reader* (New York: The Ronald Press Company, 1958), 905. The modern English rendering is by the author.

15. MWB to Marguerite C. Hearsey, undated (fall 1934), Letter 4, Fishburn.

16. MWB to Marguerite C. Hearsey, undated (November 1934), Letter 6, Fishburn.

17. MWB to Marguerite C. Hearsey, undated (November 1934), Letter 4, Fishburn.

18. MWB to Marguerite C. Hearsey, 31 December 1934, Letter 15, Fishburn.

19. Dorothy Wagstaff Ripley, interview with author, Litchfield, Conn., 3 June 1987.

20. MWB to Marguerite C. Hearsey, undated (spring 1935), Letter 2, Fishburn.

21. Elizabeth Lamb, interview with author, East Hampton, N.Y., 10 April 1984.

22. MWB to Marguerite C. Hearsey, undated (spring 1935), Letter 2, Fishburn.

23. Edith Thacher Hurd, interview with author, Starksboro, Vt., 14 July 1982.

24. Lucy Sprague Mitchell, "Pioneering in Education," an oral history conducted in 1960 by Irene Prescott, Regional Cultural History Project, The General Library, University of California, Berkeley, 1962, 155.

25. Ibid., 13.

26. Lucy Sprague Mitchell, *Two Lives: The Story of Wesley Clair Mitchell and Myself* (New York: Simon & Schuster, 1953), 119–20.

27. William James, *Talks to Teachers* (New York and London: W. W. Norton, 1958), 104.

28. Joyce Antler, *Lucy Sprague Mitchell: The Making of a Modern Woman* (New Haven and London: Yale University Press, 1987), 113.

29. Ibid., 139–58.

30. Lucy Sprague Mitchell et al., "The Working Background of Harriet Johnson's Contribution to Education," *Schools Begin at Two: A Book for Teachers and Parents,* ed. Barbara Biber (New York: Agathon Press, 1970), xv.

31. Bank Street observer notes, Box 7, Lucy Sprague Mitchell Papers, Rare Book and Manuscript Library, Columbia University (collection hereafter cited as Columbia).

32. Mitchell, *Two Lives,* 281.

33. Ibid., 279.

34. Mitchell et al., *Another Here and Now Story Book,* illustrated by Rosalie Slocum (New York: E. P. Dutton, 1937), 30.

35. Lucy Sprague Mitchell, introduction to 1921 edition, *Here and Now Story Book,* 2d ed. (New York: E. P. Dutton, 1948), 25.

36. Obituary of Anne Carroll Moore, *New York Herald Tribune,* 21 January 1961.

37. Randall Jarrell, "A Verse Chronicle," *Poetry and the Age* (New York: Noonday Press, 1972), 151.

38. Anne Carroll Moore, "About Nicholas," undated typescript, New York Public Library Office of Children's Services, New York, N.Y.

39. Anne Carroll Moore, *Nicholas: A Manhattan Christmas Story* (New York: Putnam, 1924), 3.

40. Religious leaders, moralists, and philosophers had all entered into the fray at one time or another. Since the turn of the century, as the critic Josette Frank observed, psychiatrists, psychologists, educators, and librarians had become the principal participants in the old debate over whether fairy tales might "confuse children's understanding" of the world or be otherwise harmful to them. "Did fairy tales offer easy wish-fulfillment escape from reality? Should not young children's books tell them about the things and people of their real world? There were ardent protagonists on both sides of these questions." Josette Frank, "The Child Study Children's Book Committee: Its History and Purpose," undated typescript, in the collection of the late Josette Frank.

41. Harold Ordway Rugg, review of *Here and Now Story Book, Journal of*

Educational Psychology (March 1922): 186–87; Arnold and Beatrice Gesell, review of *Here and Now Story Book, New York Post Literary Review,* November 1921, 164.

42. James, *Talks to Teachers,* 73.

43. P. Korchien, student evaluation of Margaret Brown, 25 April 1936, Bank Street Records, Milbank Memorial Library, Teachers College, Columbia University (collection hereafter cited as Milbank).

44. MWB to Marguerite C. Hearsey, undated (spring 1936), Letter 2, Fishburn.

45. Ralph Pearson, student evaluation, 12 December 1935, Milbank.

46. MWB, "The Sudden Impact of Smell in an Autumn Field," unpublished manuscript, undated, Rockefeller.

47. Bank Street observer notes headed "J—— S——, roof, 4-30-37," Box 7, Columbia.

48. Barbara Biber, telephone interview with author, 28 December 1981.

49. Dorothy Stall, "Report on Margaret Brown, student teacher at Little Red School House," 8 January 1936, Milbank.

50. *The Book of Knowledge* (1951), 79.

51. Lucy Sprague Mitchell to Louise Seaman Bechtel, 27 May 1941, Columbia.

52. Lucy Sprague Mitchell, student evaluation of MWB, 10 December 1935, Milbank.

53. Lucy Sprague Mitchell, student evaluation of MWB, 11 April 1936, Milbank.

54. MWB, Bank Street student notebook, Westerly.

55. *The Book of Knowledge* (1951), 79.

56. MWB, Bank Street student notebook, Westerly.

57. Mitchell, *Two Lives,* 155.

58. Edith Thacher Hurd, 14 July 1982.

59. Sarah Kerlin, interview with author, New York, N.Y., 11 October 1982.

60. Sarah Kerlin, 11 October 1982.

CHAPTER THREE   Bank Street and Beyond

1. Lucy Sprague Mitchell to John Macrae, Sr., 3 June 1936, E. P. Dutton Records, George Arents Research Library for Special Collections at Syracuse University, Syracuse, N.Y. (collection hereafter cited as Dutton Records).

2. Mitchell et al., *Another Here and Now Story Book,* 1–12. Recognizing that children do not all develop at the same rate, Mitchell preferred to think of the categories she had devised as a developmental sequence of "maturity levels," rather than as age levels in a strict chronological sense. Also of inter-

est in this connection is the fact that *Another Here and Now Story Book* contains material graded for up to the six-year-old level. The earlier book ranged a bit higher, to seven. This slight narrowing of scope probably reflected Mitchell's increasing flexibility as to the appropriateness of fairy tale and fantasy literature for the younger ages.

3. Mitchell, foreword to *Another Here and Now Story Book,* xxiii–xiv.

4. MWB to Marguerite C. Hearsey, undated (fall 1936), Letter 18, Fishburn.

5. Jessica Gamble Dunham, interview with author, Tucson, Arizona, 17 April 1984.

6. Edmund Wilson, "Aladdin's Lecture Palace," *The American Earthquake* (New York: Farrar, Straus and Giroux, 1979), 200.

7. Jessica Gamble Dunham, 17 April 1984.

8. Sophie Shoumatoff Ward, interview with author, Locust Valley, N.Y., 9 October 1982. Margaret later wrote a series of stories about her black cat with white paws, which were posthumously published in *Seven Stories about a Cat Named Sneakers,* illustrated by Jean Charlot. (New York: W. R. Scott, 1955).

9. Roberta Brown Rauch, 20 September 1982.

10. Roberta Brown Rauch, telephone interview with author, 24 April 1988.

11. MWB to Marguerite C. Hearsey, undated (February 1937), Letter 1, Fishburn.

12. Louise Raymond, quoted in MWB to Marguerite C. Hearsey, undated (February 1937), Letter 1, Fishburn.

13. MWB, *When the Wind Blew,* illustrated by Rosalie Slocum (New York: Harper & Brothers, 1937).

14. MWB to Marguerite C. Hearsey, undated (February 1937), Letter 1, Fishburn.

15. *The Book of Knowledge* (1951), 80.

16. Roberta Brown Rauch, 23 July 1982.

17. MWB to Marguerite C. Hearsey, undated (postmarked 17 May 1937), Letter 13, Fishburn.

18. Ibid. The passage quoted is from Virginia Woolf, *The Years* (New York: Harcourt, Brace & Co., 1937), 363.

19. This quote from United Press appeared in a Dutton advertisement in *Horn Book* (September/October 1937).

20. A. T. Eaton, review of *Another Here and Now Story Book, New York Times Book Review,* 2 May 1937, 10.

21. *Time,* 31 October 1938, 31. As Lucy Mitchell herself observed in the foreword to the second collection, the influence of the here-and-now approach extended well beyond the immediate circle of her Bank Street stu-

dents and colleagues: "Now every . . . [publisher's] list of children's books shows a larger and larger proportion of this type." (Mitchell et al., *Another Here and Now Story Book,* xv.)

22. Bertha E. Mahony, review of *Another Here and Now Story Book, Horn Book* (May/June 1937): 166.

23. Ibid., Phelps and MWB, "Lucy Sprague Mitchell," 159.

24. MWB to Lucy Sprague Mitchell, undated (summer 1937), Columbia.

25. MWB to Lucy Sprague Mitchell, undated (summer 1937), Columbia.

26. Joel Chandler Harris, "The Wonderful Tar-Baby Story," *Uncle Remus: His Songs and His Sayings,* illustrated by A. B. Frost (New York and London: D. Appleton & Co., 1880; revised 1924), 7–8; MWB, "The Wonderful Tar-Baby Story," *Brer Rabbit* (New York and London: Harper & Brothers, 1941), 7.

27. Harris, 9; MWB, 7.

28. Augusta Baker Alexander, interview with author, New York, N.Y., 31 January 1985.

29. MWB, *The Fish With the Deep Sea Smile,* 16.

30. MWB to Louise Raymond, undated (summer 1937), HarperCollins files, New York, N.Y.

31. MWB to Marguerite C. Hearsey, 18 August 1937, Letter 11, Fishburn.

32. MWB to Louise Raymond, undated (summer 1937), Harper-Collins.

33. Louise Raymond to MWB, 18 August 1937, HarperCollins.

34. MWB to Marguerite C. Hearsey, 18 August 1937, Letter 11, Fishburn.

35. MWB to Marguerite C. Hearsey, undated (postmarked 17 May 1937), Letter 13, Fishburn.

36. Bruce Bliven, Jr., 7 August 1984.

37. Anne T. Eaton, review of *When the Wind Blew, New York Times Book Review,* 3 October 1937, 10; *Horn Book* (September/October 1937): 283.

38. Bank Street observer notes headed "Words and Meanings," Box 7, Columbia.

39. Ellen Tarry, interview with author, New York, N.Y., 25 July 1984.

40. Lucy Sprague Mitchell, "Margaret Wise Brown, 1910–1952," 69 Bank Street (1953): 19.

41. Edith Thacher Hurd, 13 July 1982.

42. Ibid.

43. William R. Scott, interview with author, New York, N.Y., 10 September 1981.

44. MWB, *Bumble Bugs and Elephants,* illustrated by Clement Hurd (New York: Scott, 1938).

45. Clement Hurd, interview with author, Starksboro, Vt., 13 July 1982.

46. William R. Scott, Inc. catalogue, Fall 1938, quoted in Bader, *American Picturebooks,* 216.

47. Louise Seaman Bechtel, "The Art of Illustrating Books for the Younger Readers," *Books in Search of Children,* ed. Virginia Haviland (New York: Macmillan, 1969), 46. (Reprinted from *New York Times Book Review,* 10 November 1940.)

48. Esphyr Slobodkina, *Notes for a Biographer* (Great Neck, N.Y.: Urquhart-Slobodkina, 1978), 2:250.

49. Ibid., 427.

50. Ibid., 430.

51. MWB, *The Little Fireman,* illustrated by Esphyr Slobodkina (New York: Scott, 1938).

52. James MacCormick, telephone interview with author, 13 September 1985.

53. MWB to Marguerite C. Hearsey, undated (summer 1938), Letter 19, Fishburn.

54. MWB to Marguerite C. Hearsey, undated (February 1937), Letter 1, Fishburn.

55. MWB to Gertrude Stein, 18 January 1940, Gertrude Stein Collection, Yale Collection of American Literature, Beinecke Rare Book and Manuscript Library, Yale University (collection hereafter cited as Beinecke). Material from the Gertrude Stein Collection is published herein by permission of Yale University.

56. John G. McCullough to Gertrude Stein, 2 September 1938, Beinecke.

57. William R. Scott to Gertrude Stein (telegram), 30 September 1938, Beinecke.

58. William R. Scott to Gertrude Stein (telegram), 24 October 1938, Beinecke.

59. Gertrude Stein, *The World Is Round,* illustrated by Clement Hurd (New York: Scott, 1939), 1.

60. William R. Scott to Gertrude Stein (telegram), 15 November 1938, Beinecke.

61. Bader, *American Picturebooks,* 236.

62. William R. Scott, 10 September 1981.

63. William R. Scott, 10 September 1981; John G. McCullough, interview with author, North Bennington, Vt., 17 July 1986.

64. Bruce Bliven, Sr. quoted in Myer Kutz, *Rockefeller Power* (New York: Simon & Schuster, 1974), 73.

65. Bruce Bliven, Jr., "Fair Tomorrow," *New Republic,* 7 December 1938, 119.

66. Phyllis McGinley, "Primary Education," *New Yorker,* 14 January 1939, 19. Reprinted by permission; © 1939, 1967, The New Yorker Magazine, Inc.

67. Arnold Gesell, quoted in "Democracy Held Vital to Children," *New York Times,* 15 November 1938.

68. "Fund Urged to Aid Brightest Pupils," *New York Times,* 12 November 1939.

69. MWB, Bank Street observer notes headed "Trying out the story of Willie Lion on a group of Four Year Olds," 19 January [1939], Westerly.

70. MWB, "Three Year olds going on Four," observer notes dated 1 June (1939), Westerly; MWB to Gertrude Stein, 18 January 1940, Stein Papers, Beinecke.

71. MWB, "In the Blackberry Patch," undated, unpublished typescript, Rockefeller.

72. Louise Seaman Bechtel, review of *The Streamlined Pig,* by MWB, illustrated by Kurt Wiese, *Saturday Review of Literature,* 19 November 1938, 18.

CHAPTER FOUR   Everywhere and Somewhere

1. John G. McCullough to Gertrude Stein, 8 February 1939, Beinecke.

2. Clement Hurd, 13 July 1982.

3. Leonard Weisgard, 26 October–5 November 1982.

4. MWB, *The Noisy Book,* illustrated by Leonard Weisgard (New York: Scott, 1939).

5. Stein, *World,* 2.

6. MWB, "Leonard Weisgard Wins the Caldecott Award," *Publishers' Weekly* (5 July 1947): 42.

7. Stein, *World,* 18.

8. MWB, Bank Street observer notes, Westerly.

9. MWB, *Hollins Alumnae Quarterly* class notes (Spring 1939): 31.

10. Stein, *World,* 63.

11. John G. McCullough, 17 July 1986.

12. John G. McCullough to Gertrude Stein, 16 May 1939, Beinecke.

13. John G. McCullough to Gertrude Stein, summer 1939, Beinecke.

14. John G. McCullough to Gertrude Stein, 22 November 1938, Beinecke.

15. Gertrude Stein to Clement Hurd, undated (spring 1939), Beinecke, reprinted by permission of the Estate of Gertrude Stein; Clement Hurd to Gertrude Stein, 12 July 1939, Beinecke.

16. Leonard Weisgard, 26 October–5 November 1982.

17. Irwin Shaw, "Weep in Years to Come," *Short Stories: Five Decades* (New York: Delacorte, 1984), 145. (First published in the *New Yorker,* 1 July 1939.)

18. Leonard Weisgard, 26 October–5 November 1982.

19. "The Williamsburg Murals: A Rediscovery," exhibition pamphlet on American Abstract Artists group (Brooklyn: Brooklyn Museum, 1990).

20. Charles Green Shaw, unpublished diary, 5 May 1939, Charles Green Shaw Papers, Archives of American Art, Smithsonian Institution, Washington, D.C. (collection hereafter cited as Smithsonian).

21. Ibid., 6 October 1939.

22. Ibid., 9 November 1939.

23. Ibid., 14 December 1939.

24. Ellen Lewis Buell, review of *The World Is Round, New York Times Book Review,* 12 November 1939, 10.

25. M. L. Becker, review of *The World Is Round, Books* (24 September 1939): 6.

26. Louise Seaman Bechtel, "Gertrude Stein for Children" (review of *The World Is Round*), *Books in Search of Children,* 85. (Reprinted from *Horn Book* [September/October 1939].)

27. Katharine S. White, review of *The World Is Round, New Yorker,* 25 November 1939, 84.

28. Quoted in Edith Thacher Hurd, "The World Is Not Square," afterword to Gertrude Stein, *The World Is Round,* illustrated by Clement Hurd (Berkeley, California: North Point Press, 1988), 147.

29. Anne Carroll Moore, "Three Owls' Notebook," *Horn Book* (September/October 1939): 294.

30. MWB to Gertrude Stein, 18 January 1940, Beinecke.

31. MWB, "New York: The Melting Pot of Good Cuisine," undated typed proposal, collection of Leonard Weisgard.

32. MWB to Cipi Pinellis at *Vogue,* 7 February 1940, collection of Leonard Weisgard.

33. William R. Scott to MWB, 22 April 1940, Rockefeller.

34. Ursula Nordstrom, 7 March 1981.

35. Ursula Nordstrom to Marc Simont, 25 January 1952, Harper-Collins.

36. John G. McCullough, 17 July 1986.

37. Edith Thacher Hurd, 14 July 1982; Lucille Ogle, 8 September 1982; Virginia Mathews, telephone interview with author, 1 May 1987.

38. "To do" was never published as a children's book. The manuscript is in the Stein Collection, Beinecke.

39. MWB, "The Scent," unpublished typescript, undated, Rockefeller.

40. MWB, "Luncheon," unpublished typescript, undated, Rockefeller.

41. MWB, untitled, unpublished, undated typescript beginning "It was a strange group that sat down to dinner that night," Rockefeller.

42. Lytton Strachey, *Queen Victoria* (New York: Blue Ribbon Books, 1921), 123. Michael Strange's copy is in the house MWB built for her on Vinalhaven.

43. Books of poetry by Michael Strange include: *Miscellaneous Poems* (New York: M. Kennerley, 1916); *Poems* (New York: Brentano's, 1919); *Resurrecting Life,* illustrated by John Barrymore (New York: Knopf, 1921); and *Selected Poems* (New York: Brentano's, 1928). Her play was published as *Clair de lune; a play in 6 scenes and 3 acts* (New York: Z. & L. Rosenfield, 1921), and as *Clair de lune: a play in 2 acts and 6 scenes* (New York and London: G. P. Putnam's Sons, 1921).

44. Hollis Alpert, *The Barrymores* (New York: Dial Press, 1964), 214.

45. Charles Green Shaw, "Through the Magnifying Glass," *New Yorker,* 3 December 1927, 36, 38.

46. Michael Strange, *Who Tells Me True* (New York: Charles Scribner's Sons, 1940), 142.

47. Alpert, The Barrymores, 220. See also Margot Peters, *The House of Barrymore* (New York: Alfred A. Knopf, 1990), 224–26, 264–65.

48. Diana Barrymore and Gerold Frank, *Too Much, Too Soon* (New York: Henry Holt, 1957), 21.

49. Michael Strange, undated publicity brochure (National Concert and Artists Corporation, New York), Rockefeller.

50. Maxwell Perkins to Michael Strange, 14 May 1941, Scribner Archives, Princeton University Library (collection hereafter cited as Princeton).

51. Katherine Woods, review of *Who Tells Me True, New York Times Book Review,* 12 May 1940, 9.

52. Maxwell Perkins to Harrison Tweed, 26 November 1940, Princeton (Scribner CO 101, Box 148). Published with permission of Princeton University Library and Charles Scribner's Sons, an imprint of Macmillan Publishing Company.

53. MWB to Lucy Sprague Mitchell, undated (June 1940), Columbia.

54. Ibid.

55. MWB to Lucy Sprague Mitchell, 1 July 1940, Columbia.

56. MWB to Lucy Sprague Mitchell, 21 July 1940, Columbia.

57. Lucy Sprague Mitchell to MWB, 31 July 1940, Columbia.

58. MWB, *Hollins Alumnae Quarterly* class notes (Fall 1940): 18.

59. Edith Thacher Hurd, interview with author, Vinalhaven, Maine, 11 September 1983.

60. MWB to Lucy Sprague Mitchell, 5 August 1940, Columbia.

61. Esphyr Slobodkina, interview with author, Hallandale, Fla., 10 January 1983.

62. Slobodkina, *Notes,* 2:541.

63. MWB to Lucy Sprague Mitchell, 14 September 1940, Columbia.

64. Esphyr Slobodkina, 10 January 1983. Slobodkina also describes this incident in detail in *Notes,* 2:552–53.

65. Esphyr Slobodkina, 10 January 1983.

66. MWB to Lucy Sprague Mitchell, 14 September 1940, Columbia.

67. MWB, "Oh Gentle Jew," unpublished typescript, undated, Rockefeller.

68. Slobodkina, *Notes,* 2:502.

69. Strange, *Who Tells Me True,* 212.

70. MWB to Gertrude Stein, 28 November 1940, Beinecke.

71. MWB, "In the Blackberry Patch," unpublished, undated typescript, Rockefeller.

72. Stein, *World,* 58–59.

73. MWB to John Macrae, Sr., 11 February 1941, collection of Roberta Brown Rauch.

74. MWB, "The Earth Will Have Us," unpublished play manuscript and related notes, Westerly.

75. Leonora A. Orr, *Hollins Alumnae Quarterly* class notes (Spring 1941): 21. The article referred to is E. J. Kahn, Jr. "Tallyho!," *New Yorker,* 8 March 1941, 49–55.

76. Kahn, "Tallyho!", 49.

77. MWB, "The New York Evening Post, April 3, 1941," unpublished typescript, undated, Rockefeller.

78. Virginia Woolf, *The Waves* (1931; reprint, New York and London: Harcourt, Brace Jovanovich, 1978), 239.

CHAPTER FIVE   Other Houses, Other Worlds

1. MWB, "Author's Biographical Data," prepared for Simon & Schuster, 1945 or thereafter, Westerly.

2. MWB to Lucy Sprague Mitchell, 29 July 1942, Columbia.

3. Clement Hurd, "Remembering Margaret Wise Brown," 560.

4. MWB as Golden MacDonald, *The Little Island,* illustrated by Leonard Weisgard (Garden City: Doubleday, Doran, 1946).

5. MWB to Lucy Sprague Mitchell, 30 August 1941, Columbia.

6. MWB, untitled, undated manuscript beginning "They were two people alone in the fog," Rockefeller.

7. Polly Schoyer Brooks, telephone interview with author, May or June 1986 (date not recorded in notes).

8. Preston Schoyer, *The Foreigners* (New York: Dodd, Mead, 1942). MWB's copy with Schoyer's inscription is in Michael Strange's house on Vinalhaven.

9. MWB to Lucy Sprague Mitchell, 30 August 1941, Columbia.

10. MWB to Lucy Sprague Mitchell, 14 September 1940, Columbia.

11. MWB, *The Runaway Bunny,* illustrated by Clement Hurd (New York: Harper & Brothers, 1942).

12. MWB to Lucy Sprague Mitchell, 11 October 1941, Columbia.

13. *The Book of Knowledge* (1951), 78.

14. MWB to Lucy Sprague Mitchell, 30 August 1941, Columbia.

15. MWB, Bank Street student notebook, Rockefeller.

16. Rose Bliven to Lucy Sprague Mitchell, 21 February 1951, Columbia.

17. May Lamberton Becker, review of *The Runaway Bunny, Books* (15 March 1942): 6. In 1966, Clement Hurd began work on a reillustrated edition of *The Runaway Bunny,* hoping to prepare new art which would reproduce more effectively than had the originals. The new edition, which appeared in 1972, was an immediate success. (The final full-color illustration in the 1972 edition is the same painting that Hurd first prepared as a sample for *Wait Till the Moon Is Full,* a project from which he was eventually dropped in favor of Garth Williams.) See Clement Hurd to Mr. (Eugene M.) Scheel, undated, collection of Edith Thacher Hurd; and Ursula Nordstrom to Clement Hurd, 31 January 1966, collection of Edith Thacher Hurd.

18. MWB, "Leonard Weisgard Wins the Caldecott Award," *Publishers' Weekly* (5 July 1947): 42.

19. MWB, "Writing for Children," *Hollins Alumnae Magazine* (Winter 1949): 1.

20. MWB as Golden MacDonald, *Red Light Green Light* (Garden City: Doubleday, Doran, 1944).

21. MWB to Michael Strange, undated (early 1942), Rockefeller.

22. MWB to Lucy Sprague Mitchell, 29 July 1942, Columbia.

23. Ibid.

24. Frances Clarke Sayers to Bertha E. Mahony, 20 August 1942, *Horn Book* Archives, Simmons College, Boston.

25. Jean Charlot, "Illustrating Children's Books," *An Artist on Art: The Collected Essays of Jean Charlot* (Honolulu: University Press of Hawaii, 1972), 1:363, 366.

26. John G. McCullough, 17 July 1986.

27. MWB, *A Child's Good Night Book* (New York: Scott, 1943).

28. John G. McCullough, 17 July 1986.

29. Jean Charlot's diary is quoted in Peter Morse, *Jean Charlot's Prints: A Catalogue Raisonné* (Honolulu: University Press of Hawaii and Jean Charlot Foundation, 1976), 249.

30. Miriam L. Wesley and Alice W. Hollis, transcript of interview with Jean Charlot, 18 August 1961, Archives of American Art Oral History, Archives of American Art, Smithsonian Institution, Washington, D.C.: 19.

31. MWB, "Publishers' Biographical Material," Westerly.

32. Clement Hurd, interview with author, Vinalhaven, Maine, 11 July 1983.

33. Lucille Ogle, 8 September 1982.

34. Wallace B. Putnam, interview with author, Yorktown Heights, N.Y., 2 December 1983.

35. Leonard Weisgard, 26 October–5 November 1982.

36. Dorothy A. Bennett, interview with author, El Cerrito, California, 23 April 1984.

37. Colette Richardson, interview with author, New York, N.Y., 17 January 1983.

38. Dorothy Wagstaff Ripley, 3 June 1987.

39. Shaw, diary, 28 July 1949, Smithsonian.

40. See Alpert, *The Barrymores,* 220.

41. A letter from Ursula Nordstrom to MWB dated 20 April 1943 is addressed to her at 10 Gracie Square (HarperCollins); a notation in MWB's Bank Street student file dated October 1943 lists 10 Gracie Square as her "last address" (Milbank).

42. Transcript of "The Baby Institute" radio broadcast on the Blue Network, 18 November 1943, Westerly.

43. Leonard Weisgard, 26 October–5 November 1982.

44. MWB, "Room and a River," unpublished manuscript, undated, Rockefeller.

45. Yvonne Thomas, interview with author, New York, N.Y., 24 April 1985.

46. Dorothy A. Bennett, 23 April 1984.

47. Lucius Beebe, "This New York," *New York Herald Tribune,* 6 July 1940.

48. Ted Scott Peckham, interview with author, New York, N.Y., 16 December 1984.

49. Joseph D. Ryle, 27 October 1983.

50. Barrymore and Frank, *Too Much, Too Soon,* 51.

51. Ibid., 214–15.

52. In an undated letter to Michael Strange from late 1947, MWB wrote: "Diana looks wonderful and is in better and sweeter spirits than she

has been in a long time and things seem to be turning her way. Bob [Wilcox] seems very steady and loves her a lot and I think is giving her pride in her self because he is proud of her." (Rockefeller.)

53. Yvonne Thomas, 24 April 1985.

54. Morrell Gipson, interview with author, New York, N.Y., 21 January 1987.

55. In 1967, when Cobble Court was threatened with demolition, its current owner arranged to move the structure to a new location. On Sunday, 5 March 1967, the wooden cottage was hoisted onto a steel dolly and towed to its present site at the corner of Charles and Greenwich streets in Greenwich Village.

56. Strange, *Who Tells Me True,* 319.

57. M. C., Harper internal reader's report on MWB manuscript of *The Dark Wood of the Golden Birds,* 29 February 1944, HarperCollins.

58. M. C., Harper internal reader's report on MWB manuscript "War in the Woods," 22 March 1943, HarperCollins.

59. MWB, "Some Facts About Yourself," author's questionnaire, William R. Scott, Inc., stamped as received 29 May 1944, Scott files, HarperCollins.

60. MWB, "Civil Defense for Five Years Old [*sic*]," proposal for a book apparently to be titled "The Bomb Proof Bunnies," Westerly.

61. MWB to Louise Raymond, undated (spring 1938), HarperCollins.

62. Michael Strange, *Resurrecting Life,* 19.

63. M. C. on *The Dark Wood,* 29 February 1944, HarperCollins.

64. Nordstrom's notation appears in the left margin of the 29 February report cited above.

65. Shaw, diary, 9 March 1944, Smithsonian.

66. Judi Culbertson and Tom Randall, *Permanent New Yorkers: A Biographical Guide to the Cemeteries of New York* (Chelsea, Vt.: Chelsea Green Publishing Company, 1987), 172.

67. Barrymore and Frank, *Too Much, Too Soon,* 226.

68. Ursula Nordstrom, 7 March 1981.

69. MWB to Ursula Nordstrom, undated (early 1945), HarperCollins.

70. MWB, undated, untitled autobiographical note beginning "Born in New York of a family," Westerly.

71. MWB to Ursula Nordstrom, 27 April 1945, HarperCollins.

72. MWB to Ursula Nordstrom, undated (early 1945), HarperCollins.

73. Edith Thacher Hurd, 14 July 1982.

74. *Five Little Firemen* was published in 1948 under the authors' actual names. Only one of their many collaborations, *The Man in the Manhole and the Fix-It Men* (New York: W. R. Scott, 1946), which was the first of their joint efforts to be published, bore the pseudonym Juniper Sage.

75. The author was unable to learn what became of Smoke.

76. The passage from *Henry V,* Act IV, Scene iii, is: "This story shall the good man teach his son; / And Crispin Crispian shall ne'er go by, / From this day to the ending of the world, / But we in it shall be remembered— / We few, we happy few, we band of brothers; / For he today that sheds his blood with me / Shall be my brother . . . " Margaret modified the óriginal spelling by the addition of an " 's." She proceeded to use "Crispin" and "Crispian" interchangeably as the dog's name.

77. Leonard Weisgard, 26 October–5 November 1982.

CHAPTER SIX   In the Great Green Room

1. MWB, *Goodnight Moon* manuscript notebook, Kerlan Collection, University of Minnesota Libraries (collection hereafter cited as Kerlan).

2. Ursula Nordstrom to Clement Hurd, 8 February 1946, Harper-Collins.

3. MWB to Evelyn F. Burkey, 14 January 1946, Authors League of America, New York.

4. Ursula Nordstrom to MWB, 25 January 1946, HarperCollins.

5. Ironically, it was Moore who had encouraged White to write a children's fantasy in the first place. See *Letters of E. B. White,* comp. and ed. Dorothy Lobrano Guth (New York, Hagerstown, San Francisco, London: Harper & Row, 1976), 266–67.

6. Ursula Nordstrom, 7 March 1981.

7. MWB, *Goodnight Moon,* illustrated by Clement Hurd (New York: Harper and Brothers, 1947).

8. Mark Twain, *Adventures of Huckleberry Finn,* ed. Walter Blair and Victor Fischer (Berkeley, Los Angeles, London: University of California Press, 1985), 39.

9. Alfred Kazin, "Creatures of Circumstance: Mark Twain," *An American Procession: The Major American Writers From 1830 to 1930—The Crucial Century* (New York: Alfred A. Knopf, 1984), 208.

10. Gaston Bachelard, *The Poetics of Space,* trans. Maria Jolas (Boston: Beacon Press, 1969), 67–68.

11. MWB, *Goodnight Moon* manuscript notebook, Kerlan.

12. Clement Hurd to "Dear Misses Brown, Nordstrom et als [*sic*]," 3 March 1946, HarperCollins.

13. Clement Hurd and Edith Thacher Hurd, "Leonard Weisgard," *Horn Book* (July 1947): 281.

14. MWB as Golden MacDonald, *The Little Island,* illustrated by Leonard Weisgard (Garden City: Doubleday, Doran, 1946).

15. Shaw, diary, 13 April 1946, Smithsonian.

16. P. H. (staff member, Harper & Brothers) to Michael Strange, 23 May 1946, HarperCollins.

17. MWB, *Hollins Alumnae Quarterly* (Summer 1945): 24.

18. MWB to Ursula Nordstrom, undated (late July or early August 1946), HarperCollins.

19. Ursula Nordstrom to MWB, 28 August 1946, HarperCollins.

20. Garth Williams, interview with author, New York, N.Y., 1 March 1983.

21. Bruce Bliven, Jr., 7 August 1984; Bruce Bliven, Jr., "Child's Best Seller," *Life,* 2 December 1946, 64.

22. Clement Hurd to Ursula Nordstrom, 2 September 1946, Harper-Collins; Clement Hurd, interview with author, Starksboro, Vt., 14 July 1982.

23. Clement Hurd, "Remembering Margaret Wise Brown," 556.

24. MWB to Lillian Lustig, undated (September 1946), Scott files, HarperCollins.

25. Ibid.

26. MWB and Garth Williams to Ursula Nordstrom (telegram), 29 October 1946, HarperCollins.

27. Ursula Nordstrom, marginal notation on telegram cited above, HarperCollins.

28. MWB to Ursula Nordstrom, undated (November 1946), Harper-Collins. (During the war years, Bennett Cerf conducted a weekly radio program called "Books Are Bullets," in which he interviewed authors of war-related general trade books.)

29. Bliven, "Child's Best Seller," 59.

30. Ibid. 66.

31. MWB to Evelyn F. Burkey, 17 October 1946, Authors League.

32. Louise Seaman Bechtel to Bertha E. Mahony, dated January 1947, *Horn Book* Archives, Simmons College, Boston.

33. Bertha E. Mahony to Louise Seaman Bechtel, 3 January 1947, *Horn Book* Archives. Evidently Mahony's and Bechtel's letters crossed in the mail.

34. B. Gratz Brown, Jr., 20 September 1982.

35. Leonard Weisgard, 26 October–5 November 1982.

36. Leonard Weisgard, "Caldecott Acceptance Paper," *Horn Book* (July 1947): 285.

37. Lee Bennett Hopkins, "Leonard Weisgard," *Books Are By People* (New York: Citation Press, 1969), 309.

38. Clement and Edith Hurd, "Leonard Weisgard," 281.

39. Inscription on watch, collection of Leonard Weisgard.

40. Dummies with Caldecott medallions pasted on the cover are in the MWB Collection, Westerly.

41. MWB to Michael Strange, 17 August [1947], Rockefeller.

42. MWB to Michael Strange, 18 August 1947, Rockefeller.

43. MWB to Michael Strange, undated, Rockefeller.

44. MWB to Michael Strange, undated (postmarked 26 August 1947), Rockefeller.

45. MWB to Michael Strange, undated (late October 1947), Rockefeller.

46. MWB to Evelyn F. Burkey, 24 October 1947, Authors League.

47. MWB to Michael Strange, undated (25 October 1947), Rockefeller.

48. Ibid.

49. MWB to Michael Strange, undated (postmarked 27 October 1947), Rockefeller.

50. MWB to Michael Strange, undated (postmarked 29 October 1947), Rockefeller.

51. Ibid.

52. MWB to Michael Strange, undated (postmarked 10 November 1947), Rockefeller.

53. MWB to Michael Strange, undated (November 1947), Rockefeller.

54. MWB to Michael Strange, undated (9 November 1947), Rockefeller.

55. Michael Strange to MWB, undated (November 1947), Rockefeller.

56. Leonard Weisgard, 26 October–5 November 1982.

57. MWB to Michael Strange, undated (postmarked 12 November 1947), Rockefeller.

58. MWB to Michael Strange, undated (November 1947), Rockefeller.

59. Marilyn Iarusso, telephone interview with author, 24 September 1986.

60. Rosemary C. Benét, review of *Goodnight Moon, New Yorker,* 6 December 1947, 132.

61. A. T. Eaton, review of *Goodnight Moon, Christian Science Monitor,* 30 September 1947, 12.

62. Other reviews of *Goodnight Moon* include: Virginia Mathews, *New York Times Book Review,* 7 September 1947, 35; M. L. Becker, *New York Herald Tribune Weekly Book Review,* 26 October 1947, 10; Yvonne Poirier, *San Francisco Chronicle,* 16 November 1947, 10.

63. Sales figures from Clement Hurd's log were supplied to the author by Thacher Hurd. William Morris of HarperCollins calculated the approximate total of U.S. sales as of February 1992.

64. The 1949 printings of *Two Little Miners* were: 338,772 (first), 168,852 (second and third each). The single printing for the following year was significantly smaller.

65. MWB, *Hollins Alumnae Quarterly* (Winter 1947–48): 20.

66. Rosemary C. Benét, review of *The First Story,* by MWB, illustrated by Marc Simont, *New Yorker,* 6 December 1947, 132.

67. Ursula Nordstrom to Marc Simont, 2 December 1947, Harper-Collins.

68. Ursula Nordstrom to MWB, 2 December 1947, HarperCollins.

69. Ursula Nordstrom to Marc Simont, 2 December 1947, Harper-Collins.

70. Barrymore and Frank, *Too Much, Too Soon,* 249.

CHAPTER SEVEN   "Graver Cadences"

1. Margaret Cousins to author, 10 January 1985.

2. MWB, "One Eye Open," *Good Housekeeping,* April 1948, 94.

3. MWB to Clement Hurd, undated (early 1948), Kerlan.

4. Slobodkina, *Notes,* 2: 495–9.

5. John G. McCullough to MWB, 6 April 1948, Scott files, Harper-Collins.

6. MWB to Evelyn F. Burkey, 15 February 1948, Authors League.

7. Shaw, diary, 4 April 1948, Smithsonian.

8. MWB to Evelyn F. Burkey, 10 April 1948, Authors League.

9. MWB, *The Important Book,* illustrated by Leonard Weisgard (New York: Harper and Brothers, 1949).

10. Helen G. Trager, "Story of a Unique Publishing House," *Publishers' Weekly* (24 April 1948): 1796–1802.

11. MWB, undated memo headed "The Important Book," Harper-Collins.

12. Adelaide Dana Parker, telephone interview with author, 23 June 1985.

13. MWB to William R. Scott, 23 May 1948. Quoted in Slobodkina, *Notes,* 2: 491.

14. Ursula Nordstrom to MWB, 10 August 1948, HarperCollins.

15. Michael Strange, unpublished diary, 21 April 1948, 29 April 1948, Rockefeller.

16. MWB to Ursula Nordstrom, 13 August 1948, HarperCollins.

17. Ursula Nordstrom to MWB (telegram), 24 August 1948, Harper-Collins.

18. J. P. Miller, interview with author, New York, N.Y., 20 January 1984.

19. Slobodkina, *Notes,* 2: 487. Underlying the debate over the exclusion of facial features from some types of picture book art was the idea that less detailed images might prove a greater stimulus to the younger child's imagination. The same theory lay behind the widespread use at progressive schools of largely featureless blond wood unit blocks as play materials. See

The Block Book, ed. Elisabeth S. Hirsch (Washington, D.C.: National Association for the Education of Young Children, revised ed., 1984).

20. Ibid., 488.

21. Clement Hurd, 14 July 1982.

22. S. J. Johnson, review of *The Runaway Bunny, Library Journal* (15 April 1942): 368.

23. MWB to Clement Hurd, undated, collection of Hurd family.

24. Clement Hurd, 14 July 1982.

25. MWB, *Wait Till the Moon Is Full,* illustrated by Garth Williams (New York: Harper & Brothers, 1948).

26. MWB, unbound diary notes, undated (February 1949), Rockefeller.

27. Judith Thorne Stanton, interview with author, New York, N.Y., 22 December 1982.

28. Clement Hurd, "Remembering Margaret Wise Brown," 557.

29. Clement Hurd to Ursula Nordstrom, 26 February 1949, HarperCollins.

30. Ibid.

31. Clement Hurd to Ursula Nordstrom (postcard), 25 April 1949, HarperCollins.

32. Ursula Nordstrom to Clement Hurd, 27 April 1949, HarperCollins.

33. Esphyr Slobodkina, 10 January 1983; Billy Brown, interview with author, Vinalhaven, Maine, 12 September 1983.

34. Ethel M. Scott to MWB, 23 November 1949, Scott files, HarperCollins. (This is the version of the letter actually sent. An undated preliminary draft is in the same file.)

35. MWB to Ethel M. Scott, 13 December 1949, Scott files, HarperCollins.

36. Morris L. Ernst to Michael Halperin, 23 January 1950, HarperCollins; Morris L. Ernst to Frank S. MacGregor, 23 January 1950, HarperCollins.

37. Ted Scott Peckham, 16 December 1984.

38. Ibid.

39. MWB to Michael Strange, 26 January 1950, Rockefeller.

40. MWB to Michael Strange, 1 February 1950, Rockefeller.

41. MWB to Michael Strange, undated (early February 1950), Rockefeller.

42. Michael Strange to MWB, 11 February 1950, Rockefeller.

43. MWB to Ursula Nordstrom, undated (March 1950), HarperCollins.

44. Ursula Nordstrom to MWB, 28 March 1950, HarperCollins.

45.   Virginia Mathews, 18 July 1984.

46.   MWB, "Brief Summary of the Theme," typed synopsis of *The Dark Wood of the Golden Birds* prepared as a proposal for a ballet adaptation, Westerly.

47.   MWB to Evelyn F. Burkey, undated (1950), Authors League.

48.   MWB to John G. McCullough, dated August 1950, Scott files, HarperCollins.

49.   MWB, *Hollins Alumnae Magazine* (Fall 1950): 27.

50.   *The Book of Knowledge* (1951), 77.

51.   Shaw, diary, 27 July 1950, Smithsonian.

52.   MWB to Irene (a publicist for Golden Books, last name not recorded), 1 October 1950, Westerly.

53.   Mrs. Hoffman Nickerson, interview with author, Locust Valley, N.Y., 9 October 1982.

CHAPTER EIGHT   "The Fidget Wheels of Time"

1.   Obituaries appeared on 6 November 1950 in the *New York Times,* the *Boston Herald,* and the *New York Herald Tribune,* among many other papers.

2.   Barrymore and Frank, *Too Much, Too Soon,* 258–59.

3.   MWB to Alvin Tresselt, undated (probably October 1952), collection of Alvin Tresselt.

4.   The phrase "orange juice and crust" is from a letter from MWB to Michael Strange, undated (probably November 1947), Rockefeller.

5.   Lucille Ogle, 8 September 1982.

6.   The contents of Nordstrom's letter to MWB, which is not in the Harper files, may be inferred from MWB's response dated 16 March 1951, HarperCollins.

7.   MWB to Ursula Nordstrom, 16 March 1951, HarperCollins.

8.   MWB to Ursula Nordstrom, undated (marked as received 28 March 1951), HarperCollins.

9.   Lucy Sprague Mitchell to MWB, 29 March 1951, Westerly.

10.   MWB to Clement and Edith Thacher Hurd, undated (May 1951), Kerlan.

11.   *The Book of Knowledge* (1952), 166.

12.   Bliven, "Child's Best Seller," 64.

13.   Burl Ives to MWB, 8 August 1951, Westerly.

14.   MWB to Louise Seaman Bechtel, undated (dated by Louise Seaman Bechtel 28 July 1951), Bechtel Papers, Vassar College Library (collection hereafter cited as Vassar).

15.   Ibid.

16.   MWB to Clement Hurd, undated (July 1951), Kerlan.

17. Edith Thacher Hurd, interview with author, Vinalhaven, Maine, 12 September 1983.

18. MWB to Vincent Astor, 12 December 1951, MWB file, Weil, Gotshal and Manges, New York.

19. MWB to Harriet F. Pilpel, undated (probably December 1951), MWB file, Weil, Gotshal and Manges, New York.

20. Ursula Nordstrom to Louise Seaman Bechtel, 17 November 1952, Vassar.

21. MWB to Clement Hurd, undated (late fall 1951), Kerlan.

22. Sue Dickinson, "Former Virginia College Student Leads in Children's Book Writing," *Richmond News Leader,* 1 April 1952.

23. MWB, *Mister Dog.* Regrettably, recent editions of *Mister Dog* have been abridged.

24. James Stillman Rockefeller, Jr., to author, undated (postmarked 25 October 1984).

25. Ibid.

26. "The Early Milkman" draft manuscript and correspondence are in the Kerlan Collection.

27. Dorothy A. Bennett, 23 April 1984.

28. MWB to Georges Duplaix, 16 May 1952, MWB file, Weil, Gotshal and Manges.

29. MWB to Lucille Ogle (telegram), 15 May 1952, MWB file, Weil, Gotshal and Manges. (Leon Shimkin and Albert R. Leventhal were publishing associates of Duplaix.)

30. Harriet F. Pilpel to MWB, 3 June 1952, MWB file, Weil, Gotshal and Manges.

31. MWB to Harriet F. Pilpel, 19 May 1952, MWB file, Weil, Gotshal and Manges.

32. MWB to Margaret Lesser, undated (June 1952), Golden MacDonald file, Doubleday Books for Young Readers, New York.

33. MWB to William R. Scott, undated (June 1952), Scott files, HarperCollins.

34. William R. Scott to MWB, 1 July 1952, Scott files, HarperCollins.

35. MWB to Ursula Nordstrom, 23 May 1952, HarperCollins.

36. MWB to Alvin Tresselt, undated (summer 1952), collection of Alvin Tresselt.

37. MWB, "To My Executors," memo, 28 August 1952, MWB file, Weil, Gotshal and Manges.

38. Herbert A. Wolff, Jr., to United States Coast Guard, 29 August 1952, MWB file, Weil, Gotshal and Manges.

39. R. R. Curry to Greenbaum, Wolff and Ernst, 3 September 1952, MWB file, Weil, Gotshal and Manges.

40. Shaw, diary, 18 September 1952, Smithsonian.

41. MWB to Dorothy Wagstaff Ripley, undated (September 1952), collection of Dorothy Wagstaff Ripley.

42. Luther Greene, interview with author, New York, N.Y., 10 March 1984.

43. MWB to Ursula Nordstrom, 9 November 1952. A copy of this letter was sent by Nordstrom to Louise Seaman Bechtel and is in the Bechtel Papers, Vassar.

44. MWB to Edith Thacher Hurd (postcard), undated (October 1952), Kerlan.

45. MWB, codicil to last will and testament, 30 October 1952, MWB file, Weil, Gotshal and Manges.

46. Garth Williams, 1 March 1983.

47. James Stillman Rockefeller, Jr., to author, undated (postmarked 25 October 1984).

48. Nordstrom makes reference to this letter to MWB in a letter to Louise Seaman Bechtel, 17 November 1952, Vassar.

49. MWB to Ursula Nordstrom, 9 November 1952. Nordstrom's copy for Bechtel is in the Bechtel Papers, Vassar.

50. MWB to Leonard Weisgard, undated (November 1952), Rockefeller.

51. MWB to Judith Thorne Stanton, undated (postmarked 12 November 1952), collection of Judith Thorne Stanton.

52. Elizabeth Lamb, interview with author, East Hampton, N.Y., 10 April 1984.

53. Shaw, diary, 14 November 1952, Smithsonian

54. Garth Williams, 1 March 1983.

55. The simple stone marker bears the following inscription:

> Margaret Wise Brown
> Born New York May 23, 1910
> Died Nice, France Nov. 13, 1952
> Beloved owner of THE ONLY HOUSE
> Writer of Songs and nonsense
>
> Dear Margaret,
>   You gave us all so much—
>   A chance to love
>   A place to rest
>   A window into living.

The lower portion of the stone is inscribed with an excerpt from *The Little Island*.

56. James S. Rockefeller, Jr., *Man and His Island* (New York: Norton, 1957), 20.

57. Lucy Sprague Mitchell, "Margaret Wise Brown: 1910–1952," 69 *Bank Street* (1953): 19.

58. Shaw, diary, 102–3, Smithsonian.

59. Judith Thorne Stanton, 22 December 1982.

60. Garth Williams, 1 March 1983.

61. Dustjacket note, *The Duck,* by MWB, illustrated by Ylla (New York: Harper & Brothers, 1953).

62. Anne Carroll Moore, "The Three Owls' Notebook," *Horn Book* (June 1953): 192.

63. Information concerning MWB's earnings and expenses for the last five years of her life is from the MWB file, Weil, Gotshal and Manges.

64. MWB, handwritten last will and testament, 22 December 1949, HarperCollins.

65. Sue Dickinson, *Richmond News Leader,* 1 April 1952.

66. MWB, *Four Fur Feet,* illustrated by Remy Charlip (New York: Scott, 1961).

67. These manuscripts are to be found in the MWB Collection, Westerly.

68. MWB, "The Monkey Man and his Monkey: A Television Program," typed memo, undated, Westerly.

69. MWB, "The Unquiet Heart," unpublished poem, undated, Westerly. The title is taken from Tennyson's "In Memoriam. A. H. H.," canto v:

> I sometimes hold it half a sin
> > To put in words the grief I feel;
> > For words, like Nature, half reveal
> And half conceal the Soul within.
>
> But, for the unquiet heart and brain
> > A use in measured language lies;
> > The sad mechanic exercise,
> Like dull narcotics, numbing pain

70. Louise Seaman Bechtel's talk was reprinted in revised form as "Margaret Wise Brown: Laureate of the Nursery," *Horn Book* (June 1958).

71. *The Book of Knowledge* (1951), 81.

72. Clement Hurd, "Remembering Margaret Wise Brown," 556.

Bibliography

The Works of Margaret Wise Brown

BOOKS (FIRST AMERICAN AND BRITISH EDITIONS)

Animals, Plants and Machines. Written with Lucy Sprague Mitchell. Illustrated by Clare Bice. Boston, New York: D. C. Heath & Co., 1944.

Baby Animals. Illustrated by Mary Cameron. New York: Random House, 1941.

The Bad Little Duckhunter. Illustrated by Clement Hurd. New York: W. R. Scott, 1947.

Big Dog, Little Dog. Written as Golden MacDonald. Illustrated by Leonard Weisgard. Garden City, New York: Doubleday, Doran & Co., 1943.

The Big Fur Secret. Illustrated by Robert de Veyrac. New York and London: Harper & Brothers, 1944.

Big Red Barn. Illustrated by Rosella Hartman. New York: W. R. Scott, 1956.

Black and White. Illustrated by Charles G. Shaw. New York and London: Harper & Brothers, 1944.

Bumble Bugs and Elephants: A Big and Little Book. Illustrated by Clement Hurd. New York: W. R. Scott, 1938.

A Child's Good Morning. Illustrated by Jean Charlot. New York: W. R. Scott, 1952.

A Child's Good Night Book. Illustrated by Jean Charlot. New York: W. R. Scott, 1943.

Christmas in the Barn. Illustrated by Barbara Cooney. New York: T. Y. Crowell, 1952.

The Color Kittens. Illustrated by Alice and Martin Provensen. New York: Simon & Schuster, 1949.

Country Noisy Book. Illustrated by Leonard Weisgard. New York: W. R. Scott, 1940.

The Dark Wood of the Golden Birds. Illustrated by Leonard Weisgard. New York: Harper & Brothers, 1950.

David's Little Indian. Illustrated by Remy Charlip. New York: W. R. Scott, 1956.

The Dead Bird. Illustrated by Remy Charlip. New York: W. R. Scott, 1958.

The Diggers. Illustrated by Clement Hurd. New York: Harper & Brothers, 1961; London: Hamish Hamilton, 1961.

Doctor Squash, The Doll Doctor. Illustrated by J. P. Miller. New York: Simon & Schuster, 1952.

Don't Frighten the Lion! Illustrated by H. A. Rey. New York and London: Harper & Brothers, 1942.

The Dream Book: First Comes the Dream. Illustrated by Richard Floethe. New York: Random House, 1950.

The Duck. Illustrated by Camilla Koffler (as Ylla). New York: Harper & Brothers, 1953; London: Harvill Press, 1953.

Farm and City. Written with Lucy Sprague Mitchell. Illustrated by Anne Fleur. Boston, New York: D. C. Heath & Co., 1944.

The First Story. Illustrated by Marc Simont. New York: Harper & Brothers, 1947.

The Fish with the Deep Sea Smile. Illustrated by Roberta Rauch. New York: E. P. Dutton & Co., 1938.

Five Little Firemen. Written with Edith Thacher Hurd. Illustrated by Tibor Gergely. New York: Simon & Schuster, 1948.

Four Fur Feet. Illustrated by Remy Charlip. New York: W. R. Scott, 1961.

Fox Eyes. Illustrated by Jean Charlot. New York: Pantheon Books, 1951; London: Collins, 1979.

The Friendly Book. Illustrated by Garth Williams. New York: Simon & Schuster, 1954.

The Golden Birthday Book. Illustrated by Leonard Weisgard. Racine, Wis.: Western Publishing Co., 1989.

The Golden Bunny, and Seventeen Other Stories. Illustrated by Leonard Weisgard. New York: Simon & Schuster, 1953.

The Golden Egg Book. Illustrated by Leonard Weisgard. New York: Simon & Schuster, 1947.

The Golden Sleepy Book. Illustrated by Garth Williams. New York: Simon & Schuster, 1948.

Goodnight Moon. Illustrated by Clement Hurd. New York: Harper & Brothers, 1947; Kingswood, Surrey: World's Work, 1975.

The Hidden House. Illustrated by Aaron Fine. New York: Holt, 1953.

Home for a Bunny. Illustrated by Garth Williams. New York: Simon & Schuster, 1956; London: Hamyln, 1961.

Horses. Written as Timothy Hay. Illustrated by Dorothy Wagstaff (as Wag). New York and London: Harper & Brothers, 1944.

The House of a Hundred Windows. Illustrated by Robert de Veyrac. New York and London: Harper & Brothers, 1945.

The Important Book. Illustrated by Leonard Weisgard. New York: Harper & Brothers, 1949.

Indoor Noisy Book. Illustrated by Leonard Weisgard. New York: W. R. Scott, 1942.

The Little Brass Band. Illustrated by Clement Hurd. New York: Harper & Brothers, 1955.

Little Chicken. Illustrated by Leonard Weisgard. New York and London: Harper & Brothers, 1943.

The Little Cowboy. Illustrated by Esphyr Slobodkina. New York: W. R. Scott, 1949.

The Little Farmer. Illustrated by Esphyr Slobodkina. New York: W. R. Scott, 1948.

The Little Fat Policeman. Written with Edith Thacher Hurd. Illustrated by Alice and Martin Provensen. New York: Simon & Schuster, 1950.

The Little Fir Tree. Illustrated by Barbara Cooney. New York: T. Y. Crowell, 1954.

The Little Fireman. Illustrated by Esphyr Slobodkina. New York: W. R. Scott, 1938.

The Little Fisherman: A Fish Story. Illustrated by Dahlov Ipcar. New York: W. R. Scott, 1945.

Little Frightened Tiger. Written as Golden MacDonald. Illustrated by Leonard Weisgard. Garden City, New York: Doubleday & Co., 1953.

Little Fur Family. Illustrated by Garth Williams. New York: Harper & Brothers, 1946.

Little Indian. Illustrated by Richard Scarry. New York: Simon & Schuster, 1954; London: Golden Pleasure Books, 1964.

The Little Island. Written as Golden MacDonald. Illustrated by Leonard Weisgard. Garden City, New York: Doubleday & Co., 1946.

Little Lost Lamb. Written as Golden MacDonald. Illustrated by Leonard Weisgard. Garden City, New York: Doubleday, Doran & Co., 1945.

Little Pig's Picnic, and Other Stories. Illustrated by the Walt Disney Studio. Boston: D. C. Heath & Co., 1939.

The Man in the Manhole and the Fix-It Men. Written as Juniper Sage, with Edith Thacher Hurd. Illustrated by Bill Ballantine. New York: W. R. Scott, 1946.

Mister Dog; The Dog Who Belonged to Himself. Illustrated by Garth Williams. New York: Simon & Schuster, 1952; London: Muller, 1954.

My World. Illustrated by Clement Hurd. New York: Harper & Brothers, 1949.

Nibble Nibble: Poems for Children. Illustrated by Leonard Weisgard. New York: W. R. Scott, 1959.

Night and Day. Illustrated by Leonard Weisgard. New York and London: Harper & Brothers, 1942.

The Noisy Bird Book. Illustrated by Leonard Weisgard. New York: W. R. Scott, 1943.

The Noisy Book. Illustrated by Leonard Weisgard. New York: W. R. Scott, 1939.

The Noon Balloon. Illustrated by Leonard Weisgard. New York: Harper & Brothers, 1952.

O, Said the Squirrel. Illustrated by Camilla Koffler (as Ylla). London: Harvill Press, 1950.

On Christmas Eve. Illustrated by Beni Montresor. New York: W. R. Scott, 1961; London: Collins, 1963.

Once Upon a Time in a Pigpen, and Three Other Stories. Illustrated by Ann Strugnell. Reading, Mass.: Addison-Wesley, 1980; London: Hutchinson, 1981.

The Peppermint Family. Illustrated by Clement Hurd. New York: Harper & Brothers, 1950; London: Hamish Hamilton, 1950.

The Polite Penguin. Illustrated by H. A. Rey. New York and London: Harper & Brothers, 1941.

The Poodle and the Sheep. Illustrated by Leonard Weisgard. New York: E. P. Dutton & Co., 1941.

Pussy Willow. Illustrated by Leonard Weisgard. New York: Simon & Schuster, 1952.

A Pussycat's Christmas. Illustrated by Helen Stone. New York: T. Y. Crowell, 1949.

The Quiet Noisy Book. Illustrated by Leonard Weisgard. New York: Harper & Brothers, 1950; London: Hamish Hamilton, 1950.

Red Light Green Light. Written as Golden MacDonald. Illustrated by Leonard Weisgard. Garden City, New York: Doubleday, Doran & Co., 1944.

The Runaway Bunny. Illustrated by Clement Hurd. New York and London: Harper & Brothers, 1942.

The Sailor Dog. Illustrated by Garth Williams. New York: Simon & Schuster, 1953; London: Muller, 1954.

The Seashore Noisy Book. Illustrated by Leonard Weisgard. New York: W. R. Scott, 1941.

Seven Little Postmen. Written with Edith Thacher Hurd. Illustrated by Tibor Gergely. New York: Simon & Schuster, 1952.

Seven Stories about a Cat Named Sneakers. Illustrated by Jean Charlot. New York: W. R. Scott, 1955.

SHHhhhh . . . BANG: a whispering book. Illustrated by Robert de Veyrac. New York and London: Harper & Brothers, 1943.

Sleepy ABC. Illustrated by Esphyr Slobodkina. New York: Lothrop, Lee & Shepard Co., 1953.

The Sleepy Little Lion. Illustrated by Camilla Koffler (as Ylla). New York: Harper & Brothers, 1947; London: Harvill Press, 1960.

The Steamroller. Illustrated by Evaline Ness. New York: Walker, 1974.

The Streamlined Pig. Illustrated by Kurt Wiese. New York and London: Harper & Brothers, 1938.

The Summer Noisy Book. Illustrated by Leonard Weisgard. New York: Harper & Brothers, 1951.

They All Saw It. Illustrated by Camilla Koffler (as Ylla). New York and London: Harper & Brothers, 1944.

Three Little Animals. Illustrated by Garth Williams. New York: Harper & Brothers, 1956.

The Train to Timbuctoo. Illustrated by Art Seiden. New York: Simon & Schuster, 1951; London: Muller, 1952.

Two Little Gardeners. Written with Edith Thacher Hurd. Illustrated by Gertrude Elliott. New York: Simon & Schuster, 1951.

Two Little Miners. Written with Edith Thacher Hurd. Illustrated by Richard Scarry. New York: Simon & Schuster, 1949.

Two Little Trains. Illustrated by Jean Charlot. New York: W. R. Scott, 1949.

Wait Till the Moon Is Full. Illustrated by Garth Williams. New York: Harper & Brothers, 1948.

Wheel on the Chimney. Illustrated by Tibor Gergely. Philadelphia: Lippincott, 1954.

When the Wind Blew. Illustrated by Rosalie Slocum. New York and London: Harper & Brothers, 1937.

Where Have You Been? Illustrated by Barbara Cooney. New York: T. Y. Crowell, 1952.

The Whispering Rabbit, and Other Stories. Illustrated by Garth Williams and Lillian Obligado. New York: Golden Press, 1965.

Whistle for the Train. Written as Golden MacDonald. Illustrated by Leonard Weisgard. Garden City, New York: Doubleday & Co., 1956.

Willie's Adventures: Three Stories. Illustrated by Crockett Johnson. New York: W. R. Scott, 1954.

Willie's Walk to Grandmama. Written with Rockbridge Campbell. Illustrated by Lucienne Bloch. New York: W. R. Scott, 1944.

The Winter Noisy Book. Illustrated by Charles G. Shaw. New York: W. R. Scott, 1947.

The Wonderful House. Illustrated by J. P. Miller. New York: Simon & Schuster, 1950; London: Muller, 1950.

Wonderful Story Book. Illustrated by J. P. Miller. New York: Simon & Schuster, 1948.

Young Kangaroo. Illustrated by Symeon Shimin. New York: W. R. Scott, 1955; Kingswood, Surrey: World's Work, 1959.

ADAPTATIONS AND TRANSLATIONS

Brer Rabbit: Stories from Uncle Remus. Adapted from the text of Joel Chandler Harris. Illustrations based on those of A. B. Frost, redrawn for reproduction by Victor Dowling. New York and London: Harper & Brothers, 1941.

The Children's Year. Adapted from the French of Y. Lacôte. Illustrated by Feodor Rojankovsky (as Rojan). New York and London: Harper & Brothers, 1937.

The Comical Tragedy or Tragical Comedy of Punch & Judy. Adapted from the text of John Payne Collier. Illustrated by Leonard Weisgard. New York: W. R. Scott, 1940.

The Fables of La Fontaine. Translated from the French. Illustrated by André Hellé. New York and London: Harper & Brothers, 1940.

Homes in the Wilderness. Adapted from the journal of William Bradford and others. Illustrated by Mary Wilson Stewart. New York: W. R. Scott, 1939.

The Log of Christopher Columbus' First Voyage to America in the Year 1492. Adapted from the abridgement of Bartolomé de las Casas. Illustrated by J. O. Cosgrave. New York: W. R. Scott, 1938.

STORIES AND POEMS (ARRANGED CHRONOLOGICALLY BY MAGAZINE)

Good Housekeeping

"One Eye Open" (April 1948)

"Where Have You Been?" (May 1948)

"What Next in the Garden!"; "Whoopsie Daisy!"; "Said a Bug to a Bug—" (June 1948)

"The Big Red Barn" (July 1948)

"Sheep Don't Count Sheep" (August 1948)
"Little Brown Tug" (September 1948)
"Pusscatkin and the Pumpkin" (October 1948)
"The Brave Little Weathervane" (November 1948)
"Santa Claus Upside Down" (December 1948)
"3 Fish Go Fishing" (January 1949)
"The Magic Car" (February 1949)
"Pussywillow" (March 1949)
"In the Sugar Egg" (April 1949)
"The Bear and the Butterfly" (June 1949)
"The Moon Balloon" (July 1949)
"Three Little Pigeons" (August 1949)
"Scarecrow School" (September 1949)

Jack and Jill
"How the Animals Took a Bath" (January 1939)

Pictures and Stories: A Story Magazine for Primary Children (Methodist Publishing House)
"The Shining Stones" (12 July 1942)
"The Birthday Present" (19 July 1942)
"A Surprise" (26 July 1942)

Primary Quarterly (Sunday School Board of Southern Baptist Convention)
"Missy's Christmas Shopping" (March 1940)

Story Parade
"Never Worked and Never Will" (August 1937)
"One Night" (June 1939)
"Land Ahead" (September 1940)
"Cats from a Story Book, or Cat Medley" (November 1942)
"The Sad Sliced Onion" (March 1946)
"Two Little Miners," written with Edith Thacher Hurd (July 1948)
"Boats" (September 1951)

COLLECTIONS AND ANTHOLOGIES

Another Here and Now Story Book. Ed. Lucy Sprague Mitchell. Illustrated by Rosalie Slocum. New York: E. P. Dutton & Co., 1937.
Fun and Frolic. Ed. Barbara Nolan. Boston: D. C. Heath & Co., 1955.
Let's Read a Story. Ed. Sidonie Matsner Gruenberg. Garden City, New York: Garden City, 1957.
Lost and Found. Boston: D. C. Heath & Co., 1955.
Poems to be Read to the Very Young. Ed. Josette Frank. Illustrated by Eloise Wilkin. New York: Random House, 1982.

Read Me Another Story. Ed. Child Study Association of America. New York: T. Y. Crowell, 1949.

Read Me a Story Book. Ed. Child Study Association of America. New York: T. Y. Crowell, 1947.

ARTICLES AND ESSAYS

"Creative Writing for Very Young Children," *Book of Knowledge Annual* (1951): 77–81.

"Leonard Weisgard Wins the Caldecott Medal," *Publishers Weekly* (5 July 1947): 40–42.

"Lucy Sprague Mitchell," written with Mary Phelps, *Horn Book* (May 1937): 158–63.

"Stories to be Sung and Songs to be Told," *Book of Knowledge Annual* (1952): 166–70.

"Writing for Children," *Hollins Alumnae Magazine* (Winter 1949): 14.

AUTHOR'S NOTE: I have not attempted to solve all of the knotty bibliographical problems posed by the work of this extraordinarily prolific writer. Margaret Wise Brown's unpublished manuscripts, reissued editions of her books, reillustrated editions, foreign editions other than English firsts, recordings of and filmstrips based on her writings do not appear in these listings.

Index